S0-BWV-483

Our
Natural
Resources

and Their Conservation

Our Natural

Harry B. Kircher, Ph.D.

Professor Emeritus
Department of Geography,
    Earth Science and Planning
Southern Illinois University
    at Edwardsville

Donald L. Wallace, M.S.

Certified Professional Soil Scientist
Southwest Illinois Metropolitan and
    Regional Planning Commission

Lecturer
Southern Illinois University
    at Edwardsville

Seventh Edition

Resources
and Their Conservation

Dorothy J. Gore, Ph.D.

Former Professor of Earth Science
Southern Illinois University
   at Edwardsville and
Hardin–Simmons University
   Abilene, Texas

Consulting Geologist

Interstate Publishers, Inc.
Danville, Illinois

OUR NATURAL RESOURCES
and Their Conservation

Seventh Edition

Copyright © 1992
by INTERSTATE PUBLISHERS, INC.

Prior Editions:

First 1954
Second 1964
Third 1970
Fourth .1976
Fifth 1982
Sixth .1988

Order from

Interstate Publishers
510 North Vermilion Street
P.O. Box 50
Danville, IL 61834-0050
Phone: (800) 843-4774
FAX: (217) 446-9706

Library of Congress Catalog Card No. 91-70741

ISBN 0-8134-2923-4

2 3
4 5 6
7 8 9

*To Sue and Chuck
and all other young people*

May this book help you
realize your rich heritage
of resources.

The above symbol (also shown on the cover) represents the spheres of nature that are our resource base. The large circle encompassing all the others represents the noussphere, the realm of intelligence. The cycles within the large circle represent the four major spheres of the earth's ecosystem: the atmosphere, the hydrosphere, the lithosphere and the biosphere.

Preface

During the years since P. E. McNall wrote the first edition of this text in 1954, the world has jumped into the nuclear and space age. We orbited the earth, walked on the moon, and launched communication satellites, sending one 1.8 billion miles to the planet Uranus. The awesome fury of nuclear fission was harnessed to generate about two-thirds of the electricity in France, almost one-fifth in the United States and significant amounts in some 25 other countries. The possibilities for the growth and development of resources appeared unlimited.

But then, a series of disasters shook our presumption of earth domination. The three largest continents, Asia, Africa and South America, were wracked by famine, drought, debt, development problems and wars. Within a few months in 1986, the western world of North America and Europe, and the Soviet Union, reaped technological catastrophe. Spaceship *Challenger* blew up in the sky; U.S. and French satellite-bearing rockets had to be destroyed at launch; and the Chernobyl nuclear plant spewed contaminants across international boundaries and created havoc at home. In 1988, acid rain threatened to ravage large areas of forests in Europe and North America, and toxic wastes threatened to shorten the lives of thousands of people. Were we headed for another Dark Age?

Notwithstanding tragic and sometimes devastating losses, the authors still believe in the possibilities of a bright future for this world of ours. Resource development has always had a cost. We need to ask: Are the costs necessary? Are the benefits sufficient to justify the costs? As this text shows, over the centuries, despite sometimes staggering costs, we have multiplied by the hundreds our resources through development of the natural resource base. Furthermore, the "goods" have exceeded the "bads." This may be small consolation, if any, to the mother who has lost her son or daughter in war or because of toxic chemicals or a "natural" disaster. We must continue with sure confidence in the vision that humans have the ability to work compassionately with each other and harmoniously with nature. We must not lose faith because of the failures we see at hand.

To assure "good," that is, net benefits, from resource development, the world must practice conservation of natural resources, defined by author Kircher as "The management and use, which may include preservation, of natural resources for quality life—life in harmony with aesthetic, ecological, economic and ethical principles."

The goal of conservation, as we see it, goes far beyond creating material wealth. Its goal is no less than to help bring about an environment in which world peace as well as prosperity can be realized along with individual liberties, health and security. Such a goal may seem impossible to achieve. But, as we pursue the task, the only real failure is to quit trying.

So, the authors present this new edition of *Our Natural Resources and Their Conservation* with faith in the future. A new chapter on environmental/conservation careers and a glossary have been added. In addition, line drawings by David McClellan provide attractive motifs for chapter headings. The book continues to be a study of the evolution of natural resource development, based on the concept that inspiration, intelligence and knowledge are the foundation of resources.

Dr. Dorothy J. Gore, a geologist, and Mr. Donald L. Wallace, a certified professional soil scientist continue as associate authors. Dr. Harry B. Kircher remains the senior and principal author. The authors base their presentation on diversified academic, practical and geographic backgrounds. Besides years of teaching experience in conservation, between them they have conducted research on and written about conservation, geography, geology and soils; have farmed and been farm managers; have worked in business and finance; and have travelled widely in the United States and abroad.

Author Kircher was born in the state of Washington; Wallace in Illinois; and Gore in Oklahoma. During their working years, Kircher has resided in Florida, Massachusetts, Illinois, Missouri and North Carolina; Wallace in Illinois and Michigan; and Gore in California, Texas and Illinois. Kircher has degrees from Clark University, Worcester, Massachusetts; The University of North Carolina-Chapel Hill; and Washington University, St. Louis; Wallace from Michigan State University-East Lansing and Southern Illinois University at Edwardsville; and Gore from the University of Illinois at Urbana-

Champaign; Principia College, Elsah, Illinois; and the University of Wisconsin-Madison.

This edition of *Our Natural Resources and Their Conservation* is dedicated to Chuck and Sue and to all other young people all over the world. The earth's resource base can support a quality life for all peoples. May this book help bring this goal closer to realization.

Acknowledgments

The authors gratefully acknowledge the help received during the preparation of various editions of this text. Dr. Kircher, the senior author, especially appreciates the encouragement and help given to him by Professors Melvin Kazeck and Robert Koepke, Southern Illinois University at Edwardsville, and by Robert Ring, former Director of Conservation Education, state of Illinois; the inspiration of his formers teachers, particularly Professors Raymond Murphy and Henry Warman, Clark University, Worcester, Massachusetts; Erich Zimmermann, the University of North Carolina–Chapel Hill; and Lewis Thomas, Washington University, St. Louis; and the assistance of his former colleague, Norman Bowsher, economist, Federal Reserve Bank of St. Louis, and Robert Fortado, in charge of U.S. Documents, Lovejoy Library, Southern Illinois University at Edwardsville. Dr. Kircher also wishes to thank his wife, Edith, for her patience, endurance and support during the many editions of this text while he was engrossed in research and writing.

David Clelland, an artist and drafter with the Regional Research and Development Services, Southern Illinois University at Edwardsville, designed and prepared all the line drawings for the chapter openings, as well as those on the front and back covers. Manuscript preparation and thoughtful help was provided by Janis Moore.

The authors are indebted to various government agencies, private businesses, nonprofit private research organizations and associations and the news media. Various sources have been credited in the text.

As a final note, thanks to Patricia A. Ward, Production Editor, The Interstate Printers & Publishers, Inc., for her valuable editing.

Contents

1

The Character of Natural Resources

Most of the world's phenomena are natural, but they are not necessarily resources. To be resources, they must be of use to people. Put in the words of the first two definitions of the *American Heritage Dictionary of the English Language*, a *resource* is "1. Something that can be turned to for support or help. 2. An available supply that can be drawn upon when needed." We can see that a mild, sunny climate; productive soil; valuable minerals; and the "cool, cool" water sung of on our western plains are all natural resources because they are useful to people. Likewise, a harsh, cloudy climate; boggy lowlands; craggy mountains; and warm sulfur springs are all natural resources *if they are useful to people*. Water which is trapped far beneath the earth's surface and inaccessible to us, however, is not ordinarily considered a resource. Nor is the common plantain weed. It is important to realize, however, that such "neutral" or "nuisance" materials or forms of life are essential to our earth life system and thus, indirectly, to our own lives, and some of them may even become valuable to us. Oil was once more of a curiosity than a fuel.

We humans and our works are not superior to nature. We are part of it. As we travel down the superhighway in our compact automobiles, eyes glued to the ribbon of concrete and ears attuned to the radio, we feel

1

FIGURE 1-1. Frank Robinson, hired in the spring of 1988 as the new manager of the Balti-more Orioles, is having a few friendly words with the umpire. Robinson broke the color line in 1975 as the first black manager in baseball when he was hired by the Cleveland Indians. The labor power of blacks and other minorities is a key factor in the development of resources in the United States and throughout the world. Increased use of their management and other skills will increase the amount and the quality of resources developed from the natural resource base. (Courtesy, Associated Press)

isolated from nature. But, this is only an illusion. We are riding through, on and by reason of the availability of the resource base. It is the air we can breathe, the light we can see and the ground over which we can move. It is the base for the frame, body, motor, tires, upholstery and other parts of the car and for our body. It is the source of energy for both the vehicle and us. Finally, the availability of the resource to us humans depends upon inspiration, ingenuity and intelligence.

Under traditional classification, resources were put into three categor-ies: natural, human and cultural (economists use the terms *land, labor* and *capital*). Earth materials and life forms, except humans, which are "free gifts of nature" were classified as natural. These included the air above and the water beneath, soils, and natural (wild) vegetation, every creature except humans and all the rocks and minerals.

Humans were classified as a human resource. To state it in doggerel:

Bushman or Bulgar, Kirghiz or Kurd
No matter how different sounding the word.
Is really the same kind of species of course,
Called *homo sapiens,* a human resource.

All human works were traditionally classified as cultural resources. Here was included everything these creatures made from abacuses to zwieback.

The preceding division of resources into three groupings is both convenient and useful for many purposes. But, it has one serious flaw which we should recognize at once. Such a division tends to make us forget the interrelatedness of all resources. We become labor specialists and boast that little would be produced without our brawn. We develop a love affair with cultural hardware, such as electronic computers. "Our computers will solve all problems," we say. And, sometime we become natural resource specialists. We insist, "Don't change nature!" But, as good natural scientists, we should know that nature itself is constantly changing.

NATURAL RESOURCES MANIFEST ENERGY

All resources are interrelated. This becomes clear when we think of resources as manifestations of energy. We are accustomed to thinking of matter and energy as being different. They are really just different expressions of the same thing, energy. These expressions differ in form, animation and exhaustibility.

Forms of Energy

In form, energy may be manifested as solid, liquid or gaseous, or as a wave of energy—heat, light or electricity. These forms are often convertible or substitutable, one for the other. This transferability is very significant in evaluating our resource base. For example, energy from coal can be used directly to furnish heat energy or converted as steam—electric power; or natural gas or oil may be used instead of coal. Our analysis of resources available for heat energy should take into account these and other forms of energy capable of doing this work.

Animate and Inanimate Energy

A second important distinction of natural resources is their manifestation as animate (living) or inanimate (nonliving) energy. Coal expresses inanimate energy. Animal and plant life are animate energy. The advantage of substituting the one form of energy for another to carry out physical work can be readily understood. A horse may pull a plow. Or a tractor may pull it. The first is the use of animate energy, animal muscle power. The second is the use of inanimate energy, gasoline, diesel oil or propane gas operating through solid energy forms of the tractor. In both cases, natural resources are being employed. The tractor, using inanimate energy, will be far more productive per unit of input than the horse in most situations. (Compare Figures 1-2 and 1-3 for other examples.)

FIGURE 1-2. Animate energy is illustrated by this team of oxen pulling a cart at Kings Landing Historical Settlement, located on the St. John's River, New Brunswick, Canada. Oxen were soon replaced by horses and mules. About 20 million horses and 5 million mules were used for work in the United States in 1910. (Courtesy, Kings Landing Historical Settlement Tourism, New Brunswick, Canada)

FIGURE 1-3. This International S-Series heavy truck, equipped with a DTA-66 direct injection, intercooled, turbocharged diesel engine, can pull up to 80,000 gross vehicle load (in tandem). And, in less than an hour it can cover a distance that would be a normal day's trip in a wagon, making the cost per unit carried cheaper, considering all factors involved. Inanimate energy, represented by this truck, has multiplied many times the resources obtained from the resource base because materials are now available that would not have been without the machine. (Courtesy, International by Navistar)

Conversion to use of inanimate energy on a large scale, which began over 200 years ago, wrought such a change in our productive methods and capacity and even in our way of living that it has been called the Industrial Revolution. Machines permitted increased specialization and division of labor, the basis of the factory system. Much of our population moved from farm to city, yet the farmers produced more than ever before. Manufacturing output fairly "leaped forward." The increased productivity and freedom from many of the limitations of time and space were a great blessing to humankind. But, these benefits were accompanied by an accelerating and severe drain on and abuse of our natural resources. To solve this dilemma has not been easy.

Inexhaustible Resources

Another classification of the energy resource is according to its apparent exhaustibility. Is its supply diminishing with use? Or, is it constantly being replenished?

Three natural resources which are classified as inexhaustible are solar energy, radiant energy renewed by the sun; the atmosphere renewed constantly by sun interaction with plants, animals and bacteria; and water replenished constantly as water is carried from the oceans as clouds and vapor overland where it is "dumped," renewing inland water supplies in a movement known as the *hydrologic cycle* (see Figure 1-4). Unfortunately, we have so contaminated the air and water in recent years that these resources may have been impaired even though they have proved inexhaustible over billions of years. Plant and animal life under natural conditions is also constantly replenishing itself and thus may be considered inexhaustible. However, since such conditions are becoming the exception rather than the rule, we label them as exhaustible **replaceable** resources.

Exhaustible Resources

The exhaustible resources are those which are available in more or less limited quantities or which must be processed for use from somewhat limited sources. Aluminum, for example, is an exhaustible natural resource. It may be found in clay soils all over the world, which makes the total amount of aluminum in its natural form practically inexhaustible; yet, the aluminum we use comes mostly from a few mines where there is a high concentration of bauxite ore. It is practical to recover aluminum from bauxite, but it is not economical or feasible to recover aluminum from the tremendous deposits of common clay. Nor is aluminum, like the sun's energy, being replenished as it is used.

There are two classes of exhaustible resources: (1) irreplaceable resources and (2) replaceable or renewable resources.

Irreplaceable Resources

This class includes those resources which cannot be replaced or

FIGURE 1-4. Water power is an inexhaustible resource as long as rain falls and there is surface run-off. (Courtesy, Wisconsin Conservation Department)

renewed when once used up. Our mineral resources, such as iron, copper, nickel, sulfur, phosphate, potash and salt, are in this class. Nor can coal, oil and natural gas be renewed when present supplies are exhausted.

In most instances even our soils must be classified as irreplaceable because once they are eroded (washed away) they cannot be renewed or replaced during our lifetime or even during the lifetime of our nation. The only way to build up a soil again when once it has been lost is through the slow action of weather and time.

It has been estimated that 2,000 years is required for nature to make 1 inch of soil from the original rock of the earth. Whether the time be one-half or several times 2,000 years, it is so long that for all practical purposes a soil once eroded cannot be replaced.

Replaceable Resources

The second general class of exhaustible natural resources consists of those which can be renewed after being wasted or used up, providing some seed stock still exists. Our forests, our grasslands and some kinds of wildlife are examples of this class of resources. Even though these plant and animal resources are completely destroyed in certain areas, they can generally, to some extent, be renewed. For example, a few decades ago, the moose population was almost wiped out. It has been replenished in parts of its former range in numbers greater than 12,000, with another 120,000 in Alaska. In 1925, the number of pronghorn antelope ranged between 13,000 and 26,000. According to the U.S. Fish and Wildlife Service, the population is now up to 750,000. White-tailed deer in 1900 were estimated at ½ million, while in 1986, they were estimated at nearly 15 million, thus establishing the deer as the most abundant large wild animal. In 1900, elk were estimated at 41,000; presently there are close to one-half million total in 16 states. These facts are impressive, especially considering the rate at which our wildlife habitat is disappearing.

Even some elements of our soil are replaceable. The depletion or using up of plant nutrients from a soil may result in its abandonment as a source of production for plants. As long as the soil has not eroded, the elements used up may be successfully replaced in some cases, making the soil to become productive again.

DISTRIBUTION OF NATURAL RESOURCES

Another important characteristic of natural resources, especially minerals, is that they are unevenly distributed. The United States east of the 100th meridian generally has adequate rainfall for abundant vegetation, but west of this line much of the region is arid. Productive brown forest soils prevail in the northeastern United States, but infertile red desert soils prevail in the Southwest. Mountains and associated plateaus and valleys occupy the western third of our country, and lowlands, the central section. Major bituminous coal deposits are found in Appalachian and central states, while lignite fields are characteristic of the western states.

The unequal distribution of resources throughout the world often severely limits their availability to the United States. In the beginning of the energy crisis in 1973, many of us who were for the first time faced with empty gasoline pumps at filling stations refused to believe that our country had limited resources. We thought it was just a scheme of the domestic oil companies to raise prices. A major factor was that the Arab nations sat on the world's greatest proved oil reserves and for political and economic reasons chose not to release them.

Because of erratic distribution, the United States imports many other basic minerals and raw materials essential for our standard of living. In late 1974, John Keil, then the Assistant Secretary of the Interior, forecasted that we were heading into a shortage of minerals and materials that would "make our present fuel crisis look like a Sunday School picnic!" Subsequent petroleum discoveries and political changes led to a sharp drop in prices in the 1980's. But, the United States continues heavy use of minerals and materials and heavy dependence upon imports. No nation today, including the United States, has everything it needs.

Some nations have demonstrated great ability to overcome deficiencies of natural resources through trading manufactured goods for raw materials. But, history teaches that they may lose their ability to maintain this complementary relationship. The United Kingdom (UK), 150 years ago, was known as the "workshop of the world." Drawing upon local reserves of coal and iron, that country obtained from abroad the raw materials, such as cotton, that it needed and became an immensely wealthy nation. Today, the UK's coal and iron reserves are less accessible, and the factories of other nations are outproducing those of that country. One financial crisis after another has made the UK a debtor nation whose imports exceed its exports. In the 1980's, the United States for the first time in over six decades, became a debtor nation as well.

The relationship between the location of natural resources and the location of industry may be quite indirect and often is, even when both are within the same country. The iron and steel industry in the United States is a good example of this. After an early start in Massachusetts in colonial days, based on bog iron deposits and wood for fuel, the center of production shifted westward to the Scranton–Wilkes-Barre area, based on local iron deposits and anthracite for fuel. The next center was the Pittsburgh-Youngstown district. Here coking coal proved superior to the anthracite, and local iron deposits were adequate at first. Besides, newly developing markets of the Midwest were more easily reached from Pittsburgh than from farther east. As Pittsburgh grew, a very large body of iron ore was discovered west of Lake Superior in the Mesabi range. Why not center the steel industry there? It would not have been economical. While a steel plant was eventually located at Duluth, Minnesota, not far from the iron mines, it never became a serious competitor of Pittsburgh. Shipment of the ore to Pittsburgh was found to be more efficient, in view of its good market position and nearness to fuel. And, since it took the equivalent of 1½ tons of coal to process 1 ton of iron, it was less expensive to move iron to Pittsburgh than coal to the Mesabi. In other instances, the location of a steel complex at Sparrow's Point, Maryland, was related to markets and convenient access by ship to ores from South America; steel manufacture at Birmingham, Alabama, developed on the basis of local iron and coal deposits and markets; manufacture of steel and steel products in the Chicago district, now the U.S. production leader, began at Gary, Indiana, because it provided a good site accessible to the large Chicago market for steel.

Among the most generally used and widespread resources are our forests. Their distribution is shown in Figure 1-5. Note that even this "common" resource is unavailable locally in some regions, such as the Great Plains.

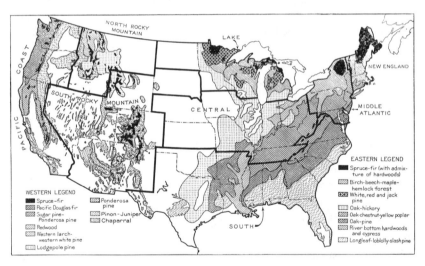

FIGURE 1-5. Forest areas of the United States. Note that most of the area east of the Mississippi River is classed as forest area, while practically no forest land is shown in the plains and prairie area east of the Rocky Mountains. (Courtesy, U.S. Forest Service)

The Midwest became known as the "breadbasket" of the nation, reflecting its outstanding natural resources of productive soil, humid climate and abundant water supply, which have made possible an enormous output of crops and livestock products. Other natural resources have helped it become a leading manufacturing region as well. But, even this diverse region must import raw materials and fuels from other parts of the United States and from foreign nations in order to meet its needs. Although the Midwest (the East North Central and West North Central states) remains the most prolific region in the United States in agricultural output, California is the leading state.

SUMMARY

Natural resources are useful manifestations of energy that occur in nature. Humans and their works, although separately classified as human and cultural resources, are interlinked with and dependent upon natural resources.

Natural resources are distinguished from one another in form, animation and exhaustibility. In a different form, one resource may sometimes be converted to or substituted for another, affording flexibility in resource use and conversation. The substitution of inanimate energy for animate energy on a large scale has brought about a radical change in our way of life. While the resultant outpouring of goods and the release from drudgery has benefited us, the accelerated drain of our natural resources and the pollution of our environment threaten our very lives.

Inexhaustible resources do not diminish with use. The sun's energy, the atmosphere and water are principal examples. But their effectiveness has been reduced by pollution of the environment.

Exhaustible resources are classed as either irreplaceable or replaceable. Minerals, including fuels, are irreplaceable. Plants and animals may be replaceable. Soil is largely irreplaceable, but some elements in it are replaceable.

Natural resources are very unevenly distributed. Nations or any regions within them which possess a wealth of available natural resources have an advantage over the "have-nots." For the welfare of a region depends to a great extent upon the ease with which it can obtain and develop natural resources.

QUESTIONS AND PROBLEMS

1. When does energy become a natural resource?

2. What advantage might be gained by substituting one resource for another? Give an example.

3. Why is our performance at school and work dependent upon natural resources?

4. Is there any need to be concerned about the future of inexhaustible resources? They can't be used up, can they? Explain your answer.

5. Give an example of an exhaustible, but nevertheless renewable, resource.

6. What is the most basic resource of all?

7. Is all matter a resource? Why or why not?

8. What effect does the uneven distribution of natural resources have on the wealth of the United States?

9. How did the Industrial Revolution affect the relationship between people and natural resources?

10. Name three important irreplaceable exhaustible resources. Are any of them important to your community?

11. Name three natural resources classified as inexhaustible.

12. What is the difference between natural, human and cultural resources? What do they have in common?

13. What areas of the United States have been developed because of the use of the following resources: (a) coal, (b) iron, (c) coal and iron and (d) soil?

14. Which one of the resources found in your area is most important to your community? Why?

2

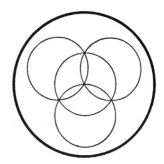

The Evaluation of
Natural Resources

The worth of a resource to society or to an individual is often quite different from its **economic** value. How much is Independence Hall in Philadelphia, the beauty of the free-flowing Klamath River in Oregon or even a single rose worth to us? How much is a dog worth to its master?

The economic worth of a resource is dependent upon its quality, accessibility and scarcity. Consider the value of a piece of land, for example. Farm land with excellent soil, thus of high quality, is ordinarily relatively valuable, even though it may be located remote from farm markets and may be relatively inaccessible, because such quality land is scarce. By contrast, a very poor-quality land—with highly acidic soil and poor drainage—might be very valuable if in the center of a city because it is readily accessible and because building sites for that particular city are scarce. In the third case, a piece of land with poor-quality soil may be rather inaccessibly located on the outskirts of a rapidly growing city, but it may sell for a relatively high price since land for urban expansion has become scarce.

One measure of the economic worth of a good is its market value— that price for which a good will sell. If market forces work efficiently, they are reliable indicators of the value of commerical goods at a particular time. But, they do not work for treasured pets. Nor, is the market place a good judge of value for many other items, such as those which have great historic, scenic or biologic value, but little cash value. And, unfortunately, even for commercial goods, the market is often imperfect in its appraisal of value. Despite these difficulties, we must try to determine the "true" worth of resources if we are to use them wisely.[1]

SUPPLY FACTORS AND NATURAL RESOURCES

The potential of a supply of a natural resource to meet demand is determined by its availability. Availability is dependent upon the way the resource is manifested in nature and its distribution, as discussed in Chapter 1, and the utilities given it.

It May Cost to Make Resources Available

Because an inexhaustible resource, such as air, is freely available, it generally has no economic value. No one markets the air we breathe. However, in view of growing pollution, "pure" air has become scarce and thus has acquired economic value. It is, for example, a major asset of resorts in the mountains (see Figure 2-1). In certain circumstances, such as in underground mining operations, submarines or air-conditioned buildings, it costs to supply air to people. But, this is not because air itself is scarce; rather, it is the cost of getting the air to the restricted area. Resources that abound in excess of human needs or desires have market value relative to the costs of making these resources accessible at the places and times they are wanted.

Residents pay higher prices for drinking water in desert places, not because the water is superior in taste or quality but because it costs more to make it available. The water may have been transported for many miles, it may have required expensive filtering or exceptionally deep wells may have been needed in order to obtain it.

---

[1]How much money is a life worth? A massive gas leak at Union Carbide's plant in Bhopal, India, caused some 2,000 deaths in 1985. The resultant litigation has highlighted the problem of estimating how much a human life is worth. While putting a value on someone's life may be repugnant, such valuation is necessary for cost-benefit analysis, besides insurance claims. Life evaluation by government agencies has ranged as follows, according to *Fortune*: (a) United States Home Administration (USHA)—$2 million to $5 million; (b) Environmental Protection Agency (EPA)—$1 million to $7.5 million; and (c) Federal Aviation Administration (FAA)—$650,000. (Daniel Seligman, "How Much Money Is Your Life Worth?," *Fortune*, March 3, 1986, pp. 25–27.)

FIGURE 2-1. A snow-covered ridge of the high Sierras, some 150 miles southeast of San Francisco. The magnificent scenery, the "pure" mountain air, the snow, the streams and lakes, the wildlife and the forests are all important resources here. People in adjacent valleys depend upon snow melt for their water supply throughout the dry summer. (Photo by Susan Kircher)

An example that all of us are familiar with is the pumping of water from wells and piping it to our houses. We are willing to pay whatever costs are necessary to bring the water to us in our homes where we wish to use it. We sometimes dig wells hundreds of feet deep just to get a continuous supply of pure, clear water, and we are willing to pay this cost. The value to us in this situation is what economists call *place utility*. If we go to a stream or a spring to get our drink of water, we pay no money for it. It costs us only the time and energy used in going to the spring. It is only when the water is moved from its source of supply to us in our homes or at our work that it has a value to us which makes us willing to pay money for it.

Economists use different names to describe or to qualify the type of use of any article or service that satisfies our wants. This process is spoken of as the creation of utility.

We have already mentioned *place utility* It costs to move an article or a service from one place to another, and this cost is usually added to the price that consumers have to pay.

The common method of creating utility is to change the form of a resource. This is called *form utility*. Changing the form from a product that is of no use to us to something that we as consumers or users want and are willing to pay for is the basis of our industrial development.

Cotton, wool and flax are made into bedding, draperies, rugs, clothing, etc. Iron, copper, aluminum and other metals are converted into engines, automobiles, structural steel and a thousand and one other articles used in our everyday living. These are illustrations of *form utility*.

A farmer harvests grain after it ripens in the summer or early fall. When that process is completed, economists speak of the farmer as having created *elementary utility*.

The grain is then moved to some mill where it is worth a little more because of the shipping cost. Place utility enters here. The miller produces flour, bran and germ meal from the grain, and form utility is created. More costs are added, and more place utility is created, when the flour is shipped to some organization where it is stored until a consumer wants to buy it. Holding or storing the product until it is bought by a consumer creates *time utility*.

All these functions and services are for our convenience and add to the cost. The creation of these various utilities results in our so-called higher standard of living, as well as in increasing the cost of living. When evaluating a resource, we need to take into account its scarcity and accessibility.

DEMAND FACTORS AND NATURAL RESOURCES

Demand for a resource can be defined as "the amount that is wanted at a given price." To create effective demand, we must have the ability to pay. Simple Simon of nursery rhyme fame did not create an effective demand for pie, for when the pieman asked Simon for his penny, the latter replied, "Indeed, I have not any!" Simple Simon went hungry. And, so do over half the people in the world today—not because they do not want to eat—they cannot afford to!

Total effective demand for a good at any given time is figured by multiplying the number of effective demand units by the amount each consumes. Of great significance to our natural resource base is that we can reduce the claims on our natural resources from a *demand* standpoint, either by reducing the total number of demand units or by reducing the amount each requires or, of course, by reducing both. Thus, if we have a sufficiently smaller population, we can maintain or even increase the amount each of us uses with no greater drain on our natural resources. But, should our population rise sharply within the next few decades, as world population is doing at present rates, we would need to limit greatly our use of resources to maintain the same total demand unless new discoveries, greater efficiencies of use and avoidance of waste more than offset the increased demand.

Elasticity of Demand

Another important factor in the nature of the demand for a resource is the flexibility of its response to price changes, which economists call its *elasticity*. For example, the demand for items made primarily from metal, such as automobiles and home appliances, is generally *elastic*. If buying lags, it can generally be revived by lowering prices. But, a rise in prices causes buying to fall off. Since goods such as automobiles and appliances generally continue to operate for a long time, we can postpone buying new ones without having to "do without."

The demand for certain resources, especially staple foods, is *inelastic*. "Enough potatoes is enough potatoes" may be incorrect English, but it is correct economics. If we are wealthy, we eat all the potatoes we want and will buy no more just because the price drops. Even if we are poor, assuming that potatoes are the mainstay of our diet, we will buy no more if the price drops because we are already eating all we can. Vice versa, ordinarily higher prices will not cause the rich or the poor to purchase fewer potatoes. If we are wealthy, cost makes no difference. If we are poor, we need to buy potatoes regardless of how much the price rises since they are still probably the cheapest food we can get.

These flexibilities (elasticities) of demand have an important effect upon the use of our natural resource base and our ability to conserve it. In times of prosperity, we drive around in high-powered, gadget-equipped sportscars which have low passenger-carrying capacity and high fuel consumption.

The manufacturer of supersports cars steps up their assembly in order to sell while the market is "hot." Prices rise, but sales continue to climb, for cost seemingly is no object. Rising prices at this point are ineffective to control the waste of our metal and fuel resources in what has been called "conspicuous consumption." But, few of us are aware of this. Should a severe economic recession set in however, the cars would be repossessed by the finance companies and could not be sold to anyone at any price. The waste of resources because of changes in taste would become obvious to everyone.[2]

Inflexible (inelastic) demand, when it is not taken into account in resource development, can also lead to waste. To help support the price of agricultural commodities, our government has paid farmers to plow under crops and to destroy livestock. The Brazilian government at times has destroyed more than $1 billion worth of coffee to prevent it from glutting the U.S. market, where most of it is sold.

THE MARKET SYSTEM: EXTERNALITIES AND RESOURCES

While the market system is an extremely valuable help in the allocation of resources, we can see from the previous discussion that the distribution may not be the best one for us or the resource base. In addition, there may be various side effects to the environment, called "externalities" by economists, which are not taken into account by the market place. These may be good or bad effects. A forest is selectively harvested in order to sell its timber. By opening up the forest in this process, we increase the food supply for wildlife—an external, good effect. However, one part of the forest, through carelessness, is overcut. Although the timber cut from it brings a good profit, the soil is exposed by the overcutting and severe erosion results—a bad effect. In using resources, we need to provide incentives to maximize the "goods" and penalties to minimize the "bads."

---

[2]Some sport sedans are relatively low-powered and provide maximum fuel efficiency and because of shock-absorbing construction, reasonable safety for small families. Heavy sedans may provide safety and comfort, but they seldom effect fuel economy.

WANTS AND ABILITIES AND RESOURCES

We have seen how the mechanics of supply and demand—the number of buyers, response to price, and so on—have an important effect upon our resource base. But, we have not considered, except by a few random examples, what gives us our ability to convert natural resources into useful products (supply) nor why we desire to do so (demand). One of the leading authorities on resource evaluation, the late Professor Erich Zimmermann, classified the motivations for our desires under the headings of **wants** and **social objectives**.[3] Our abilities, he stated, depend upon the state of our **technological abilities** and **societal arts**. Let us consider how these factors affect the appraisal of natural resources.

Human Wants and Social Objectives

Zimmerman explained that our wants may be divided into two groups: **creature wants** and **culture wants**. Creature wants are the basic needs of food, shelter and clothing. Culture wants are the desires for things in addition to those that meet our basic needs. Books, television sets and air-conditioned houses are examples. The early North American Indians used relatively few natural resources. They satisfied their creature wants and little else. Modern society demands more and more culture wants. Accordingly, the demand on our research base has multiplied many times. The next chapter is devoted largely to explaining the impact of this expanding demand upon our natural resources.

Maintaining a healthful, peaceful and productive community is a social objective. To achieve this objective, we must frequently modify our culture wants, and especially our individual culture wants. For one family or a small group of families in a village, the quaint outhouse privies, with or without a halfmoon on their doors, were adequate and generally of little danger to health. But, for 1 million families living in a city, they would be disaster! Likewise, the exhaust fumes from 100 automobiles are insignificant. From 100 million, they are deadly! The conflict between what we

---

[3] Erich Zimmermann, *World Resources and Industries*, rev. ed., New York: Harper & Brothers, 1951. The first edition appeared in 1933. A paperback version (Henry L. Hunker, ed.), called *Introduction to World Resources*, was published in 1964. Thus, Zimmermann's concepts have been taught for more than a generation!

would like to have as individuals or small, isolated groups of people and what we can have in our close-knit, industrial world has to be resolved in favor of wise group objectives if we are to have a life-supporting environment. For example, we may need to reduce our use of the large family automobile and increase the use of mass transit facilities, such as buses and passenger trains, if we are to prevent air pollution and to save space. That this is becoming recognized is illustrated by the millions of dollars which have been granted by the federal government for research in rapid transit systems and by federal law which requires automobile manufacturers to reduce the fuel consumption of their products drastically.

Technological Abilities and Societal Arts

While wants and social objectives set our course in resource development, technological abilities and societal arts determine how well we are able to use our natural resources to reach our objectives. The **technological abilities** consist of both our ability to operate machinery and the machinery itself. The **societal arts** are our ability to organize for effective action; in short, they are the arts of living together harmoniously.

The U.S. space program from successful *Apollo*, which went to the moon, to disastrous *Challenger*, which exploded, illustrates how important it is to achieve a harmonious melding of technological abilities and societal arts to develop the resource base successfully. Technologically, the National Aeronautics and Space Administration (NASA) worked to master the art of building and operating rockets, guidance systems, space capsules, lunar landing ships and other complicated space hardware. NASA was able to assemble and organize a working force of thousands of technicians and administrators, or to contract for them. And, the agency collected and disbursed billions of dollars. All of this was possible because the United States has a capable political and industrial system and labor force.

The almost unimaginable accomplishments of the program, such as sending a robot spacecraft to the surface of Mars, showed effective coordination of art and science. The tragic explosion of *Challenger* showed how a breakdown in technological abilities—the failure of the sealed rings on the booster rocket—and in societal arts, the failure to communicate the problem and to act on it—can result in a waste of resources, including human life.

THE FUNCTIONAL CONCEPT OF RESOURCES AND CONSERVATION

The force of wants and abilities together operates as a culture wedge which is constantly converting raw materials of nature into resources. In short, resources are a function (product) of our wants and abilities. Thus, resources are not constant but are ever-changing as a function of our changing wants and abilities and, of course, depending upon the resource base. Zimmermann called this concept "the functional concept of resources" (see footnote 3).

This concept also includes the idea that the creation of a resource results in a resistance. Thus, when we produce steel, we pollute air; when we raise corn, we erode soil; and when we mine coal, we fracture rocks. It is impossible to eliminate resistances in resource development. Conservation means reducing such costs or if the costs are too high or unjustified, letting the resource remain in its natural state. More completely stated, **conservation of natural resources** is the management and use, which may include preservation, of such resources for quality of life—life in harmony with aesthetic, ecological, economic, and ethical principles.

Technologically, we communicate with ease, whether by radio, telephone or jet plane. But socially, we have great difficulty understanding each other. Because of this gap between our technological and societal abilities, our ability to destroy each other has too often exceeded our ability to live together peacefully; many times our natural resources go up in smoke and flame instead of in houses and schools.

OUR HUMAN RESOURCES AND NATURE'S SYSTEM

As has been noted in both this chapter and the preceding one, when we develop a resource, we need to be concerned about the effect of this development on the rest of the world, especially the world of nature. All things are interrelated. As an example, a new highway was planned to cut across the Great Smoky Mountains National Park. It would have relieved traffic congestion. But, at the same time, it would have cut across the headwaters of streams, polluting them; it would have destroyed a wildlife habitat; and it would have threatened the forest through which it passed. To try to assure full consideration of the environment by federal government agencies, Congress passed the Environmental Protection Act in 1970. This act requires federal agencies to prepare Environmental Impact Statements to justify all proposals for legislation and other major federal actions that significantly affect the quality of the environment. (A further discussion of this act and its enforcement is included in Chapter 24.) Here we will consider some of the relationships between our human resources and nature, according to the science of ecology.

The Science of Ecology

Ecology is the study of how living organisms and their nonliving environment function together. One approach to an understanding of this interrelationship is to begin with the sun. From it comes most of the energy on earth. But, this energy is largely unavailable to animals directly. It must be transmitted to them by green vegetation through a process known as *photosynthesis*. In this process, the sun's energy is transferred through a substance in the vegetation called *chlorophyll* (from the Greek, *chloros*, "green," and *phyllos*, "leaf") in the presence of water to become free oxygen and food sugar. Animals can obtain their energy by eating plants or other animals (which have eaten plants at some stage). As plants and animals decay, with the help of bacteria and fungi, they release chemicals in the earth which, in turn, help feed plants. This cycle is illustrated by the diagram in Figure 2-2. While this explanation is oversimplified, it reliably illustrates the general principle of a cycle in nature.

Such a circular movement as just described may be viewed as one complex cycle or as a series of interlocked smaller cycles. This circulation enables the earth's basic substances—carbon, oxygen, nitrogen and water—and others to move between the earth's major stratums: air (the *atmosphere*), water (the *hydrosphere*), soil and rocks (the *lithosphere*) and living organisms (the *biosphere*).

All these spheres can be visualized as being embraced within a larger sphere, the stratum of mind, called the *noussphere* (see Figure 2-3).[4] *Nous* is a Greek word meaning "*mind, sense, reason, intellect.*" The word *noussphere* has been coined by author Kircher, who defines it as "the field of energy expressed in intelligence, inspiration, ingenuity and knowledge."

---

[4]Daniel G. Koslovsky, *An Ecological and Evolutionary Ethic*, Englewood Cliffs, New Jersey, Prentice-Hall, Inc., 1974, p. 20.

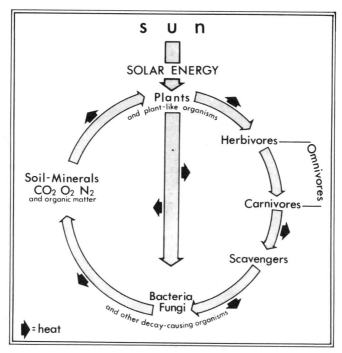

FIGURE 2-2. The energy cycle. All life on earth depends upon the sun's energy. The diagram represents the flow of energy in both living and nonliving matter. Solar energy is transferred through the chlorophyll of plants to serve as food for animals, which may be preyed upon by other animals. Animal wastes and plant and animal remains succumb to decay organisms. They may be converted to fossil fuels or become concentrated as other minerals. Or, they may aid in the formation of soils. Heat is given off as the cycle proceeds.

This concept is similar to but yet different from Daniel J. Koslovsky's *noosphere*. Koslovsky describes the noosphere as a "whole *new human mental sphere*." In contrast, Kircher sees the noussphere as a "vast field of mental energy" of which the human intellect is but one expression.

Consequently, the earth is one great interlinked system. Ecologists sometimes refer to this entire earth system as an *ecosystem*. However, just as there are smaller cycles of life within larger ones, so are there smaller ecosystems within one large earth system. Thus, a forest, pond or field may be an ecosystem. It must contain sufficient living organisms and nonliving environmental components of certain characteristics for it to operate as a system. This is a scientific problem for ecologists to determine. But assuming it has enough variety to qualify as an ecosystem, the ecosystem

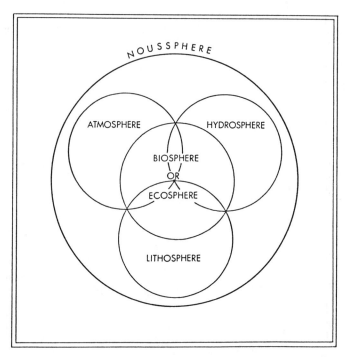

FIGURE 2-3. The ecosystem is shown above as four interlocked spheres—the biosphere, atmosphere, hydrosphere and lithosphere—surrounded by a larger sphere, the noussphere.

itself goes through various stages, or cycles, of development. The forest is young and full of grasses, bushes and a variety of saplings. By maturity, the forest floor is relatively clear, and a few species of trees, now grown tall, dominate. Finally, the old trees die out, and the cycle repeats itself.

As long as early peoples met all their needs by hunting, fishing and gathering, they were part of a particular natural ecosystem. The early North American Indians were an example. But, today's generation, with its many inventions, has made this interplay with nature often indirect. Is this an ecological relationship? The scientific relationship of cause and effect is difficult to prove. Nevertheless, however remote, the relationship is there. Even a highly human-altered system such as the city may contain many small ecosystems, such as marshes, ponds or woodlands; but they may function very poorly. There is one important distinction to bear in mind— natural ecosystems such as forests, fields and ponds can survive without us, we cannot survive without them! The problem of resource development by us, therefore, is to work in harmony with these natural ecosystems so that they are life-sustaining as long as possible.

Environmental Perception

What does a mountain mean to you? Is it a great place to hike or a poor place to farm? A storehouse for minerals or a wall from the world? Or, do you think it is all of these?

One of the problems in resource development and the environment lies not in the limits of the ecosystem, nor in questions of our greed or short-sightedness, nor in the imperfections of our economic system. The problem is in comprehension. No two people think of the environment in the same way or have the same levels of knowledge. Some individuals' views may be colored by superstitions.

The study of why we think and act the way we do toward the environment, as well as toward each other, is carried out by behavioral scientists such as psychologists and geographers who differ as to the reasons for various behaviors and attitudes toward our resources and the impact of the environment on us. We can leave the arguments to them. But, it is fit for all of us as we develop resources to realize, with humility, the limits of our own environmental perceptions and, with tolerance, those of our neighbors. Meanwhile, we should work toward more understanding for all.

FREEDOM AND NATURAL RESOURCES

One of the most cherished social goals in our nation is to assure freedom of the individual. Our business system is one of "free enterprise." Largely freed of government interference, it helped develop the country much faster than might otherwise have been possible. We rejoiced in an unequaled increase in the output of goods. But, we came to realize that many natural resources had been wasted and spoiled in the process. Continuation of abuses would mean the end of our economic system and our personal freedoms as well. We would be prisoners of want and despair. Our experience showed us that our liberties could be maintained only if individuals and organizations were willing to assume responsibility for and cooperate in a national resource policy set according to the total requirements of the environment.

Thus, we have begun to put these lessons of history into action. We have adopted an economic system in which business, labor and government are asked to cooperate. Economic history teaches that productivity is stimulated by the incentives of a competitive market and the private profit system. But, we have also found that it will not always operate to our advantage without the establishment and enforcement of standards for business and labor and control of nonmarket factors (externalities). We, as consumers, have accepted some controls over our rate of resource use—for example, the Pure Food and Drug Act and the Environmental Protection Act. The situation can be likened to that of the sport of baseball. The game would be chaos, as it often was in the old sandlot days, without well-planned and agreed upon rules and regulations, observed in a cooperative manner by the players with the help of the umpires and a well-marked baseball diamond.

Markets are valuable, but imperfect, allocators of resources. And, many of the most important benefits or costs from resource use are external to the market. Therefore, we need to consider more than economic incentives in developing our natural resources. We must consider goals such as health, happiness and peace. We should consider beauty and nature's system—the ecosystem. We should take into account the limits of our environmental perception. And, we need to consider the impact of resource development on individual freedom. Such considerations, along with sound economic goals supported by laws which are enforced and practices which are carried out, will help to conserve our environment.

QUESTIONS AND PROBLEMS

1. Give an example of how the economic worth of a resource is different from its value in other ways.

2. Is water a free resource, or does it cost to make it available? Explain your answer.

3. Why didn't Simple Simon get any pie? What does this example have to do with the demand for resources?

4. Is the demand for staple food products generally elastic or inelastic? Why might inelastic demand result in a waste of resources?

5. Distinguish between creature and culture wants. What effect do these have upon our resources?

6. How does the space program illustrate the successful carrying out of both technological abilities and societal arts?

7. Are we generally successful in getting our technological abilities and societal arts to work together to achieve our goals? Why or why not?

8. What are some worthwhile conservation goals for your neighborhood, town, city or rural area? What societal arts are needed to reach them?

9. How can maintaining our individual freedoms and achieving our economic goals be likened to the playing of a game of baseball?

10. What is meant by *environmental perception?* How do you think yours differs from the perceptions of your parents?

11. Think of a good example to illustrate how living organisms and their nonliving environment are dependent upon one another. Why is this important to you?

12. What act did Congress pass in 1970 to protect the environment? What does the law require government agencies to do to help protect the environment?

3

The Increasing Use
of Natural Resources

We, as a nation, enjoy one of the highest standards of living the world has ever known. Not only do we have more food and better shelter than most other countries, but we also have more comforts to lighten our work and to add to our enjoyment.

Many foreign students who come to the United States and live here for a few years no longer want to return home. They want to share in our exceptional national wealth and personal liberties. Despite its problems, the United States is still the great land of opportunity. The immense expansion of our national wealth, however, has placed an increasing strain upon our natural resource base. If this nation is to remain a land of opportunity, we must learn to use resources more wisely and to abuse them less.

THE POPULATION EXPLOSION

One reason we use more resources than ever before is the accelerating rate of population growth, called the population explosion. The explosion has occurred because of an increase in the birth rate which has been combined with an especially sharp drop in the death rate and a longer life span. Population at the beginning of the Christian era has been estimated as 250 million. It took over 1,650 years for it to double—to 0.5 billion by the year 1650; but only 200 more years for it to double again—to 1 billion by the year 1850; then, only 80 more years to double again—to 2 billion by the year 1930; then, just 50 more years to double again—to 4 billion by 1980. By 1988, world population had reached over 5 billion. If this rate of growth continues, it will double to 10 billion in about 40 years.[1]

In contrast to the current high rate of world population growth, that of our country has been moderate—about half the world rate. While our growth rate may seem small, it still results in large *numbers* of additional people each year. By 1988, our population had reached at least 244 million. If current rates of growth continue, we will have added 23 million people to our nation in the decade 1980–1990. This would be a number of people roughly comparable to the population of Canada. To the pressures of our own population growth on the resource base of our nation will be added the pressure of the large population growth of the rest of the world.

Population growth has a much greater impact on resources than is represented by the increase in numbers of people. In the United States especially and in other advanced nations as well, the tremendous per capita consumption of goods has been multiplying the impact exponentially. *Fortune* commented in a special issue in February 1970:

> If the population declined and technology continued to breed without any improvement in the arrangements for its prudent use, a small fraction of the present U.S. population could complete the destruction of the physical environment while justling one another for room.[2]

EARLY USE OF ANIMATE ENERGY

The best use of our natural resources could not be obtained as long as most of our efforts had to be used in obtaining food, clothing and shelter. It was only after we learned to harness the running stream, unlock the

---

[1] Population data from statistics reported by the U.S. Bureau of the Census and the Population Reference Bureau. A report by the Population Institute forecasts that world population could stabilize around 7.4 billion if family planning measures were promptly taken around the globe ("Good Sense on Population," [editorial] *St. Louis Post-Dispatch*, April 23, 1987, p. 2b).

[2] "The Environment, National Mission of the Seventies," *Fortune*, February 1970, p. 101.

power in our coal and release the energy in our oil and gas resources and then to use this knowledge to create new things for our enjoyment that our standard of living began to expand beyond the three elemental necessities of life—food, clothing and shelter.

Early nomadic peoples depended mostly upon grass and the animals which ate grass for their living. When they forsook their wanderings and settled down to a more sedentary life, they immediately began making greater use of natural resources. Wooden tools were among the earliest inventions of our ancestors. As they learned to use various natural resources, they enjoyed life more and increased their standard of living.

RELATIVELY FEW RESOURCES DEMANDED

Even as late as colonial times, our ancestors had only the power of horses or oxen to produce what they wanted. The tools used then were crude and ineffective when compared with present standards. The colonists had tapped none of the natural resources except wood, water and the soil to help them in their struggle for the better things of life (see Figure 3-1).

It required the total effort and planning of the whole family to supply the bare necessities—food, clothing and shelter. The typical family in those times had two horses, or the equivalent of 20 people, to create all the material things available for its use and enjoyment.

If we turn back the pages of history from colonial days to the time of the height of Athenian culture (500 B.C.), which was built almost exclusively on slave labor, we find it also required around 20 people (slaves) to serve one free family. This means that the progress made during the intervening centuries to colonial times amounted to substituting 2 horses per family for the 20 slaves. Although this was truly a remarkable development, it meant that the colonial family still had available for its use about the same amount of power as the free Athenian family.

CHANGE TO INANIMATE ENERGY USE

Our present standard of living is built upon more than 340 horsepower in automotive energy and about 20 horsepower in nonautomotive energy

FIGURE 3-1. The first source of energy used by the colonists was wood from surrounding forests, which supplied not only building material but also the fuel so necessary to keep them warm. The second source was flowing streams, which turned stones for grinding grain and spindles for making cloth. (Courtesy, National Park Service)

for each household in the nation. Our skills and machines used for agricultural output have become so productive since the change to inanimate energy that fewer people (3.4 million) are employed today to produce in abundance the agricultural raw materials for our present population of 244 million than were employed (3.6 million) to produce for the population of only 4 million in colonial days. Furthermore, today, we send vast quantities of agricultural products overseas.[3]

Stepped-Up Demand for Resources

This immense amount of inanimate energy, which is used to make life easy and pleasant, comes from nature. We can continue to have all this

---

[3]Data from U.S. Bureau of the Census. Nonautomotive energy is that used by factories, mines, railroads, merchant ships and sailing vessels, farms, electric central stations and aircraft.

and more too, as long as reserves of natural resources are abundant. The use of resources such as iron, copper, coal, oil, gas and water power has freed us from the dreary drudgery of the past. But, what assurance have we that these various resources will continue to be available for our use and enjoyment into the indefinite future? Will we always have enough iron and coal to produce these labor-saving wonders of our machine age? Will our oil and gas reserves continue to meet our needs in the future? Will other resources continue to be plentiful as long as we need them?

ENERGY (POTENTIAL POWER) MOST NECESSARY

It is *power*—wind, water and solar power—from coal, oil, gas, nuclear and other sources—that expands our ability to convert other natural resources into useable products. The immense amount of energy used in this country contributes to making life pleasant, easy and secure, but it also has its costs, such as pollution and social unrest. Nevertheless, without this power (energy), our other resources would be much more limited.

Since the iron, copper and other metals that we need for making the machines, tools and other appliances of our present machine age would be worthless for these purposes were it not for the sources of power, let us look at our energy base to see if it appears likely that there will be enough available to meet our present and future needs.

Macro Unit of Energy

It is not possible to compare directly unlike quantities of energy, or sources of power, such as tons of coal, barrels of oil, cubic feet of gas and feet of water head. Some unit of energy common to all sources of power must be used, and for this purpose the British thermal (heat) unit—BTU—is used. The British thermal unit is a technical term meaning the amount of heat required to raise the temperature of a pound of water $1°F$. at or near its point of maximum density, $39.1°F$. This amount of heat is 252 calories.

The amount of energy used in this country runs into exceedingly large number of British thermal units. Because of this, let us call 1 trillion BTU a "macro unit" (MU) of energy.

FIGURE 3-2. The tremendous increase in our use of energy and our ability to make energy available is graphically illustrated by this powerful steam-electric generating plant compared with the water wheel shown in Figure 3-1. It would probably require over a million small mills like that one to have the capacity for work of the Baldwin Plant of the Illinois Power Company. Its summer capacity is rated at 1,800,000 kilowatts. The plant also evidences industry's increasing concern for the environment. The lake in the foreground, of 2,000 acres, was constructed by the company to recycle water for cooling the power station's condensers. As an extra bonus, the warmed lake provides year-round fishing. The metal hopper-like structures between buildings and stack are electrostatic precipitators which remove 99.6 percent of the solid particulate matter from the flue gases. (Courtesy, Illinois Power Company, Decatur, Illinois)

Amounts of Energy Used in the United States

Since the turn of the century, while our population has increased about 3.2 times, the total use of energy has increased about 9 times. Thus, use of energy in the United States has increased almost three times as fast as population. Even more efficiency of use must be achieved for the continued existence of our modern, dynamic production system is dependent upon the ready availability of a vast supply of energy for power. Furthermore, there will be more consumers. Even if low fertility rates are maintained and immigration is controlled, we will have about 20 million more citizens by the year 2000.

In 1900, this nation was using approximately 8,000 MU (8 quadrillion BTU) of energy for all purposes. By 1930, the amount had increased to 22,000 MU. The depression in the early 1930's resulted in a drop in energy use to 16,000 MU. By 1940, however, business had recovered so that 25,000 MU were produced, while during World War II this total became more than 30,000 MU. Since then, there has been a gradual expansion in energy use until, in 1984, more than 73,700 MU were used. Some reduction in the rate of energy use occurred in the early 1980's, reflecting the impact of energy shortages and conservation, and new, more efficient technologies. But, by 1987, use was on the rise again.

Superconductors

A breakthrough in research on superconductors which may, when practical application is realized, revolutionize electric power transmission, was excitedly reported by many physicists at the March 1987 meeting of the American Physical Society. The conductors are a ceramic compound (metal and oxygen) through which electricity can move at attainable temperatures with little resistance.

We may be able to send trains along the ground, relatively securely, and to replace the tens of thousands of wires serving cities with electricity with a few cables by using the new superconductors. They have promise of facilitating nuclear fusion, among countless dramatic applications. They would, in effect, multiply our energy resources many times. In fact, they could make possible as radical a change in energy transmission as occurred in land transportation when we moved from animal power to fossil fuels.[4]

Sources of Energy for Power

Coal was the source of practically all of the inanimate energy that was used for power in this country in 1900 (see Table 3-1). By 1920, oil and gas

---

[4]Many current articles are available on superconductors. One thorough and very readable article is "Breakthrough That Could Change Our World," *Time*, May 11, 1987, p. 63 ff. Another somewhat more technical article is Arthur Fisher's "Superconductivity," *Popular Science*, April 1988, pp. 54–58.

were supplying slightly more than one-sixth of our energy, while the use of coal dropped over 10 percent. The energy obtained from water power remained at practically the same percentage.

By 1940, coal was supplying only about half the power, while the proportion from oil and gas had increased approximately three times. This trend has continued. In 1980, the proportion obtained from oil and gas had dropped from its high of 76 percent in 1970. Power derived from coal is on the rise again, after having declined, supplying 30 percent of our energy.

TABLE 3-1. Sources of Energy Used in the United States, in Percentages

Year	Coal	Petroleum (Oil)	Gas	Total from Minerals	Water	Nuclear	Total Energy
1900	89	5	3	97	3	–	100
1910	85	8	4	97	3	–	100
1920	80	12	4	96	4	–	100
1930	63	24	10	97	3	–	100
1940	53	31	12	96	4	–	100
1950	42	33	20	95	5	–	100
1960	25	46	28	99	1	–	100
1970	23	43	33	99	1	1	100
1980	29	28	34	91	5	4	100
1984	30	28	31	89	5	6	100

[1] Less than 1 percent.
Source: U.S. Bureau of Mines. Figures rounded to nearest digit.

Percentages alone, however, do not always tell just what happened in the use of energy (see Figure 3-2). For example, from 1900 to 1930, when the proportion of energy supplied by coal was reduced from 89 to 63 percent of the total power used, the amount of coal used practically doubled. But, during this time, the energy derived from oil and gas increased from 623 MU to 7,356 MU, an increase of nearly 1,200 percent.

In 1979, Sam H. Schurr, et al., prepared one of the most comprehensive studies of our future energy needs undertaken in recent years for Resources for the Future, a private research organization. The study observes:

Except for coal and uranium (as extended by breeders /reactors/), domestic mineral resources seem small when compared with cumulative energy consumption for the rest of this century. However, with coal as a source of liquid and gaseous fuels—and both coal and uranium as a basis for generating electricity—the long-term domestic outlook for mineral energy is good. Costs (in the broadest sense) are the major constraints.[5]

New Sources of Energy of Power

The consumption of power discussed in the preceding paragraphs involves those energy sources that have furnished most of our power in the past and are expected to continue to do so during the next few decades. But, shifts to other sources are now occurring. There is a new awareness of pollution problems from the use of extraction of a number of the conventional sources of supply. And, we have a renewed concern about our dependence on foreign markets for oil. Therefore, the pressure is on to develop potentially cleaner or domestically available power sources that have been barely tapped. These now include geothermal energy (heat from underground); various new water sources, such as tides and the waves of the ocean; the heat of the Gulf Stream; the heat differences between various layers of water in the seas; oil shales; and energy from combustion of wastes. Also, we may reintroduce some of the power sources which were important at one time but which are largely neglected today, such as wind power.

Chapters 4 through 9 consider the present status and future prospects for our fuel and nonfuel mineral reserves, including both conventional and new sources.

QUESTIONS AND PROBLEMS

1. Illustrate how the use of natural resources has resulted in the creation or invention of new items which add to our material well-being.

2. What natural resources did primitive peoples use?

3. What are the elemental and most important needs of humans?

---

[5] Sam H. Schurr, *et al.*, *Energy in America's Future: The Choices Before Us*, Resources for the Future, Baltimore, The Johns Hopkins University Press, 1979, p. 25.

4. Approximately how much power did a family during colonial times have to supply it with the necessities and luxuries of that period?

5. How did this compare with the amount of power each family used during the height of the Athenian culture?

6. How much power per family is now available in this country, and how does this affect the living standards of our people?

7. In what ways would our minerals and forests be useful to us if there were no power from coal, gas, oil and water with which to convert the raw resources to finished products?

8. To what degree had the energy used in this country increased in relation to the population?

9. Which of our natural resources could you do without most easily in your locality? Why?

10. In what ways are the natural resources found in your area useful to your community?

11. What is meant by the term *population explosion?* How does it affect the United States?

12. What are our major sources of energy for power today? Which ones are being used the most?

4

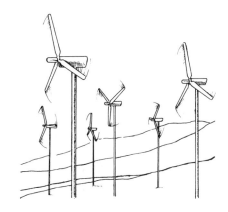

Wind and
Water Power

Everyone knows that water from running streams and from lakes is the source of a considerable amount of power, but few of us appreciate the importance that wind power had to the ancient peoples of the world, as well as to sections of this country in its earlier development. In recent years, because of the need to conserve energy, to be less dependent upon foreign supplies and to have cleaner power, there has been renewed interest in wind and water power.

Wind power from the early use of windmills to the development of modern wind turbines is discussed in this chapter. But, the discussion of water power in this chapter is limited to single-purpose use. An explanation of the characteristics of the water supply, conservation of water and multiple use of water in a river basin system is delayed until Chapter 10 so that in Chapters 5 through 9 we can learn about mineral fuels, which compete with or complement water power, and nonfuel minerals, which can be a help or a hindrance to water quality.

WIND FIRST USED FOR SAILING

Wind was one of the early used resources upon which no monetary values have been placed, mostly because of the vagaries of this universal yet most undependable of nature's gifts. Its early use was most commonly in connection with water traffic. Sailing vessels were the major form of long-distance water transportation for hundreds of years before and following the old galleys of Roman days when workers heaved and sweated and died over the tiers of oars in the dark holds of slow-moving, clumsy boats.

The Phoenicians of about 3,000 years ago were the first people to build a great maritime trade through coastline commerce, and sailing vessels were their most important means of water transportation. Cedars of Lebanon were moved by sails from the Syrian coast to Egypt. Sails replaced oars early in the history of the Phoenicians and added to their sphere of influence as well as to the speed and volume of their business.

Greece followed Phoenicia in developing an empire through the use of sails, and it in turn was followed by Rome. Although not dependent upon sails for her control, Rome, too, disintegrated, and pieces of the empire were picked up by other nations, which continued to use sails in sending and receiving products from the then known world.

Compass Expanded Navigation

It was not until after the invention of the compass, about A.D. 1400, and its application to ocean navigation that sailing vessels could head for distant ports out of the sight of land. During the next 400 years, sailing vessels moved into every nook and corner of the known water world. They even explored and opened up new worlds beyond the dreams of earlier navigators, and it was only through the use of sails that the commerce of the world was carried on.

Steam Replaced Sails

Steam-driven vessels appeared around 1820 and continued to increase in numbers until they finally all but eliminated sailing vessels from the trade lanes of the world. In the meantime, all ocean traffic increased in volume. Sailing vessels carrying the U.S. flag dotted the seven seas. The sailing ship reached its greatest perfection as a seagoing vessel about 1860. The clipper ship represented the sailing vessel at its best, but with variable winds, no winds at all or winds which had to be driven against much of the time, even this vessel was no match for a ship powered by steam in dependability of delivery, in speed and in size of cargo carried. Between 1860 and 1880, sailing vessels made the most use of this natural resource (wind) and carried their greatest amounts of world shipping. But, steam gradually took over, and, by 1900, steam tonnage outstripped sailing vessel tonnage. Since that time, sailing vessels are almost gone from the trade lanes of the world, and this once valuable resource (wind) no longer is important as a source of oceangoing power.

Different Types of Sailing Vessels

During this period of sail domination, U.S. ingenuity was responsible for the development of various types of vessels that won world recognition for their usefulness in different situations. In 1745, Andrew Robinson of Gloucester, Massachusetts, built a square-sterned vessel with two masts, a sloop sail and a bowsprit with jib. As this vessel was launched, it sped over the water so fast after coming from the ways that a bystander remarked, "See how she scoons." (*Scoon* is a word used to express the skipping of a flat stone over the surface of the water.) Mr. Robinson heard the statement and, not having named his newly rigged outfit, immediately called the vessel a "schooner." Schooners were used as fishing boats, merchant ships and even privateers, privately owned, but government authorized, attack vessels.

Another type of ship, for combination freight and passenger traffic, came into use before the Civil War. This was called the "packet." Coastwise traffic was first developed, but later various packet lines were established between U.S. and European ports. These were fast sailing ships, frequently making the trip from the United States to Europe in two weeks.

A third type of vessel, the clipper ship, was developed after the packet and was intended primarily for moving freight. Fast freight vessels were needed in trading halfway around the world in order to prevent heavy business losses and even sometimes ruin, which resulted from a decline in the market for goods while they were in slow transit.

The first clipper ship was made in Great Britain. U.S. ship builders improved on the construction so as to make for greater speed. A ship called the *Rainbow*, built in this country in 1843, was claimed to be the fastest sailing ship in the world. This ship made the round trip to Canton, China, from New York City around Cape Horn, in 6 months and 14 days. Three weeks of this time were spent in loading and unloading the cargo. Very few sailing ships ever equaled this record.

The total tonnage of ocean-borne freight and passenger traffic now carried by sailing vessels is negligible. The world lost a touch of color and glamor when these full-sailed, picturesque white birds disappeared from our seas.

WINDMILLS BECAME IMPORTANT

A second use of wind power was to turn the wheels of windmills for grinding grain and pumping water. Windmills were used in European countries 1,200 years ago, but despite the improvements made in them since that time, they still cannot compete efficiently with oil, gas and electricity in serving people.

When Mark Twain visited the Azores in 1867, he was impressed by the use made of windmills on those islands. He wrote that these mills would grind 10 bushels of corn a day if the wind did not change direction. Whenever that happened, it was necessary to hitch some donkeys to the upper half of each mill and turn it around until the sails were again in position to catch the wind. This illustrates one of the obvious shortcomings of the early windmills. The Dutch overcame this handicap by building mills with rotating tops. Even so, these mills were difficult to control in variable winds, and although the grinding was much more rapid than if done by hand, it was exceedingly slow when compared with present rates of grinding by other means.

Windmills on the Prairies

Windmills probably reached the peak of their usefulness and their numbers in the settling of the prairie states east of the Rockies. In fact, but for the use of windmills, it is doubtful that farming and the hundreds of small towns on the prairies would have developed so early or so rapidly. Water was needed for livestock as well as for people. Surface water was available only in the creeks and rivers, and, although most of the early towns were built on or near streams, the vast multitude of farms had no surface water available for their use. Farmers had to depend on either hand-dug or bored wells and hand-operated pumps for water, both for their houses and for their livestock. It was in this region that windmills became most useful.

FIGURE 4-1. The most spectacular type of wind is the tornado or twister, or cyclone as it is frequently called. Storms of this type generally occur in the warmer seasons of the year. More than 250 individual tornadoes have been recorded by the U.S. Weather Bureau in one season. Tornadoes unleash immense destructive power. Steady, reliable winds are needed for efficient wind power.

Pumping Water a Slow Process

The rate of pumping water by wind power was not great, but with some wind blowing almost every day, it was possible to store enough water in stock tanks and reservoirs to meet all the farm needs in normal times.

A 10-foot diameter wheel in a 16-mile wind would raise in one hour:

19.0 gallons	25	feet
9.5 gallons	50	feet
6.6 gallons	75	feet
4.7 gallons	100	feet

Reasons for the Disappearance of Windmills

Two events probably accounted for the rapid disappearance of windmills from our towns and farms—the development of gasoline and electric engines and the demand for greater volumes of water. It occasionally happened that for many successive days no wind would blow. Storage tanks would become empty, and in order to supply livestock with the necessary water, someone in the family would have to spend hours pumping water by hand for a herd of thirsty animals. This inconvenience always seemed to occur when there were many other kinds of farm work to be done. The use of gasoline or diesel engines and, later, the wide availability of the more convenient electricity were welcome substitutes for wind.

A second reason for doing away with this intermittent wind power was the desire of both city and farm dwellers for continuous water supplies. When homes had running water, they no longer had to depend upon the vagaries of the wind to keep up their water supplies. Coal, gas and oil and eventually electricity replaced the windmill.

WIND TURBINES BRING NEW LIFE TO WIND POWER

In recent years, wind power has been given new life by the development of more efficient wind turbines and increased knowledge of wind velocities and favorable sites to obtain the maximum wind potential for power. Both the federal government and various states have supported the development and installation of wind energy machines. Although wind is still not a source of power in any large segment of our society, it appears to be becoming much more important.

Present research is along three lines: (1) small wind turbines with small electrical outputs, (2) intermediate-scale systems of 100- to 500-kilowatt capacities and (3) larger-scale systems designed to produce more than 500 kilowatts.

At the end of 1985, there were 13,263 small- and intermediate-scale wind power systems in operation in the United States with a capacity of generating 1,097 megawatts of electricity, an amount roughly equal to that of a large nuclear reactor. California, Hawaii, Massachusetts, New York and Oregon have small wind farms producing power for sale. Power from wind was generating electricity equivalent to 2 million barrels of oil by early 1986. Large potentials for future generation lie in the Great Plains and coastal areas.

California has the largest installed capacity of wind turbines in the world. One typical small unit built by Wind Power Systems is 60 feet high and has a three-bladed rotor 33 feet in diameter. It generates 18 kilowatt-

FIGURE 4-2. An increasing amount of electricity is being generated by wind turbines on wind farms, such as the one shown here in Altamont Pass near San Francisco, California.

hours of electricity at wind speeds of 25 miles per hour. With capacity figured at 18 percent, this output is about equivalent to the electricity use of four average California households.

A large Bendix-Schachle wind turbine, installed by Southern California Edison Company in the San Gorgonio Pass near Palm Springs, is rated at

1.3 megawatts of annual output at wind speeds of 130 miles or more. This unit is judged sufficient to supply the average needs of over 200 families.

During 1986, total output of 1.2 billion kilowatt-hours of electricity by California wind generators was enough to meet the needs of 200,000 typical California homes. In the first two quarters of 1988, a total of 875.8 million kilowatt-hours of electricity was produced, indicating that 1988 output will exceed that of 1987 by a wide margin.

California wind system power is fed into the state's electric grid served by other sources of electric power. Despite modern developments, wind power still suffers from uneven diurnal and seasonal variation which makes it difficult to support firm power commitments.[1]

Wind industry sources estimate that by the year 2000 between ½ million and 1 million small windmills will be generating 1 percent of U.S. electrical needs and that windmills overall will account for 3 to 6 percent of all electrical power generated, thus rivaling hydropower. If federal and state financial incentives for individuals and businesses and large research contracts continue, these expectations may be realized.

WINDS RESPONSIBLE FOR RAINFALL

Of course, winds will continue to be necessary in carrying the moisture-laden air from over seas and oceans to the soils of the world. If winds should fail to blow even for one year, the vast soil areas of the country would produce nothing; and if no winds blew for a series of years, the productive lands would become deserts. Our soils would become useless, and all life would disappear except along the shores of the oceans. Winds, when considered from this point of view, will continue to be an essential resource. They generally are not viewed as an economic resource because, even though necessary for our existence, they continue to move uncontrolled and undirected across continents. Our knowledge of wind currents has increased greatly in recent years, but we still cannot predict with accu-

---

[1] California Energy Commission, *Wind Energy, Investing in Our Energy Future,* Sacramento, State of California, 1984, p. 7; California Energy Commission, *Results from the Wind Project Performance Reporting System, 2nd Quarter 1985; Ibid.,* 1986, p. 3; Sam Rashkin, Project Manager, California Energy Commission, Interview, April 5, 1988. Average use of electricity by California households is relatively light by national standards. Estimates of deliverable power make allowances for capacity which take into account variability of the wind.

racy just when, where and how much winds will blow, especially in the middle latitudes. Nor have we mastered the technology of controlling winds.

WATER POWER FROM FLOWING STREAMS

Let us look at water power from flowing streams, the earliest important resource of inanimate energy in this country. Water power is thought of as a continuing resource—one not depleted with use. It was one of the most commonly used sources of power during our early history. Water wheels were placed in streams for grinding grain and sawing lumber. These operations represented the principal manufacturing purposes for which inanimate energy was used at that time.

Later on, as invention added to our inanimate energy requirements, the water power of streams was used to turn spindles for the textile industry and to generate electricity. Its use did not continue to keep pace with the need for power, however, so that by 1900 only a small proportion, less that 4 percent, of the power used in this country was derived from water. Water will continue to supply a relatively small portion of the power

FIGURE 4-3. Lake Hokah in Minnesota was constructed for power nearly 100 years ago, and it was used as a resort by the citizens of nearby communities. Railroad shops and a flour mill were built here to take advantage of the power. (See also Figures 4-4 and 4-5.) (Courtesy, Soil Conservation Service)

used in the United States, even though great strides have been made since 1900 in storing our flood waters for use in industry and agriculture, as well as in reducing flood water losses. This has resulted in water power production's keeping pace with the overall increase in power used.

COSTS OF CONVENTIONAL SOURCES OF WATER POWER

One of the misconceptions about water power is that since it is derived by harnessing free-flowing water in nature, it is relatively cheap. But, this "ain't necessarily so," to use the phrase made famous by composer George Gershwin many years ago. There are many costs involved in making water power useful to industry. Some of these, such as costs of installation, are more or less common to all sources of power, but others pertain only to the use of water power.

Let us consider the following costs: (1) installation costs, (2) operating costs, (3) costs because of irregularity of water supply, (4) costs of loss of benefits under natural stream conditions and (5) non-economic environmental costs. The latter two types of costs are apt to be borne by others than the development agency.

Installation costs.—The costs of constructing dams and of installing water wheels, generators and other equipment necessary to convert water into usable power are substantial for most streams. The size of streams cannot be increased, and since most streams are small, only a small amount of power can be produced from each installation. Installation costs per unit of power generated usually are disproportionately large for the smaller sources of water power, and in many instances, these costs are relatively so great that it is not profitable to harness these small streams. Larger streams, especially those which are fairly fast-flowing, ordinarily can be harnessed profitably. When once the installation has been made, keeping it in repair is not an expensive task.

Operating costs.—The costs of carrying electrical energy are fairly high because copper wire, used because it is a good conductor, is costly. Even when aluminum-coated steel wire is used, the expense remains high. Also, losses of power into the air, along the transmission lines, are considerable, especially when energy is carried long distances.

FIGURE 4-4. Clearing of timber from the steep hillslopes, plowing up and down hills and absence of vegetation on the surface to slow the water run-off filled Lade Hokah with silt. All that was left of the little lake when this picture was taken was a swamp with a small stream running through the middle. (See also Figures 4-3 and 4-5.) (Courtesy, Soil Conservation Service)

FIGURE 4-5. Fifteen years after the photo in Figure 4-4 was taken, the swamp had filled in enough to make possible the raising of some garden produce on a part of the old lake bed. There fields continue to be subject to flooding so that it is not always possible to use this small area for crop production. (Compare with Figures 4-3 and 4-4.) (Courtesy, Soil Conservation Service)

Most water power installations made in earlier times used the power directly through water wheels and gears to run spindles, grinding stones, etc., so that the power of small streams could be used effectively. With the coming of big industry, large-scale production and lower relative costs, the installation of more of these small units became unprofitable. Those already installed were used either until the water storage space back of dams filled with silt or until the machinery needed to be replaced. Many of these early installations were then abandoned, either because replacement costs were so great that power could be supplied by coal or some other source more cheaply than through the local water supply or because the specific product being made could be shipped in at less cost than it could be produced locally. An illustration of this change is the harnessing of small streams all over Kansas and other sections of the Wheat Belt. In the early years of settlement, the power produced from these small streams was used to make wheat flour and to grind feed. The area served by each of the mills was limited to a few townships or at most a few counties An owner wishing to expand operations, could do so only by installing a supplemental power unit, wherein the additional energy was supplied by coal or oil shipped in over the railways which stretched across the prairies. Such a mill continued to operate as long as the milling or power machinery did not have to be replaced or the mill pond back of the dam did not fill with sediment.

Competition became so severe, however, because of the inexpensiveness with which flour could be made in large mills that these local mills could not meet all necessary repairs and improvement costs, pay for labor and still make money. It is for these reasons that whenever any catastrophe overtook the local mill it was not replaced; instead, it went out of existence.

Costs because of irregularity of water supply.—In addition to obtaining power from the drop of water from the distance between spillway and generator levels, storing water in back of dams is done in order to obtain a more nearly constant supply of power. If rains fell once or twice a week and about the same quantity of water fell within every four- to six-week period throughout the year, there would always be a fairly constant supply of water in the smaller streams. This does not happen, however, because storms vary in frequency as well as in intensity. Rainfall varies also with the different seasons, so that during one part of the year an area may have many times the precipitation of another season.

FIGURE 4-6. The Grand Coulee Dam in Washington is one of the largest concrete structures in the world. Potential capacity of the dam is almost 10 million kilowatts. It is also one of the most powerful hydroelectric installations in the world. Irrigation and recreation benefits are provided as well by this and other dams in the Columbia River Basin. (Courtesy, Bureau of Reclamation)

The larger rivers have more nearly constant water supplies because they drain much larger areas. They, too, are subject to seasonal variation, however, so that immense dams are built to impound flood waters of one season in order to feed generators during seasons of little rainfall.

Costs of loss of benefits under natural stream conditions.—When a river flood plain is flooded by dams, the use of the river bottomland for agriculture, as a base on which to locate highways and railroads, and for many other uses, will be effectively precluded for tens, perhaps hundreds, of years—or even forevermore. The dam builders point out that the protection of the flood plain below the dam helps offset such losses. But, such protection may be more theoretical than real. If rain continues after water has filled the reservoir to capacity, the impounded water must be released. No more can be stored. Thus, severe flooding may occur below the dam. Calculation of the cost of any dam should include a charge-off against "lost" resources.

Non-economic environmental costs.—The non-economic environmental costs of damming a stream may be the most critical to society. But, they are generally difficult to assess because they have no clear market value. Who can express in dollars and cents the value of the loss of the beauty of canyons now under the waters impounded by the Glen Canyon Dam on the Colorado River? Or, who can weigh the cost when the wild rushing torrent of water in a stream is brought to a quiet halt? How much are the delicate wildflowers and exotic wildlife worth that may be destroyed by damming a stream? And, how do we evaluate the loss of free-flowing water for recreation—canoeing, kayaking or rafting? Economists have devised ways to estimate such "external" costs. Such figures are gaining increasing acceptance.

Silting Back of Dams

One important problem in connection with practically all dams is the filling with silt of the reservoirs back of them as fine soil particles are dropped from slowed-down stream waters. This silting takes place most rapidly in streams which carry the most sediment.

Most of the streams that drain cultivated land are muddy, silt-carrying streams. Practically all the streams of the prairie states, as well as of Indiana and Ohio and many of the southern and southeastern states, are muddy. Even when these streams originate in mountainous or forested areas and start as clear water, they become dirt filled as soon as they pass through cultivated land. Dams built on these streams after they reach cultivated land may be expected to fill with silt and to lose their water-holding capacities within a few decades.

Whenever a reservoir is filled with silt, it is no longer a continuing source of power. The amount of water that can be stored becomes so limited that only a fraction of the seasonal water run-off can be stored so as to be available later on in the year. No practical method has yet been devised for flushing the deposited silt out of the reservoirs. Silting can be reduced and the life of the reservoir lengthened, however, by controlling erosion on the banks of the stream and adjoining watershed, by building dams on small tributary streams to help precipitate silt before it reaches the main stream and to aid in controlling flood waters, and by providing a siltation basin at the upstream end of the reservoir.

The dams which are built on clear water streams may not fill with silt for hundreds of years. Snow-fed streams and those which drain forest and woodland areas carry the least amount of sediment. Also, many streams that drain mountain country are clear water streams.

DISTRIBUTION OF WATER POWER

One limitation of hydroelectric power is the uneven distribution of generation capacity (see Table 4-1).

TABLE 4-1. Estimated Conventional Hydroelectric Installed and Potential Power Generation Capacity in the United States by Water Resource Regions

Water Resource Region	Percent of U.S. Total
West	
Pacific Northwest................................	50
California	11
Other Major Western	10
Upper Colorado	
Lower Colorado	
Missouri River	
Arkansas—White–Red	
Four western regions in arid Southwest	1
Total Western	72
East	
Major Regions	20
South Atlantic Gulf	
Great Lakes	
Tennessee	
Others	8
New England	
Middle Atlantic	
Ohio	
Upper Mississippi	
Lower Mississippi	—
Total Eastern	28
Total	100

Source: Percentages computed by author Kircher from estimates up to 1993 in U.S. Water Resources Council, *Water for Energy Self-Sufficiency*, Washington, D.C., 1974. Percentages are rounded to nearest whole number.

Table 4-1 shows that the West dominates in the availability of conventional hydroelectric power generation capacity. Great differences occur in the capacity of the various water resource regions.

BENEFITS OF CONVENTIONAL WATER POWER

The benefits of using free-flowing streams as a source of power for manufacturing in colonial days are clear. Wind was the only alternative source of inanimate energy power until steam engines became available. Today, many other sources of energy are available and, also, are more efficient. Where multiple use of dams for flood control, navigation and power is effectively done, as by the Tennessee Valley Authority (see Chapter 10) the benefits of power are a sort of bonus received when the other desirable functions are carried out. Water power thus figured as a share of other costs is relatively cheap.

In one respect, hydroelectric power remains outstanding. It is clean power. No air pollution, super-heated water or waste-disposal problems, such as are typical of other power plants, occur.

Despite its problems, conventional water power is a significant energy resource. At the present time, it provides over 5 percent of the power used in the United States and 13 percent of the nation's electricity. The electricity produced is only slightly less than that generated by nuclear energy.

NEW SOURCES OF WATER POWER

Sources of water power other than free-flowing streams have been little researched and even less used in the United States. Yet, they offer astonishing possibilities to supplement our energy needs. New sources of water power that have been proposed include tidal power from the sea, heat interchanges in the sea and use of the Gulf Stream current.

Tidal Power from the Sea

Use of tidal power as an energy source is especially appealing because the rising and falling of the tides are as regular in their occurrences as the movement of the moon around the earth and the rotation of the earth itself. Here is a never-failing source of energy. However, the problems are to: (1) find areas where the rising and falling of the tides are enough to generate a worthwhile amount of power: (2) store or provide for alternate power in times of change in the tides or low tides; and (3) devise a profitable system for harnessing the surge of water.

The first proposal to use the power of the tides in this country was for Passamaquody Bay, located off the Bay of Fundy on the Maine coast. This bay has an effective tide of 18 feet. Schemes to harness its immense power were developed in the 1930's through encouragement of President Franklin Delano Roosevelt, who had vacationed in that picturesque area as a young man. But a tidal plant still had not been realized as of 1987 in the United States, even though France has had a successfully functioning tidal plant on its northern seacoast for several years. Furthermore, a 20-megawatt Canadian demonstration plant, built in Nova Scotia on the Annapolis River, which carries the Bay of Fundy tides, started generating power in 1984.

Two technological developments that have made the U.S. venture more possible in recent years than half a century ago are refinements in turbines to be used in generating the power and economies in extra high voltage transmission of the power.

The project is massive. One estimate was that it would require 7½ miles of dams and 15 years to complete. It would trap some 70 billion cubic feet of sea water and generate a million kilowatts of power. But, if successful, the benefits would also be great. For it would bring cheaper power to a traditionally power-short region—New England.

Heat Interchanges in the Sea

One possibility for water power that has yet to be demonstrated commercially, but has such vast potential it is worth noting, is to obtain energy by exploiting the great heat difference that exist between surface waters and those deep down in the seas. Off the Florida coast, for example, the ocean surface may be 75° to 90°F., while several thousand feet down, it is near freezing. A fluid with a low boiling point would be heated near the surface to drive a turbine, then condensed in the cold water below.

Use of the Gulf Stream Current

The Gulf Stream is a warm current of water which flows eastward out of the Gulf of Mexico and then northward along our eastern coast at a rate of about 4 miles per hour, gradually diminishing in velocity. Some scientists have suggested that a huge underwater paddle be installed to use the force of this current to drive a generator of electrical power. Such a project is still visionary. But, we need to dream more about the possibilities of our ocean resources. The oceans' potential as a power source has largely been overlooked.

WATER POWER POTENTIAL

Water power is a clean, inexhaustible resource. But, it is not always readily available. And, free-flowing streams should only be obstructed by dams if benefits exceed costs, including environmental costs.

Use of tidal power and manipulation of ocean waves, currents and heat interchanges offer interesting possibilities, largely untested.

Overall, it is unlikely that water power will in the foreseeable future contribute more than $\frac{1}{10}$ of our energy needs, assuming present technology. Multiple uses of installations for water power are discussed in Chapter 10, along with an analysis of characteristics, use and conservation of the water supply.

QUESTIONS AND PROBLEMS

1. What ancient nations used a common natural resource to develop their trade and increase their influence and power?

2. What invention about A.D. 1400 greatly extended the use of this resource?

3. At about what time did sailing vessels reach their peak of usefulness, and why were they replaced by steam-powered ships as the carriers of the oceangoing freight of the world?

4. What types of sailing vessels were developed in this country, and for what was each noted?

5. Name a second common use of wind as a power and name the countries which became noted because of the use of this power.

6. What caused windmills to disappear from the farms and the cities of our prairies?

7. In what way will the winds of the continent continue to be useful to the nation?

8. In what ways is water power better than wind power?

9. What are some of the costs that must be met in harnessing the water power of our thousands of streams throughout the land?

10. What are non-economic environmental costs that may result from the damming of a stream?

11. What are some of the benefits of water power? In what respect is water power outstanding?

12. What are three possibilities of obtaining more power by harnessing the energy of ocean waters?

13. Will water power ever be able to meet all our energy needs? Why or why not?

14. How much water power is developed in the county in which you live, and for what purposes is it used?

15. Does present research indicate that wind power may again be used extensively in the United States? Explain your answer.

5

Coal

Coal, which is the source of about one-third of the energy used in the United States (see Table 3-1), is the most widely distributed of our current major energy resources. Yet, very little of it was used in this country 150 years ago. China used a little coal as long ago as 100 B.C., and there is evidence to show that the Romans used it in Britain in 400 B.C. It was not used commonly as fuel, however, until about 800 years ago, or about A.D. 1200. The English people themselves used coal as a household fuel as early as A.D. 850.

The early colonists had little need for coal because they had plenty of wood. Not only did these pioneers use firewood as a source of fuel, but clearing the land of timber served the double purpose of supplying fuel and making available more land upon which to produce food and fibre crops. Fathers Marquette and Joliet reported the discovery of coal in the "Illinois Country" around 1673, while anthracite coal was found in northeastern Pennsylvania in 1790. At that time these discoveries were of little importance.

The growth of the coal-using industry in this country has largely taken place since the 1860's. In 1824, only about 81,000 tons of coal were mined in the United States, while, in 1947, the total output was 676 million tons—about 8,300 times as much. Coal production then dropped off to about 420 million tons in 1961. Since then, demand has again risen; output was about 600 to 650 million tons per year in the early 1970's and

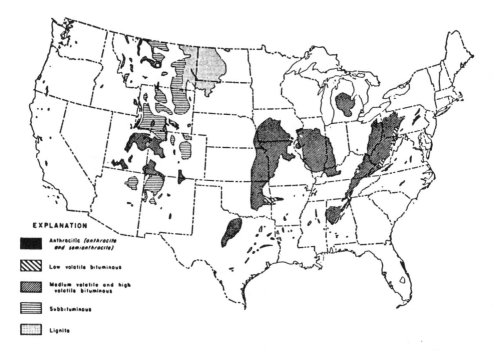

EXPLANATION

■ Anthracitic (anthracite and semianthracite)

▨ Low volatile bituminous

▨ Medium volatile and high volatile bituminous

▤ Subbituminous

☐ Lignite

FIGURE 5-1. The major coal-producing areas of the United States. Most of our soft coal comes from the "medium volatile and high volatile bituminous" areas. (Courtesy, U.S. Geological Survey)

over 800 million tons per annum during the early 1980's, reaching 897 million tons in 1987.

A grand total of more than 40 billion tons of coal has been mined in the United States since the beginning of coal-mining operations about 200 years ago. While this amount represents less than 2 percent of the estimated coal reserves in this country, some of the reserves are not easily accessible. As is explained in the following paragraphs, the potential for economically feasible reserves depends upon many variable factors.

LOCATION OF COAL RESERVES

The wide distribution of coal makes it available to every corner of the country. Over 30 states have mines, and coal is available to practically any community with no more than a 500-mile haul. There are three general coal regions which are identified as major coal-producing areas: the Appalachian field, the Interior field and the Rocky Mountain field (see Figure 5-1).

The largest and most extensive of the three is the Appalachian field. This field is found in nine states, stretching from Pennsylvania in the North to Alabama in the South. This field has the highest grade coal to be found in North America and is the largest soft coal field in the world.

The Interior field is next in importance, though it is much less extensive than the Appalachian field. There are several separate producing areas in this general location, the most important of which is the area of Illinois, Indiana and western Kentucky. Another field touches the six states of Iowa, Nebraska, Kansas, Oklahoma, Missouri and Arkansas, while smaller fields are found in Texas and Michigan.

The third field, the Rocky Mountain field, extends brokenly from Montana through Wyoming, Colorado and Utah to New Mexico. It has vast reserves of lignite, sub-bituminous and generally low-grade bituminous coals with a BTU potential estimated to be nearly as much as, or possibly even more than, that of the fields east of the Mississippi River. Production has increased greatly in this field because of the lower sulfur content of coal than in the Appalachian and Interior fields, and more coal is expected to be produced there. But, impending changes in laws controlling pollution, in technology and in use of alternative fuels make the future difficult to predict.

A little coal is found in the three Pacific Coast states, but mining operations are not extensive.

HOW COAL IS FORMED

Coal is the fossilized remains of trees and other vegetation which formed immense, dense forests millions of years ago. The clay or other material over which coal is always found was once the soil which supported the vegetation that later became coal.

Many coal beds are separated by layers of clay, shale, sandstone or limestone. These layers indicate that not all the coal-forming vegetation grew in one age. Each bed of coal between the different layers of clay, limestone, etc., represents a period of thousands of years wherein new trees and other vegetation grew and thrived. The layers of non-carbonaceous material between the coal beds were deposited on land or in shallow seas as the land slowly subsided and rose after each coal bed was deposited. The deposition of each layer took thousands of years. It is estimated that it required at least 1,000 years to form a layer of coal 1 foot thick.

KINDS OF COAL, RESERVES AND USES

Coal is made of hydrocarbons (compounds of hydrogen and carbon) and moisture. When coal is burned, that which burns with the clearest flame and leaves the least ash has the highest carbon content. The moisture, mineral content and sulfur compounds produce gaseous sulfur compounds, while the mineral compounds produce the ash.

At any given site, assuming the coal is equally accessible, coal's economic value and use is dependent upon the ratio of hydrogen to carbon, other mineral content and moisture.

Although there is enough coal in this country to last several hundred years, not all of it is of sufficient quality or in thick enough beds for commercial recovery. Other beds lie so deep in the earth that the costs of recovery are too high at the present time to be economically feasible. Bending and breaking of coal beds by movements of the earth's crust makes coal mining expensive and difficult. The U.S. Geological Survey considers the following thicknesses of coal beds as minimum for most commercial production or recovery:

Bituminous coal . . . . .30 inches
Sub-bituminous coal . . . . .24 inches
Lignite . . . . .36 inches
Anthracite . . . . .36 inches

Underground production equipment has recently been designed to work either bituminous or anthracite coal seams of less thickness than those just listed, and operators using small-scale, hand-loading equipment in underground production sometimes mine from beds no thicker than 24 inches.

Coal reserves in this country at depths less than 6,000 feet below the earth's surface are estimated to be more than 3,900 billion tons with about one-half of it (1,700 billion tons) at depths to 3,000 feet in mapped and explored areas. Demonstrated reserves are 490 billion tons, according to estimates of the U.S. Department of Energy, Energy Information Administration, 1983. At least one-half of this demonstrated reserve can be recovered. One-third to one-half of these usable reserves are close enough to the surface to be recoverable by surface mining methods.

The quality of coal mined varies greatly, and each type of coal has its best uses as well as certain drawbacks. Some coals burn more completely than others (that is, with less ash), while others give off more volatile gases from which by-products can be made, and still others have considerable waste in the form of moisture. This means that coals must be carefully selected for different purposes if they are to be most effectively used.

Characteristics of Different Types of Coal

The different types of coal and the uses for which they are especially suitable are as follows:

1. **Peat.** The first step in the development of coal from plants is the formation of peat. This always takes place under water. Not much is known about just how peat becomes coal, but it is believed that the various types of coal are formed by different amounts of heat and pressure. Large peat bogs occur in northern Europe. Some peat is found in the northern part of the United States, although much more is found in Canada. It is used for fuel in countries such as Ireland, Scotland and England, as well as in the Netherlands, Denmark and in some parts of northern East and West Germany. Charcoal is made from peat, and this product is used for working and tempering the finer kinds of cutlery.

2. **Lignite.** A great deal of the coal on the European continent, as well as much of Canada's supply, is lignite. The word *lignite* is taken from the Latin word *lignum*, meaning "wood." Thus, lignite is "half-made" coal and is usually quite woody. Most lignite is brown in color, although some is so black it is called jet. This black lignite is sometimes used for making buttons, toys, jewelry, etc., because it takes a high polish.

3. **Bituminous.** Bituminous (soft) coal is next in hardness after lignite. One of its chief varieties is called coking coal, which swells up into a porous mass when heated. Non-coking coal, which does not melt into a mass when heated, is the kind used in home furnaces. Most of the coal used in this country is bituminous coal.

4. *Anthracite.* Anthracite coal is the hardest and most brittle of coals. It is jet black and practically free from pitch or bitumen, and, when ignited, it burns slowly with a clear blue flame. It generates a great amount of heat and burns with little or no smoke. It is so difficult to ignite that one of its early uses was not as fuel but as road-building material. Later, anthracite was used for heating homes in the picturesque base-burners. A pail of coal would burn for 10 to 12 hours in one of these stoves, and it gave out enough heat to warm the normal-sized living room. The important use of anthracite now is for making gas, which is used primarily for heating and cooking.

The different types of coal with their ranges in fixed carbon, volatile matter and moisture are shown in Table 5-1.

TABLE 5-1. Ranges in Fixed Carbon, Volatile Matter and Moisture of the Different Types of Coal in Percentage by Weight

Type of Coal	Range in		
	Fixed Carbon	Volatile Matter	Moisture
	(%)		
Lignite	30–55	30–10	43–30
Bituminous	47–65	41–32	72– 3
Low-volatile bituminous	75–83	22–12	5– 3
Anthracite	85–96	2– 1	6– 2

As the fixed carbon content become greater, the volatile matter becomes less. The final product is graphite, which is practically pure carbon. Anthracite coal, which was burned in the old base-burners, burns with very little color and leaves very little ash, since about 90 percent of it is carbon. On the other hand, bituminous coal varies greatly in the way it burns and in the amount of ash it leaves after the carbon is burned out of the coals.

COAL DETERMINED THE SITES FOR INDUSTRY

Coal is important to the development of factories in every country in which there is much manufacturing. In England, iron and steel manufacture are carried on in the North Country and the Midlands where coal is found. Areas with no coal have few factories. The Ruhr development on the European mainland is the result of the coal and iron deposits located there and nearby. In the United States, the first great concentration of industries was in the coal-producing regions of Pennsylvania. Birmingham, Alabama, has many factories because of its coal.

While ready access to an energy source is still important today for high energy-using manufacturers, the ease with which coal is moved by barge, ship or rail or after conversion, sent over power lines as electricity and the availability of other sources of power have greatly lessened the significance of coal fields as location sites for industry. Transportation, however, can be costly. Most long-distance hauling of coal in the United States is by rail, and in many cases, the cost of moving the coal is more than the cost of mining it.

REDUCING COSTS AND INCREASING THE AVAILABILITY OF COAL

Reduced mining costs have enhanced the ability of coal to compete with other energy sources. One way of reducing mining costs has been by the use of more efficient machinery. In some mines a three-person team with a push-button machine can turn out coal at the rate of 250 tons an hour and work seams no thicker than 3½ feet.

Allowing for changes in the value of the dollar, it costs less to produce coal than it did 30 years ago, even though wages have risen sharply. Surface mining has especially low costs, with giant shovels lifting over 200 tons of overburden (the cover of soil or stone) at a bite (see Figure 5-2)! Small shovels then load the coal into trucks (see Figures 5-3 and 5-8). Surface mining is safer than shaft mining and thus less costly in terms of human lives.

One of the newest methods of underground mining is long-wall mining (see Figure 5-4). This method permits subsidence of the land at the surface of the ground, if it is to occur, to take place under control and in a relatively short time, thus reducing the problem. Long-wall mining recovers a much higher proportion of the coal than when numerous pillars are left. Surface mining recovers 90 percent or more of the available coal. Other mining operations are shown in Figures 5-5 and 5-6.

Environmental costs directly add to the cost of producing and using coal and indirectly affect the ecosystem. Direct costs include the cost of

FIGURE 5-2. Big Muskie, the world's largest dragline, cost $27 million to build and has a reach the length of a football field. It weighs 27 million pounds and lumbers back and forth on mammoth "feet" at a central Ohio surface mine. Its 220-cubic yard bucket can move 325 tons of overburden at a single pass. Note how the workers and even the cars and trucks are dwarfed by comparison. (Courtesy, Bucyrus Erie Company)

FIGURE 5-3. After topsoil and overburden are removed, a loading shovel scoops coal from a seam averaging 55 feet thick at the Cordero Mine south of Gillette, Wyoming. This surface mine is operated by Sunoco Energy Development Co. (SUNEDCO), a unit of Sun Oil Company, Inc., and produces 3 million tons of low sulfur coal a year. (Courtesy, Sun Oil Company, Inc.)

FIGURE 5-4. Long-wall mining machinery has been instrumental in improving productivity at the Powhatan No. 4 Mine. (Courtesy, The North American Coal Corporation)

land restoration, water protection and control of emissions from coal-burning plants. Coal mining and burning are regulated under several federal laws, including the Surface Mining and Reclamation Act, which requires that surface mined land be restored to its original contour and productivity; the Clean Water Act, which requires mine operators to restore water quality affected by mining; and the Clean Air Act, which limits emissions from coal-burning plants. Complying with these acts is costly, but when properly applied, it is essential for environmental protection.

Indirect costs of coal production and/or consumption include air and water pollution and soil disturbance and land subsidence. Indirect environ-

FIGURE 5-5. Far underground, Sue Eagleston tends a conveyor belt which carries coal out of the Wabash mine of Amax Coal Company in Keensburg, Illinois. Women, once taboo in underground mines in the United States, now hold an increasing number of jobs in the industry. The full use of all labor resources is essential to the full development of natural resources. (Photo from Amax Coal Company; courtesy, National Coal Association)

FIGURE 5-6. A roof-bolting machine bores a hole in the roof of a coal mine. A steel expansion bolt will be inserted in the hole and tightened, binding overlying rock layers together like plywood to make a firm roof without traditional wood props. Bolts already installed are visible elsewhere in the roof. Miner stands under protective canopy. (Photo from Lee-Norse Company; courtesy, National Coal Association)

mental costs are borne by society in general but may affect one group or area much more severely than others. Such costs are discussed later in this chapter.

Gasification and Liquefaction

Processes to produce coal-derived fuels are being developed. Gasification processes would produce either a high heat content, pipeline-quality substitute for natural gas or a low heat synthetic fuel for utility boilers. The liquefaction process (also called **hydrogenation**) would wring crude oil out of coal, which in turn could be converted into gasoline or lubricating oils.

Gaseous and liquid fuels derived from coal were used by Germany to fuel its military vehicles during World War II and are commercially produced today in some countries, such as South Africa, which have abundant coal and little or no petroleum.

USES OF COAL

The largest use of coal is for generation of electricity. In recent years about four-fifths of the coal used in the United States has been for this purpose. Industrial use has been taking about $\frac{1}{10}$, and coke production most of the remainder. About 55 percent of the energy generated by electric utilities in 1987 was powered by coal.

Other Uses of Coal

When bituminous coal is heated without access to air, it does not burn but gives off gases. The remaining product is no longer called coal; it is coke, which is mostly carbon. Coke is used for fuel, but its most important use is for changing (reducing) iron oxide to iron, essential to the production of iron and steel. Since not all coals will form satisfactory coke, those that will should not be diverted to other uses. In past years, the gases were used for lighting dwellings and businesses, but this practice has largely been discontinued.

Another by-product in the manufacture of gas and coke from coal is coal-tar. This is useful in many ways because of the products that can be made from it. It is used as a paint and as a preservative of timber in its crude form. It is also used in making tar paper. Practically all aniline dyes are made from coal-tar, and the shades of color obtained from these dyes compete with the rainbow. Ammonia, carbolic acid, benzine, alum and picric acid, used in the manufacture of explosives, all are by-products of coal. Few would expect to find that some delicate perfumes are made from coal, yet that is the case.

Why Coal Use Has Declined Relative to Gas and Oil

In view of the many advantages of coal as a source of power, why has it fallen from 90 percent of the source of energy in the United States in 1900 to 30 percent in 1984 (Table 3-1)? Why have we turned from a resource with reserves within our national boundaries that, by even the most conservative estimates, will last many decades and is readily available at economical costs? By contrast, as the following chapter relates, oil reserves have become more costly to obtain domestically, and we are dependent upon foreign supplies. Nuclear energy, through fission—the current process—has serious security and environmental risks. Other promising sources of clean power, such as nuclear fusion and geothermal energy, are still in the developmental stages.

Two major reasons for coal's subordination to gas and oil as an energy source are predominant. The first reason is economic and technological. Gas and oil proved to be more suitable and economical for some industrial processes and many motor age developments. Coal furnaces in homes were replaced by gas or oil furnaces which required less labor and attention, and many factories switched as well. Petroleum provided the gasoline and diesel fuel powering automobiles, locomotives, ships and many stationary motors. The second major reason for coal's relative long-term decline is environmental. The exploitation of no other mineral had resulted in so much ravaged land or polluted air, so there was great pressure to develop alternative fuels.

An estimated 3.2 million acres of land, 5,000 square miles, had been disturbed by surface mining in the United States prior to 1965. An additional 500 miles was affected by mine-access roads and exploration activities. Coal mining accounted for the largest share of the acreage (41 percent).

Sand and gravel (26 percent); stone, gold, clay, phosphate and iron together (8 percent); all others (5 percent) made up the balance.[1]

In recent decades, nuclear energy has also cut into the coal market. The growth of the nuclear power industry was aided by massive government funding and enthusiastic support from both private and publicly owned public utilities. The government saw nuclear power as an energy source which, while abetting industry, would help support our nuclear base for defense. Utilities saw atomic power as clean, and it believed, less costly. (See Chapter 7 for a discussion of nuclear power.)

Why Coal Use Has Risen in Recent Decades

Notwithstanding the inroads of nuclear power and other recent power alternatives, the use of coal has been increasing both relatively and absolutely in the last two decades. This gain is the result of greater efficiencies in mining and combustion of coal, some stagnation in nuclear power growth, reflecting technical problems and accidents, and some successes in reducing pollution from coal combustion.

The gain in coal use also is, in part, a result of the United States energy crisis in the 1970's when a shortage of oil was triggered by a Middle East embargo on petroleum shipments to this country. This was followed by shipments at greatly increased prices. The disruption caused some conversion to coal for electric generation and for general industrial purposes. Such conversion, however, was not accomplished rapidly. Short-term relief came from more efficient use of energy, less wastage and cutbacks in usage.

SURFACE MINING

As has been noted, surface (strip) mining is both the least expensive and the safest method of obtaining coal. In 1984, surface mining accounted for 59 percent of all coal mined in the United States. It can be done where there is relatively thin rock and soil, called the **overburden,** covering horizontal coal beds.

---

[1] U.S. Department of the Interior, *Surface Mining and Our Environment*, Washington, D.C., 1967, pp. 39, 42.

Prior to the federal Surface Mining Control and Reclamation Act of 1977, or earlier laws in some states, surface mining left the land covered with huge, steep-sided piles of rock and clay and unfit for economic productivity. Surface mining was especially devastating in hilly country, where sediment and acid run-off from the mine wastes contaminated streams for many miles away from the mined areas. Primary responsibility for developing and enforcing surface mining regulations rests with the individual states. However, the U.S. Department of Interior, through its Office of Surface Mining (OSM), was given oversight of state programs to ensure that minimum national standards were met in each state. Each state plan had to be submitted and approved by the Office of Surface Mining. If state enforcement of its plan was not achieving minimum national standards, the Office of Surface Mining could take over the operation of all or part of a state program.

FIGURE 5-7. A thick cover of new western grasses grow on reclaimed mined land in a Wyoming dry region where the Belle Ayr mine of Amax Coal Company is located. Note surface mining operations continuing in the background (Courtesy, Amax Coal Company)

In 1984, the Committee on Government Operations of the U.S. House of Representatives found that the Office of Surface Mining had issued over 30,000 notices of violation to mining companies but collected only 9 percent of the penalties imposed. Violations of orders to cease mining numbered over 1,700 and penalties had not been assessed in 1,100 of these cases. Such delays and breakdowns in enforcement have lost the federal treasury at least $150 million in penalty payments. The Committee found that the OSM

> ... has failed miserably to efficiently and effectively carry out its responsibilities for assessing and collecting civil penalties and for implementing other enforcement provisions of the Surface Mining Control and Reclamation Act. ... Policy decisions regarding staffing, the reorganization of O.S.M. and basic enforcement policies made while James G. Watt served as Secretary of the Interior contributed significantly to the growth of a backlog of cases which overwhelmed the agency and made the Department vulnerable to lawsuit. ... Because O.S.M. has failed to establish itself as a credible regulatory agency, [coal mine] some operators have virtually ignored its enforcement efforts.[2]

In recent years the Department of the Interior has tried to improve OSM operations and "undo the damage resulting from years of inattention and misdirection." Considerable reclamation has been done (see Figure 5-7).

There is still controversy between state governments, the federal government, mining companies, the National Coal Association and environmental and citizens groups monitoring compliance with the surface mining laws, as to the adequacy of regulations and enforcement to achieve in a cost-effective manner the results mandated by the act.

Reclamation of Surface Mines

Surface mining of coal involves six steps, including reclamation. First, the topsoil layer, up to 2 or 3 feet in thickness, is removed and stored. Second, the remaining overburden, up to 100 feet or so, is stripped from the coal bed by huge shovels, draglines or scrapers. Third, the coal is removed, Fourth, the overburden is replaced and graded to slopes similar to those the land had prior to stripping. Fifth, the topsoil is replaced, Sixth, vegetation is planted. Productive agriculture or forestry can be resumed on the reclaimed surface-mined land within a year or two of

---

[2] 98th Congress, Second Session, House Report 98-1146, pp. 43, 44.

mining. Crop types are similar to those that were grown prior to the mining. Costs of restoration are partly recovered by farming profits or sale of the land after mining.

Many mineral and rock products besides coal are obtained by surface mining (copper, gravel, barite, bauxite, clays, for example), but the land acreage stripped for coal far exceeds that for all other products. All surface mining is regulated under the federal Surface Mining Control and Reclamation Act of 1977. Among control provisions, this Act prohibits surface mining of coal in certain areas, such as prime agricultural land and land with steep slopes. Mining legislation needs to be coordinated with other land-use policy legislation.

AIR POLLUTION PROBLEMS

Uncontrolled emissions from coal combustion get clothes and buildings dirty, corrode materials and harm people, other animals and plants. Elimination of such air pollution has been a particularly thorny problem. On the positive side, SO_2 emissions because of coal burning have dropped since 1973, a time when coal use was increasing over 60 percent. The simplest method of reducing pollutants is pre-combustion treatment. The coal is crushed into fine particles and cleaned of impurities before it is burned. Also, pollution has been reduced by the use of lower sulfur coal.

More advanced control is through use of scrubbers. These are devices placed in the smokestack. The gas formed by the burning coal passes through a limestone-based chemical mixture that removes most of the sulfur. More improvement is expected. Advanced stack gas-cleaning processes are being developed by government and commercial companies.

Direct combustion processes using fluidized bed boilers are under development with commercial use foreseen within the decade. In this process, powdered coal is mixed with limestone and burned while suspended on a bed of air. Calcium in the limestone picks up sulfur in the coal, which becomes solid waste, reducing the flow of pollutants into the air.

The EPA has established ambient air quality standards for the various regions of the United States. Measurement and monitoring have improved. Also, Congress has authorized $¾ billion to be spent on clean coal research.

On the negative side, much remains to be done. (See Chapter 23 for a further discussion of the air pollution problem.) This problem, of course, involves much more that the coal industry.

COAL – OUR ENERGY MAINSTAY

"As it was in another era, coal is again becoming the energy mainstay for our nation's business and industry . . . coal has been transformed by technology into a uniquely modern and versatile fuel . . . ,"[3] the National Coal Association comments. Our examination of the resource position of coal supports this statement.

FIGURE 5-8. A stripping shovel operator's view of the pit, Sinclair Mine, Peabody Coal Company, Kentucky. The dipper of the big shovel holds 125 cubic yards of earth and rock. The loading shovel in the background scoops coal into 135-ton trucks. (Courtesy, National Coal Association)

---

[3] National Coal Association, *1985–86 Facts About Coal,* Washington, D.C., 1985, p. 4.

The United States should keep full steam behind programs of coal research and development. Such programs would anchor our energy resource base to a reliable source of proven abundance within our own national boundaries. They would lessen our dependence on oil and natural gas and would help hold down prices by affording more competition between fuels. We would then be in a better bargaining position to obtain, at a reasonable price, the oil we need from abroad. We would gain time to develop other promising sources of power, aiming for that day when we can tap directly, on a massive scale, the radiant energy of the sun—the ultimate answer to the need for clean, unlimited power.

QUESTIONS AND PROBLEMS

1. What portion of the total energy used in the United States comes from coal?

2. How many tons of coal were used in this country in the early 1970's in comparison with the amount in 1824? How much more was used in 1987?

3. Would you say that coal is widely available? How do reserves west of the Mississippi River compare to those east of it?

4. How is coal formed?

5. Why is coal always found over a layer of clay or shale?

6. Name the three kinds of coal commonly found in this country and explain how they differ.

7. Which coal burns with the least flame and gas and leaves the least ash?

8. Name some industrial centers which owe their existence to the presence of coal. Is coal as important to manufacturing locations today as formerly? Explain your answer.

9. Name some of the items that are made from by-products of coal.

10. What is one system of coal use that is being tried out in an effort to reduce the cost of converting coal to energy?

11. What percent of the total estimated coal reserves are actually usable under our present capabilities? Why is this percentage so small?

12. What kind of coal, if any, is found in your state? Name several uses to which this coal is put.

13. How will the process of gasification and liquefaction extend the use of coal?

14. Although surface mining is cheaper, how is it apt to be more expensive than shaft mining? Are there any disadvantages to shaft mining?

15. Why has coal development lagged, since it is such an abundant and useful fuel?

16. How does long-wall mining deal with the problem of land subsidence?

17. Name two ways by which harmful emissions from burning coal can be reduced.

18. What is the energy source used to heat your home?

6

Oil and Gas

No energy sources have been more a matter of public concern in the United States in recent years than oil and gas. For these are the fuels we use to provide two-thirds of our energy needs. Yet, in the early 1970's, we suddenly discovered that we were in short supply. For the first time since the introduction of the automobile, millions of us found ourselves waiting at the gas pumps. More alarming, a sudden increase in the costs of these fuels and our dependence upon foreign supplies to fulfill our needs threatened to wreck our economy. Although oil prices had dropped sharply by 1986 and gasoline had become readily available, our country remained heavily dependent upon Middle East crude oil supplies. Reflecting especially these high oil imports, the United States in 1986 became a debtor nation for the first time in three generations! This heavy dependence upon oil and gas continues today. Yet, only some 125 years ago they were little known substances. The story of their development is a dramatic example of the functional concept of resources, described earlier in this text. In response to our wants, we used our technological abilities and societal arts to develop oil and gas from the uncommon to the common—the major fuels of our energy base.

EARLY PETROLEUM USE

One of the earliest known oil products was asphalt. Asphalt is a black or brownish solid substance, which when heated, becomes somewhat runny and sticky. The smell suggests that it is derived from petroleum. It is formed from the evaporation and oxidation of petroleum on or near the surface of the earth. There are many sources of this substance over the world; the most noted source in this hemisphere is the island of Trinidad, off the coast of Venezuela, which has a lake of asphalt, or pitch, at La Brea.

Asphalt was used 7,000 years ago in ancient Egypt to embalm bodies and to waterproof various river craft. The baby Moses was set adrift amidst the rushes on the Nile in a basket made waterproof through the use of this same product.

Oil, or petroleum,[1] from Sicily was burned in the Temple of Jupiter at Rome about 2,600 years ago. We know that natural gas was used about that time because the "eternal fires" of Baku, Persia, were natural gas burning in what became one of the major oil fields in the world.

OIL A NUISANCE

The development of our oil and gas industry is the story of unappreciated resources. Early in the history of this country, the finding of oil and gas was distinctly a nuisance. Drilling was done to obtain water and brine for salt making, and wherever oil or gas was encountered, the location was no longer useful.

It was not until 1859 that a salt-well driller was hired to put down a well for oil. Crude petroleum at that time was selling for $18 a barrel, but since it was used primarily for medicinal purposes, only a small quantity was needed. Even so, the Drake well at Titusville, Pennsylvania, was put down in the hopes of finding some of this scarce, precious petroleum. This famous strike proved so productive that the market was soon flooded, and the price of crude petroleum dropped from $18 to 10 cents a barrel—a price so low that the containers used to take it away were worth more than the product itself.

---

[1] The words *oil* and *petroleum* are used interchangeably in this chapter.

From that small start about 125 years ago, oil and gas have become the fastest growing of the energy-producing industries. Oil and gas rank above all other sources of energy used in the United States.

MANY USEFUL PRODUCTS FROM PETROLEUM

Besides its importance as a fuel, petroleum has become one of the most useful of our natural resources because of the vast number of products that can be made from it. It is broken down by a process called distillation, whereby various parts, or fractions, of the petroleum are driven off then collected. In addition to gasoline, kerosene and lubricants, the list of other useful products derived from petroleum is long and varied. We know that paraffin and petroleum jelly come from this source, but it is surprising to learn that in the list, which is too long to enumerate, are enamels, water-proof cloth, electric insulating material, plastic, rayon, nylon, radiator antifreeze, a food moistener and mold growth retarder for baking products and even a blackstrap molasses for cattle feeding.

SOURCE OF OIL AND GAS

Nature's method of making oil is not definitely known. The more common belief among geologists is that oil came from the deposits of both animal and vegetable life. The principal evidence for this belief is that petroleum contains certain complex chemical compounds called **porphyrins,** which are derived from hemin and chlorophyll—the materials giving the red color to blood in animals and the green color to plants respectively. Most petroleum hydrocarbons have the power to rotate the plane of polarization of polarized light, a property known to occur in sugars and cholesterol, which are produced by living organisms as part of their biochemical processes.

WHERE IS OIL FOUND?

The organic matter from which petroleum and natural gas was derived was deposited as small particles along with clay and carbonate mud in layers on the bottom of shallow seas. These muds were slowly buried by later deposited sediments, sands, shell fragments and other muds. The weight of the overlying sediment compressed the organic-containing mud (the "source beds" of oil and gas), the temperature increased somewhat to a maximum of about 392°F. (probably less) with depth of burial, and the plant-animal tissues contained in the source bed were chemically or biochemically altered to hydrocarbons in a liquid and/or a gaseous state.

Bacterial activity is believed to be a major factor in producing petroleum compounds from plant and animal tissues. They were squeezed out of the source bed by further compression, much as water is squeezed from a saturated sponge. The petroleum then entered an adjacent porous rock and migrated through it until it reached the land surface where it seeped out or until it reached some type of trap which stored it underground.

Oil and gas must be trapped in order for them to be sufficiently concentrated for drilling. Traps consist of a number of different types of geological structures. All, however, feature a porous reservoir rock (in which the oil and gas can be stored) underneath a nonporous or impermeable "cap rock" through which the fluids cannot migrate. The cap rock may be shaped like an upside-down bowl and may be miles in width and several hundred feet in depth. Oil and gas source beds and reservoir rocks formed into suitable traps are found in rock ranging in age from 600 million years (Cambrian Period) to only a few million years (Tertiary Period). The younger rocks have produced much more oil than the older ones.

RESERVES OF OIL AND GAS

The known recoverable reserves of oil and gas are sparse compared to those of coal. Domestic coal reserves have a prospective life of hundreds of years, as has been noted, even with expanded demand. By contrast, our **proved** reserves of oil (verified by testing, recoverable by existing methods and economically feasible to develop [see "Mineral Reserves and Their Estimates"] of some 27 billion barrels in 1988[2] were sufficient to last less than nine years at current rates of production. If we add 40

    [2]Joseph P. Riva, Jr., "Oil Distribution and Production Potential," *Oil & Gas Journal*, January 18, 1988, pp. 58–61. See also U.S. Department of Energy, Information Administration, *Annual Energy Review*, Washington, D.C.

billion barrels oil equivalent of natural gas and natural gas liquids to proved oil reserves, we could conceivably meet all our domestic needs from our own supplies for about a decade. But, this will not happen. In recent years, we have had large oil imports. Thus, since 1973, oil imports have varied from about one-fourth of our total use to one-third—the approximate rate in early 1988. We will need to continue to import oil in order to keep our reserves for an emergency. For defense and industrial strength, U.S. productive capacity and the economic viability of the U.S. petroleum industry need to be maintained. Meanwhile, we need to develop alternative energy sources rapidly and to increase conservation.

Of course, our proved oil reserves will last longer than suggested by the above figures because we are making new discoveries and thus adding to our reserves. But, in recent years, more domestic oil and gas has been produced than discovered. And, even estimated **potential** reserves are not great. Potential reserves can be estimated by taking into account all the rock layers thought to be oil-bearing, estimating the amount of oil they likely hold and then multiplying this by the proportion recovered from such rock experienced in past years (around 30 percent). Other methods allow for the declining yields with additional exploration and drilling activity. Such estimates of undiscovered, recoverable reserves in this country vary widely. (See Figure 6-1, which shows how estimates varied over a decade.) These estimates may be high. Joseph Riva's table, which appeared in the *Oil & Gas Journal* in January 1988 (see footnote 2), showed that inferred and undiscovered reserves together totaled only a little over twice proved reserves. The United States has only about 7 percent of the world's remaining conventional oil.

The reserve estimates for the United States are for an area in an advanced state of exploration and production. The United States has found and used a much higher proportion of its total supply of oil and gas than most countries have. Scientific and technological advances are needed to increase our probable reserves drastically. Better recovery of oil that must now be left in the rock is one example. (See the discussion in the section "Better Recovery Developed.")

Alaskan and Outer Continental Shelf Reserves

Often asked is the question "How important are Alaskan and offshore (called outer continental shelf—OCS) reserves as part of the total potential

CRUDE OIL
Selected Estimates of Undiscovered Recoverable Resources
for the United States

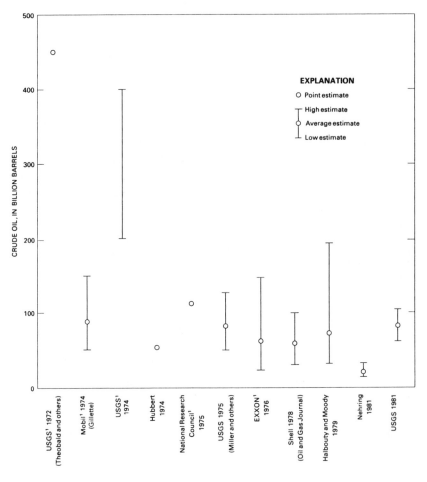

¹Includes natural gas liquids

FIGURE 6-1. These selected estimates of undiscovered recoverable resources of crude oil for the United States, made from 1972 to 1981, indicate that future potential U.S. reserves are quite limited. (Source: *Geological Circular 860*, U.S. Geological Survey, 1981)

reserves?" Alaska and the OCS may be the last frontier for major new oil and gas finds in the United States. Both government and industry estimate about 40 to 50 percent of our undiscovered oil and natural gas reserves may be located there.

A new Alaskan area proposed for oil exploration and development lies within part of that state's Arctic National Wildlife Refuge. Potential estimated reserves may be capable of meeting for quite a few years some 10 percent or our annual petroleum needs. Secretary of the Interior Hodel and spokepersons for the oil industry claimed that negative environmental impacts of this development would be minimal. Development proponents cited lack of any significant environmental damage by the Alaskan pipeline and Prudhoe Bay drilling as proof that this would be so. Leaders of prominent conservation organizations such as the Sierra Club and the Environmental Defense Fund strongly disagreed. They claimed that oil production at Prudhoe Bay has been polluting the tundra, resulting in hundreds of violations of environmental regulations. Political sentiment in early 1988 appeared to favor development.

Department of Energy preliminary estimates of oil and gas production for the period from 1985 to 1995 suggest, however, that in the near future the OCS contribution to our energy needs will be rather small. It is projected that oil output may almost double, but natural gas production will decline.[3]

While OCS reserves are some of the most accessible, possible adverse environmental impacts make their development highly controversial. The Council on Environmental Quality, after several years of study of the problem of developing these offshore reserves, has recommended improvements in these areas: (1) in equipment design and operating practices to protect the people involved; (2) in technology to meet harsher conditions in the Atlantic and Alaskan OCS than in many others; and (3) in technology and practices to minimize the impact in underdeveloped areas. Environmentalists have been disappointed because the Council has not flatly ruled out exploration in high risk areas. The oil companies feel that adverse economic impacts have been overestimated. And, the governors of some of the coastal states have opposed development in part because of disagreement over state versus federal jurisdiction of the areas.

---

[3]Council on Environmental Quality, *Environmental Quality, The Tenth Annual Report of the Council on Environmental Quality*, Washington, D.C., 1979, p. 333.

Perhaps societal problems such as those just enumerated can be resolved. Many thousand of wells have been drilled in waters off the coasts of the United States. The Gulf of Mexico is a current example of heavy offshore drilling activity. One stretch of productive oil and gas reserves is 225 miles long. Its wells are record breakers. One is described and shown in Figure 6-2. Another, Texaco's Mississippi Canyon Block 2285, located

FIGURE 6-2. The large drilling platform shown here is representative of those used to work offshore oil deposits. This one, Mississippi Canyon Block 194 (Cognac), is located in a Gulf of Mexico field. Shell Oil Company is the operator and part owner. Installed in 1982, Cognac holds the world water depth record for production from a conventional platform. In 1987, this platform produced an average of 16,650 barrels daily of oil and 81 million cubic feet of gas daily from 50 wells.

Cognac's development costs were over $800 million. The costs included leases, exploratory wells, building and installation of a three-section drilling and production platform, 28 miles of pipeline and 62 development wells. The field is expected to produce 150 million barrels of oil and 500 billion cubic feet of gas eventually. (Courtesy, Shell Offshore, Inc., a subsidiary of Shell Oil Company)

about 100 miles southeast of New Orleans, was drilled a record depth of 13,100 feet in 3,161 feet of water.[4]

Such offshore wells are truly engineering marvels. And, they are tapping our most promising reserves of oil and gas. In doing so, they have some environmental costs that cannot be avoided (see Chapter 2). But, some are inexcusable. The problem of avoiding severe environmental costs is both societal and technological. On the technological side, applied science can generally mitigate or eliminate harmful impacts by procedures such as proper siting of wells and controls of materials and by environmentally sensitive engineering and operation. Through applied research monitoring, scientists can identify areas where petroleum development should be avoided. On the societal side, the United States has passed laws and set up agencies to protect the environment. And, environmental ethics are being taught in schools of business. But, these technological and societal abilities will not be effective unless they are put into action!

Relief from Foreign Supplies?

Even foreign supplies of oil, were they to become readily available, afford no long-term prospect for meeting our fuel requirements. The world's undiscovered recoverable oil was estimated to be about 2,000 billion barrels in 1980, according to *The Global 2000 Report to the President*.[5] Proved world reserves were estimated to be about one-third of potential reserves. With world production running 40 to 50 billion barrels a year, the world supply of proved reserves would last perhaps 15 years, with potential reserves extending that life another 50 to 100 years. Joseph Riva, Jr., in 1988 (see footnote 2), using somewhat different figures, estimates the potential life at "50 years before being ultimately constrained by a declining resource base." Because there has been little exploration for oil and gas in much of the world, the chances of making major discoveries there are much more favorable than in the much explored United States. Furthermore, world demand is expected to become much greater. World gas reserves likewise afford no satisfactory long-term answer to our fuel needs.

---

[4]"Flexure Trend Yields More Oil in Gulf of Mexico," *Oil & Gas Journal*, March 14, 1988, p. 24.

[5]Council on Environmental Quality and the U.S. Department of State, *The Global 2000 Report to the President: Entering the Twenty-First Century*, Vol. II, Washington, D.C., 1980, pp. 186, 187.

The Global 2000 Report states that the Middle East contains 67 percent of the world's proved oil reserves and 25 percent of the natural gas reserves, whereas the USSR and Eastern Europe possess 9 percent of the oil and 43 percent of the natural gas reserves.

Despite promising potentials for oil discoveries, the fact that our proved reserves lead our annual consumption requirements by only a few years indicates the more critical nature of oil reserves than coal. Some potential reserves may never "prove out," while developing others may be unwise.

Some New Gas Fields

The quantities of known recoverable gas supplies in the United States, like those of oil, depend on the discovery of new fields and changes in the process of withdrawal from the underground reserves. As new locations are found and improved recovery methods are applied, more underground reserves are brought to the surface.

The proved reserves of natural gas in the United States at the beginning of 1980, according to the *Oil & Gas Journal*, were more than double those 30 years ago. But, the increase in proved reserves has been greatly offset by an increase in the demand for natural gas. The U.S. Geological Survey has estimated potential reserves to be 10 to 20 times as great as proved. But, because of the physical nature of the source and the cost-price relationships in recent years, such estimates are apt to be unreliable. A 1973 report of the Joint Committee on Atomic Energy states: "[Domestic gas]...is probably the hardest [of energy resources] to estimate. Most engineers will agree that the nation will be fortunate if long range projections of gas availability are 50% either way of actual production."[6] Various estimates from 1971 to 1981 are shown in Figure 6-3.

BETTER RECOVERY DEVELOPED

Early methods of recovering both oil and gas from their underground reservoirs were most wasteful. In many instances as little as one-fourth of the oil in an underground pool was brought to the surface, and this

---

[6]Joint Committee on Atomic Energy, *Understanding the National Energy Dilemma*, Washington, D.C., 1973, p. 17.

NATURAL GAS
Selected Estimates of Undiscovered Recoverable Resources
for the United States

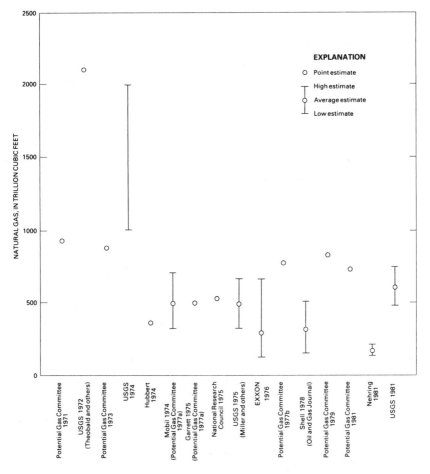

FIGURE 6-3. These selected estimates of undiscovered recoverable resources of natural gas for the United States indicate that like oil, potential U.S. gas reserves are very limited. As the text notes, natural gas estimates are generally considered less reliable than those for oil. (Source: *Geological Circular 860*, U.S. Geological Survey, 1981)

proportion was considered good. A recovery of 32 percent of the oil in a field is now average.[7]

In many instances a much larger percentage of the underground reserves could be recovered if a field could be controlled and operated as one producing unit rather than as many independent units. When neighboring wells are owned and operated by different producers, it is ordinarily to the advantage of the producers to take out all the oil they can from this commonly owned underground pool. If they do not, neighboring producers will profit by removing it through their wells.

In order to conserve these underground supplies better, most of the oil-producing states, as well as the federal government, have developed plans for allotting to individual producers certains proportions of the permitted production of a given reservoir, or "field." The rate of depletion also is regulated because the total supply of oil that may be taken is frequently increased greatly by slowing down the current rate of removal.

Various devices and procedures have been developed to recover a larger proportion, up to about one-half of the oil and gas within the reservoir rock, but in no instance is it economically feasible or even physically possible to recover the complete supply of fuel trapped in the underground reservoirs. These processes are known as secondary and tertiary production methods or collectively as enhanced oil recovery. Injections of natural gas, carbon dioxide gas, water, solvents for petroleum, heat in the form of steam or another hot fluid have all been used. Usually the injection points are wells that formerly have been producers in the field. The injected material is forced through the reservoir rock under pressure and flushes out or dissolves oil trapped in small pores in the rock, from which primary production methods could not remove it. The oil is pumped from selected wells in the field by conventional means. Costs of enhanced oil recovery must be covered by the value of the additional oil produced.

PROSPECTING AND MINING DEVELOPMENT

Since certain types of deposits were formed along with and are regularly associated with certain types of rocks, broad-scale geological map-

---

[7]U.S. Department of Energy, *Enhanced Recovery of Oil and Gas*, Washington, D.C., 1973, p. 17.

ping is usually the first tool used in estimating the possible and probable amount of ore or fuel deposits. Then, for detailed exploration and prospecting, close examination of geological structures and of the mineralogical, chemical and physical (such as electrical, magnetic and seismic) properties of the rock bodies is frequently done. Some examination is done on the surface by collecting samples for analysis and by carrying measuring instruments to the field. Some is accomplished by taking measurements from airborne instruments, by using air photos or satellite images and other data, which are quite useful in correlating mineral prospect locations.

When several favorable indicators are found in an area, then subsurface testing must be done by drilling. Analysis of the chips or cylinders of rock cut out by the drill and the fluid, such as oil or gas, found in the rock answers the question "Is there anything valuable here?" If there is, further drilling is done to outline the size and shape of the deposit.

If it is an oil or a gas deposit, a plan for rate of withdrawal and location of withdrawal points is made which will result in the most production under available technology. Too rapid a withdrawal rate or failure to maintain fluid pressure in the oil and gas reservoir underground results in some otherwise producible oil or gas being left unobtainable in the ground. Under present technological and economic conditions, as noted, one-half or more of the oil in every oil field reservoir cannot be produced. Probable future rise in the price of oil and good conservation mandates the maximum oil and gas extraction which is economically feasible and environmentally acceptable.

If an ore deposit has been located, the underground and surface workings necessary to produce it must be constructed. The mine plan will depend on the size, shape and ore grade of the deposit. First, a shaft must by sunk. This is costly and time-consuming because only a few workers and a small amount of equipment can get into the small area at the bottom of the shaft and because all the broken rock must be lifted to the surface by some type of temporary hoisting equipment. When the shaft has reached its planned depth, then horizontal and other vertical openings required in the mine can be advanced more rapidly as there is now a large permanent hoist available which fills a large proportion of the shaft. Ore processing buildings, waste disposal sites, offices, laboratories, dressing room and showers for the miners and transport facilities must all be built at the surface.

Prospecting through test drilling often requires two to five years. Mine construction frequently requires an additional four to five years for a large mine. There will be anywhere from hundreds of thousands to many millions of dollars invested before 1 pound of ore is shipped!

MINERAL RESERVES AND THEIR ESTIMATES

A mineral reserve is a valuable mineral material which has not been produced and is still in the ground. It is not available for use until it is mined.

While most geological processes at some time or other concentrate useful mineral materials, it is often difficult to determine their location and amount. Most mineral deposits are in bedrock, but some are in loose, weathered materials found on the surface of the ground. Almost all are covered with soil and vegetation. Therefore, there are built-in uncertainties in all mineral reserve estimates.

The U.S. Geological Survey and the U.S. Bureau of Mines have adopted this ranking of reserve categories:

> *proved—* These amounts are *measured* from drilling data.
>
> *probable—*These are *indicated* to be there by a favorable combination of geological factors adjacent to known deposits.
>
> *possible—* These are *inferred* to be present from the indication of some evidence and favorable geological factors.

Perhaps we should add one more category, namely "undiscovered."

There is greater and greater unreliability in tonnage estimates from proved through probable, possible and undiscovered reserves. U.S. reserves of oil and gas in these categories determined by geologists for the U.S. Geological Survey are represented in Figure 6-4.

The diagram shows 34.25 billion barrels of proved reserves, an additional 4.636 billion barrels of probable reserves, still another 23.1 billion barrels of possible reserves and, finally, 50 to 127 billion barrels of undiscovered reserves. Some confusion in interpretation results because the U.S. Geological Survey separates measured and indicated as proved and probable, but the oil industry commonly calls the total of the two "proved" (shown as "demonstrated" on the chart). All of these are further classified as "economic" which means they can be recovered at a reasonable cost.

Figure 6-4 also indicates a large amount of sub-economic reserves—an additional 166 to 251 billion barrels altogether. Such reserves are not

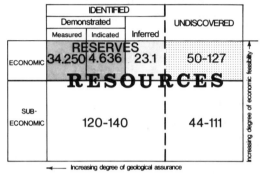

CRUDE OIL RESOURCES OF THE UNITED STATES (BILLION BARRELS)

Total U.S. Cumulative Oil Production 106 Billion Barrels

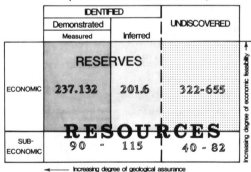

NATURAL GAS RESOURCES OF THE UNITED STATES (TRILLION CUBIC FEET)

Total U.S. Cumulative Gas Production 481 Trillion Cu Ft

FIGURE 6-4. Geological estimates as of January 1, 1975, but they are representative of the situation in the 1980's. (Source: Betty Miller, *et al.*, *Geological Estimates of Undiscovered Recoverable Oil and Gas Resources in the United States*, Geological Circular 725, U.S. Geological Survey, 1975)

ordinarily counted in any projections as being capable of meeting demands in the future, for it is assumed it would be prohibitively expensive to do so. But, there is a probability that they exist.

A similar scheme of reserves is shown for natural gas.

The cumulative figure provided below each chart shows how much oil and gas production there had been in the United States from the first well in 1859 to January 1, 1975. It is from comparing these kinds of figures that one can make the observation that the United States has more petroleum reserves underground now than all the oil and gas this nation has ever consumed. This is true—if *undiscovered recoverable* reserves are included. As the analysis of Figure 6-1 shows, however, even if the undiscovered recoverable reserves indeed prove out, we can continue present consumption rates for only a few more decades. And, this is also true for the world as a whole.

But, one may say, "The chart was prepared in 1975. I have read of new finds in the Overthrust Belt of the West that might double our proved reserves and in the Ob Valley of the Soviet Union that might equal those of the Middle East—over one-half of worldwide reserves. Doesn't this indicate that the earlier figure is too pessimistic?"[8]

In fact, the 1975 estimate did allow for, by including the undiscovered recoverable reserves, just such additions to our supplies. But, it is a long step from indications of new reserves to actual production.

All the published reserve figures, whether for fuels or nonfuel minerals, and the concepts of recoverable, submarginal, etc., are based entirely on economic and technological conditions at the time the studies were made. They tell the degree of certainty of the existence of the commodity as well as the economic practicability of this recovery. If someone were to find a cheap and easy method of extracting aluminum from clay, billions of billions of tons of aluminum which were submarginal would become recoverable. Thus, progress in science (such as an improved understanding of how ores form and the geological factors governing their deposition), technology (such as development of drilling methods capable of going deeper than at present) and exploration (such as a method of sensing the presence of oil thousands of feet underground without drilling), as well as economic considerations, would change reserve information.

---

[8]"Rocky Mountain High." *Time*, December 15, 1980, p. 31 and Thomas Watterson, "Bearish Soviet 'News' Routs Investors," *The Christian Science Monitor*, December 8, 1980, p. 11.

Let us consider an example of how this principle works. Suppose the price of a metal is $2 per pound. A mine producing it is able to drill, blast, move to the surface and extract the ore mineral from 20 tons of rock at a cost of $1.95 per pound. If ore containing less metal per ton is utilized, the cost would exceed $2 per pound because more rock would have to be handled, and this costs more. There is much low-grade ore down below which doesn't have enough metal in it to pay for the cost of mining and processing. If the price of the metal rises to $3 or more, the low-grade ore will beome profitable to mine.

In general, then, the total amount of metal available increases as the economically minable ore grade decreases.

OIL SHALES AND TAR SANDS

If oil shales in our western states and tar sands in our own territory and in Canada could be made to produce all the oil theoretically possible from their reserves, we would double, triple or even more our potential reserves. Colorado oil shales alone have some 600 billion barrels of oil, acording to U.S. Geological Survey estimates. The Canadian tar sands, which are located adjacent to Lake Athabasca, are said to have a potential of some 1,000 billion barrels of oil.

Oil shale development poses serious environmental problems. Oil shale may be surface mined, shaft mined or processed underground. Surface mining would despoil the landscape. Both would require costly reclamation. Shaft mining would leave large piles of spent shale on the surface. Processing underground might disturb and contaminate the ground water supply. Another obstacle to development is the large water requirement for mining. A 1973 study by the Committee on Science and Astronautics, House of Representatives, estimated that a 3- to 5-million-barrel-per-day industry using current technology might require all the surface water in the oil shale regions. Nevertheless, in early 1974, large tracts of public lands were leased from the Department of the Interior at a cost of almost half a billion dollars. At that time petroleum prices were rising rapidly, and some projections of an increase to $60 to $70 per barrel by the late 1980's were made. This energy crisis mentality stimulated oil and mining companies, with financial help from the federal government, to develop plans to produce oil from shale. Two of the largest operations that were designed and built were the Colony Oil Shale Project of Exxon Co., U.S.A., and Union Oil Co. of California's Parachute Colorado plant. Higher than anticipated costs combined with technical problems encountered in operations plagued the oil shale producers while they were getting the plants into full operation.

Meanwhile, the rising price stimulated some very successful exploration for conventional oil and increased production from existing oil fields. This, plus various economic and political factors, led to a decline of crude oil prices in the early to mid-1980's. Exxon halted its multibillion dollar oil shale project in May 1982. Most other oil shale projects also were terminated or put on hold. In most cases the oil shale plants had not been operating long enough to make the inevitable adjustments required to reach planned productivity and efficiency of operation. Our nation, as well as the private corporations involved, suffered considerable economic loss as a result. The Synthetic Fuels Corporation (SFC), a government corporation set up in 1980, was terminated in 1986. Administration of its five grants was transferred to the Treasury Department. Two coal gasification projects and a heavy oil recovery project were still operating in 1987.

The rapid boom and bust of the oil shale industry raises a number of questions. Should we develop this high cost fuel to ensure a supply we can depend on in case of national emergency? How can we avoid such costly crisis response in the future? To what degree should federal or state tax money be used to aid in starting or sustaining oil or other mineral production within our borders? At this writing the outcome cannot be reliably forecast. In similar developments, many financial and technical problems have arisen.

The Canadian tar sands have also experienced a flurry of renewed development. Although known about for many years, the tars were so locked in the sands that extraction had seemed unlikely. Then, in the early 1960's, a pilot program was begun at a cost of around $200 million. Development costs proved to be more than anticipated, and although some oil was produced, the operation ran up losses in the millions before finally making a profit in 1974. Since then, renewed financing of several billion dollars, including Canadian government funds, has been undertaken and production has continued. Whether or not the venture will become a major producer will depend upon the costs and availability of conventional oil and gas and alternative fuels.

WHAT IS THE FUTURE?

Briefly, the known reserves of oil and gas in the United States are definitely limited. The development of offshore oil wells has become increasingly costly, and the pollution threat may limit their potential. On balance, in the short run, we should be conserving our use of oil. Otherwise, we will become hopelessly dependent upon foreign supplies, for the United States will continue to depend heavily on oil and natural gas for its fuel needs for the near future. In the long run, we must turn to other sources of energy to meet the bulk of our energy needs.

QUESTIONS AND PROBLEMS

1. How does the development of oil and gas illustrate the functional concept of resources (that is, the resources are a function of our wants and abilities)?

2. Discuss the various problems of prospecting for minerals.

3. How many millions of years have coal and oil been in the process of forming? What does this suggest about our ability to replace them?

4. What is meant by **proved** petroleum reserves? What is the difference between the U.S. Geological Survey definition and the oil industry definition?

5. In general, how do reserves of oil and gas compare to those of coal?

6. Do you think we can rely on undiscovered recoverable reserves for our supplies of oil and gas? Explain your answer.

7. Can we expect to discover new oil fields as rapidly as we deplete the older ones, or should we expect the demand for both oil and gas to outrun the supply? Explain your answer.

8. List some of the products that are now being made from oil.

9. If oil and/or gas is found in your state, find out when both or either was first developed and what has happened since then.

10. How large are the proved reserves of these two sources of power in our nation compared with annual use?

11. How long will these reserves last if they continue to be used at the present rate?

12. What should be our long-run national policy regarding dependence upon oil and gas? Explain why we should or should not base our strategy on the amount of undiscovered recoverable resources?

7

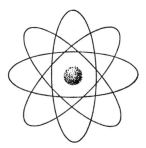

Nuclear Energy

The most striking development in sources of power has been the
release of the energy in the atom. We are apt to think, therefore, that
the knowledge of atoms is very recent. The fact is, the ancient Greeks
included atomic theory as one of their philosophical studies. Systematic
knowledge about atoms was developed in the seventeenth century. In the
early 1900's, theory became clarified. Then, in the 1940's, the atom was
split, and the resulting energy was put to work. The first large-scale use
of fission power was in the atomic bombs used by the United States in
1945 to knock Japan out of World War II. Since then, increasing attention has been given to the peaceful uses of nuclear energy. In 1986, the
amount of electrical power generated by nuclear power plants was about
16 percent of the total electrical supplies in the United States and over
5 percent of the total energy used in the United States. In 1987, there
were 107 U.S. licensed nuclear plants, and construction permits for 18
others had been issued. But, no orders for new plants had been given
since 1973, and over 100 proposed plants had been canceled. Development of nuclear power is highly controversial.

ENERGY FROM NUCLEAR FISSION

Atomic energy in the United States today is produced by *nuclear fission.* In this process, the nuclei of heavy atoms are split under bombardment by neutrons. When a sufficient amount of fissionable material is brought together, a chain reaction occurs, splitting the atoms and releasing tremendous heat. About 20,000 times as much heat and other energy is released from uranium fuels, for example, as from an equivalent amount of coal.

The fission reactors are attractive to electric power companies. The most commonly used are light water reactors (LWR's), so called since they use ordinary water. Such reactors have been in commercial use since 1957 and have been found to be workable, producing electricity at competitive operating costs. Most important, LWR's are free from the environmental problems of coal-fired electric power plants, which the utilities had begun to despair of overcoming. The principal disadvantages are the potential of a reactor explosion, leakage of radioactive materials and/or contamination from the atomic wastes left by the plants, which has led to widespread public objection to them. Also, soaring construction costs and technical problems have slowed their growth.

THE QUESTION OF SAFETY

In 1974, the Ford Foundation brought out a preliminary report of a three-year study undertaken by responsible authorities in a number of fields. Regarding nuclear power, the report noted that "its use poses serious environmental issues, including reactor safety, radioactive waste management and nuclear theft.... The wisdom of a commitment to nuclear power ultimately rests on the capability of our technology and institutions to manage, perhaps indefinitely, a very hazardous enterprise."[1] The report also noted that reasonable individuals differ substantially in their judgement about the safety of nuclear power.

Also in 1974, 47 U.S. scientists and engineers completed a two-year study for the Atomic Energy Commission in which they assessed the possibilities of accident risks in atomic reactors. The report concluded that "the odds against an American dying from a nuclear-power accident are

---

[1] The Ford Foundation, *Exploring Energy Choices*, Washington, D.C., 1974, pp. 49, 51.

FIGURE 7-1. The Callaway Nuclear Plant of Union Electric Company, located near Fulton, Missouri, has a generating capacity of 1,120 megawatts. More than 14 million ceramic pellets of low enriched uranium dioxide are encased inside 50,952 zircaloy metal tubes, each 12 feet long. These tubes are bundled together into 193 fuel assemblies, each of which is 8½ inches square. About one-third of the fuel is replaced every 18 months. The company also operates steam-generated plants and the large hydroelectric plant shown in Figure 3-2. Over 90 percent of the 7,200-acre plant site is administered by the Missouri Department of Conservation as a wildlife management area. (Courtesy, Union Electric Company)

FIGURE 7-2. The Clinton Nuclear Plant of Illinois Power Company, centrally located in Illinois, is another example of multiple use of land for industry, wildlife and recreation. The plant has a generating capacity of 950 megawatts. The lake, which covers 5,000 acres, provides cooling water for the plant and affords opportunities for fishing and water sports. Camp grounds and other recreational facilities are provided by the company on the 16 square miles of land acquired for the plant site. A 60-acre prairie remnant has been set aside, and some 700 acres have been reforested. (Courtesy, Illinois Power Company)

300 million to one." Subsequently, a list of 34 eminent scientists signed and released for publication a policy statement calling for nuclear development because ". . . the benefits of a clean, inexpensive, inexhaustible domestic fuel far outweigh the risks."

Since these early studies, there have been two especially alarming commercial nuclear power plant accidents. The first was in March 1979 at Three Mile Island, a large power installation near Harrisburg, Pennsylvania. A chain of events, involving both mechanical and human failure, led to the release of a considerable amount of radioactivity and the evacuation of preschool children and pregnant women within 5 miles of the plant. There was, however, no direct loss of life. The plant was closed.

The second major reported nuclear plant breakdown in April 1986, at Chernobyl, USSR, was catastrophic. The Soviet leadership announced that the accident cost at least $3 billion and 28 lives and contaminated almost 400 square miles of land in the Ukraine. Thousands of residents were evacuated. Radiation that spewed from the reactor drifted westward across Scandinavia and other countries in Europe and on westward spreading fear of contamination. It was feared that of those who had been affected by the radiation cloud, thousands would eventually die of cancer. The Soviets reportedly hope to put the station back into operation by using other reactors and burying the damaged one.

Three Mile Island has brought about a new effort on the part of both business and government to develop and carry out better safety. A special commission, chaired by John Kemeny, was set up to analyze the mishap and to make recommendations. The commission found that both reactor improvements and better operation training were needed. Utility executives formed two new safety institutions: one, the Nuclear Safety Analysis Center, which monitors performance of safety, and the other, the Institute of Nuclear Power, which inspects existing reactors and evaluates them.

Chernobyl has shaken the complacency of nuclear power proponents. The safety, reliability and economy of nuclear power are being questioned. Nuclear safety measures have already been shored up. More international cooperation appears to be one certain beneficial result.

While not opposing the development of nuclear power *per se*, the Union of Concerned Scientists (UCS), an organization of scientists supported in part by donations from about 100,000 individuals nationwide, severely criticized the Atomic Energy Commission in a 1977 report assessing the safety of nuclear power plants. Congress subsequently abolished that agency and created the Nuclear Regulatory Commission (NRC). The Union of Concerned Scientists, however, is still concerned about nuclear plant safety problems. More recently, the organization has focused its attention on arms control, especially Star Wars. "UCS," it declares in a small informational brochure, "has long recognized the need to protect America's national security interests. But the shortsighted development of certain weapons technologies—such as space weapons—will make the world less stable and our nation less secure."[2]

Some risks for a nuclear-powered society remain to be solved. No one knows how safe reactors would be in case of deliberate acts of sabotage, or how vulnerable a United States largely dependent upon atomic power would be to potential destruction by a hostile power.

RADIOACTIVE WASTE DISPOSAL

Safe atomic waste handling and disposal is another problem. Nuclear-fueled electric generators as well as the mining, milling, refining, fabrication and use of uranium and other radioactive elements produce large quantities of both low-level and high-level radioactive wastes. Some of these waste products, particularly plutonium, are, in addition, chemically highly toxic. These materials must be collected, transported and stored in a location that will isolate them from contaminating the environment. Radioactivity at levels dangerous to life lasts thousands of years from these wastes. To date, only temporary storage sites have been available.

The Nuclear Waste Policy Act of 1982 set up criteria for disposal sites and a schedule for their development. The selection of the first site was narrowed to locations in Washington, Nevada and Texas. Debate on selection was heated. Finally, an agreement on nuclear waste disposal was included in a House-Senate compromise on December 22, 1987. Under the compromise it appeared that all of the nation's nuclear waste would be stored in Nevada. A site at Yucca Mountain, about 50 miles from Las Vegas, was selected. The site, however, needed to be proved geologically suitable. And, Nevadans continued to protest the decision vigorously.

---

[2]Public Information Office, *Union of Concerned Scientists*, Cambridge, Massachusetts, circa 1988, p. 2.

Locations favorable for nuclear repository sites should be geologically stable (not subject to earthquake or crustal movement) and without significant ground water circulation. Rock materials that have been considered suitable are granites (sometimes called crystalline rocks), older volcanic rocks and salt beds. The rocks chosen must be essentially free of fractures to prevent ground water circulation from dissolving radioactive material and dispersing it widely into water supplies. Besides geology, questions about waste packaging need to be considered. Also, there should be continuous monitoring once storage has been made.

BREEDER REACTORS

Fast breeder reactors, which are more efficient to operate than LWR's, are undergoing experiment. Heat output of these nuclear reactors per unit compared with that of coal would be as high as 1,500,000 to 1. There are two types of fast breeder reactors: the liquid metal-cooled fast breeder reactor (LMFBR) and the gas-cooled fast breader reactor (GCFBR). Called "breeders" because they produce more fuel than they consume, these reactors are much more efficient than LWR's and can use thorium more readily that LWR's and uranium without enrichment. They can use 50 to 70 percent of the uranium mined, in contrast to only 2 percent by the LWR's. Thus, they could greatly expand the life of ore reserves if they were to replace the latter.

The U.S. government has spent many billions of dollars on breeder reactor research. Funding has varied greatly in amount from time to time. After very low to no amounts provided in the early 1980's, renewal of this research funding is now pending in Congress. Commercial breeder reactors are probably at least 15 to 20 years from producing electricity.

ADEQUATE FUEL SUPPLIES IN
THE UNITED STATES

The major elements for nuclear power are uranium and thorium, from which fissionable isotopes U^{235} and plutonium^{239} can be produced (see Figure 7-1). In our present processes, uranium is preferred over thorium

FIGURE 7-3. This is the site of the first mill in the United States built for the refining of uranium ore. The community of Uravan is on the Dolores River in the plateau region of Colorado and is 90 miles from a railroad. Uranium for the first atomic bomb came from this mill. (Courtesy, International Harvester Company)

as a source and is used almost exclusively for the production of fissionable fuels.

In the early stages of development, the United States relied heavily on imports of uranium from South Africa and Canada. Then, during the 1950's and 1960's, western U.S. deposits were developed to the extent that the U.S. Bureau of Mines reported, ". . .domestic production is adequate to supply present and near-future domestic requirements."

In 1981, the United States was the world's leading miner of uranium. Uranium production, however, fell in 1984 to the lowest level since 1956. This reflected declining prices, adequate stocks and competition from imports. Most U.S. uranium mines in 1986 were shut down or at production far below capacity.

Reserves have been predicted adequate because it has been assumed that if shortages were to develop, lower-grade ores would be available to meet needs. Professor Eric S. Cheney, however, casts doubt on this assumption. He warns that "If we are to avoid the consequences of being dependent upon foreign ores, some very large domestic reserves must be discovered almost immediately."[3] He suggests, fortunately, that adequate reserves may be discovered (in this country) in heretofore untested rock of the pre-Paleozoic Age. Present sources in the United States are Mesozoic sandstones or Cenozoic volcanic rocks. Should breeder reactors, which require small amounts of fuel, become the principal source of nuclear power, almost unlimited supplies of high-cost uranium would become economical.

NUCLEAR FUSION

Dwarfing *nuclear fission* in possibilities of almost unlimited energy is *nuclear fusion.* Fusion is a *combining together.* The atoms are fused together rather than split apart. The problem is that the process is so difficult to control that it is questionable whether commercial adaptation will ever become economically feasible. Fusion requires extreme pressure and temperatures as high as 100 million degrees! Such heat was achieved in the hydrogen bomb by first setting off a fission explosion. While control of the process is a problem, fuel is not. Fusion reactors would be fueled by deuterium, an isotope of hydrogen, available in almost unlimited supply in sea water.

The U.S. government has been pumping about half a billion dollars a year into the development of several different fusion reactor programs and hopes to have a "demonstration" reactor in operation by the year 2015.

Fusion in the laboratory is being studied by two major methods: (1) fusion of gases in a magnetic container called *Tokamak* (an acronym for "toroidal magnetic chamber") and (2) internal fusion through lasers. In the first method, hot (100 million °C.) gas and hydrogen nuclei fuse to produce helium and the released energy is contained by magnetic forces. In the second method being researched, laser beams compress pellets of hydrogen fuel until their inertia is overcome and they explode.

The enormous power output potential of a fusion accelerator is almost unbelievable. The accelerator at Sandia National Laboratories, Albuquerque,

---

[3] Eric S. Cheney, "The Hunt for Giant Uranium Deposits," *American Scientist,* January–February 1981, p. 37.

New Mexico, called PBFA-II (Particle Beam Fusion Accelerator) is designed to deliver at least 100 trillion watts of power—greater than the instantaneous output of all the power plants on Earth! In December 1985, this machine had its first successful firing, a major breakthrough, even though the burst of ions lasted only 50 billionths of a second.[4]

NUCLEAR ENERGY FOR DESTRUCTION?

The most terrible human-made threat to the environment in the short run is the prospect of nuclear war. Both the United States and the Soviet Union are said to have overkill potential—stockpiles of nuclear weapons sufficient to wipe each other out many times over! And, other nations have, or will have shortly, nuclear destruction capability.

On the encouraging side, both superpowers appear to be moving from a policy of mutually assured destruction (MAD), which relies on the threat of the revenge killing of millions of civilians as a deterrent, to a missile defense shield, which would destroy incoming missiles before they could reach their targets. This latter system is known as the Strategic Defense Initiative (SDI) in the United States, or more popularly called "Star Wars." The cost of Star Wars apparently would be in the trillions of dollars, and some scientists argue that it is too complex to be workable. Others disagree. Even critics of the program consider that the research in laser defense being generated is potentially important.[5]

War, whether nuclear or otherwise, is the antonym of conservation. We conservationists must work for international understanding and peace if we are to save the ecosystem—if we are to save ourselves! Arms limitations need to include both nuclear and conventional arms. We should work together to strengthen and improve world organizations such as the United Nations and the World Court. We should encourage the world's peoples to talk rather than fight. If the funds that are spent for munitions by the nations of the world were to be channeled into peaceful research, education and production and nations linked in friendship and mutual cooperation with conservation, the world would be able to wipe persistent poverty from the face of the earth.

---

[4] Arthur Fisher, "Fusion Milestone," *Popular Science*, April 1986, pp. 8, 12.

[5] For an evaluation of spin-off benefits, see Michael Brody, "The Real-World Promise of Star Wars," *Fortune*, June 23, 1986, p. 92 ff.

INDUSTRIAL SIGNIFICANCE OF NUCLEAR ENERGY

The move toward more peaceful use of nuclear energy has been striking. In 1986, nuclear reactors were operating in 26 countries and generating about 15 percent of the world's electricity. In Belgium, France and Taiwan over one-half of the electricity was being generated by nuclear reactors. Our own nation was generating about 16 percent of its electricity by nuclear power. According to *U.S. News & World Report,* May 12, 1986, 101 reactors in the United States were producing 16 percent of the electric power. Twenty-nine reactors were on order in the United States, *Time* magazine noted in an article of the same date.

Progress in the development of underseas and space nuclear power, in the medical use of radioisotopes and in research in nuclear physics has been made. But, the industrial development of nuclear energy, while showing great promise, has become ensnarled by many problems—technological, economic, political and social.

In the 1960's, the Atomic Energy Commission forecasted that by the year 2000 all new power plants under construction would be atomic powered and that nuclear plants would account for one-half of all electricity generated. However, this forecast does not seem likely to be realized. It takes 10 to 20 years for a nuclear plant to become operational from the time it is first planned. And, no plant orders have been signed for plants in the United States since the Three Mile Island accident. Although the U.S. government is spending vast sums to develop breeder reactors and to support research on fusion power, fossil-fueled plants will continue to supply the bulk of our electric power for some time to come. Because of soaring costs, nuclear power faces increasing resistance from the general public, dismayed by actual, or the threat of, sharp increases in rates charged for electricity for homes.

QUESTIONS AND PROBLEMS

1. How long ago were atomic particles first speculated about? When did commerical development of nuclear energy begin?

2. Look up the description of the atom in a reference book in your library. Explain what is meant by **nuclear fission.**

3. What are the advantages and disadvantages of LWR's? How many are planned for your state? Where will they be located?

4. What are fast breeder reactors? What are their advantages and disadvantages compared with LWR's?

5. Are nuclear energy fuel supplies a problem? Why or why not?

6. What is the difference between nuclear fission and nuclear fusion? Why don't we convert all atomic plants to nuclear fusion now?

7. What are some of the nonmilitary uses of atomic energy? (Consult the library to add to your list.)

8. Will atomic energy plants replace those fueled by coal, oil or gas? Explain your answer.

9. Write an essay comparing the environmental hazards of nuclear plants to the pollution problems of coal-fired steam plants.

10. Find out from your local power company how your electrical power is produced. How does this compare with how it is produced in your state? With the nation as a whole?

8

Other Sources
of Energy and Our
Natural Energy Dilemma

So far, we have considered wind and water power, the fossil fuels—
coal, oil and gas—and nuclear energy. While our full potential from these
resources is far from realized, they are nevertheless well known. They
are conventional sources of power. Four unconventional sources of power
are now considered: solar energy, geothermal energy, hydrogen and energy
from solid wastes. Also, we will take an overall look at our national energy
situation.

SOLAR ENERGY

The sun, as well as the tides of the oceans, remains a source of largely
unutilized energy. Yet, the energy from either or both of these sources
of power may sometime in the future be more fully harnessed. If ways
are found to convert this energy to usable power, there would be enough
power from solar radiation alone to meet all our needs.

Let us consider the power that could be developed in one of our areas
that has little rainfall and much sunshine. Suppose that only $\frac{1}{10}$ of the

area of the state of New Mexico were covered by heat collectors and that only 15 percent of the energy thus produced were converted to mechanical work. Allowing for cloudy weather and for nights, this state could supply from solar radiation alone over 10 trillion horsepower per year of mechanical power. Imagine one source of power from one state producing all the energy used in the United States for heat, light and power combined! It can easily be seen that if and when it becomes feasible to harness the energy of the sun, we will not want for power.

The large expense associated with a venture of this type is the installation of heat collectors. After this is done, operating expenses will be light. Solar energy has the handicap of any intermittent source of power because no power can be generated at night or on cloudy days. Power which is used as it is transformed from the sun's heat will involve small expense, but if it becomes necessary to store the power in order to permit continuous use, the expense of storage may be very great.

One of the reasons we have neglected research on solar power is because we have thought of it in too grandiose a fashion. Relatively simple solar heat exchanger devices are being used to heat water in thousands of Japanese homes today. In India, reflectors are used by thousands of families for cooking. We could all employ solar heat to more advantage in many cases, simply by the judicious planting of trees, by the use of awnings and by the use of properly oriented glass areas and reflectors. Think of the savings if 10 million homeowners were to implement the simple conservation features of the Illinois home shown in Figure 8-1!

A number of U.S. companies now manufacture solar heating components for homes (see Figure 8-2). While the costs of constructing homes with such units are still apt to be higher that for conventional units, the costs should come down rapidly if the builders and home buyers can create a large market for solar heating. Besides, extra construction costs are paid for in fuel savings over several years.

In a major study by the TRW Systems group, it concluded that solar heating will become a billion-dollar-a-year industry. Another study by General Electric estimated that 40 million buildings will be heated by solar energy by the year 2000.

Martin Wolf, research associate professor of electrical and mechanical engineering and an associate of the National Center for Energy Management and Power at the University of Pennsylvania, reported on solar energy utilization by physical methods in the April 19, 1974, volume of *Science*

FIGURE 8-1. This home, located in Illinois, illustrates simple conservation features which can save energy. It is a condominium of two units so a common wall eliminates heat loss on one side of each unit. The view is toward the north where a screen of trees provides a buffer against cold winds in winter. On the southern end (toward viewer) shrubs shield a heat pump unit (hidden) from the sun. A maple tree (far left) shields the afternoon sun from the bay window in summer, but permits radiant heat from the sun's rays to hit it in winter. The bay window, which encloses a breakfast nook, provides outside light all day long from both the east and the west. The stacked wood in the yard will be used in a circulating fireplace (note chimneys) to supplement furnace heat in severe weather.

The house foundation was constructed in the side of a hill, providing a walk-out basement with both pleasant living space and storage room. The sun deck serves as a roof for the porch underneath for outside living. A willow tree by the lake and others near the porch will soon be tall enough to screen out the sun and to provide privacy. The house, including even the garage door, is well insulated and has double or triple glass windows. Both owners hope to add solar panels in the future. (Photo by Reiner L. Otterstedde)

(AAAS). His projections of energy use to the year 2020 indicate that by then solar energy will rank about equal with nuclear and will exceed natural gas and coal.

Because of the renewed interest and excitement over solar energy, it seems possible that its development is accelerating. Figures 8-2 and 8-3 illustrate that solar energy for home and factory use is no wild dream, but rather a present reality. In 1983, 224 manufacturers produced 17 million square feet of solar heat collectors, which were used for space and water heating in the residential, commercial and industrial markets.

FIGURE 8-2. This house was designed to make the best use of natural heating, cooling and lighting. The majority of the windows face south so that natural heating can be controlled. The lower sun of winter shines through the windows, but overhangs provide shade from the higher summer sun. Natural cooling is provided by directing southwest summer breezes through the house. Deciduous trees have been planted so that they will eventually shade the east and west windows in the summer, thus restricting direct heat from the sun's rays. Heavy insulation, specially coated window glass and heat storage materials have been appropriately used. An ice-storage unit provides air conditioning for the summer months. A passive solar water heater preheats water to 100°F. The overall thermal performance of this passive system is being monitored and evaluated, with a report targeted for 1989. (Courtesy, Illinois Department of Energy and Natural Resources)

Solar energy collectors can be active or passive. A passive system requires no moving parts. With solar-oriented design, construction, site location and landscaping, a more-or-less conventional home can be a passive energy system (see Figure 8-2).

In space heating by solar energy, we must avoid creating an overwhelming demand for supplemental supplies during very cold or prolonged cloudy periods, especially if they are supplied by electricity. In the latter case, a sudden demand by many consumers could strain available generating capacity so that many people would be literally "left out in the cold."

Photovoltaic Cells

Besides the obvious process of collecting heat from the sun, it is possi-

FIGURE 8-3. Reflectors are used to concentrate the sun's energy on photovoltaic collectors in the San Joaquin Valley, California. (Courtesy, California Energy Commission)

ble to convert solar energy directly into electricity. This photovoltaic technology utilizes no mechanical equipment. A crystalline semi-conductor, usually silicon in a very pure state, is sealed in glass or plastic, attached to wires and produces electricity when the sun shines on it. Many of us have light-powered pocket calculators which use photovoltaic cells. In 1984, U.S. companies produced 15 megawatts of photovoltaic-generating capacity, about 50 percent of the world production. Japan produced 30 percent of the world production. The future possibilities are tremendous in areas where no electric wire distribution reaches—remote areas of developed countries and most of the underdeveloped "third world." Costs are presently 5 to 10 times more than conventional electric generation (distribution facilities not included), but costs have decreased a hundredfold since the 1950's and from $20 to $8 per peak watt between 1977 and 1984. Technological improvements are inevitable in this industry which is destined to be a substantial energy supplier in the future. Photovoltaic energy may also play an important part in the production of hydrogen as a readily portable fuel in the future (see Figure 8-3).

GEOTHERMAL ENERGY

Geothermal energy is power from heat from rocks or molten magmas in the interior of the earth. Characteristically, it is transferred to the surface by means of heated water.

The amount of geothermal energy near the earth's surface is almost inconceivable. It has been estimated that the heat in the top 10 miles of the earth's crust is equivalent to 2,000 times the amount of heat potential from the earth's total reserves of coal. But, much of this geothermal energy is impossible to reach either physically or economically. About 10 percent of the world's land areas could produce usable geothermal energy. In the United States, likely sources are believed to occur in the 11 westernmost states. Some geothermal resources might be accessible beneath other states in the East as well.

The most promising U.S. area of proved geothermal resources today is the Salton Trough of the Imperial Valley in California. Unfortunately, however, the water from it issues as a corrosive brine. Another problem in some areas is keeping the liquid hot till it reaches the surface. There are 112 megawatts of capacity developed here.

In some areas, energy can be developed by sending fresh water to the hot rocks below the earth's surface, whence it returns as steam or very hot— but still nonmineralized—water. Such a dry steam field is in successful operation north of San Francisco, at power plants of Geysers, with a present capacity of about 1,650 megawatts and a probable capacity of 2,500 megawatts for about 30 years. A geothermal energy field is not inexhaustible since both heat and fluid are gradually depleted.

In some areas, such as Klamath Falls, Oregon, and Reykjavík, Iceland, space heating for homes, greenhouses and other buildings is obtained from geothermal hot water below the boiling point, which is circulated by pipes from hot water wells to the buildings.

Generation of electric power from geothermal sources has increased from almost nothing in 1960 to 1,800 megawatts in 1984. This is approximately the equivalent of two large coal-fired plants. While the present contribution of geothermal energy is only 0.2 percent of the total energy use and 0.6 percent of the electric power used in the United States, it has been estimated that 20 percent or more of our electric power could be generated from this source by the start of the twenty-first century. This potential may never be realized. Geothermal energy production has grown much more slowly in the 1980's than was predicted.

HYDROGEN

With thousands of compounds composed of hydrogen and carbon (hydrocarbons) and some three-fourths of the earth's surface covered by water (H_2O), it would appear that pure hydrogen should be a major energy resource today. A great advantage of using hydrogen as a fuel is that the product of its combustion is water, a non-polluting material.

However, the problem is that hydrogen, being not freely available in nature like natural gas, for example, must be separated from its compounds and that this separation, under present processes, uses more energy than the hydrogen will subsequently produce. Thus, there is a net loss from conversion to hydrogen.

If, however, unused or excess power from inexhaustible resources such as the sun, wind and tides could be used to convert hydrogen and the hydrogen stored, then the conversion loss would not be significant and the usefulness of these sources would be greatly extended. Hydrogen could also store up power from electric power plants during their otherwise idle periods.

A major problem of hydrogen conversion is that of technology. Most hydrogen being used today is produced from the hydrocarbon of natural gas, itself in short supply. Other methods proposed require great heat and pressure. Electrolytic conversion requires some 200 times normal atmospheric pressure and heat up to 350°F. to 400°F. Direct thermal decomposition of water would require 4,500°F.

Not only is hydrogen difficult to produce in large volume, but it is also difficult to handle and store. It will "eat through" metals and is highly explosive under certain conditions, though it can be controlled. Methods used in handling propane can probably be adapted for hydrogen.

In balance, much additional research is needed before hydrogen potentials can be realized.

SOLID WASTE ENERGY

Obtaining energy from solid municipal and agricultural wastes is one of the most desirable ways of expanding our energy base. On the one hand, we are developing a "new" resource. On the other hand, we are helping to solve a serious problem—solid waste disposal! An EPA spokesperson has estimated that there is enough energy in solid wastes from homes, businesses and industries in the United States "to light every home and office building in the country." Some 450,000 tons of waste is discarded every day, the equivalent in energy of 265 million barrels of oil per year. The energy value per pound of mixed solid wastes is estimated to be 4,500 BTU's. Refuse-derived fuel (waste which has undergone further treatment) has a value of 7,500 BTU's per pound. This compares to 10,500 BTU's per pound for bituminous coal, on the average.

Quite a few areas have already begun to use wastes for energy. In Nashville, Tennessee, the National Thermal Plant, a garbage-to-steam plant, has been in operation since 1974, generating heat and air-conditioning for downtown buildings. According to the plant's general manager, the solid waste system is reasonably competitive with conventional fuels. It has been enlarged and in 1988 was converting over 60 percent of the city's burnable waste into energy.

There are other promising potentials for energy from solid wastes. In

Guymon, Oklahoma, wastes from 100,000 cattle from feedlots have been developed into an energy source. Some 40 percent of Hawaii's electricity comes from burning sugar cane wastes to drive steam generators. In addition, ambitious plans are being developed by the federal government to increase gasohol (a mixture of alcohol and gasoline) production and to obtain methane gas from biologic sources.

In 1984, 46 plants were producing heat or electricity from solid wastes, and 36 more were under construction.[1] Furthermore, the general use of solid wastes appears to be gaining more acceptance. By 1987, about 5 percent of U.S. garbage was being burned in energy recovery plants. Proponents expected use would more than triple by 1990.

THE NATIONAL ENERGY DILEMMA

The resource and use situation for energy in the United States is exceedingly complex. But, our dilemma is clear—we have been using energy at a faster rate than we can supply it from our own resources; meanwhile, foreign sources of supply have been becoming more and more expensive and unreliable. We must increase our national supply of energy resources and the efficiency of our use. Otherwise, our nation will continue to move from one energy crisis to another.

Figures 8-4, 8-5, 8-6 and 8-7 from the *National Energy Plan II*, Appendix B, "U.S. Department of Energy," 1979, pp. 20, 23, 26, and 47)[2] help us visualize the overall energy situation.

---

[1] Center for Renewable Resources, *Renewable Energy at the Crossroads*, Washington, D.C., January 1985.

[2] The U.S. Department of Energy cautions that the user of these charts and supporting data "should not be beguiled by the complexity and detail of computer models, nor assume that they are 'black boxes' from which the truth will somehow emerge, or which will conceal bias." The computers perform the calculations, but it is the insights into the behavior of energy markets and the forces that will shape them in the future which derive the results. The Department points out, "These insights and perceptions must rely heavily on judgement, since basic truths and detailed data are lacking. The world's and Nation's energy future is far from deterministic."

In short, the Department is saying that prediction is an art as well as a science, fraught with uncertainties. The forecast attempts "to deal with uncertainties by identifying the most important ones and then using a range of estimates to bracket the range of responsible opinions."

For explanations of the various assumptions and complexities, the reader is referred to the original report, U.S. Department of Energy, *National Energy Plan II*, Washington, D.C., May 1979, and its three appendices. The projections used here are based upon assumptions that a "medium" world oil price will prevail—rather than the highest or the lowest expectations.

The estimate of U.S. primary and end-use consumption to the year 2000 is shown in Figure 8-4, based upon assumption of medium oil prices. While end-use consumption (the total figure minus conversion losses) will rise over 30 percent from 1980 to the year 2000, this will be at a much lower rate of increase than during the previous two decades when it increased about 50 percent. The reason that the rate of use has been recently dropping (note the dip in the line on the graph, Figure 8-4, prior to 1980) and is expected to continue at a lower rate is because of more efficiencies of use, such as in achieving greater miles per gallon in automobiles and less waste of heat through better design and insulation.

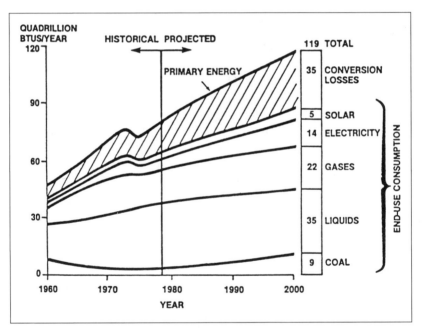

FIGURE 8-4. U.S. primary and end-use consumption. (Courtesy, U.S. Department of Energy, *Natural Energy Plan II, Appendix B: U.S. Energy Projections,* 1979)

That we must continue to press this conservation effort is illustrated by Figure 8-5, showing projections of the U.S. oil supply. Imports probably will still supply about 45 percent of our needs. Conventional oil and natural gas liquids (NGL) will supply only about 27 percent. Relatively new sources, Alaska (10 percent), shale oil (5 percent), secondary recovery—identified

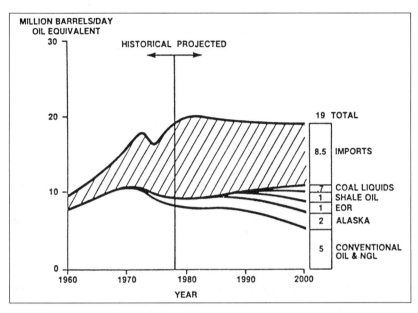

FIGURE 8-5. U.S. oil supply. NOTE: EOR—Enhanced oil recovery; NGL—Natural gas liquids. (Courtesy, U.S. Department of Energy, *Natural Energy Plan II, Appendix B: U.S. Energy Projections,* 1979)

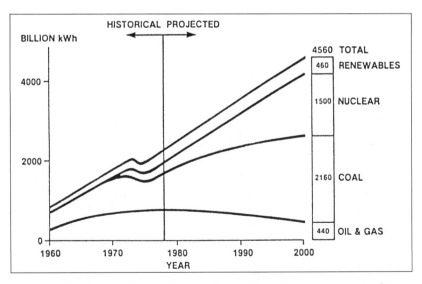

FIGURE 8-6. U.S. electricity generation. (Courtesy, U.S. Department of Energy, *Natural Energy Plan II, Appendix B: U.S. Energy Projections,* 1979)

as enhanced oil recovery (EOR) (5 percent), and *synfuels*—synthetic fuels from coal, identified as coal liquids (about 3 percent). The remaining 5 percent is accounted for by refinery loss, stock changes and "unaccounted for" crude.

The place that nuclear energy and renewables used for electricity (principally hydroelectricity, biomass, wind power and geothermal energy) are expected to play can be determined by studying Figures 8-4 and 8-6. Figure 8-4 shows sources for total end-use consumption, and Figure 8-6 shows a breakdown of that part generated by electricity.

Referring again to Figure 8-4, we see that electricity use is expected to be about 16 percent of total natural end-use consumption by the year 2000. Figure 8-6 shows that these renewables would be less than 2 of these percentage points and nuclear power about 5. The balance, 9 percent, will be accounted for by coal, oil and gas.

Direct use of energy from the renewables production (too small to be shown in the graph) will account for less than 1 percent, while solar power is expected to account for about 6 percent, according to these Department of Energy estimates, assuming a medium world oil price.

Adding direct and indirect (through electrical power) use, total end-use consumption by the year 2000 of renewable energy would then amount to about 23 percent. The remaining 77 percent will come from our conventional fuels—coal, oil and gas.

To sum up, there are not expected to be any "magical" technological developments or new natural resources which will relieve us from dependence upon fossil fuels during the next decade. Whether or not to conserve them is not a matter of choice. It is a matter of necessity. And, the need is heightened because of our continued dependence upon foreign supplies.

This view of expectations for the future would not be complete without some accounting of the ultimate consumers. Figure 8-7 shows that the industrial sector will account for most of the growth in end-use energy consumption by the year 2000. By comparison, residential and commercial use and transportation use are expected to increase only marginally.

Note that electricity and direct coal use, which will increase by 75 to 80 percent, will supply most of the anticipated new requirements of industry. More natural gas, electricity and solar power will meet the slight increase in residential and commercial demand, offset by a decline in use of fuel oil. Strikingly, transportation will continue to be almost entirely dependent upon petroleum-based fuels.

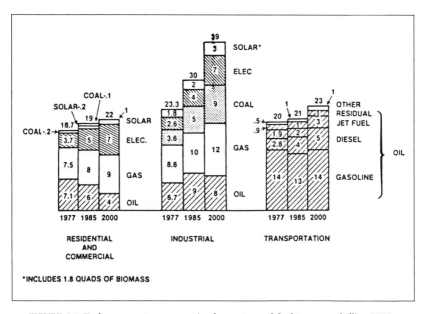

FIGURE 8-7. End-use energy consumption by sector and fuel type, quadrillion BTU's per year (medium world oil price case). (Courtesy, U.S. Department of Energy, *Natural Energy Plan II, Appendix B: U.S. Energy Projections*, 1979)

The Joint Committee on Atomic Energy's statement of the U.S. energy dilemma is as significant now in its implications for the 1990's as when it was issued in 1973.

> The United States with about 6% of the world's population is now consuming over 35% of the planet's total energy and mineral production. The average American uses as much energy in just a few days as half of the world's people on an individual basis consume in one year. This Nation has literally been developed without any significant restrictions due to lack of energy or mineral resources. However, we now see ever-increasing indications of the fact that the United States cannot long maintain the growth rate of recent years in our energy consumption without major changes in our energy supply patterns.

High use of energy is identified with a high standard of living. However, wasteful use is both unethical and costly. Through conservation we would use less energy and still be better off. In the highly acclaimed

Harvard Business School Report, *Energy Future*, Robert Stobaugh and Daniel Yergin observe:

> The United States might use 30 to 40 percent less energy than it does, with virtually no penalty for the way Americans live—save that billions of dollars will be spared, save that the environment will be less strained, the air less polluted, the dollar under less pressure, save that the growing and alarming dependence on OPEC oil will be reduced, and Western society will be less likely to suffer internal and international tension. These are benefits Americans should be only too happy to accept.[3]

QUESTIONS AND PROBLEMS

1. It seems as though solar energy should be very cheap. What factors make it expensive to develop on a large scale?

2. What are some relatively simple applications of solar energy?

3. How could you use solar energy more efficiently in your home? At school?

4. What is geothermal energy? Where is it most apt to be applied in the United States?

5. Since hydrogen is so common as a part of water (H_2O), why isn't it being used by all of us for fuel today?

6. What sources of power might be available that would make it economical to produce hydrogen?

7. How is solid waste being disposed of in your community? How could it be used to help meet our energy needs?

8. What is our national energy dilemma? Try to state it in terms of supply and demand for resources.

9. What kind of developments could help resolve our energy dilemma?

10. Suggest five ways by which you personally could help reduce the intensity of the national energy problem.

---

[3]Robert Stobaugh and Daniel Yerbin, eds., *Energy Future, Report of the Energy Project at the Harvard Business School*, New York, Ballantine Books, 1979, p. 229.

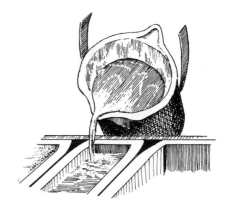

9

Nonfuel Minerals[1]

NONFUEL MINERALS – THE MUSCLES OF THE IRON AGE

Our energy supplies would do us little good if we did not have the other geological resources of rocks and minerals to house and contain them and to convert their gaseous and liquid energy into mechanical energy. The reference to one of our historic periods as the "Iron Age" speaks of the basic importance of metals to our industrial world. They might be called "the muscles of the Iron Age." Without iron, copper, lead, zinc and various combining metals, such as manganese, chromium and tungsten, we would not be able to use the mineral fuels effectively. We would not be able "to build the engines to drive the machinery to make the parts to build the factories to make the goods that 'Jack' wants"—to twist an old nursery rhyme a little. In other words, it takes metal to harness our energy resources, to drive machine tools, to make other tools to build the complicated machines to produce the airplanes and automobiles, calculators and computers and telephones and televisions of our modern world.

---

[1]Much of the data for nonfuel minerals used rather extensively in this chapter are from the standard official reference source, *Minerals Yearbook*, U.S. Department of the Interior, Bureau of Mines. The 1985 yearbook was published and distributed in 1987. Other reports, as noted, have been used to supplement and update this material. Major ones are *Minerals and Materials, A Monthly Survey*, and *Mineral Facts and Problems*, 1985, both by the Bureau.

NONFUEL MINERALS – A SOURCE OF CHEMICALS

Besides metals, nonfuel minerals are also an important source of the chemicals which are essential to life's productive processes and protection of the environment. Over 700,000 chemicals have been identified!

Chemicals can be classed as *organic* or *inorganic*. The organic are derived from plants and animals whose availability depends upon environmental factors described in other chapters. The inorganic chemicals, which are obtained from nonliving sources, can be grouped according to source as follows: those obtained from (1) air and water, (2) the mineral fuels and (3) nonfuel minerals.

One of the most widely used nonmetallic elements is sulfur. When we strike a match, write on paper, paint or use a plastic container, we may be using sulfur. Sulfur is also used, of course, to produce sulfuric acid which is required in so many industrial processes that the volume produced is used as an indicator of the level of activity of all business.

NONFUEL MINERALS – A SOURCE OF BUILDING MATERIALS AND OTHER PRODUCTS

Another, and no less important, group of nonfuel minerals is the nonmetallic mineral building materials such as stone, clay, sand and gravel. These are the materials for surfacing our highways with concrete, constructing buildings, making pipes for sewage and drainage and building dams. Such minerals are also the raw materials for the china we eat off of and the glasses we drink from, among other uses.

Mineral building materials are a mineral resource for which we can say, "Don't worry, we have plenty." For the country as a whole, the rocks, such as limestone and sandstone and the gravels and sands, are, from a practical standpoint, unlimited. But, for various localities, this is not necessarily so. Even sand and gravel may have to be transported many miles to them. And, because of quality considerations, as well as availability, we may get our marble from Vermont and our granite from Georgia. Even suitable clays for making bricks are hard to get in some places.

NONFUEL MINERALS NOT AS CRITICAL
A RESOURCE AS FUELS

We noted in Chapter 6 that proved reserves of oil and gas were those which have been verified by testing, are recoverable by existing methods and are economically feasible to develop. The same considerations hold for nonfuel minerals, but there are some important differences in supply and demand characteristics between fuels and nonfuels. It is generally easier to locate and determine the extent of deposits of nonfuel minerals; nonfuel minerals do not deteriorate once extraction has begun; they generally last much longer in use; in contrast to fuels, they are often readily reused; and they are easier to store. Both, however, face competition from substitutes.

To evaluate in detail the effects of all the preceding factors is far beyond the scope of this book. But it all boils down to this: Nonfuel minerals are not as critical a resource as fuels. There is not the frantic concern to develop nonfuel minerals that there is for fuels. Mining companies are more apt to "prove out" new resources only as needed. For world reserves, the estimated "life" (obtained by dividing the volume of use during a year into the volume of proved reserves) should generally be regarded only as a signal which must be carefully interpreted. It is useful, for example, in indicating how much more abundant the developed resources of one mineral are in comparison to those of another. It does give a good idea of how one nation stands relative to another in developed reserves.

The character of the supply and demand for nonfuel minerals means that the index of self-sufficiency for our country (net imports as a percent of consumption) shows how heavily we are relying upon supplies from abroad. But, this does not necessarily mean that we could not develop supplies from our own resources if we wanted to pay the higher costs. When the statistics are checked against the geological facts, we *are* definitely *lacking* in certain minerals.

With these reservations and considerations in mind, let us now take a look at the status of a number of our most important minerals. But, first, a word about environmental concerns and conservation needs.

ENVIRONMENTAL CONCERNS AND
CONSERVATION NEEDS

As with fuels, there are obviously many environmental problems in recovering minerals. As was pointed out in Chapter 2, all resource development encounters resistances. Mineral developments often face especially difficult problems in the task of minimizing bad impacts. Mining minerals may create great piles of waste, upset underground and/or surface water supplies, fill the air with dust and leave carcinogenic waste in the lungs of miners, to note a few.

While some environmental costs are unavoidable, generally actions can be taken to minimize the negative environmental impacts of those projects that are justified. A good place to start would be to repeal the obsolete General Mining Law of 1872. Under this law, still in effect in 1987, claims for mining can be made for only $2.50 per acre—a perhaps reasonable price in 1872 but ridiculously low 115 years later! Furthermore, no controls are provided by the law on hard rock mining—gold, silver, copper, uranium, etc.

Federal land in western states is pockmarked with abandoned mines that were claimed under this obsolete law. It permits any person with minimum proof of development potential and of work on the land to secure ownership of the land surface and underlying minerals for a pittance. In Colorado alone there are some 100,000 such claims.

The Minerals Leasing Act of 1920 governs disposal of fossil fuels. Also, the Environmental Protection Agency has enforced various provisions of the National Environmental Protection Act to correct some environmental abuses. State law enforcement has helped. Also, some corporations and individuals have been good conservationists. But, much remains to be done.[2]

PRINCIPAL METALS

The relative amounts of four principal metals produced in this country, as well as their share of our total use, are given in Table 9-1. The table makes obvious the overall dominance of iron in our present machine age. It does not show the importance of other metals, such as those used in making steel stronger, harder, more elastic, rustproof or capable of a high permanent polish.

---

[2]For a succinct commentary, see Charles H. Callison, "The Nation's Obsolete Mining Law," *St. Louis Post-Dispatch,* July 20, 1987, p. 3B.

Table 9-1 also shows that our nation is dependent upon imports to meet our mineral needs despite large production in some cases. Columns 2, 4 and 6, showing self-sufficiency, indicate the percentage of our needs we have met with our own production (this includes both mine output and recovery from scrap metal). The deficit has been made up by imports. For these important minerals, except copper and lead, we met less of our total needs with our own production in 1979 than we did in 1949. Figures for 1983 show a continuing decline in self-sufficiency, in every one of these important minerals. The general trend shown is more significant than the specific figures. Annual changes in production reflect market and labor conditions as well as the supply potential. Furthermore, the total needs include metals imported but used in exports, which accounts for a considerable share of the use of minerals such as copper.

Iron

Iron, a metal which is one of the most abundant and most generally used all over the world, was probably first used by the Egyptians about 5,500 years ago. It was not known in Europe until 3,500 years later, or about 1000 B.C. This iron probably was obtained from meteorites, and only very small quantities were used.

The first evidence of obtaining iron from smelting, that is melting the iron out from the ore with heat and a chemical-reducing agent, dates back to about 700 B.C. in Ethiopia. Its early use there was limited to items such as hinges, bolts, keys, chains and nails. The first ore was refined in the United States on the banks of the Saugus River near Lynn, Massachusetts, in 1646 (see Figure 9-1). The ore was obtained from a nearby bog, and charcoal was used as fuel and carbon to reduce the ore to metal.

Later processes used coke instead of charcoal as a source of heat (see Figure 9-2). After the ore has been brought to melting temperature, it is necessary for the mixture to remain open so that the melted iron will trickle through the mass and collect at the bottom of the furnace. Many fuels will supply the necessary heat and reducing agent to melt and reduce the iron, but coke is still the only fuel found that will form an open structure in the lower part of the mixture so that the metal melted from the ore can move down through the coke and accumulate on the hearth below.

Making coke from coal is an involved process, and when carried on

TABLE 9-1. Production and Self-sufficiency of Four Important Minerals, 1949, 1979 and 1983[1]

	1949		1979		1983	
	Production	Self-sufficiency[1]	Production[1]	Self-sufficiency[1]	Production[1]	Self-sufficiency[1]
	Million Tons	Percent	Million Tons	Percent	Million Tons	Percent
Iron ore	94.2	95	87.0	72	380[e]	63
Copper	1.1	78	1.4	87	01.0	81
Lead	0.8	81	0.8	92	01.0	86
Zinc	0.6	76	0.4	38	0.6	35

[e] Estimate

[1] Self-sufficiency is the ratio of production (from both mines and scrap) to total use. Total use includes exports.

Source: U.S. Bureau of Mines, *Minerals Yearbook*, Vol. I and II for 1949, and Vol. I for 1977, U.S. Government Printing Office, Washington, D.C., 1952 and 1980; and *Minerals and Materials, A Monthly Survey*, U.S. Government Printing Office, Washington, D.C., August 1980 and September 1985.

FIGURE 9-1. The first iron ore in this country was produced in commercial quantities near Lynn, Massachusetts, about 1646. The ore was dug from a swamp along the Saugus River, and the charcoal was made from neighboring forests. The giant waterwheel shown above supplied the power to run the huge leather-and-wood bellows for the forced air draft. This Saugus smelter has been restored to commemorate the beginning of the U.S. iron and steel industry. (Courtesy, U.S. Steel Company)

so as to save the various by-products, it results in the making of other valuable products in addition to coke. One ton of coal will make:

> 1,425.0 pounds of coke
> 19.0 pounds of sulfate of ammonia
> 2.0 gallons of crude, light oil
> 7.0 gallons of tar
> 10.5 cubic feet of gas

Not all coal can be made into coke. That which can be coked should be reserved for that purpose and not diverted to ordinary uses where only

FIGURE 9-2. "Cornwall furnace" in Pennsylvania is the oldest blast furnace in the United States. During the Revolutionary War, cannons for the Continental Army were cast here. It was in operation for 100 years and is now preserved by the Pennsylvania State Historical Society. (Courtesy, Bethlehem Steel Co.)

heat is required. This illustrates the general conservation principle that a high-grade resource should not be put to a low-grade use. Scientific research has extended the supply of coking coal in the United States by finding that blends of coking coal and some non-coking coals can produce satisfactory coke.

It was not until after 1857, after the invention of the Bessemer process, that steel, a refined commercial form of iron, was produced cheaply enough to make its widespread use practical. The Bessemer process of making steel from cast iron consists of burning out the carbon and other impurities by using a stream of air which is forced through the molten metal. All the carbon ordinarily is removed, and a definite amount is again added, along with other ingredients, to make the desired kind and quality of steel.

How Steel Is Produced

There are several general steps which are necessary to produce steel. When a body of iron ore is found and "blocked out" so that the approximate quantity of ore is known, several development steps are taken. These consist of sinking shafts, driving tunnels or stripping overburden.

The next step is the actual mining of the ore. This work is done either by hand or by machinery and involves loosening the ore from the general rock formation and moving it to some mill, where the iron ore is separated from much of the rock with which it is intermixed.

This separation process is known as "concentrating," "milling," "ore dressing" or "benefication." The resulting product is called a "concentrate," because all that actually is done here is to concentrate the ore by removing a part of the waste. Concentrating the ore usually is done near the mine, reducing the weight and bulk which must be hauled to smelters.

Smelters and other plants are used to remove from the concentrate various impurities and unwanted elements with which the metal or metals are chemically combined. They are usually located near the source of heat rather than near the mine. One reason for this arrangement is obvious when we realize that it requires 2 tons of coal to make 1 ton of steel.

The iron which has been smelted, or refined, is cast into bars known as "pigs," "ingots" or "bars." These are then ready to be made into various manufactured articles by remelting and adding the correct kinds and amounts of other metals before rolling, drawing or otherwise processing into forms such as castings, forgings, sheets, rods, tubes and wire.

Increased Use of Steel

The growth of the steel industry in the United States was very slight before 1900, when approximately 15 million tons of pig iron were made. Since then, there has been a general growth, with ups and downs related to the strengths of business activity. Steel production averaged 136 million tons from 1970 to 1979 and reached a peak of 151 million tons in 1973. Since then, there has been a drastic decline in U.S. steel production to an annual rate of about 85 million tons (roughly 55 percent capacity) from 1982 to 1986. Imports of steel averaged 18 million tons per year from 1974 to 1983, close to 10 times the amount of steel exported. The decline in U.S. production is the result of (1) economic recession, (2) increasing competition from other countries, (3) rising costs of production in the United States and (4) substitution of lighter weight materials, such as plastics, fiberglass and aluminum in vehicles.[3]

New technology will lead toward a more competitive steel industry. Plants called steel minimills that use scrap steel as raw material and produce a limited line of products have steadily increased their market share, from 3 percent in 1960 to more than 20 percent in 1985. Specialty steel plants account for about 10 percent of the industry's sales, while producing only 2 percent of its volume. The increased use of advanced technologies, such as direct reduction and continuous-feed electric furnaces, ladle technology and thin strip casting, and improved sensors for computer-controlled systems, will be needed to restore the health of the industry.[4]

World economic and trade conditions will determine what portion of this steel is produced within our country. Modernization and greater efficiency of the domestic steel industry is necessary if it is to compete successfully with imported steel. It would be contrary to conservation principles to levy restrictive tariffs to subsidize inefficient industry.

Do we have enough iron to keep up this high rate of use? Practically 85 percent of the iron ore used in the United States before 1950 came from the Lake Superior area (see Figure 9-3). Mining operations were concentrated there because of the immense supply, its availability and the high quality of the ore. This tremendous store of high-grade ore has nearly run out, but the area has been successful in developing plants to use lower-grade ores.

Lower-Grade Ores Abundant

Because the reserves of the lower-grade ores of iron are practically inexhaustible, production in the United States has turned largely to the lower-grade magnetic taconite rock. According to geologists, the supply of this ore is so great that all iron mining for generations could come from this source without exhausting the supply. The ore mineral is **magnetite**, an iron oxide formed from pre-existing iron minerals in the iron formation

---

[3]Frederick J. Schottman, "Iron and Steel," *Mineral Facts and Problems*, Bulletin 675, U.S. Department of the Interior, Bureau of Mines, Washington, D.C., 1985, pp. 405–424.

[4]Donald Paul Hodel, "The Mineral Position of the United States: The Past Fifteen Years," (excerpt of annual report), *Minerals and Materials, A Bimonthly Survey*, U.S. Department of the Interior, Bureau of Mines, August–September, 1986, p. 9.

FIGURE 9-3. Before 1950, the Mesabi range was the largest iron ore operation in the world. This and other mines in Minnesota have shipped almost 2½ billion tons of iron ore to the steel mills of the nation. The Lake Superior district is still producing a substantial proportion of the nation's yearly supply of iron ore. This area has mined its lower-grade taconite ore to maintain its position in the increasing market for iron.

when an intrusion of hot melted rock, the Duluth Gabbro, entered the area near the west end of Lake Superior. This magnetic taconite is so tough that the development of a new drilling technique has been necessary in order to mine it successfully. This technique involves using a blast of fuel oil and oxygen which is burned to heat the rock and then quenched with a spray of water which shatters it as it is quickly cooled. Because the magnetic grains are so small, they must undergo four steps in processing before they can be used in the furnace. First, the rock is ground to fine powder. Second, the magnetite is extracted by passing the powder over large electromagnets. Third, the magnetic powder is formed into pellets about ½ inch in diameter. Fourth, the pellets are baked hard in a furnace. Then, the taconite can be handled for shipping and blast furnace charging.

The expense of concentrating the iron from lower-grade ore is, of course, passed along to the consumer in higher prices of refrigerators, automobiles, tools, nails and any other products containing iron.

Finding New Ore Deposits

The alternative to using lower-grade ores is the development of new fields of high-grade ores, an unlikely development, or the importation of more ore, specifically from Canada or South America, or perhaps from Liberia which has exported some iron ore to us. Or, we might import steel products manufactured from foreign ore in foreign countries.

North America's major iron ore reserves.—Lake Superior and the Canadian Labrador-Quebec iron ores are the most important in North America. As has been noted, the ores of the Mesabi fed the mills of the United States for decades, but today they are mostly mined out. However, the Labrador Trough has the same high-grade ore as that formerly in abundance in the Mesabi range. This area and other Canadian mines provided approximately one-half of the U.S. iron imports from 1975 to 1980. Some geologists believe that Labrador may contain as much as a billion tons of high-grade ore, from which Canada could meet the iron needs of the United States for years to come. Both the United States and Canada have proved and probable iron ore reserves of 25 billion tons, with about one-half of these capable of being economically produced at present.

Some sizeable iron ore reserves are found in New York, Alabama, Missouri, Utah and Texas, while smaller reserves are found in 10 or 12 other states.

South America's major iron ore reserves.—A second source of high-grade ores for our smelters is South America. Suppliers include Brazil, Peru and Venezuela. U.S. capital has helped develop a large field of high-grade ore in Venezuela and has helped other South American countries to explore and develop their ore resources.

World iron ore reserves.—The USSR, Australia, China and South Africa have the world's largest proved and probable reserves of iron outside the Western Hemisphere. The USSR is in first place worldwide (59 billion tons), followed by Australia (33 billion tons), Canada (25 billion tons), the United States (25 billion tons) and Brazil (15 billion tons). Western Europe has only a paltry share of the world's iron ore, which is located in Sweden (4.6 billion tons) and France (2.2 billion tons).

Although reserves of iron ore of lower grade are ample to meet all U.S. demands for steel for an indefinite length of time and although high-grade Canadian and South American ores will be available for the United States to use for generations to come, the importation of these ores is based upon a continuation of friendly relations and mutual good will between these countries and the United States. These supplies, along with the immense reserves of coal within the United States, assure us of the base materials—coal and iron ore—which are necessary to continue to produce all the machines and mechanical developments of our present age.

Occurrence in Nature

The Lake Superior and Canadian Labrador-Quebec iron ores occur in sedimentary rock approximately 2,000 million years old, formed during the Huronian Age (late Pre-Cambrian). These rocks contain about 30 percent iron, too little to be at present utilized as ore. However, they have been locally enriched to about 55 percent iron, and these zones have been extensively mined.

The source of iron in the Huronian iron formations was the rock of a series of large mountain ranges which eroded down to a vast lowland. These rocks were granites and metamorphosed sediments in the form of gneisses, schists and slates. Most of these rocks contained a small percent of iron in the form of iron silicate minerals such as biotite, amphibole and pyroxene. At that time, only primitive plants, such as algae, mosses and lichens, existed on land, but their activity, plus chemical reactions of the iron silicates with oxygen, carbon dioxide and water in the atmosphere, produced solutions and colloidal particles containing iron, silica, calcium and other chemicals found in the rocks.

How did the iron become concentrated? Most of the silicon and iron were **colloids** (particles only a few microns in diameter), which carry positive electrical charges. These colloids did not stick together because of their light weight, similar electrical charges and a protective coating of organic material. Thus, they were carried to a marine basin where the salt water neutralized the electrical charges and allowed the colloids to form into masses and to settle to the bottom. This produced a sediment (iron hydroxide, iron silicate, silica, calcium and magnesium carbonates) which became a cherty iron formation known as **taconite,** which contains about 30 percent iron.

After many more thousands of years, the concentrations of iron ore varied greatly. The iron formations occurred as layers up to a few hundred feet thick, interlayered with sand and mud. These layers were folded and faulted to various degrees, depending on their location relative to the source of deforming forces. The westernmost area was less deformed than those to the east in Michigan, Quebec and Labrador; thus, it became North America's major iron range, known as the Mesabi. Called a range because the iron formation, which is more resistant to erosion than associated rocks, out-crops as a low ridge, the Mesabi is about 100 miles long and 1 to 3 miles wide.

The Mesabi had some of the richest ores in the world. It became enriched when the ore was exposed at the surface and subject for over millions of years to movement of oxygenated water from the land surface downward through it. (A few geologists believe the oxidizing agent was hot water derived from large igneous intrusions moving upward to the surface.) This process accomplished oxidation of the iron hydroxides and iron silicates and removal by solution of the silica and carbonate. In many instances, this left millions of tons of nearly pure iron oxide at or near the surface, an ore requiring no processing whatsoever. It could be dug from open pits or underground, loaded onto railroad cars and shipped directly to blast furnaces for reduction to pig iron.

Aluminum

It has already been mentioned that aluminum is one of the most com-mon metals. It is second only to iron in its abundance over the earth and in its usefulness. Aluminum comprises one-seventh of the earth's crust and occurs in many forms and combinations. Some of the better known forms are bauxite, corundum, turquoise, kaolin, feldspar, mica, ruby and sap-phire. It also occurs in all our clay soils.

The main source of aluminum is bauxite ore, although many other ores carry a considerable quantity. In most minerals in which aluminum is found, is occurs with silicon, and both are very tightly bound to oxygen. It is pos-sible to extract aluminum from these minerals, but not yet practical from an economical standpoint, since very great amounts of energy must be used to free the aluminum from the strong chemical bonds with which it is held. Bauxite, though a scarcer mineral than many aluminum silicates, is used as the main aluminum ore because the aluminum can be extracted from hydrous aluminum oxides of bauxite at much less cost. Bauxite is a product of chemical reaction between aluminum silicate minerals and oxygen, water and carbon dioxide in the atmosphere. This reaction will take place on the earth's surface only in tropical and subtropical climates where there is an abundant supply of water during at least one season of the year. Thus, world bauxite deposits are confined to regions which, during some period of time, have been in these climatic zones.

Occurrence in Nature

Aluminum ore occurs in pockets as well as in layers, or sheets. If the deposits of ore are large enough, it pays to mine them. Because bauxite is formed as a product of weathering, its deposits are confined to the thin zone of contact between rock and the atmosphere. They are generally confined to a sheet-like layer at the earth's surface which may be a few to a hundred or so feet thick. In some cases, oxygenated and carbonated water may penetrate fractures in rocks containing aluminum silicates. This

FIGURE 9-4. This is one of several open pit mines of the Aluminum Company of America at Bauxite, Arkansas, where most of our domestic bauxite is produced. The 30-cubic yard dragline, mounted on crawlers, removes the overburden. The ore is then drilled, blasted and loaded onto 54-ton trucks for transport to the processing plant. (Photo by Dorothy J. Gore)

produces pod- or wedge-shaped bauxite masses just under the earth's surface. Because of the mode of formation, residual bauxite is always strip mined from shallow pits dug into the surface deposits. Underground mines may be required if, as in Dalmatia, Yugoslavia, the residual deposits were buried, then tilted steeply during the Alpine mountain-building deformation. Occasionally, the bauxite from the weathered residue is eroded, transported and deposited elsewhere as an ordinary layer of sediment. It may be buried later by other sediment layers. If bauxite content is high enough, it may be mined at the surface or underground, but such instances are not very common.

The principal bauxite-producing area in the United States is located in Arkansas, where there is a town named Bauxite because of these deposits. Most of the ore mined in the United States is from this location. Bauxite was first discovered in this country in Rome, Georgia, in 1883, while the Arkansas deposits were not discovered until about 1900. Smaller deposits are found in Alabama, Tennessee and Mississippi.

All the U.S. deposits are in the South. This is no accident of nature, because all bauxite deposits were formed and laid down under warm climatic conditions. Also required are nearly continuous rainfall and relatively good drainage over long periods of time. Some deposits are found in the cooler parts of the world because of changes in climate which occurred after the aluminum ore was formed. Bauxite is quarried or mined in about the same way as shallow iron or copper ore.

Aluminum is extracted from bauxite by dissolving it in a hot melted salt and passing an electrical current through it. The positively charged aluminum ions in the solution are attracted to the negatively charged electrode. The temperature is sufficient enough to melt the aluminum. It collects at the bottom of the electrolytic cell and is tapped off into huge ladles and poured into molds from which it is rolled into sheets, drawn into wire or converted into one of many chemical compounds of aluminum, which have proved useful in industrial or consumer goods (see Figure 9-5).

Uses of Aluminum

The uses of aluminum are many because of its lightness, its freedom from rust and the ease with which it can be combined with other metals. We are familiar with its use in kitchen utensils, automobile parts, airplane construction and even building materials. A building made entirely of

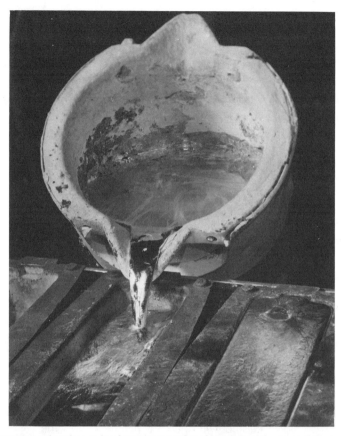

FIGURE 9-5. After the ore has been processed in electrolytic cells, the melted aluminum is drawn off into large ladles and poured into molds. When cool, the metal is ready to be shipped to various factories for production of useful articles. In 1983, about 47 percent of the aluminum produced was the result of the recycling program initiated by the industry. This conserved existing aluminum ores and saved 95 percent of the electricity that otherwise would have been needed to extract aluminum from bauxite. (Courtesy, Aluminum Company of America)

aluminum stands on the campus of Purdue Universiy in West Lafayette, Indiana. It was constructed so that the advantages and disadvantages of a structure made of aluminum could be studied.

From 1960 to 1985, the greatest growth in aluminum use was for containers and packaging, where aluminum was used for 90 percent of beverage cans. The next largest uses were for transportation and for building and construction. Electrical demand (plant construction and power line installation), consumer durables, machinery equipment and other uses accounted for the balance.

All major uses of aluminum have grown, and total use more than doubled from 1960 to 1985.[5]

Alumina (Al_2O_3) is used in making grinding and polishing compounds, bricks for lining high temperature furnaces, bearings for revolving shafts and a cement which is resistant to chemicals as well as to heat.

Supply and Distribution of Bauxite

The known world reserves of bauxite are estimated at 5.7 billion short tons, and the total resource potential is estimated at some 3.8 trillion tons.[6] The reserves are distributed widely, with 23 countries producing bauxite in 1986. Australia has the largest proven supply and is also the largest producer by far, accounting for about one-third of the world total. Major suppliers to the United States in 1986 were, in order of importance, Guinea, Jamaica and Australia. Guyana, Surinam and Brazil also exported to the United States.

In recent years, the United States has been importing practically all of the bauxite that is used to produce aluminum in this country, using our own supplies for a relatively small production of alumina. And, we will continue to rely upon imports. Our 40 million tons of proven and indicated reserves are only 0.2 percent of world reserves. Growth in use of aluminum is expected to be about 4.4 percent per annum to the year 2000.[7]

Copper

Copper was probably the second metal used by people, with gold being the first. Archeological studies lead us to believe that its discovery was about

---

[5] For a complete analysis, see Richard K. Schaefer, "Aluminum—The Past 35 Years of Production and Consumption," *Minerals and Materials*, U.S. Department of the Interior, Bureau of Mines, July 1986, p. 16 ff.

[6] Council on Environmental Quality and the U.S. Department of State, *The Global 2000 Report to the President: Entering the Twenty-First Century*, Vol. I, U.S. Government Printing Office, Washington, D.C., 1980, p. 31. (Figures converted from metric tons to short tons by authors.)

[7] Luke H. Baumgardner and Ruth A. Hough, "Bauxite and Alumina," *1986 Minerals Yearbook*, U.S. Department of the Interior, Bureau of Mines, preprint, available 1988, p. 7.

6000 B.C. Ancient Egypt used a great deal of the metal, much of which came from the island of Cyprus. This island gave copper its name—*cyprium,* or *cuprum.* Copper mining in Cyprus began about 2500 B.C.

Copper was produced in the American colonies in 1709 from ore deposits in Connecticut. Deposits were later found in Vermont and New Mexico. However, it was not until the discovery of the ore in northern Michigan in the early 1840's that the U.S. production exceeded a few hundred tons a year. Still later, extensive ore deposits were found in Arizona, Utah and Montana. It was these later discoveries that gave the great impetus to copper production.

Native (pure) copper is found in the Lake Superior region where there are pockets of various sizes, while veins of the ore are found in the Butte, Montana, area. The deposits of Arizona, Nevada and Utah contain copper minerals scattered through the mass of large igneous rock intrusions. Some pyritic (copper-iron) deposits are located in Tennessee as well as in northern California.

Most Versatile Metal

Copper is among the most versatile and beautiful of metals. It is distinguished from all other by its peculiar red color. It has many of the characteristics of gold in that it can be drawn into a fine wire (ductile), is easily hammered or pressed into sheets (malleable) and yet is very tenacious. When 11 parts of copper are mixed with 2 parts of zinc, the combination may be hammered into foil comparable in appearance to goldleaf. In this form it is called "Dutch metal."

Copper becomes very soft and malleable when heated to red heat and immediately immersed in water. This is opposite to the behavior of steel under similar treatment. On the other hand, if it is heated to a higher temperature than red heat, it becomes brittle, another trait which shows its versatility.

Copper is the only metal which occurs in relatively pure or native form abundantly and in large masses. It is also found chemically combined with carbonate and sulfur in many ores and gives to these ores their beautiful shades of green and blue.

Mining Development of Copper and Other Metals

Minerals are sometimes widely dispersed in rocks, or they may be concentrated. Some understanding of their occurrence helps us appreciate why they may be costly and difficult to mine.

Copper, lead, zinc, manganese, chromium, tungsten, columbium, cobalt and many other metals, including gold and silver, occur in similar types of deposits. In fact, most rocks contain slight traces of these metals in them. When a rock mass is pushed deep within the earth's crust (at least several thousand feet up to perhaps 30,000 or 40,000 feet) and sufficient heat is encountered to melt or recrystallize the rock, the metals are freed to migrate. None of these metals (except manganese) are the same size as iron, aluminum, calcium, sodium and potassium atoms, which are much more abundant and go into making up the rock minerals. Thus, the metals first noted do not fit into the crystal structure of any common mineral. Furthermore, there is not a sufficient amount of them to form minerals of their own. So, they collect in residual hot water which is freed from the melted or recrystallized rock mass. This hydrothermal (hot water) solution moves laterally or upward from the new rock mass, in whatever direction the resistance is least. It moves through small interconnected pores which occur in some rocks, through fractures or faults or along contacts between different rock masses.

The ore minerals are precipitated when the hydrothermal solutions either react chemically with rocks through which they seep (this is especially true of limestone) or cool sufficiently to saturate the solution with some particular ore mineral. In either case, the ore minerals may fill pre-existing openings in the rocks (filling) or take the place of some rock mineral which is dissolved by the hydrothermal solution (replacement).

Deposits may occur in many different shapes and grades of ore, each requiring a different mining method. Massive or scattered replacement deposits may be irregular or blanket shaped and range in size from a few hundred to many thousands of feet in dimension.

Deposits made in fractures and faults are commonly narrow veins in near vertical position. These are the lode or vein deposits frequently mentioned in popular fiction. One mining area may contain several sets of intersecting veins which are sometimes broken and offset by rock movements which occurred after the ore was deposited.

Minerals from the sea floor.—More and larger massive and disseminated ore deposits in layered volcanic and sedimentary rocks of all ages, and fewer and fewer vein deposits have been found in recent years. Understanding the origin of these deposits has presented many problems until the recent discovery that hot water seeps on the sea floor contain copper, lead, silver, zinc and other metals in large quantities. These seeps occur in many places along the major fracture systems of the earth's crust which mark the pulling apart of huge crustal plates of the earth, and are also marked by the extrusion of large volumes of basaltic lava to form new sea floor. Not only do the hot waters from these rift systems contain metals in solution, but both volcanic rocks and sediments near them have been found to contain metal sulfides and other ore minerals. Gorda and Juan de Fuca Ridges off the west coasts of Oregon and Washington, Southern Juan de Fuca Ridge in the Gulf of California and southwards to 25° south latitude, and the Red Sea are the best known of these.

Another major area for undersea minerals is the Atlantis II Deep, one of 18 hot brine pools known within the Red Sea. With a surface area of 23 square miles, it is estimated to have 2,000,000 metric tons of zinc, 400,000 metric tons of copper, 4,000 metric tons of silver and 60 tons of gold in a layer of fine-grained mud about 100 feet thick. Large-scale laboratory tests have indicated a probable 70 percent recovery of metals from these muds suction pumped into a processing ship. The environmental impact of submarine dredging and disposal of 400,000 tons of waste mud per day has been studied by the Red Sea Commission and, so far, found to be slight.

Most known sites of underwater minerals lie on the sea floor under several thousand feet of water. Many are international waters, beyond the claimed ownership of any nations. Recovery of metals from the brines, sediment and rock will require technologic advances in hydrometallurgy. Mining of rock, sediment and brines from the sea floor will require development of new types of equipment to handle a large volume of materials. Processing must be done in an environmentally sound manner. It is to be hoped that the United Nations Law of the Sea Treaty will be ratified by all countries and will provide a means of monitoring and regulating sea floor mining for the protection of the environment and the benefit of all nations and peoples of the world.

The sea floor rift system extends over 25,000 miles, and relatively little of it has been explored for metals. These new discoveries offer one of the most exciting possibilities for obtaining large future supplies of metals.

Mineral development expensive.—Development of most mineral prospects is expensive and financially risky. Sufficient test hole drilling must be done to outline the volume and shape of the ore body. Extensive physical and chemical tests must be made in order to plan the mining, processing and waste disposal methods. The mine shafts, hoists and underground equipment must be installed. From initial ore discovery to first ore shipment frequently takes as long as 10 years and an investment of hundreds of millions of dollars. Mines of any kind—metal or coal, underground or surface, new or reactivated—cannot be quickly developed. Long-range planning, stable markets and consistent government policies (regulations, taxes, tariffs, etc.) are all required for profitable mining ventures to exist.

Many Uses for Copper

The uses to which copper is put are as varied as its colors in its many different mineral ore compounds. Ornaments, tools and weapons of copper and of bronze, an alloy of copper and tin, have been found in the ruins of prehistoric dwellings. The metal probably was used before iron. Early North American Indians used it as evidence of wealth—Samuel de Champlain in 1610 was given a sheet of copper a foot long by the Indians who reportedly had found the metal on the bank of a river near one of the Great Lakes. The Indians gathered the copper in lumps, and after melting it, they spread it into sheets and smoothed it with stones.

A mixture of copper and zinc, called brass, is one of the most commonly used copper alloys at the present time.

Copper coins were common throughout the world for many years. Kitchen utensils have long been made of copper, and roofing, screens and other building materials are made of this metal. Copper piping is used where some non-corrosive metal is necessary.

The ability of copper to conduct electricity makes it an essential metal in most electrical installations. Fully one-half of all copper used is in connection with electricity and electrical appliances. Electric power production, transmission and use would be most seriously handicapped, if not impossible, without copper. There would be no extensive wire or radio communication, and the life of power machinery and equipment would be greatly reduced if these were made without copper.

Nothing has yet been found to take the place of copper in making shell cases, as well as other necessary military weapons. In medicine it is used as an astringent (a shrinking agent) and occasionally as an emetic to cause vomiting. It is also used as an antiseptic. Care must be exercised in the use of copper because it is poisonous in all soluble salt forms.

Reserves Adequate for Near Future

When estimating copper reserves, we should remember that it is possible to recycle much copper from scrap. Also, the known reserves reflect how intensive exploratory activity has been at prevailing prices. As prices rise, more reserves become available. In 1984, world estimated reserves available from 272 deposits in market economy countries were estimated to be about 500 million tons. The survey accounted for 90 percent of the reserve base of all such countries. The United States, over the years, has had about one-third of known reserves. Reserves are widely distributed.

At prices prevailing at the time of the study, known deposits could economically produce an estimated 88 million tons of copper. Assuming world consumption continued at about 7.7 million tons of copper a year, this would be only a 12-year supply. But, with higher prices, using the known deposits, they would last almost six times as long, or almost 70 years. To this should be added supplies available from scrap, which have been around 20 percent in recent years. This would extend the copper supply indefinitely— but at least 14 years. And assuming the 10 percent of the reserve base not surveyed is added, even more years, to a grand total of 90 to 100 years, can be assumed. Such estimates are complicated. But, they illustrate the principles of changing resources in accordance with our wants and abilities as explained in Chapters 1 and 2. Potential undiscovered reserves could add further to the supply of copper if found developable and economically feasible.

Since the beginning of heavy industrial use of copper at the turn of the century, the United States, with minor exceptions, has been a net exporter of copper. World War II and its aftermath caused us to import heavily. But, this was a temporary situation. In recent years (1982–1986), cumulative imports have supplied about 17 percent of our needs, recycled scrap about 20 percent and primary mine production about 46 percent. The balance was made up from inventories minus exports, which have been running less that 2 percent of total use. Chile, Canada, the USSR and Zaire, along with the United States, accounted for over half the world's copper mine production in 1986.[8]

Annual mine production capacity was 1.8 million short tons in 1985, with domestic consumption about five times production. Domestic copper mining was mostly unprofitable in 1985, reflecting international debt and exchange rate problems, chronic oversupply, excess world capacity, competing alternative materials and weak economic activity within some markets. Even though copper is a metal with a high reusable rate, and our production and reuse will undoubtedly increase in the years ahead, we will probably continue to import sizeable amounts to meet our future needs, reflecting the advantages of complementary trade.

Lead

Lead is one of the few metals mentioned in the earliest known writings of civilized people. King Midas, the miser of history, is credited with its discovery 1,000 years before Christ was born. There is evidence, however, to indicate that lead was used as money by the Chinese 1,000 years before that, and some authorities claim that the Egyptians used lead as long ago as 7000 B.C.

Even in those early times, lead was used for many purposes. In addition to employing it for money, the Chinese are credited with using it to mix with and debase (cheapen) the more valuable forms of metallic money. It was used by the Egyptians for glazing pottery and as one of the ingredients of solder. Ancient Babylonians held iron clamps in sockets with lead, and the Hanging Gardens, one of the Seven Wonders of the Ancient World, was floored with sheet lead. Other people used it as a roofing material for cathedrals and as a covering of basement pillars to prevent moisture damage. White lead was used as an ointment by the Egyptians, while red lead was the source of a cosmetic.

---

[8]Data compiled by author Kircher from U.S. Department of the Interior, Bureau of Mines, *Minerals and Materials, A Bimonthly Survey*, December–January 1987, circa 1987, p. 50; Janice L. W. Jolly and Daniel Edelstein, "Copper," *1986 Minerals Yearbook* (preprint 1988), pp. 51, 52; R. D. Rosenkranz, E. H. Boyle, Jr., and K. E. Porter, *Copper Availability–Market Economy Countries*, U.S. Bureau of Mines Information Circular 8930, 1983 (circa 1984). See abstract in preface; and earlier reports of the Bureau of Mines. Tonnage figures converted from metric tons to long tons on the basis, 1 metric ton equals 1,224 pounds.

Distribution in the United States

Lead was mined and used in Virginia in 1621, and its discovery in the Upper Mississippi Valley was reported as early an 1690. The French attempted to establish lead-mining operations in the valley region, but it was not until the latter half of the eighteenth century that production was on a permanent basis. This area was the important source of lead for this country until the latter part of the nineteenth century.

Lead ores were worked by the French in what is now the Southeast Missouri Lead District during the early 1780's, but production was negligible. In 1867, discoveries at new depths led to the development of one of the most productive lead-mining areas in the world. Missouri continues to be the largest producer, accounting for 90 percent of the total mine output in 1985. Idaho, Colorado and Utah produce most of the remainder.

Still Many Uses of Lead

About 50 to 60 percent of the lead that is used yearly in this country is reused. Present uses include paint pigments, chemicals, storage batteries, cable covering, type metal and building construction. Approximately 10 percent of the lead is used primarily because of its weight; 30 percent because of its softness, malleability and corrosion resistance; 25 percent because of its alloying properties (tendency to melt and blend with other metals); and 35 percent because of its chemical character in various compounds. Although it can be rolled to a foil so thin that it requires 2,000 sheets to make an inch in thickness, it does not have tensile strength, so it cannot be drawn into a wire. It is both the softest and the heaviest of our common metals.

Supplies in This Country Limited

The United States has depended upon some imports of lead to meet its yearly needs since 1931. Imports were relatively unimportant during the early part of the 1930's, when the imports of lead never exceeded 10,000 tons, or 2 percent of our total yearly supply. Beginning in 1940, however, this country sharply increased its supplies from abroad. During the 1970's, we were importing about 17 percent of our annual lead used, but our imports dropped to around 10 percent from 1980 to 1985.

Two important facts about lead are its indestructibility and its reusability. It will not corrode or rust away, and in most cases at the end of the useful life of the product containing it, it can be recovered and used again. This helps account for the fact that, although we use three of four times our yearly production, we do not depend upon foreign lead to the extent that our production figures suggest.

The use of lead in the United States varied from 1.1 to 1.5 million tons a year during the 1970's and early 1980's, while mine production was from one-third to nearly one-half this amount. Imports were about one-quarter to over one-half as great as mine production. The difference was made up from our reused lead.

Thus, although we will continue to look to foreign countries for a considerable part of our lead, our supply does not present a critical problem in the near future because of our large reserves and quantities of reusable lead. U.S. proved and probable reserves are 27 million tons, lead content, which is 20 percent of world reserves.

Sulfur

Sulfur is a nonmetal mineral used since antiquity. It was used to bleach linen, and it was used in religious rites about 2000 B.C. Egyptians used it as a paint component 400 years later. About 1000 B.C. it was used as a fumigant. Five hundred years later, it appeared as a component of the explosives of that time.

Commercial production of sulfur began in Italy early in the fifteenth century, but it was 300 years later, with the development of a process for making sulfuric acid, that it acquired industrial importance. Sicily was the major, and practically the only, source of sulfur until near the end of the nineteenth century.

Where Sulfur Is Found

Sulfur is found free in nature and combined or mixed with many other elements. Until the beginning of the present century, practically all sulfur in this country was obtained by separating it from gypsum and other minerals it was mixed with in sedimentary deposits.

Since early in this century, much of the sulfur has been obtained from the rock caps of salt domes. The largest known of these deposits are in the United States and Mexico. There are also notable deposits in Iraq, Poland and the Soviet Union.

These formations are dome-shaped bulges of salt, probably forced up into denser sedimentary rock while the salt was in plastic form. They vary in size and percent of recoverable sulfur. Only a few of the salt domes discovered in this country to date contain enough sulfur to warrant development. Of more that 230 of these deposits found in Texas and Louisiana,

FIGURE 9-6. This is part of a half-million–ton mountain of sulfur which was pumped from underground beds after being melted by superheated water at about 260°F. Sulfur is one of the most important of our mineral resources. It is used in making items such as matches, gunpowder, fireworks, medicines, fertilizers, paints, insecticides, paper, rayon, vulcanizing rubber and sulfuric acid. When the price of sulfur justifies recovery from smaller, deeper and marsh land deposits, known supplies in this country will probably meet our needs for the next generation. (Courtesy, Texas Gulf Sulphur Company)

only 21 have been commercially productive. The process of mining, known as the Frasch process, uses superheated water (see Figure 9-6). All the native (not naturally combined chemically with any other element and not recovered secondarily, as from coal, oil or smelting of ore) sulfur produced in this country is from Frasch mines in Texas and Louisiana.

Frasch process sulfur was 36 percent of the domestic production of sulfur in all forms in 1986. Recovered sulfur, a by-product from natural gas and petroleum and coking operations, sulfide ore smelting and utility plants, accounted for 53 percent of the total domestic production in that year. The balance of our needs was obtained from imports, from pyrite, hydrogen sulfide and sulfur dioxide.

Uses of Sulfur

Both free sulfur and sulfuric acid are required in various industries. Much more sulfuric acid than free sulfur is used. About 70 percent of all sulfur in 1986 was first shipped as sulfuric acid which was then consumed. The U.S. Bureau of Mines lists nearly a hundred uses of sulfur in industry, but it notes that the list is far from complete. Figure 9-8 shows the wide range of application of the two forms of sulfur.

What Is the Future of Sulfur?

Sulfur and sulfur-bearing materials in the United States and the rest of the world are ample to supply "any demand," the U.S. Bureau of Mines assures us. Native deposits in the Gulf Coast area alone may exceed 200 million tons. Recoverable reserves from fossil fuels, sea water and other secondary sources are in the billions of tons. An orderly transition to these alternate sources of supply appears possible.

Zinc

This metal was little known until around 200 B.C. when both the Romans and the Greeks produced brass by melting together copper and zinc. The metal itself was apparently forgotten or unknown from that time until the sixteenth century when the Portuguese brought zinc back from China. The Chinese were evidently familiar with this metal before

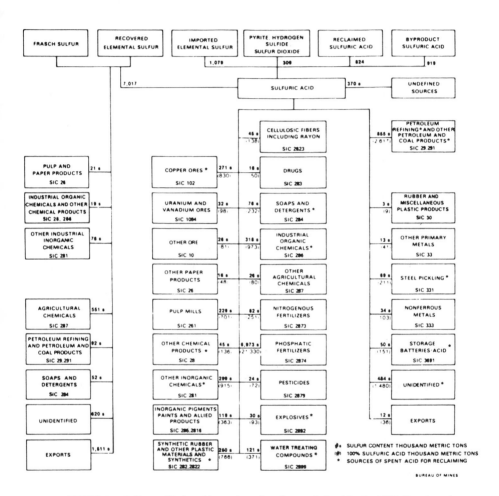

FIGURE 9-7. Sulfur–sulfuric acid supply and end-use relationships in 1986. Frasch and recovered sulfur from domestic sources provided most needs (top boxes across). About 2.7 million tons of the sulfur went directly into food, paper products, chemicals, other uses and exports (column 1). Over 7 million tons were first shipped as sulfuric acid, which was then consumed (other columns). The Standard Industrial Code numbers are used for identification by the U.S. Department of Commerce. (Courtesy, U.S. Department of the Interior, Bureau of Mines, *1986 Minerals Yearbook*, Washington, D.C., preprint, available 1988, p. 12)

the Greeks and Romans. Zinc was first smelted in England about 1740, and the first continental European smelter was erected in 1807.

Production in the United States

The commercial production of zinc in the United States began in 1858 when smelters were built in Pennsylvania and Illinois. The industry grew rapidly from the beginning, and by 1890, the yearly average production of zinc was 64,000 tons.

From 1900 to the time of the depression in the early 1930's, production had increased to where the yearly average was 725,000 tons. One-half of this production was from the tristate district of Missouri, Kansas and Oklahoma. At that time our production met all our needs and furnished some zinc for export.

During World War II, our production of zinc reached a peak of more than 942,000 tons. This was the largest production in our history. Since then, mine production has dropped to less than 500,000 tons annually, being only 203,000 tons in 1986. Secondary production has nearly equaled mine production during recent years, including 1986. We also have been importing half or more of our requirements in recent years.

The source of supply also has changed. Eleven states are now in commercial production. The tristate district that formerly produced one-half of our zinc is now accounting for a negligible amount, although other deposits have been developed in Missouri. Tennessee now leads the nation in zinc output, followed by New York and Missouri.[9]

Uses of Zinc

Currently, most zinc is used in galvanizing steel products to prevent rusting. Rust damage to unprotected steel products amounts to billions of dollars each year. In 1983, 46 percent of the total consumption of slab zinc was used for galvanization.

The second most important use is in zinc alloys. In this category of uses, 39 percent of our total consumption was used. Automobile parts

---

[9]Current figures from James H. Jolly, "Zinc," *1986 Minerals Yearbook*, U.S. Department of the Interior, Bureau of Mines, Washington, D.C. preprint, available 1988, pp. 2, 12, 13.

such as radiator grills, fuel pumps, carburetors, hydraulic brakes, instrument panel parts, door and window accessories, heaters and air-conditioners are commonly zinc die castings, as are business machines, electrical appliances, building hardware and tools. The aircraft industry also uses die-cast alloys. The amount of zinc in brass ranges from 3 to 45 percent, with the average brass containing about 30 percent. Zinc is also used in wet batteries, weather stripping, radios, washers, oil burners, vacuum cleaners, slide projectors and kitchen appliances.

Domestic Reserves Not Large

U.S. proved and provable zinc reserves are 22 million tons. The present rate of consumption, including ores and secondary recovery, is between 0.7 and 2 million tons per annum. The present mine production of about 300,000 tons a year is expected to continue. Even with secondary recovery, we still have to look abroad for a major part of our zinc. The chief sources of imports are expected to continue to be Canada, Mexico, Peru and other South American countries and Australia. It is quite possible if prices increase enough over costs and new smelters become available that new deposits will be developed to add to our present known reserves. The Council on International Economic Policy has stated that "world reserves are ample to provide zinc in the quantity likely to be demanded at current price levels for the rest of the century."

SCARCE METALS

There are many other metals which, though used in relatively small quantities, are as essential as coal and iron for making the various types and kinds of metal alloys, as well as the many machines so necessary in this age of mechanical and industrial development. A modern automobile, for example, requires about 20 different metals for its construction and operation. An electric motor requires the use of many of these same materials, and the more nearly automatic these machines become, the greater the number of metals required in their construction.

We need metals such as nickel, tungsten, chromium, cobalt and manganese for making the various kinds of metal mixtures (alloys). Some alloys are harder than steel, others are more elastic or tougher, while still others are brilliantly colored, rustproof or capable of high permanent polish.

Table 9-2 lists 35 minerals and metals according to the percent we imported in 1980 in order to meet our needs. Table 9-2 also shows that we depended upon other countries for over one-half of our supplies of 18 of these metals and minerals and that we even imported almost all of some of them.

TABLE 9-2. Net Import Reliance of Selected Metals and Minerals Used in the United States, 1980 (net import reliance[1] as a percent of consumption[2])

More than 50 Percent Reliance[3]		Less than 50 Percent Reliance	
Metals and Minerals	**Percent**	**Metals and Minerals**	**Percent**
Columbium	100	Titanium (ilmenite)	47
Mica (sheet)	100	Silver	42[4]
Strontium	100	Selenium	40
Titanium (rutile)	100[4]	Barium	38
Manganese	97	Gypsum	38
Tantalum	97	Gold	28
Bauxite and alumina	94	Iron ore	22
Chromium	91	Vanadium	15
Cobalt	93	Copper	14
Platinum group metals	87	Iron and steel products	13
Tin	84	Sulfur	13
Asbestos	76	Salt	8
Nickel	73	Lead	8[4]
Cadmium	62	Cement	7
Potassium	62	Aluminum (metal)	4
Zinc	58	Pumice and volcanic cinder	3
Tungsten	54		
Antimony	53		

[1]Net import reliance = imports − exports.

[2]Apparent consumption = U.S. primary and secondary production + net import reliance.

[3]Substantial quantities are imported for fluorspar, graphite, rhenium and zircon. Data withheld to avoid disclosing company proprietary data.

[4]1979 figures.

Source: U.S. Department of the Interior, *Mineral Commodity Summaries, 1981*, U.S. Government Printing Office, Washington, D.C., August 1981, pp. 4, 5.

Figures for 1983 confirm a continuing heavy reliance upon imports: manganese, 99 percent; cobalt, 95 percent; chromium, 90 percent; and platinum group metals, 89 percent, for example. Location and relative share of foreign mines producing these minerals are shown in Figure 9-8.

Since the United States is dependent upon imports of many minerals and metals that are necessary for making machinery, equipment and utensils, if we expand the use of these, we must of necessity depend upon imports for the increased supplies more than we do now. This means that we are limited in the use and enjoyment of many products by imports of strategic minerals and metals to the United States from foreign countries.

A host of foreign policy considerations complicates mineral imports for the United States. Embargos, revolutions, monopolistic sales practices, restraint of trade for political or strategic reasons, prohibition of foreign control of mines, etc., must all be considered. For example, South Africa is particularly rich in many strategic minerals, yet its apartheid policy has caused many U.S. businesses to cease investing and trading there. It is probable that the United States could encourage mineral-producing countries to sell to us needed minerals through economic and technological aid to develop mines and manufacturing and supplies of food and other materials needed by these countries. Some U.S. businesses are doing this now, and federal laws and regulations are needed to encourage this.

The U.S. government maintains a stockpile of many strategic materials. The amounts are supposed to be enough to supply both military and civilian needs for a three-year periods of conventional war. The mandated levels have consistently not been maintained. Some supplies have even been sold off to help balance the federal budget. The stockpile is not a long-term solution to mineral supply and is probably not even an adequate protection in case of wartime cutoff of imports.

Some substitutes for minerals which the United States lacks are possible. For example, ceramic or metal-ceramic materials developed for the space program may well be adapted for high-temperature engine parts, thus saving the importation of cobalt, chromium or other materials we lack. That educated human ingenuity is a most important natural resource is well illustrated here.

Manganese

More manganese is used in making various kinds of steel than any other

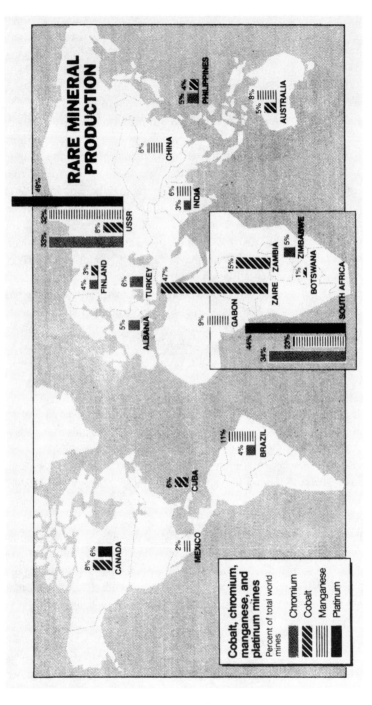

FIGURE 9-8. The large share of mines producing some important rare minerals outside our country is illustrated here. These scarce metals are needed by the United States for products such as high-strength tools, electric resistors and parts for jet engines, nuclear reactors and submarines. (Map by Forbes in *The Christian Science Monitor,* © 1986, The Christian Science Publishing Society)

metal except iron, for it is needed in every ton of steel produced. Yet, in 1985, less than 1 percent of the amount used in this country was supplied from within our boundaries. Other uses of this metal are for electric dry batteries, driers for varnish, Japanese lacquer and printing ink, glass, porcelain enamel, some building brick, welding rods, pottery and tile. We require ½ to 2 million tons of manganese ore yearly to meet our normal needs.

Chromium

Chromium is familiar to all of us because of its use on the bumpers and trim of some automobiles. It was used in these places because it carries a high polish and will not rust. It is called the "work horse" of the alloy steel industry because it makes steel harder and tougher, does not rust and is the key ingredient in practically all stainless and heat-resisting steel. It is also important to the chemical industry. Unfortunately, domestic mine production of chromite essentially ceased in 1961, and we must now import almost our entire supply of this metal. We use about one-half million tons a year.

Tungsten

Tungsten is one of our most needed metals. As an alloying metal, it helps steel retain its hardness and toughness at high temperatures. It is especially useful in alloys employed in cutting tools which must keep sharp edges, even when red hot. An important military use is in making armor plate, as well as gun barrels and armor-piercing shells. Tungsten is used in about 1,500 different military items.

Domestic production during normal periods of the past 20 years accounted for one-third to two-thirds of our consumption, with most of it recently produced by two California mines. Tungsten is also recovered as a by-product of molybdenum mining in Colorado. U.S. mines are projected to supply one-third or less of our domestic needs per annum up to the year 2000.[10]

---

[10]U.S. Department of the Interior, Bureau of Mines, The 1984 Report to the Secretary of the Interior, Washington, D.C., pp. 2.7–2.58.

Columbium

Columbium is used to make the steel needed for the walls of jet engines which will withstand the terrific heat of the burning gases. Columbium, first discovered in 1801, was not commercially used in significant amounts until recently. It is also employed in making stainless steel, fast cutting tools, nuclear reactors, heavy construction and electrical equipment needing to withstand heavy strain or intense heat. Very little is found in this country, and no production has been reported since government contracts were terminated in 1959. Paying quantities have been found in Australia, Canada, Norway, Portugal, Malaysia, the Congo and Nigeria. We must continue to look to foreign countries for most of our columbium.

Cobalt

Cobalt is another rare metal found mainly in other countries. It is necessary in making electric generators, as well as in making porcelain enamels, pigments and hard facing steel. Like most of the other scarce alloying metals, it has important uses in atomic energy projects. Canada has some deposits of cobalt, as do the Congo, New Caledonia, Morocco, northern Rhodesia and the United States. Use in the United States must be met by imports, except for secondary recovery.

PLANT LIFE NEEDS MINERALS

The Puzzle of How Plants Grow

Records of early peoples show they were interested in and puzzled by the growth of plants. How did plants grow from small seeds and become large and woody? Where did the material come from out of which the woody, more permanent parts of plants were made? It was known that water was necessary to grow plants, but the question of where the solid or firm parts of plants came from remained unanswered.

It was thought that all plant growth came from water alone through some mysterious transformation by nature. One of the earliest recorded experiments attempting to solve this puzzle was carried on by John Woodward in London about 350 years ago. He grew spearmint in pots containing identical kinds and amounts of soil. In these experiments he supplied each plant for 77 days with all the water needed for satisfactory growth. The water for each pot was taken from a different source.

The difference in growth of the various pots of plants was so much as to be startling, as is shown by the following figures:

Source of Water	Gain in Weight After 77 Days
Rain	17.5 grains
River Thames	26.0 grains
Hyde Park conduit water	139.0 grains
Hyde Park conduit water plus 1.5 oz. of garden mold	284.0 grains

There was also a very slight decrease in the weight of the soil used in the different pots.

Real Need of Plants for Minerals

Woodward's conclusion was that since the soil lost only a very small proportion of its weight, the increase in weight of the spearmint was not caused by any ingredient in the soil. Neither was it caused by water alone, but by some "peculiar" terrestrial matter in the different waters. His explanation was that there was more of this terrestrial matter in some waters than in others and that the rain water contained the least. No thought was given to the very small loss in soil weight following the experiment.

Although the reason for plant growth as given by Woodward was incorrect, it did open the way for other experiments that finally resulted in showing the need of plants for various plant nutrients, such as phosphates, potash, nitrogen and numerous other elements, in exceedingly small amounts, as well as for water and sunshine.

We now know that the three plant foods needed by most plants for healthy growth and seed production are phosphates, potash and nitrogen, which frequently are not readily available in the soil in sufficient amounts. These three elements are needed in the largest amounts and are found in practically all fertilizers.

Phosphates

Phosphorus is never found free in nature. It is usually combined with other elements as phosphates.

Most commercial deposits have been laid down in sea water and are of organic origin. When sea water containing phosphates in solution seeps through limey deposits, such as layers of broken shells on the sea bottom, the phosphate may replace the carbonate of the shell material if temperature, acidity and concentration are favorable. This results in phosphorite, a rock rich in calcium phosphate.

U.S. deposits are found in Florida, North Carolina, Tennessee, Idaho, Montana, Utah and Wyoming. Florida has the largest known proved and probable reserves, and along with North Carolina, accounts for 90 percent of U.S. phosphate production. Idaho has the largest inferred reserves. Only Morocco exceeds the United States in proved and probable reserves. Our country produced about one-half of the total world output during the 1970's and early 1980's and is a major exporter.

Potash

Potassium is found almost everywhere in nature. It is estimated that 2.5 percent of the earth's crust is composed of potassium. It is found, for example, in rocks, soils and salt lakes as well as in the waters of oceans, fresh water lakes and streams.

Where guano is found.—Guano (droppings of birds and bats) is a source of phosphates and nitrogen as well as potash. Deposits are found in regions of limited rainfall and in caves where the soluble elements are not leached out.

Peruvian natives were probably the first people to use guano as an aid to crop production. They had been using it for generations before Baron Humboldt took some of it to Europe in 1804. That was the Europeans' introduction to guano as a fertilizer.

Guano used in the United States.—Peruvian guano was first brought to this country for use as a fertilizer in 1843 when a shipload arrived in Baltimore. It was widely used from then until the late 1850's and was the first commercial fertilizer to gain widespread use in the United States. After the 1850's its use declined rapidly because of the increasing availability of mixed chemical fertilizers. Guano from the Mammoth Cave in Kentucky was used during the Civil War in the manufacture of explosives.

Early sources of guano were the islands off the west coast of South America and off the African coast. These deposits are becoming depleted, but other nitrates of a mineral source are found in various regions throughout the world.

How potash deposits were formed.—Most U.S. deposits of potash, as well as those of Europe, originated in past geological times. Some of the deposits are the result of sea water having been cut off from the ocean and gradually drying up through evaporation. At times of heavy ocean storms, additional sea water was washed into these salt lakes so that over the centuries deposits of potash and other salts became deeper.

In other situations inland lakes with no outlets have become so filled with salts as to be workable for potash as well as for other salts. The Great Salt Lake in Utah and the Dead Sea between Israel and Jordan are the two bodies of water with the heaviest concentrations of salts. Each has about six times the concentration of sea water.

Ages ago when the Great Salt Lake was formed, it was larger than Lake Huron. Geologists call it Lake Bonneville. As it dried up over the centuries, several smaller lakes were formed in addition to the Great Salt Lake.

Potash from wood ashes.—One of the earliest sources of potash commonly used in the past was from wood ashes. It is from this source that potash obtained its name. It was orginally obtained by running water slowly through wood ashes and boiling the resulting liquid down in open kettles. The solid white residue was called potash because it was made in pots from ashes. Potash was first produced in this country at Jamestown, Virginia. One of the reasons given for England's establishing colonies here was to obtain potash from wood ashes to meet her growing need for this product.

Where potash is found.—The main source of potash for the United States as well as for the rest of the world from 1860 until the beginning of World War II was Germany. Our first serious effort to develop our potash resources was during World War I. As soon as that war was over, however, and foreign potash again became available, we turned to using these supplies and lagged in the development of our own deposits.

Our present supplies are obtained mostly from mines near Carlsbad, New Mexico, and the Williston Basin of North Dakota and imported from Saskatchewan, Canada. The mineral occurs in beds like coal and is mined in a somewhat similar manner. Smaller quantities are obtained from California and Utah. Other possible sources are kelp (sea weeds), recovery from industrial waste, Georgia shales and subterranean deposits in Texas and a few other states.

Nitrogen

Nitrogen is one of the most nearly universal of our natural resources. Seventy-eight percent of the air is nitrogen. It is estimated that 400 million tons of nitrogen are removed from the air each year by plants, rainfall and electrical discharges and that a like amount is added to the air through decaying organic matter and other ways. This is an abbreviated statement of the process called the nitrogen cycle. This yearly transfer represents only one-millionth of the total nitrogen in the air.

Nitrate deposits.—The world's most extensive deposits of natural nitrates are in northern Chile. These deposits supplied most of the world's needs for nitrogen until the 1920's when German chemists developed a cheap and efficient method of manufacturing synthetic nitrate from the air.

The Chilean nitrates accumulated along the western coast of South America ages ago as a result of the decay of the plant life of that time. They escaped being washed away when the climate changed from a moist climate that encouraged the growth of luxuriant vegetation to one of almost perpetual drought.

Nitrogen from the air.—Nitrogen compounds were synthesized from the air in Germany before World War I for use mainly in explosives. After the war, demand for commercial fertilizers showed the need for more phosphates and nitrates. This need was partially met when the Muscle Shoals Dam was constructed in the Tennesseee Valley and a part of the power was used to produce fertilizer. The first fertilizer produced in the United States for agriculture was made from phosphate rock. Before World War II, however, the prospective need for nitrates both for the military and for agriculture hastened the conversion of phosphate plants to nitrate production.

Nitrogen from natural gas.—Today, most of the nitrogen used in farm fertilizers is produced from natural gas. During the fuel crisis of the early 1970's (see Chapter 6), natural gas prices rose sharply and so did those for fertilizer, even though the production of ammonia used for fertilizers accounts for only a small part of total natural gas consumption (about 2 percent in recent years). In the 1980's, the cost of imported natural gas and oil declined and so did the cost of fertilizers.

The production of no other element has increased as rapidly as has that of various forms of nitrogen during the last few years. We are now using about 15 million tons of nitrogen in various forms annually, and the nitrogen in fertilizers for agriculture accounts for nearly three-fourths of this amount. Other uses include explosives, resins, fibers, plastics and animal feeds. Two decades ago we were producing about $\frac{1}{10}$ as much nitrogen, and only about $\frac{1}{2}$ was used for agriculture.

The use of fertilizers on the farm is discussed in Chapter 18.

RECYCLING OF MATERIALS – GOOD CONSERVATION

Many materials are not used up or damaged when an item containing them is worn out, broken or discarded. Some examples are the metal in the body, frame and engine of an old car or truck, food and beverage containers, discharged batteries and the fiber in yesterday's newspaper. These items are valuable, but their value is not commonly recognized by most people.

Reuse of these materials is possible if a system for such reuse has been devised. The scrap metal and auto salvage yard are traditional ways in which some materials have been reused. For example, some Girl Scout and Boy Scout troops earn money by collecting aluminum cans or newspapers for sale.

It is logical to reuse materials for a like purpose such as making new paper from old or new metal parts from scrap metal. Sometimes materials can most easily and economically be put to an entirely different use. Scrap glass and ceramic materials have been used in street paving mixtures, old paper has been made into cellulose insulation for homes and commercial buildings, municipal trash has been used as a fuel for electric generation and heat.

One problem with reusing "trash" is the great variety of materials mixed together. It takes equipment and labor to separate and prepare them for reuse. Consider municipal trash. By weight it contains:

```
paper—cardboard . . . . . . . . . . . . . . . . . . . . . . . . . . . . . . . . . .50%
iron . . . . . . . . . . . . . . . . . . . . . . . . . . . . . . . . . . . . . . . . . . . . .9%
aluminum . . . . . . . . . . . . . . . . . . . . . . . . . . . . . . . . . . . . . . . .1%
glass—ceramic . . . . . . . . . . . . . . . . . . . . . . . . . . . . . . . . . . .10%
garbage—yard clippings . . . . . . . . . . . . . . . . . . . . . . . . . . .20%
plastic—fabrics, etc. . . . . . . . . . . . . . . . . . . . . . . . . . . . . . .10%
```

All of these are reusable in some way. These materials are generally hauled to a dumping place and buried there under a layer of clay. Suitable sites are becoming more expensive and located farther from cities, thus increasing the cost of disposal. More cities should think of recycling their trash. The sale of materials can pay for part of the cost of collecting and processing the trash. Land required for future dumps can be put to other uses, and fuel, metals and paper recovered for reuse will mean extending the mineral and forest resources available. In 1983, for example, 46.7 percent of the 1.23 million tons of aluminum beverage cans manufactured were recycled. Nine states have mandatory beverage container deposits. In most of these, aluminum container returns have exceeded 90 percent.

What's in a junked car? Several different types of steel (axles require a steel different from that used in doors, doors from engine blocks, etc.), zinc, aluminum, copper, rubber, plastic, fiberglass, fabrics, glass, etc. As with municipal trash, the dispersed location of the resources and the economical separation of different materials are problems.

As economic and environmental costs of locating, mining and milling ore deposits increase, and as more demand occurs for forest products, recycling of used materials makes sense in today's world. (Solid waste disposal is discussed in Chapter 23.)

NONFUEL MINERALS – ENOUGH FOR EVERYONE?

Our nation's current resource position on nonfuel minerals, in sharp contrast to that on fuels, is a strong one. We have abundant resources of many of the most basic and widely used minerals. And, we have convenient, friendly access to many of the others. But, we are dependent upon foreign sources to meet our needs for all or a very large share of a number of nonfuel minerals critical to our industrial production and national defense.

The Global 2000 Report to the President foresees "steady increases in demand and consumption" of nonfuel minerals on a worldwide basis. But, the study adds that the "projections point to no mineral exhaustion problems but . . . further discoveries and investments will be needed to maintain reserves and production of several mineral commodities at desirable levels.

In most cases, however, the potential is still large . . ., especially for low grade ores."[11]

Commenting on the mineral position of the United States, the Secretary of the Interior declared in his 1985 annual report:[12]

> Two countries that may change the pattern of worldwide demand for and supply of minerals are China and the U.S.S.R. A number of Soviet deposits, primarily in Europe, are being exhausted. If the U.S.S.R. continues with a policy of relative self-sufficiency in minerals, it will have to pay the increased cost of developing, producing, and transporting them from new mines in remote locations in central Asia and Siberia. On the other hand, the U.S.S.R. may seek to purchase at least some of its future mineral needs in world markets. China already has burst upon the world economy both as a major supplier of minerals (tungsten, coal, rare earths) and as a purchaser of metal-intensive equipment. China could be both a major market opportunity of U.S. companies and a formidable competitor in the production of a number of commodities.

While we should continue developing our domestic reserves and strengthening our international friendships, we must not neglect to consider our role as consumers. Conservation through recycling of minerals and other materials by both industries and individuals will reduce costs and extend the life of reserves. If we practice wise use instead of misuse and abuse, our nonfuel minerals resource position will remain strong.

QUESTIONS AND PROBLEMS

1. Try to name 20 important products we get from nonfuel minerals.

2. Why are nonfuel mineral resources said to be less critical than fuel minerals?

3. Indicate the steps necessary to produce iron from the ore in the parent rock.

4. Steel production has declined sharply from levels in the 1970's. Give at least three reasons for this drop.

5. Is the United States in danger of not having enough iron to meet its needs in the future? Give reasons for your answer.

---

[11] Council on Environmental Quality and the U.S. Department of State, *The Global 2000 Report to the President*, p. 27.

[12] "The Mineral Position of the United States: The Past Fifteen Years," excerpted from the 1985 annual report of the Secretary of the Interior, in *Minerals and Materials, A Monthly Survey*, U.S. Department of the Interior, Bureau of Mines, August–September 1986, pp. 6–9.

6. In what part of the country are aluminum ores found? How do you explain this distribution of these ores?

7. How is aluminum ore mined?

8. What are the characteristics of aluminum that make it so useful for various purposes? Name some of the common uses of aluminum.

9. Is aluminum likely to become a scarce metal during the next 50 years? Give reasons for your answer.

10. Why is copper called one of the most versatile of metals?

11. Why do you suppose copper was used by prehistoric peoples long before there was any evidence of their using iron or other metals?

12. Name some of the more common uses for copper and tell why you think the metal is especially adapted to various special uses.

13. Where are the more important concentrations of copper in this country, and what one of nature's activities is responsible for most of the deposits?

14. How is our nation's mineral reserve situation for copper different from that for aluminum?

15. What are some of the reasons why lead was so useful in early times?

16. Where does most of our lead come from at the present time?

17. Name some of the ways in which sulfur is used.

18. What is the outlook for the sulfur resources of the United States?

19. What are some of the special uses for zinc?

20. What are the functions of the scarce metals that are used in relatively small amounts and yet are so important to our mechanized development?

21. Name the important uses to which the following metals are put: (a) manganese, (b) chromite, (c) tungsten, (d) columbium and (e) cobalt.

22. Name some metals that are found in your state and tell how they are used.

23. Describe John Woodward's efforts to find the reasons for plant growth.

24. What are the sources of phosphates used in fertilizers?

25. How did potash get its name?

26. What is guano and where is it found?

27. Tell how mineral deposits of potash were formed.

28. What country first synthesized nitrogen from the air?

29. What limits the production of nitrogen? What is the principal use?

30. The United States depends upon foreign sources for over half of its supply of many metals. Name five of them. Describe the use of one of them.

31. Compare the resource position of fuels to nonfuel minerals. Which is more critical? Explain why.

10

Water Supply for Industrial and Private Uses

In the past we thought of water for the home, the farm and the various industries as an inexhaustible resource. How can we be short of water when three-fourths of the earth's surface is covered with water; when rain or snow falls periodically and brings new supplies of clear, cool water from our oceans and lakes; and when below us, under the surface, are vast supplies of water held in the pores of sand and rock, which are continuously being replenished from these rains and snows? Yet, we find cities that are critically short of water, not only for industries but also for street cleaning, yard watering and household purposes, such as laundering, cooking and cleaning. New York City has rationed its water during several droughts. Miami, Florida, has had problems in keeping salt water out of its system, and some of the West Coast cities have to use water supplied a hundred or more miles away in order to meet the increasing demand for this invaluable resource.

WHY ARE WE SHORT OF WATER?

The reasons for our water shortages can be grouped under three major headings: (1) unequal distribution, (2) abuse and (3) misuse. Intensifying these problems has been the strain put upon our supply by increased use.

The Hydrologic Cycle and Unequal Distribution

The unequal distribution of water occurs because of the vagaries of the hydrologic cycle, which we first noted in Chapter 1. This process by which water is evaporated from the oceans by the sun, moved overland by the winds and precipitated over the surface of the earth is a very imperfect one.

Distribution of water is uneven both from place to place and from time to time. The map of areas vulnerable to drought (see Figure 10-1[1]) shows that while the eastern half of our nation is humid, most of the West is dry. Even in the humid regions, however, droughts can occur. And, cloudbursts are not uncommon in the desert regions.

Water is also unequally distributed after initial precipitation. For the United States, exclusive of Alaska and Hawaii, it is estimated that of the water precipitated over land, some 70 percent is either evaporated or transpired (called **evapotranspired**) back into the atmosphere. Of the remaining 30 percent, which stays on the surface or sinks into the ground, about one-fourth is diverted for human use.

Abuse of the Water Supply

Adding to the problems of nature's erratic disposal of water is the pollution and often wasteful allocation of water by humans. Water pollution problems have become very serious in the United States. Many of our major streams have become open sewers. The Cuyahoga River near Cleveland actually caught fire on the surface because of accumulated waste. The

---

[1]While the U.S. Geological Survey has not classified drought areas for Alaska and Hawaii on the map, the general situation is well known. In Alaska, annual rainfall is heavy (up to 200 inches) in the southern and western areas and much lighter (under 25 inches) in the northern areas. In Hawaii, the reverse generally holds true. The northeast coast and the mountainous areas usually have heavy annual amounts (up to 200 inches), and the southern and western areas, light amounts (less than 20 inches). The effect of these variations in rainfall on vegetation and human occupation is quite different because of the great temperature differences, reflecting the northern, more continental location of Alaska and the southern, trade wind location of Hawaii. Moisture deficiencies occur in the drier areas of both states.

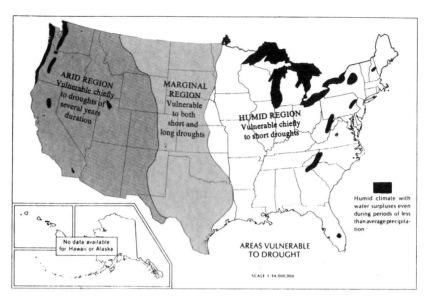

FIGURE 10-1. Drought potential. Drought occurs when precipitation is less than the long-term average and when this deficiency is great enough to hurt people. In humid regions, a drought of a few weeks is quickly reflected in soil moisture deficiencies and other water resources. In arid regions, the inhabitants protect themselves from short droughts by depending upon surpluses of ground or surface water, and a drought becomes critical when it is sufficiently prolonged to reduce these supplies. Prolonged droughts occur rarely in humid regions, but they reduce the normal ground or surface water supplies. In semi-arid regions, some people may be affected by every drought, whether of short or long duration. (Courtesy, U.S. Geological Survey)

Connecticut River was called by one nauseated native "the world's most beautifully landscaped cesspool." George Washington's Potomac River, which featured a popular "bathing" beach at Washington, D.C., in the 1920's has become so polluted that swimming is prohibited. Instead, its foul odor offends sightseers who come to visit the seat of government of our nation. A few years ago, Lake Erie had become so filled with industrial and sewage wastes that scientists despaired that it could ever be returned to desirable purity.

Pollution of streams must be stopped at its source. Industry has been the chief offender over the years, accounting for twice as much organic waste in streams as the sewage of all cities combined. The organic chemicals that wash from farm lands are another serious source of pollution of streams.

We are all aware of some of the properties of water—its color, odor, transparency, taste, hardness, saltiness, foaming qualities and temperature. Farmers, engineers and public health officials are concerned with the dissolved oxygen content, acidity, dissolved salts, plant nutrients and toxic substances. They are especially concerned—as we all are—with the amounts of suspended matter and with disease-producing bacteria, the worst offenders of all.

FIGURE 10-2. To help compensate for the uneven distribution of water in California, water from Mt. Shasta, and other sources in the northern part of the state, is carried by aqueducts to the southern part of the great valley—a distance of over 400 miles. (Courtesy, Bureau of Reclamation)

Misuse and Increasing Use of the Water Supply

Misuse of water can mean that we are wasting it and/or that we are not using it efficiently. Or, in the case of ground water, we may be drawing it down faster than it is being recharged.

Waste of water appears to be a way of life in the United States. We use twice as much water as actually needed to wash the car, take a shower, clean the porch, etc. Industry also has not paid sufficient attention to water economy. Savings could be made especially by recycling—treating the water that has been used in a process to remove impurities and then using it over again. With better national and state clean water laws and better enforcement, we can anticipate much reclamation of waste water in the future.

Misuses of other resources also often critically affect the water supply. Our resources are interdependent. To destroy one resource frequently is detrimental to, or wasteful of, some other resource, or even the wise use of one resource may be harmful to some other resource. We drain our marshes in order to produce more food, and in so doing, we ruin the homes and feeding places of many of our wild animals and birds. We break up our prairies in order to feed our growing population, and we lose the buffalo, the antelope and the prairie chicken. We cut our forests, thus changing our clear, cool, bowered streams into stark-naked, dirty, mud-filled water courses.

Another reason why water shortages will become more critical in the future, unless corrective steps are taken now, is the expanding use of water for all purposes. Much more water for domestic use is needed by our growing population than in other countries of the world. A study of 10 of the largest cities of the United States showed them to be using nearly three times as much water per person as was being used by 10 cities of equal size in Europe. All new industrial techniques, such as those associated with the development of new explosives, synthetic fuel production and chemical industries, necessitate the use of more water. Even the bringing of new land into crop production requires more water, because much of this undeveloped land is in those parts of the country which need irrigation to produce crops.

CLEANING UP OUR WATER SUPPLY

A Task Group on Coordinated Water Resources Research of the Federal Council for Science and Technology, made up of leaders in government, business and science, has suggested how we should go about cleaning up our water supply. To improve the quality of our water supply, we must first determine the quality requirements for various uses. Water used by humans must be free of disease organisms. Water used for recreation must look clean as well. Water used by industry must be relatively free of damaging chemicals and abrasive particles. Water for agriculture, as well as that serving as a habitat for fish and other creatures, must not contain damaging toxic substances.

After we have determined the various requirements, we must find out what effect the various substances we now add to our water supply have on it. These additives include detergents, pesticides, chemical fertilizers and various industrial wastes.

After successfully researching the problems of requirements and the causes of pollution, we can then establish water quality standards and a plan to achieve them. Finally, we must enforce the standards and management practices.

Since the Task Group report, the question of water pollution and our requirements have received renewed public interest and action. The Federal Water Pollution Control Administration (now part of the U.S. Environmental Protection Agency), established in 1965, requires the state governments to submit water quality standards to it. In the last few years, it has authorized hundreds of millions of dollars to help municipalities build sewage treatment plants.

Progress in Water Cleanup

Congress, reacting to the serious water quality problems, has enacted legislation and funding to clean up our waters. The Water Pollution Control Act of 1972 was amended in 1977. Its goal was to make all waters of this country fishable and swimmable by 1985. It provided funds for the identification of all sources of pollution and for the development of implementable plans to control these sources.

It also was intended to help local communities solve their water quality problems. Areawide water quality plans as well as state water quality plans were established. The areawide plans covered relatively small areas within a state, usually consisting of several counties centered about a common problem such as acid water run-off from mines, urban storm water run-off or erosion of agricultural lands. The state plans usually addressed all water quality problems of the state outside the areawide planning areas. As this effort proceeded, all plans within a state had to be compatible. The entire water quality program was often referred to as the 208 Program because Section 208 of the act spelled out the actions that were to be taken by the states.

To observers, the high goals of the act had obviously not been met by 1985. And, there were some misapplications. But much had been accomplished. Some 47,000 miles of monitored streams were in noticeably better condition. Lake Erie, declared biologically dead a few years ago, again had game fish. Elsewhere however, the quality of 1,000 miles of water had remained unchanged or had deteriorated.

Fortunately, Congress overrode President Reagan's veto to pass a new bill called the Clean Water Act. The act provides for $20 billion to continue clean water projects through 1994. At that time new water legislation must be passed, or water pollution control will be left largely to the states.[2]

Another 1986 bill, the Safe Drinking Water Act, gives the Environmental Protection Agency three years to set acceptable limits for 83 different contaminants of water and provides for eventual monitoring of additional substances. Since it will be years before we will see the results of EPA action, states need to set up their own stream monitoring programs if they want to protect their citizens in the interim.

The establishment and enforcement of a uniform set of standards is an absolute essential to control of industrial and municipal pollution. All industries need to be treated alike under the law if they are to be able to compete with one another. Unevenly enforced laws favor one producer at the expense of another. If one industry cleans up and another does not, the one cleaning up is apt to lose its competitive ability to stay in business. Its costs will rise, while its negligent competitor will keep costs down and be able to undersell it. If, on the other hand, a uniform code of water management is enforced, the costs will be fairly borne by all firms. The higher costs will eventually be passed on to us as consumers. The cost of pollution control should be recognized as a necessary cost of production.

Case of the Illinois River

How pollution of a stream develops is illustrated by the case of the Illinois River. This is the largest river within the state of Illinois, flowing over 300 miles from near Chicago to enter the Mississippi near St. Louis.

---

[2] Robert A. Taylor, "Clean Water: Adding Up the Balance Sheet," *U.S. News & World Report*, February 16, 1987, p. 2.

The Illinois was noted by the early Native Americans for its fishing. In the 1600's, Marquette and Joliet, the famous French explorers, remarked on its beauty. By the 1800's, it had become the most important commercial fishing stream in the United States. But, this distinction came to an end when beginning in 1901, all the sewage of the Chicago area was dumped into the Illinois through the newly constructed 37-mile sanitary district canal. The water in the river became so contaminated that even with the diversion of 10,000 cubic feet of water per second from Lake Michigan to the river, all fish were destroyed for 150 miles downstream. After 1930, Chicago installed more efficient sewage treatment facilities and, more recently, banned pollution. Fish life has recovered somewhat, especially in the southern part of the river basin. Nevertheless, pollution of the river bottom mud, thus destroying the clams, snails and other organisms and aquatic vegetation upon which fish feed, affected the quality of the fish and may have made the northern basin sterile for generations.

INCREASING THE AVAILABILITY OF OUR WATER SUPPLY

The hydrologic cycle provides us with four sources of water supply: (1) atmospheric moisture, (2) surface water, (3) vadose water (that held in the topmost layer of earth) and (4) ground water. Let us consider briefly the nature of these and the possibility of increasing their availability.

Atmospheric Moisture

Atmospheric moisture is water carried in the atmosphere in various forms of water vapor or in condensed form. As noted earlier, some 70 percent of the water is returned to the atmosphere. Moisture-laden air is indeed an important potential source of supply. Changing the weather to induce precipitation is one of the most intriguing ways of obtaining this supply.

Modifying the Weather

If the needed water supply in a particular place could be obtained from the atmosphere, this would certainly solve many water shortage problems.

This idea reminds us of the rain dances of the American Indians. Modern methods, however, are based on scientific reasoning. A common method has been to release fine particles of chemicals into a moisture-laden cloud from an airplane. The particles make a base around which water droplets form, thus starting rainfall.

Modern rainmakers have been quite successful in inducing rainfall in this manner. But, regardless of how successful the triggering of rain from clouds may be, there is one critical factor which suggests that artifically induced rainfall can never by a panacea for water shortages. The limiting factor is that there must be moisture in the air before moisture can be obtained from it. Our severe drought conditions are generally characterized by relatively dry air masses. With little water in the air, there is little for the ground.

Another problem of changing the weather is the danger of loss of control. Would light showers become "gully washers"? Would the rain fall where unintended? These questions are particularly thorny ones. They might give rise to thousands of lawsuits against rainmakers by irrate landowners. And, even with perfect control, *who* is going to decide *who* will get the rain?

Reducing Evapotranspiration

Since so much of the water in the hydrologic cycle is evaporated and transpired, we could greatly increase our available supply by preventing the return of moisture to the atmosphere. Removal of undesirable phreatophytes (plants which send their roots deep in the earth to reach water) is one method. Other methods include covering or lining with cement canals which transport water for irrigation purposes; spreading a thin film of chemicals on reservoirs; irrigating less wastefully and with the distribution pipes placed underground; and fallowing (plowing and tilling but leaving unseeded) fields in semi-arid areas.

Surface Water Supplies

The use of surface water is the most obvious way to help meet our water needs. This source is large enough to provide water to meet most needs in the foreseeable future—if it is accessible and if excessive water pollution is stopped. Water consumption figures are deceptively large because, of course, it is the same water used again and again in its progress to the ocean. The water of the Wisconsin River, for instance, is harnessed by 13 dams along its rather short course and therefore is counted 13 times in computing the amount used for power. Even after passing over the last dam, the water can still be used for industrial or other purposes.

Practically all the water that flows again into the ocean does so through our rivers, with only a small portion returning through ground water. When streams are dammed, the availability of their water supply is greatly increased. Many factors should be considered in addition to water supply, however, before a reservoir can be created, as was noted in Chapter 4, which dealt with water power. The most diversified large-scale surface water control project in the United States, and probably in all the world, is the Tennessee Valley Authority.

The Tennessee Valley Authority (TVA)

In 1933, Congress passed the Tennessee Valley Authority Act "to improve the navigability and provide for the flood control of the Tennessee River; to provide for the reforestation and the proper use of marginal lands in the Tennessee Valley; to provide for the agricultural and industrial development of said valley; and for other purposes." The main river channel is over 600 miles long, and with its tributaries the TVA system extends into seven states (see Figure 10-3).

Multiple-purpose river basin development.—As a result of this act of Congress, steps were taken to place dams in the watershed of the Tennessee Valley so as to control water run-off and thus reduce the damage done by flood waters as they race down these valleys. When the Ohio River is in flood stage, the flow of the Tennessee can actually be stopped, thus alleviating additional flood damage. The whole watershed was included in the project; otherwise, complete control of the waters of the river could not have been achieved.

Not only were flood waters tamed by the work done in this valley, but land was conserved as soil from the uplands and hillsides was saved and rebuilt; forests were replanted; wildlife was restored; and more water was made available for various industrial and home uses.

The increase in agricultural productivity has been remarkable. While farm acreage in the valley has dropped from 24.5 million acres in 1933 to less than 13 million in the 1980's, farm product sales have increased

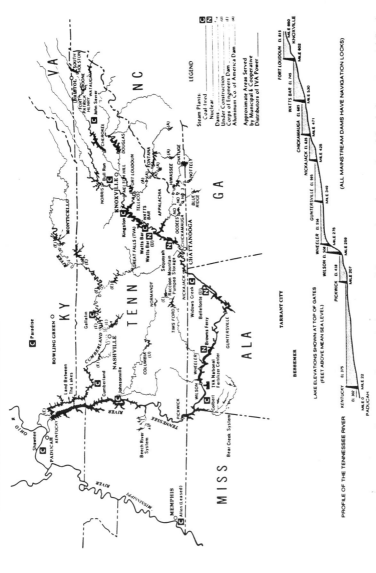

FIGURE 10-3. Map of the Tennessee Valley Region showing the location of dams, nuclear plants and coal-fired plants. Potential flood waters are stored behind the dams during wet seasons and released during dry seasons, thus allowing for flood control as well as maintaining a sufficiently deep channel for navigation. The dams also produce hydroelectric power and their reservoirs provide recreation. The coal fired and nuclear power complement the water power. Flood damages of over $2 billion have been averted since the TVA system began operation in 1936. (Courtesy, Tennessee Valley Authority)

from a little over $100 million per annum to nearly $2 billion. Soil erosion is a serious problem on this hilly land, which TVA has been fighting through research, education and demonstration farms. An offset to soil saving in this type of program is the loss of soils in the fertile bottomlands, which are now lake bottom.

Improved navigation was another asset created by the TVA. The formerly sandbar-choked, meandering stream became navigable from one end to the other during most of the year for commercial barge tows and large and small pleasure craft, as reservoirs became filled and locks were opened for by-passing the dams.

Another major development was the installation of hydroelectric plants at the dams. Within a few years after the project began, cheap electrical power became available to part of a region which President Franklin Delano Roosevelt had described as "Our Number One Economic Problem." In 1949, TVA began building coal-fired steam plants and in the 1960's, nuclear plants. Today, these steam-powered facilities provide about two-thirds of the TVA's electric-generating capacity (23 million kilowatts), with the balance provided by hydroelectric (8.5 million kilowatts) and standby gas turbines for peak power (2.5 million kilowatts).

Cumulative flood damage of over $2 billion has been averted since 1936 and over $100 million downstream along the Ohio and Mississippi rivers. Flood control benefits have been many times the outlay for the flood control system since its inception.

Tennessee River commercial freight tonnage has set new records from year to year, and savings to shippers (an estimated $150 million a year) have exceeded the federal costs of maintaining and operating the waterway.

In this region, which was once as depressed as surrounding Appalachia, private investment in waterfront manufacturing plants and terminals is in the billions of dollars. Electrical power use is common on practically all farms of the area as well as for city dwellers and industrial plants. TVA power is distributed to more than 1.5 million consumers.

Forestry programs continue to expand in the TVA region. Over 1.5 million acres have been reforested in the last 25 years. The TVA research and field workers have become leaders in developing uses for forest products, including the use of saw-mill waste for pulp and paper making. The forest products industry has millions of dollars in plant investments in the area. Wildlife habitats and demonstration areas are located throughout the forests. As an indication of the success of wildlife conservation

FIGURE 10-4. Wautaga Lake, Tennessee, is on a tributary of the Tennessee River, flowing into that river from North Carolina. It is one of the smaller lakes in the TVA system. The lake has five camping sites and six boat landings or docks. (Photo by Tennessee Valley Authority)

programs, the deer population has increased from about 100,000 head in 1940 to about 4,000,000 head in the 1980's.

Not the least of the many benefits derived from the TVA program is the development of recreational facilities. From an area which once had very few recreational developments of any kind, the Tennessee Valley has become one of the best developed playgrounds in the United States. TVA lakes in the Tennessee Valley states have more than 1,000 square miles of water surface and 11,000 miles of shoreline. The region abounds in beach developments, camps and resorts, fishing docks and other private and public works. Over 90 public parks, 400 public access areas and 100 group camps and club sites have been created, and over 350 boat docks have been built. There are over 40,000 moored boats and 13,000 private residences on lakefront property. The TVA region has received over 70 million visitors for recreation annually in recent years. In 1985, tourism contributed $6 billion to the valley's economy and accounted for 336,000 jobs.

The TVA system is not without its problems. Stream bank and other types of erosion adds to the turbidity of the water and silting up of the reservoirs. Some natives complain that damming of the tributaries has destroyed priceless natural beauty. Coal-burning electric generating plants have created air pollution and drawn upon land-destroying strip mines, although TVA now requires reclamation projects of its suppliers and has installed emission control devices at steam power plants.

Also, distressing to the TVA, in 1986 nuclear programs were brought to a halt. New order for plants were canceled, completion of others were delayed and working reactors were shut down because of safety concerns.

TVA officials are very proud of the agency's accomplishments. The problems which have beset its operations reflect human and mechanical failings of performance rather than bad intent. The drowning of historic river bottomlands and the coming of new industry has radically changed the human and land-use relationship of the Tennessee Valley. Throughout the changes, TVA management has continued to emphasize conservation. Among newer developments, it has begun water quality control and waste disposal programs. Despite problems, and, in fact, problems in dealing with them, the TVA stands as a world model for river basin development.[3]

FIGURE 10-5. This beach is on TVA's Chickamauga Lake, near Chattanooga, Tennessee. Seventh in a series of nine reservoirs on the main stem of the Tennessee River, the lake is 59 miles long with a maximum width of 1.7 miles. It has 810 miles of shoreline with many camping and boating facilities. (Photo by Tennessee Valley Authority)

---

[3]For an excellent report on TVA conservation accomplishments, see *The First Fifty Years: Changed Land, Changed Lives, State of the Environment in the Tennessee Valley—1983*, Tennessee Valley Authority, 1983.

California State Water Project

Rivaling the TVA in size, although different in purpose and construction, is the California State Water Project, which was chosen as the outstanding civil engineering project of 1972 by the American Society of Civil Engineers. Unquestionably, it is the largest and most complex water-moving project in history. This project is a 685-mile aqueduct system consisting of dams and reservoirs and hydroelectric power stations like the TVA, but unlike it, having huge concrete-lined canals and pumping plants for irrigation and domestic water supplies (see Figures 10-6, 10-7 and 10-8). The major purpose of this system is to trap excess run-off in the Feather River water-

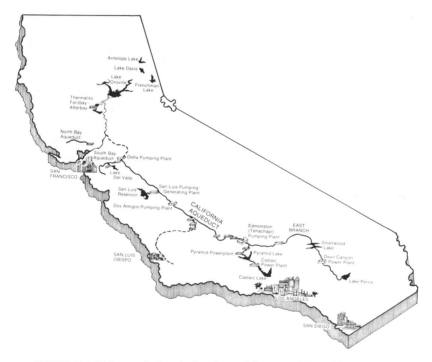

FIGURE 10-6. This map depicts the location and features of the California State Water Project, a major part of the vast and complex system of rivers, canals and aqueducts which serve California. This project extends some 685 miles, and its initial facilities, completed in 1973, include 18 reservoirs, 15 pumping plants, 5 power plants and 540 miles of aqueducts, pipelines and tunnels. This map does not show the Federal Central Valley Project or the several regional water transfer systems which, together with the state project, form a network which taps water from the mountain ranges on both sides of the Sacramento and San Joaquin valleys, their streams and the Colorado River. (Courtesy, California State Department of Water Resources)

FIGURE 10-7. This view is downstream as the California Aqueduct of the State Water Project moves water along its 600-plus-mile journey from north to south. Adjacent orchards and field crops are irrigated by the Delta Mendota Canal, a part of the Federal Central Valley Project. The two projects share facilities and storage at nearby San Luis Reservoir.   (Courtesy, California State Department of Water Resources)

shed in northern California for multiple uses in southern California, the San Joaquin Valley and the San Francisco Bay area (see Figure 10-6). The project also provides flood control on the Feather River, recreation facilities and conservation of fish and wildlife.

While engineers have been working on various aspects of the California State Water Project since the 1950's (construction began in 1957), it was not until October 7, 1971, that water was pumped to southern California by the new project. Initial facilities were completed in 1973, but the whole project is not expected to be completed until after the turn of the century.

Ecologists have expressed concern over the project. The project transports water through channels of the Feather and Sacramento rivers to the

FIGURE 10-8. This view looking downstream on the California Aqueduct of the State Water Project is about 200 miles south of the view in Figure 10-7. The Wheeler Ridge and Ira J. Chrisman Wind Gap pumping plants, which keep the water flowing, and an outcrop of the Tehachapi Mountains are in the foreground. The latter also stretch across the middle background. Beyond is the Antelope Valley, and far to the south, the San Gabriel Mountains. (Courtesy, California State Department of Water Resources)

delta and then diverts some of it to the south. Some ecologists believe the project threatens to pollute the delta and San Francisco Bay by diminishing the rivers' seaward flow. Others decry the increase in population that is almost sure to follow the increased availability of water.

Greenwood and Edwards declare: "The movement of water to people rather than people to water has been an ecological disaster."[4] However, it should be recognized that all over the world, since the beginning of the Industrial Revolution, the movement of water to people has facilitated industry, quality water supply, building of cities and disposal of wastes. And, the project engineers of the California State Water Project point out that the environment is being considered in the project. Under state law and by order of the California Water Resources Control Board, the project must maintain good water quality in the delta.

FIGURE 10-9. Here water is being turned into an almond grove. It has been carried 300 miles to supply the hot, thirsty soil. (Courtesy, Bureau of Reclamation)

As with all their water projects, the engineers have tried to provide for land subsidence, ground water pollution, earthquakes, floods and other hazards. The California Department of Water Resources is working to increase reservoir and ground water recharge capacity. It hopes to achieve

---

[4]Ned H. Greenwood and J. M. Edwards, *Human Environments and Natural Systems*, Scituate, Massachusetts, Duxbury Press, 1973, p. 173.

increased efficiency through more coordination with the Federal Central Valley Project and other water control systems in the state. It is increasing water conservation in the cities by fostering use of water-saving devices, on the farms by promoting more efficient use of irrigation and in recreation by a program to reduce water use on parks and golf courses. And, it is proud that this and earlier water projects have provided the water needed by the millions who live in southern California and have enabled the state to become the most productive of all the 50 states in agricultural output (Figure 10-8).

Other River Basin Developments

While the TVA remains unique in the scope and unified control of planning and management of an interstate river basin's resources and the California State Water Project is unexcelled in size and complexity, unified efforts are being made today in many other river basins. Projects in the arid West particularly involve development of hydroelectric power and irrigation facilities, while in the humid East, the emphasis is on hydroelectric power, flood control and navigation.

The Pacific Northwest has the greatest potential for hydroelectric development of any of our water resource regions (see Table 1-4). Its Columbia River is nearly twice as long as the Tennessee River and with tributaries has over five times the hydroelectric capacity of the Tennessee Valley. Grand Coulee Dam, on the Columbia River, alone has a potential hydroelectric capacity of 9.7 million kilowatts—more than that of major dams of the TVA (see Figure 4-6). The Columbia Basin has over 30 dams. Like the river systems of California, it has extensive irrigation works.

Other river development projects benefit our populace from coast to coast. The Colorado River has been dammed in numerous places, providing flood control, irrigation and hydroelectric power, while, fortunately, still preserving the scenic wonders of the Grand Canyon. The Missouri River basin has some 100 dams, 8 of them large, to provide for flood control, navigation and power production and to aid in development of the watershed. The Mississippi-Missouri River System, including the Ohio River and its tributaries, carries over one-third of our inland waterway commerce. It is exceeded in this regard only by the Great Lakes System, with which it is connected. Dams up north and levees on the lower Mississippi protect millions of acres of farm land in Mississippi and Arkansas from flooding, although whether the benefits have been sufficient to justify the costs is questioned by some, and the management problems are great as noted in the section dealing with flood plains.

FIGURE 10-10. Some privately financed power developments rival those built with government authority. Union Electric Company's Bagnell Dam, which began operation in 1931, forms the Lake of the Ozarks. The lake covers 86 square miles in Missouri. With 129 miles of length, longer than Lake Michigan, and 1,150 miles of shoreline, it is one of the largest human-made lakes in the world. The lake has become a year-round recreation and residential area. The average annual hydroelectric output is 440 megawatts. (Courtesy, Union Electric Company)

A remarkable water development in the northeastern and lake states is the St. Lawrence Seaway, which connects lake ports such as Chicago and Milwaukee with the Atlantic trade routes. It also provides electrical power. In New England, water power utilization directly powered the early industrial development, as we have noted. Today, hydroelectric power there runs a poor second to other sources of power, but control of the rivers to prevent floods is vital to industry.

The North American Water and Power Alliance plan.—One almost incredible water diversion proposal is known as the North American Water and

Power Alliance. It would hook up streams and lakes of Canada, the United States and Mexico, originally estimated at a cost of about $100 billion. In view of the environmental upset this would cause and the questionable economic benefits, it appears that this proposal should never be accepted.

Wild Rivers

A few rivers in our country still remain in a relatively natural condition. Their courses have been little affected by human intervention. These streams are known as *wild rivers.*

What is a wild river worth? What is it worth to taste the cool spray; wade in the rippling rapids; hear and see the white-green-blue waters of the roaring falls; hike along the bank heavy in grasses or hemlock, pine and birch; contemplate the still pools or quiet, deep, clear waters of a wild river—a river left in its unspoiled state?

The great tows moving down the Mississippi or the Tennessee, the mammoth dams and power plants of the Columbia or the Colorado, the exotic ocean freighters plying the St. Lawrence are evidence of vital industry and trade and express the beauty of science and technology. The wealth they bring is welcome.

But there is no need to destroy every wild river for the sake of commerce. If we do, we will destroy one more place where many of us can go to renew our own spirits and, perhaps, help lift up those of others. Of what avail outward pomp and circumstance if inwardly we lead lives of bitterness, frustration and jealousy? In a message of the same vein universal to all peoples in all times, the gospel according to St. Mark (Mark IX: 36) declares: "For what shall it profit a man, if he shall gain the whole world and lose his soul?"

The Allagash, Buffalo, Current, St. Croix and Rogue are a few of some 75 rivers now protected by or being considered for inclusion in our Wild Rivers System, established in 1968. We must preserve these few free-flowing streams. Our nation's economy can afford them. We cannot afford to be without them.

River Flood Plains

No discussion of our inland surface water resource would be complete without calling attention to the plight of flood plains. In the United States, as in the rest of the world, settlers migrated to these river lowlands because of their natural conveniences—flat land and flowing water. Here, as everywhere, we have paid the price—catastrophic floods with loss of property and life.

Gilbert F. White, one of America's leading authorities on flood plains, points out that, as their name implies, they will be flooded. We must provide a place for the water to go. Ian McHarg, the noted ecologist and land-use planner, says in his film *Multiply and Subdue the Earth*, " . . . the 50-year flood plain by definition should be not occupied by any residential development, the 100-year flood plain might, the 5-year flood plain absolutely never." Dr. Lincoln Brower, Professor of Biology, Amherst College, at a flood plain conference in St. Louis on February 4, 1974, pointed out that "flood damage is bad, but the overflowing is good." In other words, used for agricultural and ecological purposes, river bottomlands benefit from floods, but where unwisely occupied by people, they become casualty areas.

The advantages and problems of damming streams have been pointed out in earlier paragraphs of this chapter and especially in Chapter 4. How about levees (embankments raised to prevent the river from overflowing)? In limited areas they are helpful. They can protect part of a given urban area from flooding. They are useful for protection against moderate flooding of farm land or wild life areas. But, Brower and others have called the attempt to levee an entire river system, as is being done on the lower Mississippi, a disaster. Not only may the levees be breached, but also water may seep underneath—and emerge on the flood plain in sand boils. Major flooding can be caused behind the levees by water rushing down from the adjacent uplands through tributaries and/or ditches, only to be blocked by the water of the main stream, now cresting at a high level between the levees. This situation has occurred many times on the Illinois side of the Mississippi River at St. Louis, although it has been "protected" by a levee system for half a century.

Levees are useful. But, adequate spillways and ponding areas must be provided, and critical areas of the flood plain must be freed of permanent structures. A river serves us best when it is allowed to do what comes naturally—flood!

Vadose Water and Ground Water Supplies

Water under the surface of the earth is classified into two major types:

vadose water—that held in the topmost layer of earth, which is the source of most soil moisture—and ground water—water found considerably deeper beneath the surface in the pores and fissures of the rocks, including clays, sands and gravels.

Vadose Water Is Essential

Vadose water is essential to most plant life. Using soil moisture efficiently or being able to help drain saturated soils or to add to those deficient in water is essential to getting the maximum production from soils used for agriculture. Refraining from disturbing soil moisture conditions may be equally important to conserving wildlife habitats or natural vegetation. Such management practices are discussed in the chapters on soils, forests and wildlife.

Ground Water Supplies Are Vast

Potential resources of ground water are enormous. The volume of underground fresh water has been estimated to be at least 10 times the average annual precipitation of 30 inches. Unfortunately, it is not always available in the place where it is needed the most. And, ground water supplies may often be easily polluted or overdrawn.

Ground water is replenished by water seeping into water bearing rocks or underground channels from some source above the ground. Or, it may be recharged by stream and river water which seeps into underlying permeable materials. The water pumped from wells for a community may have moved hundreds of miles through sand, gravel and porous rock before it reached that point from which it is pumped, perhaps several hundred feet below the surface. It is estimated, for example, that the water now being pumped out of 800-foot wells for the city of Madison, Wisconsin, fell as rain and snow in the northern part of the state several hundred years ago. Because of the slow movement of these underground waters, it can easily be imagined that their replenishing may be too slow to maintain the supply if water is pumped too rapidly.

Ground water use is increasing. — While only about one-fifth of the total amount of water used in our nation is from ground water resources, they are much more important than their relative share suggests. For ground water serves areas critically short of rainfall. And it supplies two-thirds of our urban areas. Many of us are absolutely dependent upon it for drinking water.

Reflecting the growing demand from agriculture, industry and households, ground water use doubled over the decade of the 1970's and has continued to increase during the 1980's. This heavy demand, on often slowly recharged supplies, along with ground water pollution, has led to severe problems all over our nation.

The other four-fifths of our nation's water supply comes from rivers and lakes, except for a very small quantity obtained from desalted sea water. Unlike ground water, surface waters in general are rapidly recharged by nature. Therefore, the impact of increasing demand is not as severe as for ground water. But, pollution is![5]

Water table varies.—The water table (the upper level of ground water) is gradually getting lower in some regions; consequently, several problems have developed. In some sections of Ohio, the water table has dropped 100 feet in the past 50 years. In the Central Valley of California, it has been dropping around 10 feet per year, and if no other source of water had been made available to this area, approximately 400,000 acres of highly productive land would have returned to a semi-arid condition before now.

In some coastal cities, the dropping of the water table has resulted in so reducing the water pressure that instead of fresh water flowing from the land to the sea the reverse is taking place and the salty ocean water is flowing through the underground channels toward the land. Can you imagine the distress of finding salt water coming from all the faucets in the house?

In some places the ground water supply has been recharged by recycling water after it has been used for cooling purposes, as in Louisville, Kentucky, for example. In others, as in Memphis, Tennessee, the supply of clear, cool ground water has never been wanting, and the city gets its supply from this source rather than the surface waters of the Mississippi River, on which it is located. In fact, the coastal plains facing the Atlantic Ocean and the Gulf of Mexico, including a large area extending northward up the Mississippi River Valley to the tip of Illinois, and the flood plains of our eastern rivers, all have excellent ground water potentials.

---

[5]Prepared in consultation with Dr. Harlan H. Bengston, Director, Environmental Resources Training Center, Edwardsville, Illinois, April 3, 1988.

SALT WATER CONVERSION

The Use of Saline Waters

When saline water is mentioned, we usually think of sea water. The water of the various oceans represents inexhaustible supplies if and when the salinity (saltiness) can be economically removed. There are other waters in many parts of the country that cannot be used for human consumption even though they are not nearly as salty as sea water. These brackish waters contain from $\frac{1}{30}$ to $\frac{1}{2}$ as much salt, or dissolved solids, as does sea water. Sea water contains some 35,000 parts per million, or $3\frac{1}{2}$ percent, of dissolved salts, while the various brackish underground waters contain from 1,000 to 15,000 parts per million. The dissolved salts in these waters consist of many minerals and mineral compounds besides calcium, such as magnesium, sodium, bicarbonates and sulfates. The greater the number of salts and the heavier the concentration in the water, the more costly it is to remove enough to make the water usable. Drinking water should not contain more of these salts than 500 parts per million, or $\frac{1}{2}$ of 1 percent.

Removing Salts by Distillation

Sea water distillation in small quantities has been used on ships for years as a means of maintaining a supply of fresh water during the time at sea. Until fairly recently, the method employed was not economical enough to use when larger quantities were needed for whole communities. Since then, much progress has been made, with Congress appropriating millions of dollars to subsidize experiments in the desalinization of water and the building of plants.

The techniques of distillation have been so improved during the past few years and the costs so reduced that they have been widely adopted by many communities requiring larger supplies of fresh water. The two major items governing the cost of water supplied by this process are installation and fuel costs.

Other Processes

Some of the other processes that are being experimented with are (1) electro-dialysis, (2) reverse osmosis and (3) freezing. The first two processes achieve separation of excessive salt from the water by diffusion of the sea water through a semi-permeable membrane. The third process achieves separation by freezing, since ice carries a relatively low percentage of dissolved salts.

Dr. John Hult, a physicist, has a really "cool" proposal to increase the water supply of southern California. He suggests that icebergs be transported from Antarctica to be melted offshore in California and that the water then be piped inland. Hult believes that this is feasible and that the costs of delivered water would be less than half as much as the cost of that delivered over the California State Water Project.

Desalinization Plants

There are some 900 water desalting plants in the world today. Plants are operating in the United States and in the Caribbean area. An early plant built at San Diego, California, was moved to our naval base at Guantánamo Bay, Cuba, when Fidel Castro cut off the water supply, and it has successfully met all the needs of the base for years. A plant, which was built at Key West, Florida, in 1967, is no longer in use, having been replaced by

FIGURE 10-11. An artist's conception of the 72-million-gallon-per-day desalting plant being installed on the Colorado River near Yuma, Arizona, to process highly mineralized water after irrigation use. After its installation is completed, the desalinized water will be added to the river to improve its quality before it flows into Mexico, thus honoring an agreement between the United States and Mexico. The plant will be the largest membrane plant in the world. It is scheduled to begin operation soon. (Courtesy, U.S Department of the Interior, Water and Power Resources Service)

a reverse osmosis plant that operated on an as-needed basis. A new plant under construction at Yuma, Arizona, will help to improve the quality of the Colorado River water for irrigation purposes, with full operation expected soon (see Figure 10-11).

Cost of Desalted Water

Interest in desalinization of water has been heightened by the rising cost of fresh water from usual or conventional sources. One of the reasons for these higher costs is the greater distance, either horizontal or vertical, that communities must go to get enough fresh water for their needs. Also, other items of cost, such as fuel, labor and equipment, are continuously increasing. Furthermore, because the pollution load introduced into streams from all sources is much greater than formerly, maintaining the higher water quality standards which are now required costs more.

With the increase in energy costs during the 1970's, desalting sea water both by distillation and by reverse osmosis increased sharply. But, in the mid-1980's, energy costs dropped, affecting desalinization plant growth adversely. It is still more costly, in most places, to desalt highy saline water than to treat conventional water for ordinary usage.

Water desalinization does have benefits which may outweigh its higher cost, however. One major benefit is that the quality of water may be much better than conventional supplies. Also, desalted water saves plumbing fixtures and systems from premature disintegration, eliminates the need for home water softeners and removes contaminants from industrial and farming operations.[6]

Another way to extend the available water supply is to use water from wastewater treatment processes: (1) by pumping the effluent through separate distribution systems for use in lawn watering, car washing, irrigating and other nonpotable uses or (2) by pumping the effluent into the ground to recharge existing ground water supplies. Experiments and studies are now in progress to evaluate using tertiary-treated water as a new water source for potable water.

Although we have the ability to purify sea water, we cannot afford to neglect effective water managment of our fresh water supplies, for use

---

[6]C. E. Pitts, "Desalinization in Florida, 1979," *NWDA Journal*, Topsfield, Massachusetts, National Water Supply Improvement Association, January 1, 1980.

of saline water is a costly alternative which may never be feasible at many inland locations.

RECLAIMING WASTE WATER

Most water is not "consumed," for it is eventually returned to the water supply. But by then, as we have noted, it is often badly polluted. A major way to increase our water supply is to recycle the water. By this is meant that after water had been used in a process, it would be treated for undesirable impurities and used again. With better national and state clean water laws and better enforcement, we can anticipate much reclamation of waste water in the future.

PLENTY OF WATER, IF. . .

The question of the adequacy of our water supply is an "iffy" one. There appears to be plenty of water for everybody . . . *if* we increase its availability by the various methods related and *if* we clean up our waters and stop inordinate polluting of them. In addition, we must stop wasting the water we use and start using the water we waste. Finally, we will meet our requirements far more easily and cheaply *if* we move people to water instead of water to people.

QUESTIONS AND PROBLEMS

1. Give some of the reasons why water for use by cities, in homes and for industry, is becoming a scarce resource in various places throughout the United States.

2. What are the principal sources of water supply, and which ones must be depended upon at the present time to supply water for the aforementioned uses?

3. What are the two principal reasons we are short of water, not counting our expanding use of it?

4. Describe the hydrologic cycle. Why is it called an "imperfect" system?

5. Cite several examples of water pollution given in the text. Cite any similar situations in or near your community.

6. Why are uniform water control standards essential from the standpoint of the costs of businesses?

7. Illustrate how good water conservation affects other natural resources.

8. Whose responsibility is it to see that water is properly conserved as it makes its way from the small piece of land where it falls as rain or snow through ravine, lake and stream to its place again as a drop of water in the ocean?

9. Under what conditions can ocean water be used for industrial or home use?

10. Where does your city, or the one nearest you, get its water supply? What are the advantages and/or disadvantages?

11. There is so much moisture in the air. Why isn't *changing the weather* an ideal solution to our water shortage problems?

12. Should levees ever be used on flood plains? Explain your answer.

13. What is meant by describing the TVA as a "unified, multiple-purpose development?" How has it been successful? How does it differ in character and purpose from the California State Water Project?

14. What is vadose water, and why is it essential?

15. Since ground water supplies are so vast, why can't they meet all our supply problems?

16. Why is the adequacy of our water supply called an "ify" question?

17. Isn't keeping a river in a wild state a waste of our surface water resources? Explain your answer.

11

The Nature of Forests and the History of Their Growth

Probably no other resource has been as useful over the centuries as have trees. Our Native Americans always established their camp sites near wood and water. Not only was wood the source of fuel to keep them warm during the cold weather, but it also supplied them with birch bark to build canoes, not to mention shade to keep them comfortable during the warm summer months. Hickory, elm and other woods were used to make bows and arrows for hunting or for war purposes, as well as for furnishing poles, walls and roofs for shelters. The early American Indians had an appreciation of the beauty and inspiration that unspoiled forests can give, as shown in their form of religion, just as we ourselves are now realizing how important these non-material values are.

WOODS AND WILDLIFE

Some woods are composed of dense forest trees whose tops form a

FIGURE 11-1. This forest of virgin lodgepole pine in Wyoming will support very little wildlife. There is practically no low undergrowth for their food supply and protection. (Courtesy, U.S. Forest Service)

canopy over the whole area and completely shade the ground. Few animals roam these woods because there is no low growth of shrubs or grass upon which herb- or grass-eating animals can live. Neither are there many insects or small seeds to support small bird life. The vast forests of pine, hemlock and spruce are of this type, called evergreen, coniferous, cone-bearing or softwood forests.[1]

Other woods are not as dense and usually consist of a mixture of different kinds of trees. Forests of mixed hardwoods or of hardwoods and cone-bearing trees together are ordinarily open enough; that is, the trees are far enough apart to permit shrubs and some kinds of grass to flourish. It is in these woods that most of our animal and bird life is found. Grass

---

[1] This term *softwood* is used by foresters to designate cone-bearing trees, while the term *hardwood* refers to the broad-leaved trees which shed their leaves each fall.

and shrubbery are available for the animals to eat and hide in and for insects to thrive. These woods attract birds. Wherever food is available, animals and birds will be there to live on it.

DIFFERENT WOODS MEET
DIFFERENT NEEDS

We are told that when the white settlers came to this country, more than 300 years ago, about 43 percent of the land area was in woods. As more people came and settled, they found the forests both a help and a handicap in making homes and producing food. Practically all the buildings put up by the colonists and later settlers were made of timber cut from the land upon which the individual familes settled. Fuel was also supplied from the same source, and household furniture, as well as most parts of farm implements and machinery, was made from the different kinds of wood that grew on the land. But still, the job of clearing the land of trees and preparing it for crops was really uphill work.

The variety of trees was such that some kind of wood was found for every purpose. The pines, basswoods and hemlocks supplied soft, easily worked wood for fashioning kitchen and other household utensils and cheap furniture, while the oaks supplied wood for heavy use, sturdy construction and dignified appearance. Fine-grained woods, such as cherry, hard maple and walnut, where carefully finished, gave beautiful luster and color to furniture. Many of these pieces are still in use after several generations of wear. Farm use required tough, hard wood, such as elm, ash and hickory.

All these woods are found growing in greater or less profusion on practically all the land east of the Mississippi River. Only the land comprising central Illinois was free from a covering of virgin forest growth.

WOODLANDS A HANDICAP TO
EARLY FARMING

The early settlers did not regard these benefits of the forests as an unmixed blessing, however. They had to clear the land of trees before they could plant crops. It required months of work for a family to cut the trees with axe and saw and later to clear the stumps from a single acre of land before it could be used for crop production. And, because of the immense amount of work required to clear such small areas, these people considered the forests as enemies to progress in settling this country.

FIGURE 11-2. As our plane dips over the region known as the Wheaton Moraine Country of Illinois, preparing to land at Chicago, we see that farms have taken over most of the land, with only a small section (foreground) left or grown back into forest. At one time, even the prairie state of Illinois was over 40 percent forests. (Photo by Harry B. Kircher)

FOREST SOILS NOT AS PRODUCTIVE AS PRAIRIE SOILS

Another discouraging factor about forest areas is that, in general, most of their soils are not as productive of farm crops as are most prairie soils; so that even after an acre of land is cleared, the production from this acre is not large, and after it has been farmed many years, crop yields will decline even to the point that the land will be abandoned. These soils were not as productive as the soils in the homelands from which the colonists came.

George Washington once said that the early colonists found it was better to clear and cultivate new land, of which there was an abundance, than to try to maintain crop production on land already cleared and cropped for a few years. This was true despite the great cost in time required to clear the land.

There are three obvious reasons why the productivity of the cropland was not maintained at that time. First, New England soils generally were rather infertile soils, formed under woodland. The organic matter, as well as plant nutrients, was quickly used up or washed away when once planted to the crops usually grown at that time.

The second and more fundamental reason for the loss in fertility of these nearly virgin soils is that little was known of the value of crop rotations in keeping up soil productivity and less yet was known of the requirements of plants for the various plant food elements, or nutrients. The need of plants for lime, phosphorus, potash and nitrogen is so generally recognized at the present time that one can scarcely believe there was a time when farmers did not know that crops would not grow without the presence of those nutrients in usable form in the soil.

A third reason why the productivity of those soils was not maintained is associated with the experiences of the immigrants in their homelands before coming to this country. Many rains here are severe thunderstorms, in which from 1 to several inches of water may fall within a few hours. Land cleared of forest growth and depleted of leaf mold cannot absorb these heavy rainfalls; thus, soils are carried away from the water run-off. The rainfalls of the northern European countries usually are gentle, steady rains, most of which are absorbed into the soils instead of being flushed off over the surface. Only recently have farmers in this country become aware of the seriousness of these soil losses and have begun to take measures to control erosion.

It was only a little more than a century ago that chemists discovered the dependence of plants upon certain plant food elements. And, it is less than a century that artificial plant nutrients in the form of fertilizers and lime have been used to supplement the application to soils of farmyard manures, leaf mold and river bottom sediment as sources of food for plants.

OUR VIRGIN FORESTS ALMOST GONE

The early attitude that forests were obstructions to progress continued

almost to the present generation. As a result of excessive cutting and burning, this country now has left not more than a small percent of its once
magnificent stands of virgin forests.

FIGURE 11-3. This shows a part of our remaining virgin forest. These mature white pines
are growing near Pierce, Idaho. The next generation will see none of this type of timber unless
the trees that are here now are preserved. (Courtesy, U.S. Forest Service)

Even though these untouched forests are nearly gone (a great esthetic
loss), it is not the economic tragedy usually visualized by the uninformed.
Trees are growing continuously so that what was a sapling 150 years or
even 100 years ago may now be a mature tree. So, with conservation, our
stocks of saw timber can be replaced. Also, contrary to some commonly

held views, wood from these later grown trees may be as good if not better than wood from the virgin forest for practically all the human-devised uses.

SAW TIMBER GROWS SLOWLY

Why is there such a loss in standing timber when most trees grow to lumber size in 75 to 150 years? The problem is one of slow growth relative to use and losses. Some species of softwoods, such as white pines, planted 100 years ago are now large enough to cut for lumber. It is also true that trees such as walnut, maple, elm and gum will grow to maturity within 120 years. A glance at Table 11-1 shows tree growths over the country, with different lengths of time in different localities needed to produce what lumber workers call "saw timber," which is quality timber of usable size for lumber and wood-working. Whereas it requires only 30 to 40 years to grow saw log pines in the South, it takes 150 to 180 years to grow western pines of like size in the Rocky Mountain states.

TABLE 11-1. Years Required to Grow Saw Log Timber

Area	Type of Timber	Years to Grow
Southern states	Pine	30– 40
Great Lakes and	{ Pine	60–100
Northeastern states	{ Hardwoods	100–120
Western states	Fir and hemlock	100
Rocky Mountain states	Wetern pine	150–180

NATURE PRODUCES FORESTS SLOWLY

The natural reproduction of a forest is a slow process. Trees do not grow quickly. The history of any forest shows that it requires hundreds of years to develop a forest soil after the unspoiled cover has once been destroyed either by cultivation or by fire. The fine leaf mold which carpets all hardwood forests contains large amounts of organic matter which, when dry, burn readily. Even when plowed and cultivated for ordinary farm crop

FIGURE 11-4. One of the great enemies of both forests and wildlife is fire. The continued burning of undergrowth destroys all young trees, burns out the leaf mold and leaves no place for wildlife to find food or shelter. (Courtesy, Soil Conservation Service)

production, this organic matter and the organic layer of soils are quickly lost through oxidation and erosion. Oxidation in this sense is a slow process of burning. It is so slow that is may take several years for the oxygen of the air to combine with the organic matter of the soil and thus destroy it, whereas a fire will produce the same result in a day or two. The loss by erosion is the most serious loss of all, not only because the plant nutrients are lost but also because the soil itself is eroded away.

Nature must rebuild this soil before it will again produce the kind of timber that was there as a virgin or original crop at the time white settlers first saw it. The process used by nature in rebuilding forest soils requires a cycle (sequence) of different plants. When a pine forest is logged or cut over or burned, the first growth to start again is not pine. Usually some quick-growing shrubbery, berry vines or annual plants will immediately spring up to cover the ground.

The quick growth of these berry-producing plants is one reason why the Indians used to burn small forests areas. Among these low-growing shrubs, and aided by the protection they afford, some quick-growing trees will start. These trees usually are hardwoods. They include elm, ash, basswood, birch, poplar and soft maples, which grow quickly and soon outstrip the shrubs, vines and grasses in growth.

As they grow they produce more shade. This shade reduces the growth of shrubs and vines which must have direct sunlight on their leaves in order to remain vigorous and strong.

As this smaller growth becomes less dense, it offers the opportunity for the development of those trees which start and make their early growth best under some protection from direct sunlight. Many of the conifers are among these trees.

The taller-growing conifers continue to thrive in the protection afforded by the broad leaves until they ultimately grow up through and outstrip their early protectors. The conifers then cut off the direct sunlight from the hardwood trees, which in turn die off as did the shurbs and grasses a few year earlier.

Thus, nature's way of rebuilding a forest is slow. The stand also may be very irregular, being much too thick in some parts of the area for the production of sturdy, heavy-trunked trees, while in other spots, being so sparse that the trees throw out spreading branches and grow laterally almost as much as they do upward. This type of tree is desirable for shade or parks but not for timber production, which requires tall branchless trunks if timber free of knots is to be developed.

WHERE DO WE GET OUR LUMBER— WHAT SPECIES?

The leading lumber production region of our country is the West (56 percent), with the South second (31 percent) and the North a poor third (13 percent) (see Table 11-2). The South, because its trees grow faster, is eventually expected to replace the West as the major lumber resource region. The figures in Table 11-2 show that the South, from 1970 to 1983, gained 16 percent in lumber output, while the West gained only 4 percent. The data over the intervening years, however, do not show a consistent trend. Among Census divisions, the Pacific states, which include, of course, Alaska and Hawaii, are leading producers. In recent years, we have been importing about one-fifth more lumber than we have been exporting. Net imports have been gradually increasing since 1960. Then, they were less then 10 percent of our lumber exports.

TABLE 11-2. Lumber Production, by Geographic Division, 1970, 1975 and 1983[1]

Region and Division	1970	1975	1983, prel.
United States	**34.7**	**32.6**	**36.9**
North[2]	4.4	4.1	4.3
Hardwood	3.4	3.0	3.0
Softwood	1.0	1.1	1.3
South[2]	10.8	9.7	12.5
Hardwood	3.6	2.7	2.1
Softwood	7.2	7.0	10.4
West[2]	19.4	18.8	20.1
Hardwood	0.1	0.3	0.4
Softwood	19.3	18.6	19.7
New England	0.7	0.8	1.2
Middle Atlantic	0.8	0.7	0.8
East North Central	1.2	1.1	1.2
West North Central	0.6	0.5	0.4
South Atlantic	5.2	4.7	6.3
East South Central	3.4	3.0	3.8
West South Central	3.2	3.0	3.2
Mountain	4.2	3.9	4.4
Pacific	15.3	14.8	15.7

[1] In billion board feet. Data based in part on a sample of sawmills and are subject to sampling variability; see source. See *Historical Statistics, Colonial Times to 1970*, series L 113-121, data by regions.

[2] Source: U.S. Forest Service, *U.S. Timber Production, Trade, Consumption, and Price Statistics, 1950-84*, annual. Regions are as defined by the U.S. Forest Service, Table 1199.

Source: Except as noted, U.S. Bureau of the Census, *Current Industrial Reports*, Series MA-24T, annual, Washington, D.C.

TABLE 11-3. Lumber Production, and Consumption, by Kind of Wood, 1960, 1970 and 1983

Item	1960	1970	1983, prel.
Total Production	**32,926**	**34,668**	**36,871**
Softwoods[1]	26,672	27,530	31,415
Cedar	(s)[2]	633	721
Douglas fir	8,832	7,727	6,558
Hemlock	2,032	1,980	1,604
Ponderosa pine	3,169	3,429	2,899
Redwood	1,000	1,078	960
Southern yellow pine	5,660	7,063	10,406
White fir	2,224	2,063	1,276
White pine	675	898	293
Hardwoods[1]	6,254	7,138	5,456
Ash	125	159	139
Beech	195	188	89
Cottonwood	206	229	137
Elm	195	155	61
Maple	602	742	422
Oak	2,789	3,250	2,000
Sweet gum[3]	331	376	181
Tupelo and black gum	292	335	74
Yellow poplar	592	606	421
Domestic Consumption[4]	**35,225**	**38,073**	**45,138**
Percent net imports[5]	8.7	12.7	22.2

[1] Includes types not shown separately.

[2] (s) – Figure does not meet publication standards.

[3] Red and sap.

[4] Source: Through 1970, Copeland Economics Group, Inc., Stanford, Connecticut; thereafter, National Forest Productions Association, Washington, D.C., *The Economics Monthly Bulletin,* quarterly edition.

[5] Imports minus exports.

Source: Except as noted, U.S. Bureau of the Census, Current Industrial Reports, Series MA-24T, annual, Washington, D.C.

About six time the volume of softwood lumber is produced as of hardwoods (see Table 11-3). Southern yellow pine and Douglas fir are the leading softwoods. In hardwoods, no species comes even close to oak in lumber volume.

HOW MUCH TIMBER HAVE WE?

Since the first settlement in this country, more than 2,700 billion board feet of timber has been removed from our forests. One-third of the timber removed was used by people. Two-thirds was destroyed by fires, diseases and insects. Over half of this drain has occurred since 1906. We started with approximately a billion acres of forest land. It contained over 8,000 billion board feet of potential saw timber.

According to U.S. Forest Service statistics, with Alaska and Hawaii added, we have about three-fourths as much forest land left, with just over one half as much saw timber. Furthermore, in balance, the quality is poorer since many of the Alaskan forests are of poor quality naturally, and many of the other forest lands have been poorly managed.

The great reduction in our forest resources does not mean that we are critically short of supplies. It does suggest that without wise management the forests will be seriously depleted in a few decades. The demand for forest products is expected to double by the year 2000. The U.S. Forest Service concluded as a result of its study that these future demands could be met with more intensive forest mangement and utilization. The next chapter discusses ways in which these goals might be met.

The growth of all timber has been exceeding the drain from all causes. This speaks well for the work done by our foresters in combatting fires, diseases and insects and in using reforestation methods and tree species that make for faster growth than when "nature took its course."

QUESTIONS AND PROBLEMS

1. Define the terms *hardwood* and *softwood* as used by lumber producers.

2. What types of forest growth offer food and shelter to various forms of wildlife?

3. Why did the early settlers in the United States look upon forest land both as a blessing and as a handicap to settling the country?

4. Name some of the trees that were found in the areas settled by the early colonists and tell how they were used in the home or on the farm.

5. Why did the colonists find the soils of the Atlantic Coast disappointing when compared with productions from the cultivated lands of Europe from which they came? Give reasons why the production of these soils was not maintained.

6. How much of our virgin forests was still left in this country in 1945? How much standing timber do we have now in comparison with the original forests, even though there have been 100 to 150 years in which to grow new forests after the virgin forests were destroyed?

7. Are we growing forests faster then they are being used up, or is the reverse true?

8. What part of the country will grow saw timber most quickly, and in what area will it develop most slowly?

9. What is nature's way of regrowing a forest?

10. Give the names of 10 trees that grow in your neighborhood.

11. Tell how each of five of these trees is used.

12. What uses can you think of for forest products?

12

The Management and Use of Forests

MANAGED WOODS GROW FASTER

Most of our present woodland growth does not require the slow process of nature, explained in the previous chapter, to develop salable timber, even though we cannot approximate the size, dignity and majesty of our "forests primeval." We have learned that we can plant some kinds of trees to replace those cut or lost through fire or wasteful handling. Today's forests respond to a system of management which results in greater and more uniform growth than when the trees were permited to develop "according to nature's plan."

MANAGEMENT PRACTICES

Common management practices to increase the productivity of forests include planting selected varieties of trees, breeding supertrees, controlling insects and diseases, providing fire control, selective harvesting trees and clearcutting forest plots.

Planting Selected Varieties of Trees

The kinds of hardwoods which are most valuable for certain purposes are listed in Table 12-1. This table shows that some trees may be used for several purposes; and the rate of growth, as well as the use for which the wood is grown, should determine the variety of tree to plant. There is little doubt that lumber and veneer will continue to be two of the most important uses of wood, while some of the other uses shown in the table may be less important outlets in the future than they have been in the past.

TABLE 12-1. Uses for Hardwoods

Lumber	Veneer	Poles and Posts	Excelsior	Windbreaks
Ash	Basswood	Catalpa	Aspen	Green ash
Basswood	Beech	Coffee tree	Basswood	Box elder
Beech	Yellow birch	Red elm	Cottonwood	Cottonwood
Birch	Black cherry	Eucalyptus	Willow	Eucalyptus
Black cherry	Sugar maple	Black locust	Yellow poplar	Hackberry
White elm	Oaks	Honey locust		Silver maple
Hickory	Red gum	Russian mul-		Russian mulberry
Sugar maple	Sycamore	berry		Osage orange
Oaks	Black walnut	Oaks		Russian olive
Red gum	Yellow poplar	Osage orange		White willow
Black walnut		White willow		Yellow willow

Barrels	Tool Handle Stock	Railroad Ties and Mine Timbers	Hardwood Distillation
Ash	Ash	Black locust	Beech
Basswood	Beech	Honey locust	Black birch
Beech	Birch	Red oak	Yellow birch
White elm	Hickory	White oak	Sugar maple
Sugar maple	Sugar maple		
White oak	White oak		
Red gum			

Source: U.S. Forest Service.

Since the time required to grow salable timber is always a factor in its planting and care, it may pay to consider this in any planting which is to be made. The fastest-growing trees ordinarily have fewer uses than those which are slower growing. When species of trees are planted in climates most suitable to their growth, we find the eucalyptus to be among the fastest-growing trees, while the oak, birch, beech and hard maple are among the slowest (see Table 12-2).

Most so-called timber species, when planted close enough for forest planting, will grow quite tall before showing much growth in diameter.

TABLE 12-2. Average Height Growth of Hardwood Trees from Seed

Kind	10 Years	20 Years	30 Years	50 Years
	.... (feet)			
Ash, green.....................	26	41	52	70
white.....................	19–25[1]	34–50[1]	45–67[1]	62–83[1]
Aspen..........................	18–21	27–40	28–55	50–75
Basswood	–	16–32	23–44	37–63
Beech..........................	–	8–19	13–28	22–42
Birch, paper....................	13	30	44	62
yellow	–	30	18–39	15–54
Box elder[2]	20	–	–	–
Catalpa, hardy[2]	19	27	33	64
Chestnut........................	7	17	33	64
Cottonwood[2]	56	97	115	136
Elm, white	–	21	28	40
Eucalyptus[2]	24–80	70–90	85–160	–
Gum, red	35	66	88	108
Hickory, shagbark	3–7	8–18	15–32	32–51
Locust, black....................	15–20	28–45	–	44–65
honey[2]	18	27	35	–
Maple, silver[2]...................	22	44	60	80
sugar	–	18	29	40–48
Oak, burr[2]	–	–	40	60
red........................	13	32	46	72
white	11–12	22–25	32–38	53–63
Osage orange[2]	–	15–25	37	–
Poplar, yellow	20–27	36–50	50–64	78–83
Walnut, black	18	30	40	60
black[2]	15–24	35–50	–	–
Willow, white	50	73	89	109

[1]Where a range in height is given, the lower figure in each case is in poor growth situations.

[2]Plantation grown or grown under more favorable than average conditions. Others forest grown.

Source: U.S. Forest Service.

FIGURE 12-1. Practically the only virgin forests now left in this country are in the western part of the United States. It is only through the vigilant efforts of conservation-minded individuals and organizations that these forests have not been sacrified. Selective cutting, such as is being practiced in this forest, is beneficial to both the remaining stand and the users of wood, especially if the selection and felling of the timber are properly supervised. (Courtesy, National Park Service)

They will then increase in diameter at a variable rate, again depending on the variety of trees grown (see Table 12-3).

To grow a 15-inch diameter black willow, eucalyptus or cottonwood will require from 40 to 50 years. If the species grown is black walnut, one of the oaks or a hard maple, it may require about 100 to 125 years to grow a tree of the same diameter.

Plantations of conifers, as well as those of hardwoods, are common throughout the country. Wherever they are planted, they make satisfactory growth as windbreaks and for ornamental and commercial use.

TABLE 12-3. Average Diameter Growth of Hardwood Trees

Kinds	Average Number of Years to Grow 1 Inch in Diameter
Eucalyptus[1]	½–3
Cottonwood,[1] white willow,[1] honey locust,[1] black locust,[1] black willow	2–4
Silver maple,[1] white elm,[1] Russian mulberry,[1] hardy catalpa,[1] red gum, yellow poplar, chestnut	3–6
White ash,[1] green ash,[1] box elder,[1] black walnut,[1] butternut,[1] burr oak,[1] osage orange,[1] red oak, black oak, aspen, basswood	4–7
Hard maple,[1] hickory, white oak, chestnut oak, paper birch, yellow birch, beech	5–10

[1]The growths of these trees were measured from plantation growth on farm lands, while the species not marked were grown in natural forests.

Source: U.S. Forest Service.

Breeding Supertrees

In addition to selecting the proper varieties of trees, timber producers achieve maximum timber production by the breeding and planting of quality stock. To achieve this, timber producers select seeds of the fastest-growing, tallest, straightest and healthiest trees and reproduce them in nurseries. The superseedlings are then set out to produce supertrees. Millions have been planted. One corporation alone, the International Paper Company, has planted "two supertrees for every man, woman and child in the country."

Controlling Insects and Diseases

The enemies of forests are many and are increasing. Some diseases and insects affect certain varieties of trees without damaging others, and when once a disease or insect pest becomes well established, it is practically impossible to eliminate it completely or even partially. The trees attacked must develop an immunity to or a toleration for the disease or pest, or they will be completely destroyed.

Insect, Fungal and Bacterial Enemies

The chestnut blight has caused the complete destruction of our commercial chestnut from Canada to the Gulf of Mexico (see Figure 12-2). Not only has this removed a commercially valuable and beautiful tree from our landscape, but it also has deprived this generation of children of the thrill and delight of gathering and roasting the tasty nuts in the fall of the year and has removed from the woods a native food for the wildlife.

Another tragic loss has been the death of most of our magnificent ornamental and shade elms. The loss of these trees is the result of the combined destructive work of the European elm bark beetle, which makes holes in the bark, and the Dutch elm fungus, which thrives in the protection offered by these holes.

The white pine blister rust entered this country over 50 years ago. This disease does not spread from pine to pine but must live a part of its life cycle on an alternate host, such as wild gooseberries or currants. The only known way to control this disease is to destroy its alternate host. It appears now that the white pine may be saved for future generations to enjoy, but only by the destruction of our wild currants and gooseberries.

The story of the gypsy moth, which has been a pest in our forest for almost 70 years, is the story of a well-intentioned man who introduced this moth from Europe in the hope of developing a hardy, silk-producing insect. The result is the widespread prevalence of an insect which eats the leaves of both hardwood and evergreen trees.

There are dozens of other insect and fungal enemies in the United States, and there are hundreds of these pests that have the potential of getting a foothold in this country and further destroying our forests, upsetting the balance of nature and adding to the costs of control.

Providing Fire Control

The methods of fighting forest fires have radically changed. Forest managers no longer send in workers to fight every fire. First, they carefully consider which ones to fight and which ones to let burn. And, with caution, they may even light a few, for they realize that fires are nature's way of controlling distribution and succession in forests. A study of a 300-year period of part of the Boundary Waters Canoe Area, which is a protected wilderness, shows, for example, that on the average, the forest has been completely burned over by nature every 100 years.

Fires are essential to the growth of some species of trees and provide better habitat for some wildlife. Jack pine cones, for example, do not release

FIGURE 12-2. Wildlife requires both food and protection in order to survive. This forest of native hardwoods in North Carolina, with its open spaces filled with undergrowth of shrubbery and grasses, supported some wildlife. However, since the early 1900's, when this picture was made, the chestnut trees in this woods and all over the United States have been killed by the chestnut blight. (Courtesy, U.S. Forest Service)

their seeds until they are exposed to intense heat. Fires may destroy harmful insects and turn ground cover into beneficial ash. Fires open up the woods, providing new leaves, young shoots and other vegetation for wildlife to browse on, and birds find more nesting and feeding areas. Dense forest is not attractive to birds or wildlife.

Fire prevention and control.—Many forest fires are, of course, devasting. The prevention and control of fires continues to be a cornerstone of good forest management. The record of control by the U.S. Forest Service over the past few decades has been a good one (see Table 12-4).

Controlled burning of forests should be practiced only with expert advice and preferably under actual supervision of a forester. Many fires,

FIGURE 12-3. The sign "Tree Farm" on this planting of pines indicates that the owner is managing and protecting the stand in accordance with the standards of the American Forest Institute. The American Tree Farm System began in the Douglas fir region in 1941. The Soil Conservation Service promotes this program with advice on plantings and management and certification of the complying. On January 1, 1985, there were nearly 55,000 tree farms in the United States, totaling nearly 87 million acres. (Courtesy, Soil Conservation Service)

TABLE 12-4. Area Burned Over by Forest Fires in the United States Since 1930 (10-year intervals and 1983)

Year	Number of Acres
	(million)
1930	52.3
1940	25.8
1950	15.5
1960	4.5
1970	3.3
1980	5.3
1983	5.1

Sources: U.S. Bureau of the Census, *Historical Statistics of the United States, Colonial Times to 1957,* Washington, D.C., 1960, Table L98–105, p. 318; *Statistical Abstract of the United States,* 16th edition, 1985, Table 1201, p. 674.

FIGURE 12-4. The above shows a poorly managed forest of white spruce. Though these trees are but 6 inches in diameter, they are overmature and many are dead. Thus, the area becomes a fire hazard and an eyesore. Proper management would have made this a desirable young forest. (Courtesy, National Park Service)

deliberately started to thin out brush and kill insects, have done the job thoroughly—and killed the trees, too.

Sad and destructive are fires started by carelessness, such as the flip of a cigarette out the car window. The resultant fire, spreading with little warning, may trap game and people. All of us can help prevent these woodland disasters by being careful with fire.

Selective Harvesting Trees

Selective harvesting means that trees are thinned out each year in accordance with a plan so that the remaining trees grow faster, taller and healthier. The wood that has been removed is marketed. If this program is carried out year after year, it provides a steady source of income; and the forest is said to be under **sustained yield management.**

Clearcutting Forest Plots

Clearcutting is the practice of cutting off a sizeable block of trees during one harvest period. The wisdom of this practice, which leaves the land temporarily almost denuded of vegetation, is highly debated among foresters. On the one hand, clearcutting is essential for successful commercial reforestation of some species of trees, can provide good forage for wildlife and is more profitable to the timber companies. On the other hand, when steep slopes of thin soil are stripped of timber, severe gullying or sheet erosion results. If large areas are saturated with unwise clearcutting, heavy rains can send their waters unchecked down the slopes to turn streams into roaring, destructive torrents. Furthermore, whether clearcutting is profitable to the timber companies over the long run is questionable.

MANAGEMENT OF THE NATIONAL FOREST SYSTEM BY THE U.S. FOREST SERVICE

The national forests, set aside as preserves and resources of timber in the late 1800's, produced about 20 percent of the timber harvested in the United States each year from 1975 to 1984. These lands have been mandated by Congress for multiple use: outdoor recreation, range, watershed, wildlife and fish purposes, as well as timber production. Depletion and poor management of privately owned timber land has put much pressure to harvest timber from national forests. Yet, much national forest land is roadless, remote, steep, or with poor timber regeneration capacity, and should never be logged. Only part of this land is protected as part of the Wilderness Preserve System.

The poor lands, as well as better timber-producing lands within the national forests, have been logged, often returning to the federal government far less money than the costs of administration. In the 10-year period 1975–1984, it is estimated that the Forest Service spent 2.1 billion more on growing and harvesting timber than it received in payments from timber cutters. The Forest Service sells timber by using the minimum value less the purchaser's logging and milling costs and profit as a basis for bids. This ensures a profit to the logger and a loss to U.S. taxpayers. While the National Forest Management Act of 1976 provides for "not less than the appraised price" for federal timber sales, timber can be sold for its actual commerical value. It does not make economic sense for the U.S. taxpayers to subsidize commercial logging in the national forests.

Below cost timber sales have, in part, been justified by the Forest Service by "non-timber benefits" for wildlife, recreation, fishing and local employment. Considerable scientific study however shows mostly environmental and recreational damage from such logging. Every mile of logging road per square mile in Montana forests decreased the elk usage of that area by 25 percent. Six miles of road per square mile decreased elk usage of that area by 80 percent.[1]

In the Tongass National Forest of southeast Alaska, U.S. taxpayers were losing more than $50 million a year on the government-permitted timber program. Futhermore, the timber harvesting was destroying the only largely intact rain forest left in the world's temperate zones. Not only was the forest being destroyed but the area's fishing industry and tourism also were being threatened by the damage to spawning beds and scenic beauty. "Timber policy in the Tongass is a textbook example of a well-intentioned government policy gone astray,"[2] said Alice Rivlin, Director of Economic Studies at the Brookings Institution, who is also a member of The Wilderness Society's Governing Council.

The public should demand fair economic return to the federal government for all timber harvested in the national forests. Full costs of growing and selling the timber should be recovered. Logging must be done in a manner so as to protect other forest values.

The potential timber yield of the land should not be exceeded by cutting. Lands economically unsuitable for timber production, where timber values are less than the costs of managing and harvesting, should be left uncut. The managers of our national forests must not be under the control of or under undue pressure from the timber industry. Citizens must be alert to the preservation of **all** values of the national forests.

IMPORTANCE OF SMALL LANDOWNERS

Since some 70 percent of commercial timberland is held by private owners, the destiny of our present timber supply is in private hands. This

---

[1] *The Land Letter*, Vol. 3, No. 4, San Francisco, Sierra Club, December 1985.

[2] "Wilderness Watch," *Wilderness*, Washington, D.C., The Wilderness Society, Summer 1986, p. 3.

does not mean, however, that its destiny is completely controlled by large corporations, important as they are. The forest industry owns only about one-seventh of such timber-producing areas; farmers, about one-fourth; and other private owners, about one-third. The balance of timberland is held by the federal or state government, with a small share (less than 2 percent) classified as Indian holdings. Over the years, more than one-half of the saw timber produced in the United States has been grown on land owned by farmers and other small landowners.[3]

FIGURE 12-5. When cattle have the free run of woodland, they trample and eat down the growth of young trees. They obtain very little feed from the wooded area. For best woodlot management, livestock should not be allowed to graze the area. (Courtesy, Soil Conservation Service)

Forest conservation can be profitable for small landowners. But, profit is highly variable and is dependent upon many factors including site, species, costs, prices and discount rates, forester Gene Campbell points out. "For high quality sawtimber on good sites [in the Central States], I would expect real, before tax, rates of return to exceed 4 percent, and possibly as high

---

[3]U.S. Forest Service, *An Assessment of the Forest and Range Land Situation in the United States,* Washington, D.C., 1981, p. 228. Also, Robert E. Wolf, *Overview of the U.S. Forest Situation,* Congressional Research Service, Washington, D.C., 1979.

as 10 percent, depending on the management strategy followed and price assumptions made."[4] (This estimate assumes land costs to be common to all alternatives.)

Despite the prospect for profits, small timber owners are slow to respond. In Illinois, for example, where over half the timber is of the valuable oak-hickory type, much of the woodland is unmanaged and producing far below its potential.[5]

In the South, much of the farm land in crops and pasture could earn more money if planted to pine trees, a 1983 USDA study of 15 million acres showed. The study concluded that the pattern of cropland and pasture use of the late 1970's and early 1980's was a misallocation of land resources from an economic standpoint.[6]

Today, potentials for increasing productivity from small woodlands are even more attractive, for the costs of management involve few cash outlays and thus are affordable. In forest care, farmers can generally use the same equipment they use for farming, with the exception of a chain saw. They can do most of the work, such as thinning, harvesting and cutting fire lanes, in the off-season for crops. And, they can draw upon nearby state or national foresters or experts employed by timber companies for free advice in most cases. Woodlands were taxed only when harvested, and perhaps if some incentive payments were made by the federal government to support small woodland management, these lands would help us to meet our forest production goals.

RECREATIONAL USES OF FORESTS AND WOODS

Our forests, as well as smaller wooded areas, are becoming more popular each year for recreational uses. Apparently, the more the living habits

---

[4]Gene Campbell, Agricultural Experiment Station, University of Illinois at Urbana–Champaign. Letter to author Kircher, April 8, 1988.

[5]G. Campbell and R. Koenig, "A Financial Analysis of Upland Hardwood Even-aged Management in Illinois," Forestry Research Report No. 87-14, Agricultural Experiment Station, Unversity of Illinois at Urbana–Champaign, April 19, 1987, p. 1.

[6]U.S. Department of Agriculture, "Conservation of Southern Pine Tree Plantings; Conversion for Conservation Feasibility Study," Office of Budget and Program Analysis, Washington, D.C., 1983, 63 pp. Reported by John Fedkin in "The Future for Multiple Use of Land in the South," *Journal of Soil & Water Conservation*, July–August 1986, p. 212.

of people take them away from forests, woods and streams, the greater their desire to spend time in the woods or near streams or lakes where they can fish, examine trees and shrubs, study wildlife or just rest and let the world go by. We as a people agree with Byron that:

> There is a pleasure in the pathless woods,
> There is a rapture on the lonely shore,
> There is a society, where none intrudes,
> By the deep sea, and music in its roar.

Multiple Use of National Forests

For many years our national forest were managed primarily with timber production in mind. But, as our traditional recreation areas, the national forests, became more and more crowded, we realized that the national forests, which were often nearby, could provide relief. They had space and scenery which would attract and accommodate people and help take pressure off the parks. In June 1960, the Forest Service Multiple Use Act was passed by Congress, providing that: " . . . the national forests are established and shall be administered for outdoor recreation, range, timber, watershed, and wildlife and fish purposes."

Recreation in Forests More Popular Than Ever

National forests have become very popular for all kinds of recreational activities. Visitor days have increased almost tenfold from 1950, shortly after World War II, to today (225 million recorded in 1985). Overnight stays have also increased (see Table 12-5).

The favorite recreational activities in national forests are camping and sightseeing. Most of the camping is on developed camping sites; whereas, sightseeing is largely dispersed. Fishing activities are third in importance. A large number of visitors participate in downhill skiing, which is expected to have the most relative increase, among forest recreational visitors, during the next few decades. (see Table 12-6).

The U.S. Forest Service points out that these demands are growing faster than the capacity to meet them. "Thus," it concludes, "the Nation is

TABLE 12-5. U.S. Recreational Statistics: Visits to Recreational Areas, 1950–1984 (in thousands)

Recreational Areas	1950		1960		1970		1984	
	Visits	Overnight Stays	Visits	Overnight Stays	Visits	Overnight Stays	Visits	Overnight Stays
State parks	111,291	6,079	259,001	20,569	482,536	50,572	665,524	65,976
National parks[1]	33,253	4,501	79,229	9,365	172,005	16,160	332,500	16,325
National forests	27,368	5,760[2]	92,592	15,454	172,559	38,477	227,554	NA[3]
Total United States	171,912[4]	16,340	430,822	45,388	827,100[4]	105,209	1,357,584	NA[3]

[1]Visits for calendar year 1950 not adjusted for comparability with counting system as modified in 1960. Prior to 1965 excludes visits to the White House. Smaller parks not included.

[2]No category for overnight stays in national forest data for 1950. Includes campground use and hotel and resort visits.

[3]NA—Not available.

[4]Adjusted by authors.

Sources: National Recreation and Park Association, State Park Statistics, 1970; U.S. National Park Service, annual reports on recreational use; Outdoor Recreation Review Commission, Outdoor Recreation for America, 1962; U.S. Forest Service, Recreation Use of the National Forests, annual; unpublished data from the U.S. Department of the Interior, as cited in the U.S. Bureau of the Census, Statistical Abstract of the United States, 1986, Tables 381, 382 and 384; Council on Environmental Quality, Environmental Quality, The Tenth Annual Report of the Council on Environmental Quality, Washington, D.C., 1979, p. 700; and U.S. Forest Service, An Assessment of the Forest and Range Land Situation in the United States, Washington, D.C., 1980, p. 113.

TABLE 12-6. Number of Recreation Visitor Days of Outdoor Recreation Activities in National Forests in the United States by Types of Activity and Area, 1978

Activity Group and Type of Activity	Total	Developed	Dispersed
	.... *(thousands)*		
Land:			
Bicycling	434.2	11.5	422.7
Camping	59,902.6	41,539.8	18,362.8
Motor bike	4,520.7	2.8	4,517.9
Hiking[1]	10,925.6	196.8	10,728.8
Horseback riding.	3,038.3	31.5	3,006.8
Hunting	14,946.2	13.9	14,932.3
Nature study.	1,257.3	205.9	1,051.4
Picnicking	8,762.8	6,094.1	2,668.7
Pleasure walks	1,587.0	132.8	1,454.2
Sightseeing[2]	52,387.5	4,851.3	47,536.2
Other[3]	16,028.0	12,395.9	3,632.1
	173,790.2	65,476.3	108,313.9
Water:			
Canoeing.	1,099.7	209.6	890.1
Sailing.	261.1	76.1	185.0
Other watercraft[4]	6,286.7	1,416.3	4,870.4
Fishing	16,559.1	581.2	15,977.9
Swimming.	4,441.8	1,790.1	2,651.7
Water skiing	983.0	65.4	917.6
	29,631.4	4,138.7	25,492.7
Snow and Ice:			
Cross-country skiing.	760.5	–	760.5
Downhill skiing	9,335.7	9,335.7	–
Ice skating	67.8	27.8	40.0
Sledding	107.9	107.5	0.4
Ice and snowcraft	3,439.0	118.2	3,320.8
Snowplay	1,361.8	426.3	935.5
	15,072.7	10,015.5	5,057.2
Grand total.	218,494.3	79,630.5	138,863.8

[1]Includes mountain climbing.

[2]Includes viewing outstanding scenery, auto driving, aerial trams and lifts, human works and VIS related.

[3]Includes spectator sports and activities, team sports, games, other accommodations, gathering forest products and acquiring general knowledge and understanding.

[4]Includes ships, yachts, ferries and powered boats.

Source: U.S. Forest Service, Washington, D.C. (See footnote 3.)

faced with a growing imbalance between supply and the quantity of forest, range, and water products that people would like to consume."[7]

WILDERNESS

Vast tracts of mostly forested land in this nation that contribute little in commercial productivity but contribute immeasurable value in other ways are **wilderness areas.** A wilderness is "an unsettled, uncultivated natural region... a piece of land that is set aside to grow wild," the *American Heritage Dictionary of the American Language* tells us. To many of us today, *wilderness* has come to mean an area set aside by, or proposed for inclusion in, The Wilderness Act. An area designated as "wilderness" bars mining

FIGURE 12-6. This helicopter is helping personnel of the Bureau of Land Management survey land in the vicinity of 10,085-foot high Mt. Iliamna in the background. The mountain is in southwest Alaska, west of Cook Inlet. Alaska, our largest state by far has almost three-fourths of the U.S. offically designated wilderness areas, thanks to the Alaskan Lands Act of 1980. (Photo by R. A. Lytle)

---

[7] U.S. Forest Service, *An Assessment of the Forest and Range Land Situation in the United States*, Washington, D.C., 1980, p. x.

development and vehicle use. Hiking, rafting and other recreational activities are permitted. Hunting, mining by special permit and livestock grazing are allowed with some restrictions.

This act, signed into law on December 19, 1964, gives permanent protection to millions of acres of nature sanctuaries formerly subject to the whims of various administrators. Proposals for additions are to be reviewed by citizens before acceptance into The Wilderness System. This is the first law in our nation's history which gives the general public a direct input into federal land-use decision-making. Also, all forms of commercial activities, except for mining by special permit and for a number of years, are prohibited in the wilderness areas.

On December 2, 1980, President Jimmy Carter signed the Alaska National Interest Lands Conservation Act of 1980 into law, thus increasing the wilderness area protection in the United States by 56.6 million acres (see Table 12-7). Conservation System units (parks, refuges and monuments) add another 100 million acres set aside.

Additional acreage is under study for wilderness designation. Late in 1980, the Bureau of Land Management completed a review of 174 million acres in the contiguous United States to be considered for possible inclusion. Of these, 25 million acres have been designated as potential wilderness areas. The Bureau of Land Management has until 1991 to complete the process. According to The Wilderness Society, although conservationists objected to the exclusion of some areas from wilderness designation, they felt that except in Utah, the Bureau of Land Management had made a "good faith" effort. In Utah, one-third less land was set aside for wilderness than conservationists identified as qualifying for such status.[8]

The setting aside of wilderness has had a mixed reception. Conservationists are jubilant. The Wilderness Society has been credited with being primarily responsible for the successful passage of the legislation. Conservationists and ecologists point out the inspirational worth of "getting back to nature," as related for wild rivers in Chapter 10. But, more important, they note, are the opportunities such areas afford to draw upon the unique communities of diverse forms of plant and animal life found there. Such life forms constitute a storehouse upon which we may draw for possible breeding or medicinal uses. They are a base against which we can measure

---

[8]"Million Acres Selected by BLM Wilderness Study," *The Living Wilderness*, Vol. 44, No. 151, December 1980, pp. 38–39.

TABLE 12-7. Lands Set Aside by Alaska National Interest Lands Conservation Act of 1980 (thousands of acres)

National Park System			National Wilderness Preservation System	
Parks	24,599		Parks and preserves	32,355
Preserves	18,986		Refuges	18,860
Total	43,585		Forests (including forest monuments)	5,362
National Wildlife Refuge System	53,720		Total for the Wilderness System	56,577
National forest monuments	3,206			
Total for Conservation System units (except Wilderness)	100,511			
National Forest System additions	3,350			
BLM national conservation and recreation areas	2,220			

Sources: Alaska Coalition, *Alaska Status Report*, December 5, 1980, p. 2. [This was the final report of this organization.] For future reference and interpretation of wilderness areas, see periodic reports by The Wilderness Society in various issues of its periodical, *The Living Wilderness*. Environmental impact statements on all areas are also available from federal government sources.

biotic changes. They help us better understand the intricacies of the web of life.

Opponents of wilderness preservation include people living near the areas to be set aside, land developers and timber and mining companies. Local residents fear loss of jobs or loss of potential job opportunities. Some businesspersons and politicians view wilderness preservation as a "lock up" of resources. One nationally known wildlife expert was against an eastern wilderness proposal because better habitat for wildlife could be provided there by managing the land. Besides, it was not a "pure" (never used commercially) wilderness. Opposition to eastern wilderness proposals is especially strong on the latter count—that they are not "pure."

Each wilderness area is unique and should be considered for protection under the act on the basis of its own merits. All of us, either on our own competence or through being represented by an organization, can participate in the citizen's review process to help determine if protection is justified.

Wilderness is a trust established for all of us. How much respect we give it can be shown by how we act when in the woods. It is only in the wilderness areas that the last vestige of virgin woods—beautiful ferns and rare native flowers—persists in abundance. It is apparently impossible for some vacationists, intent upon enjoying the landscape about them, to appreciate the rare beauties of nature without disturbing the environment. They thus destroys the beauty they came to enjoy.

Most of us do not possess the information necessary to propagate or even keep alive wild flowers such as spring beauties, lady slippers, trilliums, gentians, arbutus and other rapidly disappearing gems of our woods. We, in our eager, selfish desire to have these beautiful plants with us, do not seem able to carry this beauty as a picture in our minds. We must pick them, and as we pick, we see them wilt and wither in our hands. Thus, both the flowers and the picture are gone.

BETTER USE OF FOREST RESOURCES

As in the case of all of our other resources, we can increase greatly the adequacy of our forest resources by less waste and more efficient use. Progress is being made. More wood chips and other forms of waste products are being used today than formerly. Once discarded material is being made into particle board or burned for energy. Houses are being redesigned to use lumber more efficiently. Waste paper and newspapers are being recycled. And, plastics and other renewable resources are being substituted for wood in many products. But, we have a long way to go before we anywhere near reach the potentials for savings.

THE KEYS TO OUR FOREST RESOURCES

The key to more abundant timber resources in our nation is good management. The ones who could turn this key to the greatest advantage are the small landowners who control over half of the forest land, which has by far the best potential for higher yields of wood products.

If all our forests were well managed and if economy of use, including substitution, were practiced, our nation might eventually become a net exporter of timber.

No less important than its value as timber is our forest resources' recreational and ecological value in parks and wilderness areas. The largest amount of such land use is in the public domain. We are the trustees. The

FIGURE 12-7. This is a forest of West Virginia where a continuous stand of good trees will persist as long as trees are cut when they reach maturity and the young growth is protected during the selective cutting. It requires good forest management to accomplish the results shown here. (Courtesy, U.S. Forest Service)

key to maintaining these values is for us to live up to our individual responsibilities as concerned citizens.

Don'ts for Forest Visitors

Whether people are picnicking, camping or traveling through the woodlands and forests as tourists, it is well for them to have a few fundamental rules in mind for their own safety and for the preservation of woods, shrubs and plants.

1. ***Don't be careless with fires.*** Drench every camp fire with water before leaving it. Be sure to extinguish cigarette or cigar butts before dropping them anywhere in the woods or along roadsides.
2. ***Don't leave papers, tin cans and other signs of camping.*** Leave every camp site looking as you would like to find it if you were to return to the same camp.

3. **Don't hack, mark, deface or place names on trees or stones.** Remember there are 20 million other people who may follow your example.

4. **Don't stray from marked trails when exploring unless you are "woods wise."** Being lost is frightening, and it can be fatal.

5. **Don't pick any flowers.** Most woods flowers wilt as soon as picked, and the picking of many of our rare flowers weakens and untimately kills the plants.

6. **Don't dig specimens to plant in your garden.** Many of the rare wild flowers will grow only in special soils, and even when a ball of earth is taken with a plant, the plant soon loses its woodland quality when "potted" in other soil.

7. **Don't disturb anything in the woods.** Even the removal of old logs which cross trails may destroy the home of some woods animal or plant.

8. **Don't depend on someone else to do what you should do.**

QUESTIONS AND PROBLEMS

1. Which makes the faster growth—forests which are managed or forests which are permitted to restock and grow naturally?

2. Approximately how much of our original billion acres of forest land is left today? How much of it is commercial? (See Chapter 11.)

3. How many management practices to increase productivity of forests can you list? Describe any one of these.

4. Name some of the trees that grow in your part of the country and list some of their various uses.

5. Name three enemies of trees, other than fire, which have destroyed completely the species attacked or which are continually being fought to keep the trees from destruction.

6. How can forest fires possibly do any good? Why should they be controlled?

7. What is the difference between clearcutting and selective harvesting?

8. What are the advantages and disadvantages of clearcutting?

9. Why are small landowners so important to our forest resources? What arguments would you use to try to persuade them to improve management?

10. What is meant by "multiple use" of forests? How can multiple use in a national forest help a national park?

11. What is a wilderness area? How does The Wilderness Act protect it? How can you help provide for and take care of wilderness areas?

12. What are some of the ways by which we can extend our forest resources by better use?

13. Name some substitutes for wood that are being used in your community.

14. List the eight "don'ts for forest visitors." Which two would you place at the top of the list? Why?

13

The Origin and Depletion of Soil

In our largely industrial society, with less than 3 percent of our employed civilian labor force directly engaged in agricultural production, the study of our soil resources is apt to be neglected, except by farmers and a few specialists. Yet, two-thirds of all businesses are said to be agribusinesses—businesses whose economic activities are dependent upon agricultural products in one way or another. And, no resource is more essential to our well-being, and to life itself, than soil. All of us need to appreciate and to understand the nature of this resource so that we can support and carry out the practices that will help preserve it. If those of us who are nonfarming citizens, for example, fail to demand that the federal government support conservation farming programs, not only will our soil be lost, but our nation will too! The first six of the following chapters describe soil processes and soil conservation in agriculture. The seventh chapter of this group, Chapter 19, which deals with the city, indicates the significance of soil in urban situations.

FORMATION OF SOIL

Soil, most simply defined, is "that part of the earth's mantle which

FIGURE 13-1. The immense sand dunes in the southwestern part of the United States represent one of the many long steps taken by nature in reducing rock to soil. These dunes will not become soil for many thousands of years. (Courtesy, National Park Service)

supports plant growth." Overlying the earth's crust, which is of rock, is a covering of loose materials called *regolith* (derived from the Greek; *rega*, meaning "covering" or "blanket," and *lith*, meaning "stone"). Soil is formed from this loose material, eventually consisting of a combination of air, water, minerals and decayed plant materials (humus).

Soil formation is a complex process. The top part of the rock mantle (combination of topsoil and subsoil) of the earth is subject to the action of heat, cold, rain, sunshine and the mild acids of plant roots so that its composition and structure are changed until it is quite different from the lower parts (see Figure 13-1). The roots of the plants which grow on the surface penetrate the upper part of this mantle in all directions. When the roots die, they become part of the mantle, and the surface growth falls to form a covering over the mantle.

The upper part of the mantle is honeycombed with small burrows caused by earthworms, beetles, moles, gophers and a host of other insects and animals as they search for food and/or seek protection from enemies. Even smaller forms of life, such as bacteria, molds and fungi, live in and on the mantle. They help in the decay of plant roots as well as in the process of making smaller particles out of the larger pieces of the mantle. As a result of all these processes, the surface layer of the soil is formed.

The mantle was formed by the disintegration of the underlying rock or was transported to its present location in one of several ways.

The sedentary or residual deposits, or soils, which were formed over the rock from which they were derived, have two general sources. The most usual source of these soils is the disintegration of underlying rock. The rock below was broken up into fine particles or disintegrated through the combined action of water, heat, cold, etc., to form a covering. Much of this covering was eroded, while other parts were dissolved in water and leached (drained off) through this covering. The material that was left forms the present residual deposits, or residual soil.

The second source of residual soil is the result of decaying plant growth in the flatter, poorly drained places. Peat, muck and swamp soils result from this process and form a small part of our general soil covering.

The transported soils, or soils which have been moved by wind or water, were formed by one or more of the following processes: (1) transportation by water—alluvial deposits (see Figure 13-2); (2) transportation by

FIGURE 13-2. The soil in this picture is alluvial, or water formed. The soil was deposited from quiet water, from a lake or a pond. It is called "lacustrine." The strip of grass between the onions reduces wind erosion. (Courtesy, Soil Conservation Service)

FIGURE 13-3. Colluvial deposits at the base of the Great Organ formation in the Capital Reef Monument, New Mexico. Deposits of this type are more common in areas of low rainfall. (Courtesy, National Park Service)

winds—aeolian, or loessial, soils; (3) transportation by glaciers—soils; (4) accumulation of deposits at the base of cliffs—colluvial deposits (see Figure 13-3).

SOIL FORMATION — A LONG PROCESS

It takes millions of years to form the rock mantle, for it requires the disintegration of many feet of the original, or parent, rock to form 1 foot of mantle. The formation of the top part of the mantle, or soil, which supports plant growth, requires a greater thickness of the parent rock and a much longer time to form than any other part of the mantle of equal thickness.

When nature is left to make and rework its soil without human interference, the rock mantle continues slowly to increase in thickness through the disintegration and breaking up of the rock upon which it rests. This accumulation at the bottom of the mantle tends to increase at about the same rate at which soil is lost from the top of the mantle. Thus, the thickness of the mantle under natural conditions tends to remain about the same, century after century. This balance of losses in soil from the top of the mantle with increases at the bottom of the mantle is spoken of as a condition of equilibrium in nature. This equilibrium, or balance, in nature is possible only because of the continued presence of plant growth and accumulation on the surface of the mantle.

How We Upset Nature's Balance

When farmers use the soil for agricultural production, they destroy the balance which natural erosion has set up because they substitute a sparce-growing plant for the natural denser growth and they take the growth off the soil instead of letting it drop and accumulate over the top of the soil. They use up the organic matter of the soil by their plowing and seeding operations, making the soil less porous. Their crops take out the plant nutrients which have accumulated in the soil; thus less plant growth is produced, making a thinner covering for the soil. The final result is a washing away of the soil by rains which previously were absorbed or a blowing away through dust storms in the drier parts of the country.

Why Some Soils Take Much Longer to Form than Others

No one knows how many thousands of years it takes for nature to pulverize the original rock of the earth in order to form the mantle (covering of loose material) from which the soil finally is derived. We do know that scratches left on the face of our harder quartzite rocks by the glaciers are still plainly visible after weathering for 25,000 to 50,000 years. More than that, we know there are polished surfaces on rock which have not lost this polish in 100,000 years. Gutzon Borglum, the sculptor who created the Mount Rushmore National Memorial in the Black Hills of South Dakota, once said that erosion will reduce the surface of this sculpture by not more than 1 inch in 100,000 years.

The rates of disintegration of some of the softer rocks of the earth, such as limestone, are much faster than that of quartzite. The rates of breaking up these rocks are much faster, too, in climates with alternate freezing and thawing temperatures than in those in which the temperature is constantly above freezing or almost constantly below freezing throughout the year. Another factor is moisture. A moist climate is thought to lead to faster disintegration of rock than a dry climate because both chemical and mechanical weathering take place under moist conditions. In a dry climate the disintegration of rock is largely a mechanical process—the result of the action of wind.

How Limestone Rock Makes Soil

Some geologists estimate that the face of limestone rock disappears at the rate of about 1 foot in a thousand years. Most of the limestone, or calcium carbonate, is slowly soluble in water and washes away with the water run-off. The remaining impurities form the residual mantle. Let us assume that the limestone rock has 5 percent impurities. If none of the impurities are carried away, it will require 20,000 years to build up 1 foot of mantle. But, it is more likely that most of the impurities will wash away. If we assume three-fourths of the impurities are carried away, it will require around 80,000 years to make 1 foot of rock mantle from limestone rock. This may seem like a long time, but it requires a much longer time to make 1 inch of soil from this mantle than it does to make several inches of the mantle itself.

Whether these estimates are high or low, once the precious mantle of soil is gone from limestone rock, this valuable material is gone forever as far as our generation or even the life of our nation is concerned. We think of limestone soils as among our most productive soils. Soil making from the original rock formation of the earth is such a slow process that we can safely say that no significant amounts of soil have been created since the beginning of human history.

WHAT IS EROSION?

The formation of soil is one of the steps taken by nature in reducing mountains and leveling hills. It is a "way station used by the rock of the earth as it journeys to the sea." The vehicle used to make this transition is erosion. Soil is built by erosion. It is also destroyed by erosion. Soil is built through the ages by geological erosion. It is destroyed in years by human-made, especially agricultural, erosion. The difference between geological and human-made erosion is essentially one of degree, not of kind.

The same forces of nature cause both kinds of erosion. Wind and water, heat and cold are the agencies which throughout the ages have made soil building possible. They are also the agencies which can destroy the land in a few short hours. Erosion began when the first rains fell. It cannot be stopped, although it can be retarded and held in check. The discussion of the formation of the rock mantle in the early part of this chapter is in reality a discussion of the results of erosion. Erosion carried away much of the original rock, leaving only a fraction of the total quantities of disintegrated rock. This residual fraction created the mantle; the eroded and leached parts were carried away to the sea where they were deposited and later became rock. Thus, wherever erosion occurs, deposition also occurs. Whenever soil is washed away, it must be deposited in some other place. In ages to come, this deposition may again be raised above the water from which it was deposited and so later become soil.

KINDS OF EROSION

There are two types of erosion which are destroying our soils and adding to our waste land—wind erosion and water erosion. Wind erosion takes place when there is little rainfall or when the soil does not support a good vegetative growth. The most disastrous effects of wind erosion are produced when land is plowed and left bare in areas of limited rainfall. Water erosion, on the other hand, takes place wherever rain falls. It, too, has resulted in most serious damage where the lands have been cultivated. The term *soil erosion* or *erosion* as used here refers mostly to human-made erosion and not to the small amount of normal or geological erosion which occurs with good vegetative cover and proper soil management.

Water Erosion

Wherever there is rainfall, there is the possibility of water erosion and wherever water runs off over the surface of the soil, there is sure to be erosion. The amount of soil washing, or soil losses, depends upon the total amount as well as the intensity of individual rains, the length and steepness of the slope, the type of soil, the kind and density of the crops covering the soil and the method of cultivating the soil (see Figure 13-4).

The surface run-off, roughly estimated to be about 30 percent of the total precipitation (rainfall and snow), results in either sheet or gully erosion. Where the water moves off over the surface as a sheet, it takes off a

FIGURE 13-4. The lower, darker 8 feet of soil were laid down by water (alluvial soil) thousands of years ago. Grass growth has added organic matter to the top 2 feet of this layer, causing that area to be darker in color than the soil lower down. The top 4 or 5 feet of lighter, stratified soil, also alluvial, was washed down from nearby hills after being broken up and put to crops. The cut of 11 to 12 feet, which shows the soil profile, is the result of recent erosion. (Courtesy, Soil Conservation Service)

complete layer of soil and is true sheet erosion. Very little of the water actually runs off any field in smooth sheets. It usually collects in numerous little rills, which may become larger and less numerous as the bottom of the slope is neared. As long as the rills can be plowed across and the field smoothed again for the next crop, this rilling is designated as sheet erosion. The concentration of the water run-off into large channels which cannot be filled in by plowing across the fields is the start of gully erosion. These gullies or channels become larger with each rainfall and ultimately may so cut up a field that it has to be abandoned.

Gully erosion is conspicuous and is more startling in appearance than sheet erosion. It was the appearance of gullies in fields that wakened the public to the seriousness of our erosion problem. Great have been the losses to agriculture by this type of erosion.

Sheet erosion, on the other hand, is more insidious and more dangerous than gully erosion. It is not so readily recognized, and much of the topsoil may be washed away before the farmer is conscious of the damage done. Because it is possible to plow across fields which are subject to sheet erosion and because the evidence of the damage is thus hidden by each plowing, the process may continue until practically all the topsoil is gone. Where sheet erosion does not lead later to the formation gullies, it frequently is difficult to alert farmers to the type of problems that must be faced if they are to continue to produce crops. We all have seen the smooth, rounded light-colored knolls or hilltops in a field which is covered everywhere else with a darker soil. When this field was first broken and planted to crops, the soil on these higher points was the same color as the other parts of the field. The change in the soil color on these knolls is the result of sheet erosion. The darker-colored topsoil which once covered these higher parts of the field is now on the lower parts of the field or has washed off the farm completely.

Wind Erosion

Wind erosion takes place only where the soil is dry and where little or no vegetative cover is maintained on the field. A soil which is very loose and fine requires more vegetative cover to keep it from blowing away than one which is coarser. Some land that is too closely pastured, or that has been burned over, is subject to wind erosion. Wind erosion is especially noticeable in the Great Plains area of the United States because of the semi-droughty character of the country and the velocities of the prevailing winds. High winds and dry soil may come at any season of the year. If they come after the ground is plowed and before a good growth of crop is produced, the whole depth of the plowed soil may be blown away.

Dry Farming with Dust Mulch Encourages Wind Erosion

A generation ago farmers in the semi-arid areas of the Midwest were encouraged to make a dust mulch of the soil surface in order to keep down weed growth and to conserve moisture. Although in this condition no weeds grew to use up the moisture of the soil, the flour-like dust mulch also prevented the water from being absorbed by the soil. When large areas adopted this practice, the situation was set for wind erosion and the historic dust storms that occurred.

The strong winds of the prairie broke up the slight crust of the surface, and "black blizzards" followed (see Figure 13-5). It is estimated that during

FIGURE 13-5. This approaching dust storm, or black blizzard, sometime during the 1930's, shows how our loessial soil was made. Many feet of wind-formed soils are deposited throughout the semi-arid parts of the country. It required hundreds of years of dust storms, such as the one shown above to deposit the loessial soils of the prairies of the Midwest. All wind-formed soils must first be made by some other forces of nature before they can be picked up by the wind and transported elsewhere. (Courtesy, Soil Conservation Service)

one day's dust storm in the "dust bowl" of the Oklahoma, Texas, Colorado and Kansas wheat lands in 1936, as much as 300 million tons of fertile top-soil were blown away. Dust from this area was deposited over the eastern half of the United States, and dust clouds were observed 300 miles out over the Atlantic. Not only were these storms destructive of soil, but they were also a most terrifying experience to live through. It was almost impossible to breathe, the air was so full of dust. Children could not find their way home from school, and all traffic was completely stopped because no light could penetrate the blackness of a mid-day storm.

Drifts as large as winter snow drifts buried fences, smothered buildings and sifted through windows and doors in unbelievable quantities. Some attics were so filled with dust that the plaster of the ceilings below gave way. The winds took the soil from where it was most useful and left it where it could do the most harm. It is not surprising that many people, now destitute, gathered up a few possessions and left this desolation (see Figure 13-6).

FIGURE 13-6. Wind erosion following soil depletion caused the loss of this farm, its neighbors and the community. Only a forsaken church bell and a few abandoned building remain to tell the story of lost effort and shattered hope. (Courtesy, Soil Conservation Service)

SOIL DEPLETION

Another aspect of soil erosion which adds to the problems of crop production is the depletion of the soil of its organic matter and plant nutrients. Dr. H. H. Bennett, known as the "father" of the Soil Conservation Service, noted that more than 90 million tons of the five principal elements of plant food are contained in the soils that are lost each year through erosion. Forty-three million tons of these consist of phosphorus, potash and nitrogen—the three plant nutrients used in commercial fertilizers. If this quantity of fertilizer were supplied to our croplands, it would be equivalent to 225 pounds on every acre of cropland throughout our country. Calcium and magnesium, though they are necessary for the best production of most crops, are not as scarce or as valuable as the three aforementioned elements.

This loss of plant nutrients is in addition to the loss through the depletion by crops, which is not replaced, and through leaching by the water that drains through the soil. It is estimated that the amount of plant food lost through leaching is equal to that lost through erosion and that the amount lost through erosion is more than 20 times the amount removed by farm crops. Thus, we see that losses through leaching and erosion are many times the losses through crop production.

BUILDING UP, TEARING DOWN

Each time a piece of rock falls from a cliff or is forced from its parent rock by the action of water or frost, the first step is being taken by nature in the ultimate formation of new soil. On the other hand, every muddy stream or every cloud of dust carried away by some vagrant wind is evidence of the erosion of the soil that took nature ages to create. Thus, the great cycle goes on through eons of time.

QUESTIONS AND PROBLEMS

1. What is the rock mantle, or regolith, of the earth?
2. How is the mantle formed?
3. What happens to the mantle so that the upper part becomes soil?
4. What is meant by equilibrium in nature?
5. What happens to the soil when the balance, or equilibrium, of nature is destroyed?
6. How long did Gutzon Borglum estimate it will take for the natural forces of wind, rain, heat and cold to cause the loss of 1 inch of the surface of the Mount Rushmore National Memorial?
7. About how many years does it take to reduce the face of limestone rock by 1 foot?
8. If we assume that limestone rock has 5 percent impurities and that none of these impurities are carried away by the water which dissolves the limestone, about how many years will it take to build 1 foot of mantle?

9. Does it take more or less time to make soil from the mantle than it does to make mantle from the limestone rock?

10. What is the difference between natural erosion and human-made?

11. What are the two kinds of water erosion, and how do they differ?

12. What conditions make for wind erosion?

13. What is a dust mulch, and is it desirable to maintain such a mulch? Give reasons for your answer.

14. How does soil depletion differ from soil erosion? Give the proportions of the loss of plant nutrients by (a) erosion, (b) leaching and (c) soil depletion.

15. Was the soil near your home made from limestone, sandstone or granite?

16. Was the soil in your community deposited there by wind or water? If by water, was it deposited by the slowed-down action of running streams, or was it formed by still lake waters?

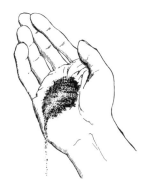

14

The Extent of
Our Soil Resources

There is no more important natural resource than our land, that is, the solid portion of the earth's surface. Soil is that part of the land surface of the earth which supports plant growth. Not only is the soil the source of all our vast forest resources, but it also is the source of practically all our food and clothing. Only some 10 percent of our food supply comes from the seas (see Chapter 22). Thus, our present living standard is especially dependent upon the productivity of our soil.

SOIL RESOURCES ONCE CONSIDERED INEXHAUSTIBLE

In colonial times there seemed to be an inexhaustible quantity of land, and the only cost to the colonists of obtaining cropland was that necessary to clear the land of its tree growth. The cost of clearing a piece of land was all that made it valuable. The first president of our nation, George Washington, in writing to Arthur Young of England concerning the use of land for the production of crops in the colonies, made the statement that it was easier to clear new land for farming than it was to attempt to maintain the productivity of land which had been used several years for crop production.

Even as late as 1909, Dr. Milton Whitney, Chief of the Bureau of Soils of the U.S. Department of Agriculture, wrote that "the soil is the one indestructible, immutable asset that cannot be exhausted, that cannot be used up." This mistaken view of soil resources as virtually unlimited unfortunately persisted for decades.

CHEAP LAND PERSISTED

Until about 1862, when the Homestead Act was passed, any man could get land for farming from the various states or from the federal government by moving onto it and taking possession. After that time, by paying a small fee, $1.25 per acre, and by living on the acres for a very few years, a man could homestead public land.

Since those early days, farm land has risen in price until farmers now pay many times as much per acre as a whole 160-acre farm cost during the latter part of the nineteenth century. This means that soil is now recognized as a valuable but limited natural resource. Unfortunately, however, industrial, commercial and residential uses still continue to take over prime farm land.

THE EXTENT OF OUR SOIL RESOURCES

The total land area of the United States, exclusive of its outlying possession, is approximately 2,271,600,000 acres. The acreage used as cropland is 313.4 million acres and is divided as shown in Table 14-1, the latest information available.

In the *1977 National Resources Inventory*, 413 million acres were classed as cropland, resulting in an average of 1.93 acres per person; whereas in The Second RCA Appraisal, it was projected that in 1990, 370.4 million cropland acres would be available, resulting in an average of 1.48 acres per person (based on the U.S. Bureau of the Census population of 249.7 million people in 1990). If this rate of increase in population continues and cropland available declines, then the conservation and management of cropland will become a priority item in our society.

TABLE 14-1. Cropland Use in 1982 (irrigated and nonirrigated)

Major Crop	Irrigated	Nonirrigated	Total
	(millions of acres)		
Corn (all purposes)	8.5	69.4	77.9
Wheat (for grain)	4.7	66.3	71.0
Soybeans	2.3	62.5	64.8
Hay (alfalfa, tame, wild small grain, grass)	8.5	48.2	56.7
Sorghums (all purposes)	2.3	11.2	13.5
Barley	1.8	6.8	8.6
Cotton	3.4	6.3	9.7
Orchard	3.3	1.4	4.7
Vegetables (harvested for sale)	2.0	1.3	3.3
Rice	3.2	0.0	3.2
Total	40.0	273.4	313.4

Sources: The Second RCA Appraisal, U.S. Department of Agriculture, Public Review Draft, July–August 1987.

Our food supplies will probably be large enough to feed this number of people, but even now we are faced with the problem of supporting our larger population and helping meet world food shortages. How can this be done? The three possibilities usually mentioned are to (1) import more food and export less, (2) consume less food or eat more cereals and fewer livestock products and (3) produce more per acre and increase the amount of land in cultivation.

The problem with trying to import more food is that most of the other countries of the world have less agricultural productivity per person than we have. With more than half the people of the world already on an inadequate diet, other countries are looking to us to export, not import, vital food supplies. Of course, we will have to limit exports, if we need the food stuffs at home.

Consumption of less food is a desirable goal for most of us in the United States. We are the first great nation in the world whose population as a whole has suffered from eating too much rather than too little! While expert opinion may be divided on just how much we can cut meat consumption without impairing our health and vitality, it seems reasonable that some reduction should be made. Some of the world's strongest animals, such as gorillas, are vegetarians; and at least one of its most witty men, George Bernard Shaw, was a vegetarian. Brawn and brains are thus not exclusively the product of red meat ingestion!

The third way to increase our food supplies, through producing high yields or putting more land in cultivation, deals with the resource base. The balance of our discussion of agriculture is largely concerned with examining these possibilities.

If all our swamp land could be drained and all our plowable pasture plowed up, we would add about 10 percent to our total cropland. To drain all the swamps and wetlands would be folly. Migratory fowl and some animals depend on these lands for habitat, and such lands help store and purify our water supply. We also know that it is poor conservation to plow up all our plowable pasture because much of this is on the rougher, more sloping parts of farms. We may think it possible to obtain more cropland from some of the grazing land, but this land is practically all in the semi-arid part of the country where crop production is low because of the limited and variable rainfall. Besides, the area is subject to violent thunderstorms and strong winds which greatly increase erosion hazards when the land does not have permanent vegetation cover. If properly managed, grazing land will produce as much feed without destructive erosion and losses as it would if plowed up for crops. So, we cannot expect to increase food production much, if any, in this way, The best way to increase our food supplies is to make better use of our present cropland.

It now appears that by using the 438 million or more acres that can be cropped and by more intensive use of all our cropland, we can so increase our production so as to feed our growing population for several decades to come. This seems possible if we use new, improved varieties of seed, proper and timely application of fertilizer and efficient weed and pest control and if we make more efficient use of our water resources.

Over 58 million acres of our good cropland are now being irrigated as a supplement to rainfall and other forms of precipitation. Another 155 million acres are having their excess soil moisture removed, and an additional 50 million acres of flood land receive flood protection. There are also another 115 million acres of flood land that ultimately may be protected from flooding. But, as is noted in the following paragraphs, much of our soil is being lost to soil erosion, and much of our cropland is being diverted to nonagricultural uses.

Much of Our Land Is Forest Soil

About one-third of our national area, including Alaska, is forest land. This figure includes woodland on farms, forest areas set aside for water management and commercial timberland. Forest land ordinarily is less subject to erosion than are lands used for other purposes. Land which carries a good forest cover will absorb most of the rainfall with little or no direct run-off (see Figure 14-1).

The sponge-like nature of these soils, resulting from many years' accumulation of decaying leaves, twigs and bark, makes an ideal absorbent for water. The excess water requires days to drain off by slow percolation through these soils, rather than rushing off over the surface within a few hours. In unpastured woodlands and forest areas which still have fairly dense stands of trees, good soil condition is thus actually being built up instead of being lost through erosion.

Marshes and Swamps Make More Soil

There is about one-fourth as much land in marshes, swamps and other

FIGURE 14-1. Water run-off from land carries with it the finest parts of the soil and much of the plant nutrients. This gives the water the dark color shown in the left jar labeled "run-off from corn-field." Run-off from protected woodlands does not carry soil particles and plant nutrients and is practically clear, as is shown in the right jar. (Courtesy, Soil Conservation Service)

low, flat areas as in forest land. Little or no soil losses take place in these areas. The land in these marshes and swamps actually may be adding to its small soil content as soil-laden water drains into it from neighboring hills. The depositing of soil in these low lying areas in this manner is sometimes called sedimentation, or silting. Also, the deposits of organic matter left by the rank plant growth in these low spots finally fill the areas, and swamps first become peat, and later muck soil. This is an exceedingly slow process, however, requiring hundreds of years to fill in a marsh or a swamp. Even then, there must be some way to control the water level, either by drainage outlets or by dams if such an area is to be used for crop production.

Nearly One-third Is Grazing Land

Nearly one-third of our acreage is public and private grazing land. These lands are in regions of low rainfall, so that without irrigation they will not support ordinary crop production. It is for this reason that they are not classed as cropland. About one-fourth as much land now in farms is classed as pasture land.

These lands are subject to severe erosion if overgrazing takes place (see Figure 14-2). Practically all these grazing lands are subject to occasional heavy rainfalls and flash floods. Since there is little grass growth on these heavily grazed areas, the flood waters rush off in torrential streams which cut channels deeply into the surface soil.

Grasses Stop Growing

The damage to these lands is not limited to erosion, even though that is bad enough. The loss of moisture is just as serious.

Before the lands were overgrazed and all grass cover was removed, these broad, level or slightly rolling prairie areas with their abundant covering of green or dry grasses absorbed most of the meager rainfall, even though much of it fell during thunderstorms, which are always of short duration but frequently of severe intensity.

Since most of the rainfall was absorbed into the soil where it fell, a good growth of grass followed. This growth was not cut or heavily grazed by the animals that roamed the region, so that it remained to catch the

FIGURE 14-2. One of the big failings of farmers and ranchers is to overgraze pasture land, as shown in the left field. The first effect of this condition is poor cattle. Later, when rains come, the soil moves off with water. (Courtesy, Soil Conservation Service)

next rainfall. The result was a continuous covering of grass which easily survived moderate wildlife grazing.

Wherever one of these broad basins or stretches of grass is overgrazed and gullies are cut through, then rainfall immediately rushes off so that even the areas between the gullies, or ravines, absorb very little water. The result is no grass growth on any of the land (see Figure 14-3). Useless, sparse weeds or inedible shrubs replace the grass. Thus, a whole grazing area is lost.

Pastures Lose Soil

Lands classed as pasture lands ordinarily are found on farms rather than on ranches. These areas receive from 25 to 50 inches of rainfall yearly, whereas the ranch country, where most of the grazing lands are located, receives less than 20 inches.

Much of the pasture land on our farms is eroding or will erode if not handled correctly. The same situation that causes grazing land to erode is causing soil losses on these lands. Summer rains frequently come as

FIGURE 14-3. Gravel, sand and dirt from overgrazed pasture land washed down into this broad valley, covering the rich soil and reducing its value for crop production. Much of the pasture land was also destroyed. (Courtesy, Soil Conservation Service)

thunderstorms in the ranch country. Since these pasture lands receive more rainfall than the public and privated grazing lands, greater care must be taken to keep these soils from washing.

These lands usually represent the steeper slopes of farms, or they may have stony outcrops or other hindrances to cultivation which place them in the pasture land class. Some fields that are now classed as pasture land were originally good farm lands. They have lost their topsoil or have been so cut with gullies that they can no longer be used effectively for crop production.

Another reason for large soil losses on these lands is the practice of pasturing them so early and so heavily that little or no plant growth remains on the surface. In most instances, farmers mistakenly think they must do this in order to "make the lands pay." The result is that most of the rainfall runs off in rivulets which come together farther down the slope to cut gullies across the fields.

Overall the range conditions improved from 1963 to 1977 (see Table 14-2). However, 60 percent of the 406 million acres of nonfederal rangeland remains in less than good condition. Range conditions have changed little between 1977 and 1982. This is a challenge in light of increasing demands for red meat and pressure to produce more livestock on grass and less on grain.

TABLE 14-2. Trends in Range Condition Class on Nonfederal Range Lands

Condition	1963	1977	1982
	. . . . (%)		
Excellent.	5	12	4
Good	15	28	30
Fair.	40	42	44
Poor.	40	18	17

Sources: Soil Conservation Service, *1977 National Resources Inventory,* U.S. Government Printing Office, Washington, D.C., December 1977; The Second RCA Appraisal, U.S. Department of Agriculture, Public Review Draft, July–August 1987.

About One-fourth Is Cropland

The most valuable of all our agricultural resources is our cropland. It must supply us with practically all of our food and most of our clothing, as well as a considerable quantity of material used in industry. Dr. Bennett, referred to earlier, stated that civilizations of the past have risen and fallen with food supplies.

The impact of loss of food supply capabilities is seen in Africa today. Severe drought there and the effects of war and land abuse have caused untold thousands of people to starve and even more thousands to roam in search of food. Sad as it is, the restoration of adequate diets will take many years to accomplish. Restoration of their soil and water resources to prior levels may not be achieved for generations—if ever.

How well are we taking care of our farm cropland? Is it losing its surface soil as rapidly as our grazing and pasture lands? The story here is brief and tragic (see Figures 14-4 and 14-5). In the past 200 hundred years, which is a short time in the life of a nation, this country has lost approximately one-third of its topsoil, according to SCS estimates.

The *1977 National Resources Inventory (NRI)* is an exhaustive bench-

FIGURE 14-4. These small gullies were made on a field in Iowa after the crop was taken off. The slope of the field in 8 percent, and fields with that slope are commonly used for crop production. The loss of surface soil here is estimated at 100 tons per acre. (Courtesy, Soil Conservation Service)

FIGURE 14-5. A 2-inch rain that fell in two hours caused the damage shown above to a Michigan field which was being summer fallowed for wheat. Many tons of valuable topsoil were forever lost from this field during that two-hour period. (Courtesy, Soil Conservation Service)

mark study still used as a guide for comparative soil erosion studies in 1987. Its estimates of erosion losses are shown in Table 14-3.

The survey indicates an average annual soil loss of 7.8 tons per acre. Other state and regional studies indicate, however, that this is a very conservative erosion estimate.

There is also evidence of low estimates in states west of the Rocky Mountains. For example, in the Palouse region of eastern Washington, the *NRI* estimate on Class IVe cropland was a 3-ton loss per acre, while a new River Basin study estimated a 24-ton loss. On Class VIe cropland, the *NRI* still estimated a 3-ton loss per acre, while the field study showed a 55-ton loss. (For a description of various classes and subclasses, see the next chapter. The *e* indicates that erosion is the main limitation.)

TABLE 14-3. Estimated Average Annual Sheet and Rill Erosion on Cultivated Cropland, by Selected Capabilities

Capability Class	Row Crops		Close-grown Crops		Total Cultivated Cropland	
	Nonirr.	Irr.	Nonirr.	Irr.	Nonirr.	Irr.
	. . . .(average tons of soil loss per acre per year).					
I	4.1	2.2	2.2	1.3	3.6	2.0
IIe	7.8	3.4	2.9	1.7	5.5	2.9
IIIe	15.1	4.7	3.6	1.6	7.8	3.3
IVe	20.6	4.6	5.9	1.2	10.7	3.1
VIe	37.3	8.4	10.0	1.5	19.4	6.2
Average	7.8	2.9	3.1	1.4	5.5	2.3

Source: USDA, Soil Conservation Service, *1977 National Resources Inventory*, U.S. Government Printing Office, Washington, D.C., December 1977.

Average annual wind erosion loss on cropland in the 10 Great Plains states is 5.3 tons per acre. These annual rates for each state range from a low of 1.3 tons per acre in Nebraska to a high of 14.9 tons per acre in Texas. Marginal cropland is the major problem. For example, Texas has 2 million acres of Class IVe cropland, losing 57.5 tons per acre per year. The erosion rate for Class VIe is almost double at 101.6 tons per acre per year.

USE OF SOILS IN URBAN AREAS

Our soil resources are also being used for many nonagricultural uses. These land uses include housing, schools, industry, recreation and transportation. Seventy-five percent of the land converted to urban uses has been from former cropland, including high value irrigated cropland. In 1967, 61 million acres were used in this way; by 1977, these had increased to 90 million. In 1987, urban and built-up land use occupied twice the acreage it did in 1967.

When land is changed from agricultural use to urban use, the problems of erosion are always present. When the surface is covered with roofs, parking lots, roads and other like construction, the water does not enter the soil. Water running off these surfaces causes local flooding and contributes to inundation in natural flood-prone areas. When houses, roads, etc., are being constructed, the soil is disturbed, and the vegetative cover is often removed. The soil in this condition is easily eroded when rains occur. This erosion contributes greatly to the sediment (silt) carried in our rivers and streams. Such soil losses can be as large as 200 tons of soil per acre per year.

GOOD SOIL IS LIMITED

In this chapter we have called attention to the vast soil resources of this country, but only about one-fifth is cropland. Also, losses of valuable soil have been enormous and will continue to be large for some years to come, even though many steps are now being taken to reduce them. We must think of land as a most valuable heritage for our children and our children's children and no longer permit it to be wasted or misused according to the whims or vagaries of individual owners.

QUESTIONS AND PROBLEMS

1. Do you agree with Dr. Whitney, Chief of the Bureau of Soils in 1909, who wrote that "the soil is the one indestructible, immutable asset that cannot be exhausted, that cannot be used up"? Explain your answer.

2. We have approximately 2,271,600,000 acres of land in the United States. How much of this is cropland?

3. How many acres of cropland per person do we have?

4. How much will we have to add to our present cropland if, by 1995, we keep the same number of crop acres per person we now have?

5. What are the problems we must solve before we can increase our production by adding our swamp land or our grazing land to our cropland?

6. Would it be desirable to plow up our forests and use that land for cropland? Give reasons for your answer.

7. Tell how our marshes and swamp land ultimately will make for more cropland, even though it may be a few hundred years hence.

8. What do you consider to be the best use for the grazing land we now have in this country? Explain your answer.

9. What happens to the land when these grazing lands are overgrazed?

10. How many acres of pasture land do we have on our farms? What causes soil losses on these lands?

11. Since our cropland is our most valuable land resource, one would logically expect it to be conserved more than our other resources. Tell what has happened to this resource during the past 200 years.

12. Can we continue to use this cropland to produce food for us to eat and feed for our livestock and still conserve the soil? Explain your answer.

13. What is needed to make the soil in your community produce more?

14. What percent of the land converted to urban land use has been from former cropland?

15

Soil Conservation on
Farms and Ranches

CURRENT LOSSES OF SOIL STILL LARGE

We must consider our soil as a resource which is not permanent and which is renewable only over a very long time. Dr. H. H. Bennett pointed out over a generation ago that we were losing our soil at the rate of ½ million acres a year. We still are. Every year we are losing more than 3.5 billion tons of soil, the equivalent of 6 inches of soil on 5.5 square miles of land surface. At present prices, this would be several hundred billion dollars' worth of fertility.

FARM CONSERVATION PRACTICES
SUPPORTED BY THE
FEDERAL GOVERNMENT

In the Great Depression of the 1930's, our federal government became directly involved in conservation on the farm. With farmers desperate

for cash, the federal government offered help if the farmers would cooperate in certain conservation programs. Soon, two important U.S. Department of Agriculture agencies were set up under the USDA to help farmers:
the Soil Conservation Service, the Agricultural Stabilization and Conservation Service to work with the previously formed Extension Service.

The Soil Conservation Service (SCS) is known as the applied branch
of the federal government's agricultural program. Conservation agents of
the SCS work directly with farmers on the farms in planning conservation
measures.

The Agricultural Stabilization and Conservation Service (ASCS) is the
USDA's financial arm, working at the local level. This organization allocates
and dispenses federal funds in accordance with government programs.

The Extension Service works under the land-grant colleges, such as
the University of Illinois, etc.—for each state—as the USDA's educational
arm. It provides information on all sorts of agricultural practices through
lectures and brochures or directly to any citizen who requests it.

By the 1940's, the government conservation program was well
established. However, during World War II, the agricultural emphasis was
on production, not conservation. Many conservation practices were
shelved in the effort for "all-out" production of food and fibers to
support world needs, especially those of our allies in the war effort. Also,
farmers were eager to take advantage of a bull market in which prices
rose sharply.

After the war, farm property also continued to rise in price for several
decades. Farmers, still supported by government programs, both state and
federal, voluntarily cooperated in conservation.

But, with the energy crisis of the 1970's, collapse of some foreign
markets, inflation of items farmers buy and some adverse natural factors,
such as drought, insect infestation and plant diseases, "the bloom was off
the rose." By the mid-1980's many farmers were in dire financial straits.
Conservation practices suffered because farmers could not afford to finance
the long-run investment such programs often entailed. Agriculture seems
to be nearing another crisis of the proportion of the 1930's. In December
1985, a new farm bill was passed by Congress, which, according to some
agricultural analysts, marked the most fundamental change in farm policy
in 50 years. This development is discussed in Chapter 24, which deals with
the history of the conservation movement through the years.

Agricultural Problems International in Scope

It should not be forgotten, in considering U.S. agricultural programs, that farm problems are international in scope. One persistent and wasteful world problem is agricultural subsidies. Such subsidies encourage surplus production, often on highly erodable farm land. Furthermore, these subsidies have been huge—it is estimated that $100 billion was spent globally in 1986 to subsidize agricultural output. One suggestion to help solve the problem is to set up an international conservation reserve. Besides fostering conservation, the set-aside lands might reduce market imbalances and the pressure to use subsidies.

Another problem is the failure of international trade agreements. The result has been waste and inefficiency. More cooperative trade agreements and less restrictive tariffs are needed.

Other world-wide problems are the lack of marketing systems which will give farmers a fair share of the market price for their products, adequate financial shelters to carry them through losses caused by natural disasters and enough funding for conservation programs so farmers can follow them in good and lean years. Faced with continuing losses and eventual bankruptcy, many farmers abandon conservation practices in a desperate attempt to save themselves. The world needs more imaginative marketing and banking. Interest rates on government-guaranteed farm loans, for example, could be made flexible in accordance with the fluctuation of market prices. The guarantee would be given with the requirements that soil conservation practices be followed on the mortgaged land.

GOOD CONSERVATION

The following five chapters describe various practices that have spread throughout the United States largely as a result of programs introduced at the state and local levels by dedicated conservation specialists in government, at land-grant colleges, in private businesses, by the press and by conservation organizations.

Any measure which helps to keep the land productive is useful in conserving the soil. Soil conservation, then, includes any practice, structure or device which will keep the land in place and make it produce more. This is a restatement of the definition often cited that "good conservation means the use of a resource in such a manner as best to serve the needs of people."

The three general problems which must be met in conserving our soils are how best to (1) keep the topsoil from washing or blowing away, (2) keep the soils from becoming depleted of their plant nutrients and lime and (3) build up soils so as to improve their water-holding capacities and their plant nutrients. When these are accomplished, better crop production will be inevitable.

Special Soil Conserving Practices

Let us look at soil conservation as a series of practices which, when put into effect, will slow down or stop erosion or will build up the soil. Different soils will require the use of different practices. Also, one soil which is on a gentle slope may require practices which are quite different from those needed for the same soil if it happens to lie on a steeper slope. And, soils on long slopes may require somewhat different practices from identical soils on very short slopes.

Some practices can be adopted by individual farmers regardless of what their neighbors do. Strip cropping, terracing, grassed waterways, pasture renovation and conservation rotations are examples of these practices. Other problems in soil conservation can be solved only, or best, through project action. This might be two landowners working together or many landowners in a large watershed working in concert.

Preventing surface run-off from a watershed (a ridge blocking large gullies as they cut their ways across farms and highways) and arresting the filling up of stream beds with silt may all require the action of a number of neighboring farmers. Some such actions by neighbors may require some legal organization or approval in order to stay within the law, while in other instances, the neighbors may act jointly without legal support or sanction.

In any case, it will be necessary to obtain technical advice from those qualified to give the desired information. Such specialists are employed by the Soil Conservation Service of the U.S. Department of Agriculture and are located in nearly every county.

Most of the work done by these specialists is by request, through local soil and water conservation districts, of individual farmers. A study of each farm shows the lay of the land, the size and slope of each field and the erosion which has already taken place. When this study is completed, the farmer receives a map of his/her farm showing how each piece of land should be handled, what practice or practices should be adopted to keep the soil in place and what crops should be grown.

LAND-USE CAPABILITY CLASSES

In order to simplify the work of the specialist, the farm land of the nation has been grouped into eight separate classes called "capability classes." When used for agricultural purposes, those soils which can be treated in the same way (with the least loss of soil) are grouped into the same class. Subclasses are also designated to indicate major limitations within each class.

It is encouraging to know that from a review of studies compiled by the Soil Conservation Service and other government agencies up to 1987, the National Association of Soil Conservation Districts concluded that the majority of the nation's lands are used in keeping with their inherent capabilities. A study of the classifications which follow will show why crop yields were found to drop sharply as less suitable land was brought into production.

Class I

Soils in Class I have few limitations that restrict their use. They can safely be used for the production of the commonly grown field crops with conventional farming methods. No special soil conservation practices need be followed on these soils except for maintenance of tilth and fertility.

Class II

Soils in Class II have some limitations that reduce the choice of plants or require moderate conservation practices. The moderate conservation practices may be one or more of the following: contour tillage (various tillage operations performed as nearly as possible on the level), protective cover crops, conservation tillage, tile drainage and conservation crop rotations which may include grasses and legumes.

Class III

Soils in Class III have severe limitations that reduce the choice of plants or require special conservation practices, or both. The special conservation practices may be one or more of the following: contour strip cropping, terraces, drainage of excess water, conservation tillage and/or conservation crop rotations which may include grasses and legumes.

Class IV

Soils in Class IV have very severe limitations that restrict the choice of plants, require very careful management, or both. Soils in this class are usually marginal cropland and probably best used as hayland. Small grains can be grown if followed by several years of grasses and legumes.

Class V

Soils in Class V have little or no erosion hazard but have other limitations, impractical to remove, that restrict their use largely to pasture, range, woodland or wildlife food and cover. Soils in this class have water at or on the surface most of the year and are not practical or economical to drain.

Class VI

Soils in Class VI have severe limitations that make them generally unsuited for cultivation and limit their use largely to pasture or range, woodland or wildlife food and cover. Soils in this class may be steep, droughty or shallow to rocky, or they may contain moderate amounts of salts which are toxic to plants or they may be combinations of these factors.

Class VII

Soils in Class VII have very severe limitations that make them unsuited to cultivation and that restrict their use largely to grazing, woodland or wildlife. Soils in this class may be very steep, rocky or extremely droughty, or they may contain an excess amount of soils which are toxic to plants or they may be combinations of these factors.

Class VIII

Soils and landforms in Class VIII have limitations that preclude their use for commercial plant production and restrict their use to recreation, wildlife, water supply or esthetic purposes. Soils and landforms in this class may be extremely rocky, steep or sterile, or they may be combinations of these factors.

Classes Ranked by Cultivability

The foregoing classification divides land according to both productive capability and land-use practices. The classification ranging from cultivation to nonagricultural use is as follows:

Those lands suitable for cultivation with:

    I. No special erosion control or other conservation practices.
    II. Simple conservation practices.
    III. Intensive erosion control practices.

Those lands suitable for limited or occasional cultivation with:

    IV. Limited agricultural use and intensive erosion control practices.

Those lands not suitable for cultivation but which can be used for permanent vegetation with:

    V. No special erosion control practices.
    VI. Moderate restrictions in use.
    VII. Severe restrictions in use.

Those lands not suitable for cultivation, grazing or forestry.

    VIII. These lands may be extremely rough, sandy, wet or arid and not suitable for cultivation, grazing or forestry. Some forms of wildlife may be found on all this land.

Land-Use Capability Subclasses

In order for users of soil survey information to understand the major limitations of the capability classes, these classes are further defined by the addition of a small letter—*e, w, s* or *c*—to the class numeral. (An example is IVe.) The letter *e* shows that the main limitation is risk of erosion unless close-growing plant cover is maintained. The *w* shows that water in or on the soil interferes with plant growth or cultivation (in some soils the wetness can be partly corrected by artificial drainage). The *s* shows that the soil is limited mainly because it is shallow, droughty or stony. And, the *c* shows that the chief limitation is a climate that is too cold or too dry.

Each of the eight classes of land is portrayed in Figures 15-1 through 15-12.

We see from Table 15-1 that the amount of land which can safely be used for crop production without the use of one or more soil erosion control practices is definitely limited. Even these lands will benefit from the use of fertilizers and the rotation of crops.

Chapter 16 deals with some of the most widespread and commonly used practices for the control of erosion.

TABLE 15-5. Distribution of the Classes of Farm Land in the United States (including Alaska and Hawaii), 1982

Class	Million Acres	Approximate Percentage
I	36	2.6
II	291	20.7
III	288	20.4
IV	187	13.3
V	34	2.4
VI	265	18.8
VII & VIII	308	21.8
Total	1,409	100.0

Source: *1982 National Resources Inventory,* Soil Conservation Service, Washington, D.C., 1982.

FIGURE 15-1. Past the storm cellar and tree on the farmstead, Class I land appears to extend to the horizon in this central Illinois farm scene. Hedges which formerly stood between fields have been removed. Many of the fields are tiled to assist drainage. Class I land must be level to nearly level and drained well enough, either naturally or artificially, to permit the growing of ordinary crops. It must not show more than the slightest erosion, regardless of treatment. (Photo by Harry B. Kircher)

FIGURE 15-2. Class II land is suitable for continuous cultivation with the use of simple practices to control erosion, conserve water, drain wet soils, supply irrigation water, remove stones or other obstacles to cultivation or add to soil productivity. Erosion control or moisture conservation practices commonly used are contour tillage, strip cropping, cover crops, rough tillage, basin listing and surface mulch. Occasionally terracing is recommended. This land ordinarily has a slight slope. (Courtesy, Soil Conservation Service)

FIGURE 15-3. Class III land usually needs a combination of practices for safe and continuous cultivation. Frequently this land requires more careful application or more intensive use of the practices recommended for Class II land: longer crop rotations, narrower strips for strip cropping, terrace outlets with terraces, buffer strips, diversion ditches and cover crops. Needed drainage or irrigation systems may be more difficult to install, or the land may be droughty or the slope of the land may be slightly greater than for Class II land. (Courtesy, Soil Conservation Service)

FIGURE 15-4. Another example of Class III land.

FIGURE 15-5. Class IV land usually is steeper than Class III land. Or, it may be more eroded or susceptible to erosion, less fertile, more droughty, more open or more difficult to drain or to irrigate. Nearly level land of low productivity that is so wet in late spring that crop yields are reduced may be regarded as Class IV land. (Courtesy, Soil Conservation Service)

FIGURE 15-6. An example of Class IV land that is too wet for best production. This wetland has been pastured over the years, and the hummocky condition is mostly the result of tramping by the grazing livestock. (Courtesy, Soil Conservation Service)

FIGURE 15-7. Class V land is fairly level and not subject to erosion. It is suitable only for grazing land or for woodland because of wetness, dryness or stoniness. The only restrictions on its use are not to overgraze or to deforest the area completely so as to reduce grass or tree growth. This land is frequently recommended for wildlife. (Courtesy, Soil Conservation Service)

FIGURE 15-8. Another example of Class V land.

FIGURE 15-9. Class VI land includes steep, stony, sandy or shallow soils. It is usually steeper or more subject to water or wind erosion than is Class IV land. It is best suited for pasture, woodland or wildlife. Pasture areas which are free from stones may be renovated to increase grass growth. (Courtesy, Soil Conservation Service)

FIGURE 15-10. Class VII land is usually very steep, rough, stony, eroded or sandy. It usually produces some wood or forage. Where the land is not so steep or rough, it may still be classed as VII land if there is scant natural vegetation and if the soil is easily subject to wind erosion. It is best suited for woodland or wildlife. (Courtesy, Soil Conservation Service)

FIGURE 15-11. Another example of Class VII land.

FIGURE 15-12. Class VIII land may be rough, stony or barren, or it may be a swamp or marsh land that cannot be used in any way for the production of forest products or grass. Some forms of wildlife may find food and shelter here. (Courtesy, Soil Conservation Service)

QUESTIONS AND PROBLEMS

1. How many acres of farm land are being lost each year through soil erosion?

2. What three conditions must be met if we are to continue to use our croplands for food production?

3. Name some of the soil conserving practices that individual farmers can put into effect. What are some practices that must be used through groups of farmers acting together or by local units of government in order to reduce soil erosion?

4. Why has the Soil Conservation Service grouped the soils of farms into different soil classes? Give the characteristics of each soil class and tell what the land in each class is best suited for. When it is desirable to use one or more soil conserving practices for a soil class, name the practice or practices which are usually recommended.

5. What percent of our farm land can safely be used with no supporting soil conserving practices?

6. What classes of land are most common on the farm lands near your home? What soil conserving practices are being used for these classes?

16

The Use of
Vegetative Cover
in Soil Conservation

Probably the simplest way of controlling erosion is to maintain cover with some plant growth. This includes the use of native or adapted grasses, close-growing biennial or perennial crops, shrubs or a mixture of grasses, shrubs and trees. Where this vegetative cover is to be used in connection with farming operations, the crops must be close-growing, and the crop residues should be left as cover for most of the year; otherwise, they will not protect the soil from eroding.

BENEFICIAL EFFECTS OF VEGETATIVE COVER

A healthy vegetative cover reduces soil losses in three ways. These are:

1. Heavy plant growth intercepts falling rain and reduces the impact on the surface of the soil. If a person were to stand under a leafy tree during the early part of a rain, he/she would find that the rain would not come through the foliage. If the rain continued, that person would be wet by small droplets of water as they dripped

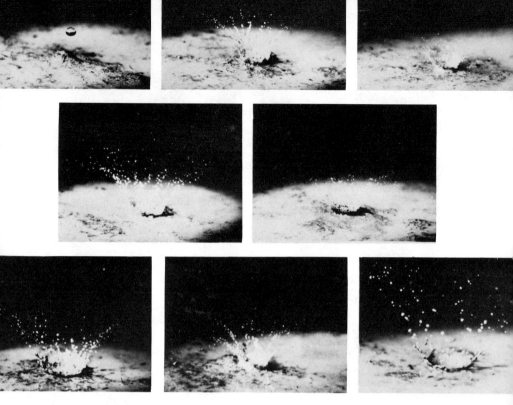

FIGURE 16-1. Rain falling on the land is ordinarily beneficial. It is harmful, however, if it falls on bare soil as this drop does. Every direct splash on bare soil dissolves in the rain drop some of the finer parts of the soil and carries them away with the water run-off. If there had been some grass growth or other surface cover, the force of the falling rain drop would have been broken and the finer parts of the soil would not have been detached in the splash of rain. (Courtesy, Soil Conservation Service)

or flowed from leaves and twigs. The heavy force of the rain would not reach him/her. This is similar to the effect upon soil of any covering, whether it be growing or dead grass, weeds or shrubs.

When rain drops strike bare soil, some of the finer particles of the soil are loosened and suspended in drops (see Figure 16-1). This is the first step in soil erosion.

2. The speed of water run-off from the surface is reduced. The fallen leaves, stems and litter on the surface slow down the rate at which the water runs off. This reduced speed carries less of the soil with it. It also allows more time for the soil to absorb a greater portion of the rainfall.

3. The growth and the decay of plant roots make the soil more porous. Thus, it absorbs more of the rainfall in a shorter time. The decaying roots also add some organic matter to the soil. Organic matter readily absorbs water.

Farmyard manure, when spread over the soil, helps to break the flow of water as well as any plant residue does and later, when turned under, opens up the soil and adds a little organic matter.

ANNUAL CROPS ONLY PARTIALLY EFFECTIVE COVER

All growing crops provide some vegetative cover to the soil. Any type of cover is more or less effective in conserving soil. The more completely the soil is covered, the better it is protected from eroding. One of the problems in connection with most cultivated crops is the length of time the soil is left unprotected by any crop growth. Crops such as corn, soybeans, potatoes, cotton, spring wheat, oats, barley and even our truck crops are planted in the late spring and harvested from three to six months later.

In preparing land for most cultivated crops, the farmer prepares the soil for planting by plowing, followed by other tillage practices, leaving the soil bare prior to planting. It remains essentially unprotected for two to four weeks after planting because the young plants offer very little ground cover. From the time the soil is plowed and until the planted crop provides good ground cover, the soil is subject to severe erosion. After the crop has matured and has been harvested, the crop residues protect the soil if they are not plowed under. However, in many parts of the country, the remaining crop residues are plowed under. This leaves the soil bare from six to nine months of the year, so that there is little surface growth or litter to break the force of the rainfall or to decrease the water run-off during that time.

HAY CROPS OFFER BETTER SOIL PROTECTION

Biennial or perennial hay crops give much better protection to the soil from erosion (see Figure 16-2). This growth offers the much-needed surface protection during times of heavy rainfall. And, it offers protection even though the plants are not growing. Seed bed preparation and planting takes place with these crops less frequently than with crops planted each year.

FIGURE 16-2. (Upper) Plant cover can stop erosion on hillsides. This is a two-year-old stand of crown vetch seeded on cut slopes of a highway in Illinois. Seed and mulch were applied by blower. Fertilizer was applied later. (Lower) A close-up taken at an Indiana nursery, showing the solid cover of this plant. (Courtesy, Soil Conservation Service)

Thus, the hazards of washing rains coming while the soil is open and exposed are reduced.

SPECIAL CONSIDERATIONS IN USING VEGETATIVE COVER

Although the use of vegetative cover is one of the easiest methods of controlling erosion, it may be very ineffective unless it fits the specific conditions that make it suitable. There are many kinds and combinations of crops and other vegetation that may be employed to help control erosion. One type of cover may succeed where another will fail. This means that each crop or type of vegetation will do best in reducing erosion if used in the right situation. Also, some methods of erosion control by plant cover apply to several sections of the country, while others are useful in one part of the country but are of no value in other parts. The best erosion control procedure in every area and on practically every farm is most often based on the use of a combination of practices. Ordinarily, no one practice alone will control erosion while the field is used for crop production. The kind of vegetative cover to employ and the best way to use this cover can be determined only after the following conditions have been considered.

1. The part of the country in which the crop is to be used. The length of growing season, the average as well as extreme temperatures, the prevailing winds and the season and severity of the heavy rains all must be considered.
2. The kind of soil—whether it is sandy or clayey, well or poorly drained, etc.
3. The physical condition of the soil. Is it fertile, or is it depleted of plant nutrients, organic matter and lime?
4. The steepness and length of the slope of the land.
5. The likelihood of the farmer's using the crops grown. These crops should be used to advantage, fitting into the farmer's system of farming.
6. Adaptability of the crop to local conditions.

The use of vegetative cover as a part of farming includes the following practices: grazing land improvement, cover crops, strip cropping, conservation crop rotations, contour tillage, gully erosion and stream bank erosion

FIGURE 16-3. The absence of vegetation started this gully which made the pasture lot an ideal place for weed growth. (Courtesy, Soil Conservation Service)

control, terraces, diversions and waterways and windbreaks. These practices will be considered in more detail in Chapters 17 and 18 (see Figures 16-3 and 16-5).

PASTURE AND RANGE LAND IMPROVEMENT

Any improvement in the grass growth on our pasture lands will serve two purposes. It will increase the ground cover, thus reducing the surface run-off, and it will increase the amount of water absorbed by the soil. When these are accomplished, there will be better grazing for livestock. Of course, when the heavier growth of grass is obtained, owners should use caution not to increase the livestock numbers enough to overgraze the lands. Overgrazing will destroy the vegetative cover, leaving the surface subject to erosion.

Grazing Lands Owned by the Federal Government

Extensive areas of grazing lands are owned by the federal government.

The policy of the government is to lease various areas to individual cattle or sheep owners. Restrictions on grazing these areas are intended to prevent overgrazing. As a result, not only is the value of the land maintained for grazing purposes, but also the soil is not subject to erosion, which in many instances causes losses that cannot be repaired.

FIGURE 16-4. Grazing on this federally owned land has not been controlled, and excessive grazing has killed off the desirable forage grasses. Unpalatable sagebrush has taken over. Unless the management of this land is changed, severe erosion will occur. (Courtesy, Bureau of Land Management)

Only the U.S. government has the power to restrict grazing in these areas (see Figure 16-4). The government leases grazing rights to individuals through local organized grazing associations. Part of the fée charges is returned to the local governments to support schools, roads and other governmental concerns. The remainder of the fee helps maintain and improve the quality of the grazing lands. The federal government limits the number of sheep or cattle for each range. It also supervises the grazing to prevent damage to the land from early grazing or overgrazing in local plots.

The management of federal lands used for grazing has been heavily criticized. The 1986 federal grazing fees are called a "subsidy of destruction" by The Wilderness Society. That society and eight other conservation groups sued Secretary of the Interior Donald Hodel in May 1986 for failing to comply with a number of federal laws. The Department of the Interior set grazing fees about one-fifth the rate paid for grazing on comparable private lands. The returns would cover only about one-third of the costs government must pay to manage the program. Data on more than 118 million acres of federal grazing land gathered over a period of seven years reveal that 84 millions acres—or 71 percent—are in unsatisfactory condition. Besides, the American Fisheries Society has estimated that livestock damage has reduced sport fish production by half on some 60 to 90 percent of 68,600 miles of streams in western national forests.[1]

Production Increased from Pasture Lands

There are several ways in which the growth on pasture and grazing land can be increased. They are delayed, rotational and controlled grazing, the application of fertilizers, and the use of different grasses or combinations of grasses which will make for a thriftier and more continuous cover.

FIGURE 16-5. Work Unit Conservationist, John Conroy, and farm operator, Gene Miller, and his daughter, Marilyn, are standing on the edge of a beautifully maintained grassed waterway as they discuss the corn crop on this southern Illinois farm. This is the principal waterway for drainage on this farm. The corn is planted on the contour. (Courtesy, Soil Conservation Service)

[1]"Wilderness Watch," *Wilderness*, Washington, D.C., The Wilderness Society, Summer 1986, p. 2.

Delayed Grazing

Most of our grazing land, as well as our farm pastures, is overgrazed. Livestock frequently are turned out so early in the spring that the grass cannot maintain sufficient root reserves to provide a vigorous growth. When livestock are turned out this early, they usually are kept on pasture continually from this time on, and the grass is grazed too closely. The results are that the total growth for the season is not as much as it should be and the individual grass plants become less able to make quick recovery growth when rains come.

Often, in addition to early grazing, too many cattle are placed on an area, and it soon becomes overgrazed. If the grazing lands of the Great Plains area are to be protected from overgrazing, the number of cattle or sheep that are placed on any range must be limited. When the land is under private ownership, the owner will benefit by placing only the number of livestock on the range that it will support throughout the growing season. The grass also should have a good spring growth before any grazing is permitted.

Rotation of Pasture Lands

Experiments have shown that a greater amount of good grazing can be obtained if a pasture or range is divided into several fields and one field pastured at a time. Each field is numbered and pastured in turn. Every field is pastured once in four to six weeks. The length of time the herd or flock is left on a field is determined by the amount of grass growth and the number of animals pastured. The animals should be moved from a field before it is completely eaten off, and each field should have a good growth of grass before the animals are turned into it. Of course, there should be water and salt available in each field if this arrangement is to work out satisfactorily.

While it is possible for a farmer to divide a pasture into 3 or 4 fields with the use of electric fences, it is not so easy to divide 100,000 acres of grazing land; but where rotation is possible, livestock will come off the grass in better condition, and in case of summer drought, selling cattle or sheep to reduce starvation losses will not be necessary. Even on the open range, herds or flocks can be moved from place to place. Grazing pressures can be reduced or transferred from area to area by providing widely spaced watering facilities and predetermined spacing of salt blocks.

FIGURE 16-6. Well-managed grazing land of the Southwest. Grazing on this land has been regulated according to the grass growth and the season. Water run-off has been checked through simple earthen structures. The result is a fine growth of desirable grasses with practically no sagebrush. (Courtesy, Bureau of Land Management)

Another benefit of rotation of pasture lands is a better permanent stand of grass with fewer weeds and good erosion protection (see Figure 16-6). As discussed earlier, the grazing lands of the nation showed little or no erosion damage until they were grazed too heavily and practically all grass growth was eaten off. The remedy for this situation on those areas which are not too badly eroded is to keep some grass growth on the land all year. This is especially true during the growing season when heavy rains occur. If a good growth of grass is left at the end of the growing season, there will be some cover of dead grass to protect the soil throughout the remainder of the year.

Management of Farm Pasture Lands

Pasture lands on farms are frequently as badly overgrazed and poorly managed as range lands. They are pastured too early in the spring and are overstocked later in the year when grasses are short and the weather is hot and dry.

It is much easier to improve most farm pastures than range lands. Most of our pasture land is in areas having enough rainfall to mature commonly grown farm crops, while most of our range land has an erratic rainfall distribution, with annual rates of less than 20 inches. This means that rainfall is usually not the important factor limiting the establishment and growth of grass in pastures.

Pasture lands are much smaller than range lands. A pasture field on a farm may be 10 to 40 acres and at most will not exceed a very few hundred acres. A section (640 acres) of pasture land is an exceptionally large field. Range land, on the other hand, ordinarily consists of thousands of acres. To manage range land may mean to look after 100,000 acres or more of land under adverse conditions.

Application of Fertilizers

Permanent pasture lands over much of the country have been pastured ever since the farms were homesteaded. In most instances, thousands of pounds of livestock growth have been taken from these lands and nothing in the form of fertilizers (plant nutrients) has been returned. The result is that most pastures produce less feed than they originally produced.

The carrying capacity of pastures may be greatly increased if the land is properly fertilized and limed. Frequently, it is necessary to re-establish a pasture in order to work calcium, nitrogen, phosphorus and potash again into the soil to replace what has been drawn out by the growing grass over the years. Where pastures have been limed, fertilized and reseeded to adaptable grasses, the carrying capacity may be doubled and in some instances tripled, when measured by the number of livestock that can be pastured satisfactorily.

Use of Different Grasses or Combinations

We usually think that our native grasses are the ones best adapted, not only to survive under local climatic conditions but also to produce the largest amount of feed while adequately protecting the soil. We find, however, that many new varieties of grasses have been introduced and many of the local strains have been improved to the point where they not only greatly outyield native grasses but also survive climatic conditions just as well.

We also find that combinations of legumes and non-legume grasses many times outyield the pure seedings, as well as protect the soil against erosion (see Figure 16-7). Here again, the best combination of grasses for an area should be obtained from the local agricultural authority. New combinations of grasses are constantly being brought out that are proving more satisfactory than previously recommended mixtures.

FIGURE 16-7. A close-up of an alfalfa-brome-ladino growth in a meadow. Where the soil is covered with a growth like this, no rain will damage it. (Courtesy, Soil Conservation Service)

COVER CROPS

Growing some crops on the land when the regular crops have been removed may reduce soil erosion impacts. When these crops are grown primarily to keep the soil from being exposed to wind and rain during the off-crop season, they are called **cover crops.** It is sometimes difficult to distinguish between green-manure crops and cover crops because all green-manure crops serve the purpose of cover crops during the time they are growing and before they are turned under. The real reason for growing green-manure crops is to conserve fertility and to improve the soil condition.

Cover crops, on the other hand, are grown primarily to hold the soil against erosion. They also will improve the condition of the soil, as well as hold the nitrogen which might otherwise be leached from the soil.

Many crops may be used for cover crops, and many times the regularly grown cereal crops are used for this purpose. The usual crops grown only to protect soils, however, are not those grown in the regular cropping system.

Fewer cover crops are grown in the northern part of the United States than in the southern part because the ground is frozen and there is less erosion in the winter. In the Great Plains, protection against wind erosion is most effective when the crops are seeded on the contour and across the prevailing winds, especially if there is any significant slope.

Limitations to the Use of Cover Crops

Probably the time of year when most soils need protection against erosion is during the winter months. In some parts of the country, however, where regular crop production is limited by the yearly rainfall, it may be more desirable to conserve all moisture for the regular crops and depend upon other practices for reducing erosion instead of planting cover crops. Cover crops should not be attempted when the late fall and winter months are so cold or snowy that little growth is made by the crops.

Conservation Tillage Comes of Age

Conservation tillage is a term now being used for tillage practices which involve the least disturbance of the soil and provide plant residues on the surface of the soil. This conservation practice was initially limited to chisel plowing. This resulted in a rough surface with a larger percentage of crop residue remaining on the surface than in conventional plowing. The next development was using a disc to incorporate a small amount of crop residue, a pre-emergence chemical spray for weed control and little or no additional cultivation. Then, a development now being accepted and used extensively was zero-till, commonly referred to as "no-till" crop production. This method involved neither plowing nor discing. And, it calls for intensive use of pesticides for both weed and insect control. One phase of no-till being studied is limited use of pesticides in the crop production process. The differences between the conventional zero-till and limited chemical control methods

FIGURE 16-8. (Upper) A deep-working chisel plow with wide and deep trash tunnels is well suited to primary tillage operations. The trash (pieces of corn stalk, etc.) left on the surface acts as a wind breaker to help prevent wind erosion of the soil. (Lower) This machine, called a conservation planter, can spread insecticides and fertilizer and sow the seeds in the field. The discs cut a furrow into which seeds are drilled, leaving the surface relatively undisturbed. (Courtesy, Deere and Company)

are: (1) the conventional method kills all vegetation prior to planting and (2) limited chemical control does not kill the vegetation but stunts its growth.

Chisel plowing. — Fields are chisel plowed after grain crops are harvested. The chisel plow consists of tines (prongs) which can penetrate about 14 inches into the soil. The tines are spread about 15 inches apart (see Figures 16-8, 16-9 and 16-10). When pulled by a tractor, the chisel plow shatters or fractures the soil. This improves water intake, yet leaves crop residue on the surface. This tillage practice helps reduce erosion by wind and water.

FIGURE 16-9. The benefits of conservation tillage are available to small-scale farming operations with the John Deere 710 mulch tiller. Tractors having 60 to 120 horsepower can operate the 710, in contrast to previous conservation tillage equipment which required substantially larger tractors.

Similar to the John Deere 712 mulch tiller introduced some years ago, the 710 consists of a row of disk or coulter blades followed by chisel plow shanks. It may be equipped with 20-inch spherical disk blades of 20-inch coulter blades. Disks provide maximum incorporation of residue. Coulters should be used in heavy residue, which requires maximum cutting and slicing action.

The chisel plow shanks are arranged in two ranks. They may be equipped with 3-inch (standard) or 4-inch (optional) shovels to stir the soil and incorporate some of the residue. Both coulters and chisel plows are mounted on spring-loaded frames to permit operation in rocky soil conditions. (Courtesy, Deere and Company)

FIGURE 16-10. An attachment for non-folding John Deere Max-Emerge planters makes the advantages of ridge-tillage available for a minimal machinery investment. The attachment permits growers to convert existing planters for ridge-tilling planting instead of having to purchase new ridge-till planters.

Mounted between the tractor and the Max-Emerge planter, the attachment tracks the previous crop's ridge, slices off the top of the ridge and leaves a 14-inch wide seed bed for the Max-Emerge units to plant into. The new 720 ridge-till attachment achieves this with stabilizing gauge wheels and center coulters which slice through residue on top of the ridges and stabilize the attachment and planter on the ridges. Horizontal rotating disks clear residue from the tops of the ridges, and deflectors push residue and excess soil into the furrows between the ridges. (Courtesy, Deere and Company)

No-till (or zero-till). — In many areas of our nation, because of soil and/or slope conditions, chisel plowing is not adequate to prevent excessive soil losses. Therefore, no-till is used. The present method is to kill all vegetation present with pesticides. When the vegetation is dead, using a drilling technique, the farmer plants the crop (see Figure 16-8). Sometimes, because of weather conditions, a post-emergence spray is needed. The decaying vegetative cover on the surface of the soil reduces soil loss to a minimum. This practice is so different from the conventional way of planting that farmers should consult their agricultural extension service specialist or soil conservationist before implementing it.

Several agricultural research stations are producing corn using a smaller amount of pesticide than usual for no-till planting. A sub-lethal dose of pesticide is applied to stunt the vegetative growth. Thus, the grasses continue to live but are surpressed by the shading of the corn plant. This cover provides a continuous living sod for protection against soil loss. This method is still in the experimental stage.

Crops Used as Cover Crops

Winter rye is the principal cover crop used in the upper Midwest, while the New England area may use hairy vetch along with winter rye. In the southern Appalachian area, crimson clover, vetch, bur clover, Austrian winter peas and red clover, either alone or in various mixtures, are commonly grown to provide winter protection.

On the Atlantic and Gulf coastal plains, Austrian winter peas, hairy vetch, crimson clover, blue lupine and bur clover are the legumes used, while in the upper Great Plains, red clover, alfalfa, biennial sweet clover and legume-grass mixtures constitute the principal winter covers. Rye grass has been used as winter cover in parts of Oklahoma and Texas. In the southern part of the Great Plains, winter grains are the most effective winter cover crops.

The Pacific coastal areas use wild oats, bur clover, alfalfa, vetches, sour clover and mustard for soil protection. It is possible to add many legumes, grasses and cereals to the crops already listed as cover crops. However, the choice of a cover crop depends upon the cost of the crop and the use to which it may be put, as well as the local climatic and soil conditions. The best information regarding the local use of cover crops can be obtained from an agriculture teacher, a soil conservation specialist or a county agricultural agent.

It must be remembered that any growth on the soil affords better protection from erosion than no growth. Ordinarily, the finer the growth and the longer it grows during the year, the better it protects. Any surface cover or crop residue, whether dead or growing, helps to slow down surface run-off and water absorption by the soil.

QUESTIONS AND PROBLEMS

1. In what ways does the growth of grasses or shrubs help reduce soil erosion?
2. What are the disadvantages of using crops such as small grains, cotton, corn or potatoes as soil conserving crops?

3. Why are perennial hay crops better for keeping soil from washing away than annual crops such as those mentioned in question 2?

4. What are some of the points to keep in mind in using vegetative cover to control erosion?

5. Name two soil conservation benefits to be derived from improved pastures.

6. What are the ways that growth on pasture lands can be increased?

7. In what ways are government grazing lands managed to maintain good cover and forage?

8. Why is it easier to improve pasture lands on farms than to improve large grazing areas?

9. Is it more important to use fertilizers for improving farm pastures or to sow other grasses than those which grow naturally? Explain your answer.

10. What are cover crops, and how can they be used to reduce erosion? What are the limitations to using cover crops? What crops are commonly used in your part of the country for cover crops?

11. What kinds of vegetative cover are being used in your part of the state to keep the soil from washing away?

17

Strip Cropping, Contouring and Terracing in Soil Conservation

The damage potential of water rushing down a slope is so great that much of the soil conservation work in the United States, and throughout the world, is done to prevent or at least to hold such damage to a minimum. Such erosion can be reduced by shortening the length of the slope or reducing the velocity (speed) of the water as it flows downhill. Or, it can be a combination of the two. Common methods of accomplishing this are strip cropping, contouring and terracing.

EFFECT OF WATER SPEED

We know that water increases in speed and in its capacity to move and carry away soil as it flows down a slope. A steep slope will lose more soil than a gentle slope of equal length, even though the amount of water run-off is but very little greater (see Table 17-1). This is because the speed of the water is greater than it is on the gentler slope. Practically every long slope loses soil because more water flows off and the velocity of the water run-off increases with the length of the slope.

The effect of increased speed of water run-off and its ability to wash and carry away soil can be very damaging to our soil resource. When water flows at the rate of over 2 feet per second, it can loosen and carry away some topsoil from fields containing no green cover or litter.

Assuming that the speed of water flowing down a slope increases from 2 feet per second at about 50 feet from the top of the slope to 4 feet per second at 100 feet farther down, what effect will this increase in speed have upon the ability of the run-off to do damage to the slope? (Four feet per second is only about 2.7 miles per hour, or the speed of a horse walking slowly. We can walk at that rate and call it a leisurely pace.)

TABLE 17-1. Soil Losses from One Soil Type but with Different Slopes, Five-Year Average[1]

Slope	Water Run-off per Acre	Soil Loss per Acre
(%)	(inches)	(tons)
3	14	5.1
8	14	10.8
13	16	22.6
18	20	28.6

[1]The above figures were obtained from the Upper Mississippi Valley Soil Conservation Experiment Station at LaCross, Wisconsin. The plots were 72.6 feet long. The amount of water run-off was not greatly influenced by slope until the 18 percent slope was reached. The velocity with which the water ran from the plots was greatly increased with steeper slope, however, and this increased speed of water flow accounts for the greater soil losses.

The first point to consider is that as the speed of the water flow is doubled, its ability to cut, or to tear away, soil is increased four times. In other words, we should expect to see four times as much damage done to the soil when the speed of the run-off is doubled. The capacity of the water for carrying away soil is even greater than its cutting ability would suggest. It can carry around 30 times as much soil as it could with half the speed. It is because of these relationships that the velocity of water run-off should be as slow as possible.

The volume or total quantity of water run-off from a given area of land also affects the amount of erosion. If the quantity of water run-off is doubled without increasing its velocity, the rate of erosion as well as the amount of soil carried in the run-off will also be doubled. This means that the volume of water run-off may be greatly increased without doing much damage if the speed is kept low. An increase in the velocity of water run-off is much more damaging to the soil than an increase in the quantity of run-off.

CROPS DIFFER IN SLOWING DOWN WATER RUN-OFF

Some crops are very effective in slowing down water run-off, while others reduce the rate very little. Corn, soybeans, potatoes, tobacco, cotton and many of the truck crops, which are planted in rows far enough apart to permit cultivating or working between them, do very little to retard the flow of water (see Table 17-2). Small grains are considerably more effective in slowing down the rate of water run-off during the three to six months the crops are on the land. During the remainder of the year, they offer little resistance to water erosion. Even so, farmers should expect only about one-seventh as much loss of soil from fields which are continuously in grain as from ones on which corn is grown continuously.

TABLE 17-2. Soil Losses from Different Cropping Practices, Seven-Year Average[1]

	Soil Lost Yearly	
Crops Grown	Tons per Acre	Inches of Soil
Fallow	162	1.12
Corn, every year	112	0.77
Grain, every year..................	16	0.10
Bluegrass, every year	0	0.00
Corn, 3-year rotation	53	0.37
Grain, 3-year rotation	30	0.21
Hay, 3-year rotation	1	0.007
Average, 3-year rotation	28	0.30

[1]The above figures were obtained from the Upper Mississippi Valley Soil Conservation Experiment Station at LaCross, Wisconsin. They show that for this soil it requires less than one year to lose one inch of surface soil under continuous fallow land, while it takes 1⅓ years to lose one inch of surface soil from a field which grows corn continuously. It can be seen that conditions which cause a large loss of soil under continuous cropping of corn will cause only one-seventh as much loss under continuous cropping of small grain. No doubt other soils, when growing similar crops, will vary from these figures, but the general relationship of losses should hold true for most soils.

FIGURE 17-1. An airplane view of strip-cropped fields in western Wisconsin. Each alternate strip should be in grass in order to retard soil losses from the strip above. (Courtesy, Soil Conservation Service)

The biennial or perennial hay or grass crops, on the other hand, show little or no loss of soil over a series of years. They furnish some surface cover to retard water run-off during the whole year, and because of this, they are exceedingly useful in any program which depends upon vegetative cover to control erosion.

STRIP CROPPING

Strip cropping is a system of growing common farm crops in which the crops are planted in strips across the slope of a field. Effective strip cropping usually requires that every other strip on the slope be a hay or grass strip (see Figure 17-1). The water run-off from the corn or grain strip tends to collect from the smaller rivulets into larger streams as it flows down the slope. The hay or grass strip will slow down and spread the water as it comes from the grain or corn strip above, and, as the water slows down, it will drop a part of the silt it has picked up from the strip above.

Shorter Slopes

Strip cropping maintains a vigorous grass and legume cover on at least one-half of the field. The strips, to be effective, must always be worked and planted at right angles to the slope or on the level across the slope.

Value of Strip Cropping

About 22.6 million acres of farm land have been strip cropped, and this fact in itself shows the importance attached to this practice by farmers. Strip cropping reduces soil losses by slowing down water run-off. It also results in a reduction in run-off and in an increase in the amount of water absorbed into the soil. These two benefits are enough to justify the practice, because without them crop yields would decrease. Not only may production be maintained but also, in some instances, it may actually be increased as a result of strip cropping a field.

FIGURE 17-2. These strips of rye are planted to protect against wind erosion on muck soil. Strips are planted at right angles to the direction of the prevailing winds. (Courtesy, Soil Conservation Service)

Width of Strips

The width of strips is influenced by many factors, and no one width can be considered best for all conditions. The length of the slope, steepness of the slope, type of soil, degree of erosion, length of rotation, amount and intensity of individual rainstorms and type of cultivation all help to determine the necessary width of strips. Other factors being equal, the wider the strips, the greater the soil losses.

Theoretically, the strips should be quite narrow so that the flow of water across the strip of a grain or corn crop will gain very little speed and will pick up very little silt before it is slowed down by the hay or grass strip. It is not practical, however, to make strips too narrow. They should be wide enough to be easily worked with ordinary tillage and harvesting machinery. This is the reason that the smallest practical width is frequently set at 40 or 50 feet. On the other hand, strips for peanut growing are frequently as narrow as 12 feet.

The greatest width should be set by the largest amount of soil the field can lose and still maintain satisfactory yields. Field practice throughout much of the Midwest suggests 6 rods or 100 feet as a reasonable maximum width. Some conditions are found where it is safe to make strips 150 or 160 feet wide. This is usually on nearly level land or on soil types which absorb water quite readily.

In much of the Great Plains area where dry farming is practical, the strips may be as much as 300 or 320 feet wide. These widths are suggested for the control of wind erosion. In areas where both water and wind erosion are prevalent, the greatest width of strip should not exceed the safe limit for either type of control when used alone.

In any case, it is assumed that when definite maximum widths are set, it is a compromise between some soil loss and the more efficient use of machinery and labor.

Kinds of Strip Cropping

There are several kinds of strip cropping. The differences are based upon the purpose for which the strip is laid out, as well as the character of the strip itself. The four general types of strip cropping are (1) field strip cropping, (2) wind strip cropping, (3) contour strip cropping and (4) buffer strips.

1. ***Field strip cropping*** refers to strips of crops which are parallel across the field. They need not necessarily remain on the exact level, or contour, because if contours were followed across a field with uneven slopes, the two sides of the contours could not remain parallel. The most frequent use of field strip cropping is on long, smooth, gentle slopes where water run-off is not gathered into a few streams as it moves down the slopes. This method is used throughout the Great Plains area.

2. ***Wind strip cropping*** is used wherever the land is fairly level and the soil is subject to wind erosion. These strips are usually parallel across a field. They are laid out at right angles to the direction of the prevailing winds and do not necessarily follow contours (see Figure 17-2).

3. ***Contour strip cropping*** is the most commonly used form of strip cropping because of its importance in controlling water erosion. These strips are laid out at right angles to the natural slope of the land, or on the contour (see Figure 17-3). When the slope is more than 5 or 6 percent but not greater than 12 percent, strip cropping is frequently used with terracing, which will be discussed later. Although these strips are used mostly for the control of water erosion, they may be used effectively on sloping land where wind erosion also may be serious.

4. ***Buffer strips*** are strips of a more nearly permanent nature. They may be wide or narrow, long or short, and they may vary in width from one end to the other. A small part of one field may be badly eroded, or it may be a very steep, short slope. In either instance, the piece should be plowed only occasionally, if at all. In this situation buffer strips of grass, legumes or shrubs may be put in and left for several years. Buffers are also used in small irregular areas, odd corners and small triangular pieces which are inconvenient to work with ordinary field implements or which have special erosion problems.

   Buffer strips may be used to break up long slopes or to give protection from erosion when a field is planted to a single crop, such as grain or some intertilled crop. In this type of circumstance, the buffer strips may effectively replace the grass or hay strips. When used in this way, the buffer strips should be as wide as the grass strips for which they are substituted.

FIGURE 17-3. The fields on this 270-acre Illinois dairy farm, located in Stephenson County, are contour strip cropped to better accommodate slopes of from 3 to 14 percent. Crop rotation will help further and will accommodate the characteristics of the eight silt loam soils found on the farm. (Courtesy, Soil Conservation Service)

When used on the contour, the buffer strips facilitate contour field operations. They are sometimes used to prevent wind erosion. They may well be called field strips when used in these ways, unless they are not grazed or harvested and are there for more than one year.

Strip cropping is a valuable method of soil conservation when conditions are adapted to its use, and its widespread usage in recent years is witness to the acceptance of this practice.

CONTOURING

Contour tillage is the practice of performing all field operations on the

FIGURE 17-4. Contour tillage has some of the advantages of strip cropping in that all tillage operations are performed on the level. Water from small showers and light rains is more readily held in place to be absorbed by the soil. Most erosion comes from the less frequent, heavier rains, as contour tillage does little to retard losses in these situations. (Courtesy, Soil Conservation Service)

FIGURE 17-5. A field of soybeans planted on the contour. Rains will not cause serious erosion of this field. (Courtesy, Soil Conservation Service)

contour, or level. Plowing, planting and other tillage operations are at right angles to the slope of the land (see Figure 17-4). This is not strip cropping because the whole field may be used for one crop, such as cotton, corn or grain (see Figure 17-5). This method of controlling erosion is recommended when soil erosion is not severe enough that other practices need to be used.

TERRACING

Terraces have been used for centuries by different people to help control erosion and to make it easier to cultivate sloping land. It is believed that terracing for rice fields in the Philippines was begun 2,000 years ago and that the Incas in Peru terraced their steep hillsides more than 4,000 years ago. Stone terraces built in France and in Phoenicia of Biblical times are still effective in controlling erosion on steep slopes after hundreds and even thousands of years of use.

What Are Terraces?

When properly installed and maintained, terraces are a positive conservation practice which will reduce soil erosion. The practice of terracing in this country grew out of the practice of contour farming and was started along our eastern seaboard at about the time of the Revolutionary War. A terrace was originally defined as a raised, level stretch of earth which is kept in place on a hillside by a wall or a bank turf. Terraces were made so that the steep hillsides could be cultivated. Terracing is now done not only to hold the land in place on a slope but also to cause rainfall to run off a field slowly or to hold it on the field until it is absorbed into the soil. The main feature of most terraces built today is a channel or a ditch to carry or hold water.

The original idea that a terrace was for the purpose of protecting some leveled out piece of land from washing away does not completely describe all terraces now. Many kinds of terraces are recognized today. A channel with a ridge on the lower side, a channel with no ridge and a lister furrow may be classed as terraces. The important function of a terrace is to reduce the length of slope and to reduce the volume and speed of any water run-off by intercepting it and carrying it across the slope of land, rather than letting it run down the slope as in the case of strip cropping, contour tillage or grass cover. Or, it may be for the purpose of holding rainfall rather than carrying it slowly off the field.

Why Should Terraces Be Used?

Terraces reduce soil losses. Studies covering a 14-year period at the Upper Mississippi Valley Soil Conservation Experiment Station at LaCrosse, Wisconsin, show that there was only one-sixth as much loss of soil from the experimental terraced areas as from the unterraced ones. There were 11 heavy rainstorms during this 14-year period, which accounted for 60 percent of the soil loss on the unterraced fields. Terraces controlled most of the erosion, even during these critical storms. In these experiments, both the terraced and the unterraced areas were treated the same.

Terraces increase crop yields (see Figure 17-6). If soil is saved and there is less water run-off from terraced areas, it is reasonable to expect some increase in crop yields over the years. Experiments show this to be true. Where longer rotations were used in tests and fertilizers were applied to both the terraced and the unterraced fields, crop yields were 7 percent greater on the terraced than on the unterraced fields.

Terraces allow a more flexible cropping system. The entire field can be used for one or many crops, depending on the yearly desires of the operator. Strip cropping, in contrast, must have alternate strips of some grass or hay crop to be effective. Most present terraces are so constructed that farm machinery can be used on them. Even drills, combines and corn pickers ordinarily are able to pass over the terraces without dragging or cutting into the ridges. The ridges are not so high or narrow or the channel sides so steep that it is hard to drive over them. Water channels ordinarily should be from 15 to 25 feet across from the top of the ridge to the farther edge of the channel. The depth of a channel usually does not exceed 10 inches, although some channels with ridges are 12 inches deep.

Types of Terraces

Most terraces can be classed as one of four types: (1) bench terraces, (2) ridge terraces, (3) diversion terraces and (4) lister terraces. However, variations found in terrace construction are so great that a classification cannot always be complete in every detail.

FIGURE 17-6. There are 18 miles of terracing on this farm, and the luxuriant growth of brome-clover–crested wheat mixture speaks for the effectiveness of this type of conservation. (Courtesy, Soil Conservation Service)

Bench Terraces

Bench terraces are constructed much like the terraces of a thousand years ago and most nearly exemplify the original meaning of the word. They are used on very steep land or hillsides in order to reduce the sharp slope to a series of narrow, level or nearly level strips. Each terrace has a retaining wall of stones or grass-covered earth to keep the soil from eroding away, and because the benches are constructed on the level, water run-off is greatly retarded. The purposes served by the bench terraces, then, are to reduce water run-off, retard erosion and make crop production possible.

Bench terraces are generally used in densely populated areas where land is scarce and where most of the land is hilly or mountainous. There are only a few places in this country where bench terracing is in place. In the southern and southeastern parts of the United States, the steep hillsides have been bench terraced for generations. It is not unusual to see corn or cotton being grown on these narrow strips. In the productive citrus and avocado areas of southern California, bench terraces are also installed.

These terraces usually cost more than other forms of terraces. Since they are used mostly on steep slopes, they must of necessity be narrow and very close together.

FIGURE 17-7. Even gently sloping fields require conservation practices if soil erosion is to be reduced. A district conservationist and a landowner are looking over parallel tile outlet terraces on this eastern Illinois farm. The terraces will greatly reduce soil erosion. (Courtesy, Soil Conservation Service)

Level Ridge Terraces

A ridge terrace, as the name indicates, has a ridge of earth on the lower side of the channel. The earth from the channel goes to make a part of the ridge, and the rest of the necessary earth is taken from below the ridge.

Ridge terraces are constructed primarily to hold the water that falls rather than to let it drain off. This means these terraces are used more in the Great Plains where water is the important factor limiting production. They are built to spread the water over large surfaces so as to facilitate absorption by the soil.

Ridge-Channel Terraces

One modification of the ridge terrace, sometimes called the channel terrace, is constructed similarly to the regular ridge terrace except that no earth is pulled up from below to form the ridge. It is all taken from the channel. Also, the channel of the channel terrace ordinarily is not made as deep as that of the ridge terrace.

Both ridge and channel terraces are built on gentle slopes. The channel terrace is best adapted to soils that are relatively impervious to water and in areas with a reasonably good distribution of rainfall throughout the growing season and enough rainfall to justify draining off the surplus through surface drainage. These conditions are found throughout the Southeast, the Middle Atlantic states and the Tennessee and Ohio valleys, as well as parts of the Mississippi Valley where there is a fairly good distribution of rainfall throughout the growing season.

Both ridge and channel terraces are left open at the ends so that excess rainfall can escape before it overtops the rim and cuts it away.

A modification of the channel terrace is built with no ridge on the lower side. In very heavy soils where the land is nearly level, it is desirable to remove excess water in order to improve the drainage. Such a heavy soil frequently has small, shallow pot holes which fill with water every spring and after each rain. Because of the imperviousness of the soil, the water is very slow to soak in or to evaporate, thus delaying any field work. The result is a delay of timely seeding and cultivation. Machinery becomes mired in these wet spots too, and crop production is reduced.

The channel with no ridge permits the use of the earth from this channel to fill the pot holes. This serves the double purpose of doing away with the wet spots and improving yields. In very heavy, nearly level soils, the ridgeless type of channel is superior to the ridge-channel type of terrace in several ways:

1. The water is carried in a channel below the ordinary surface of the ground, which means that overtopping from an extremely heavy rain does not cause severe damage.

2. Channel terraces are but little obstruction to the passage of machinery.

3. Channel terraces are easier to align in a true parallel pattern.

4. Earth removed by the excavation of channel terraces can be used to fill objectionable pot holes and draws in the field, thereby eliminating ponds and soft spots.

Diversion Terraces

Another modification of the channel terrace is the diversion terrace. Diversion terraces are built on the steep slopes (usually more than 10 percent slope—10-foot drop in 100 feet) where the erosion problem is more serious than on the gentler slopes. The channels are deeper than those of the usual terraces, and they may have steeper sides. They are constructed to carry away more water and to do it more quickly than the channels

FIGURE 17-8. Wallace Cole cultivates soybeans on his farm of parallel terraces in Moultrie County, Illinois. The terraces help reduce soil erosion. (Courtesy Soil Conservation Service)

of standard terraces. For this reason, the grade of slope of a channel may be increased to as much as 2 feet per 100 feet along the channel. In order to protect the channels from cutting and washing away, farmers should keep them permanently in sod.

Diversion terraces cannot be easily crossed by farm machinery and should never be plowed up with the intention of using the land in the rotation. All tillage operations should be on the contour between the terraces, which may be placed two to four times as far apart as standard terraces. Diversion terraces are built primarily to carry water off the steeper slopes with the least possible amount of erosion.

Lister Terraces

Lister terracing is essentially contour tillage. The implement used to make this type of channel is ordinarily the lister, which throws the earth both ways, thus creating a furrow which is not filled in by the next furrow slice as in ordinary plowing operations. In some parts of the country, this implement is called a "middle-buster" or "middle-breaker."

Lister terracing is a temporary land conditioning operation for the purpose of holding the water where it falls until it is absorbed by the soil. Frequently, the lister has an attachment that throws up a small dam or dike every few feet across the furrow (channel). This attachment is especially useful when it is not convenient to work the soil on the absolute contour.

When it is time to plant the crop, the field is smoothed out if grain is to be planted. If the field is to be planted to corn, the lister may be used to split the temporary ridges, thus creating new ridges in the old channels.

Terraces for Nonfarm Uses

Erosion can be equally serious in nonfarm areas. In urban areas soil losses can be very high. High soil losses can affect houses, streets, bridges and many other urban structures because such losses produce sediment as well as remove soil from lawns, house and bridge foundations and other critical areas. Terraces are an important erosion control feature of many hilly golf courses.

To control soil losses and to reduce erosion, terraces are often applied to intercept water and carry it slowly to a non-erosive watercourse, or channel. The design and function is similar to that of farm terraces; those terraces in an urban setting usually have permanent grass cover. As nonfarm areas generally have buildings, streets, water lines and other like developments throughout, the designs of terraces in these areas require unusual considerations. Therefore, expert assistance should be obtained from soil specialists.

Laying Out and Building Terraces

All terraces should be laid out by competent persons. Usually soil specialists or conservationists are available in every county in the United States for this work. They also will designate the type of terraces to construct, the height of the ridges, the width and depth of the channels, the distance between the channels and the type of equipment best adapted to the work. When once done properly, this work should not have to be done over again, so it is very important that it be done correctly the first time.

Outlets for Terrace Channels

Wherever there is to be water run-off from a field through terraces or other constructed channels across the slope of a field, the water must be discharged into an outlet of some sort. Outlets of terraces may be either open grassed or closed tile. The open-grassed outlets may be located in natural waterways or in constructed grassed waterways.

Any open water outlet must be sodded or grassed with a growth of fine-leaved grass (see Figures 17-9 and 17-10). It should be large enough to carry the run-off from the heavier rains. Wherever the outlet is to be crossed by machinery, the sides should slope gently. In any situation the slope of the outlet should be such that the flowing water will not cut away the sides. One common standard for size of outlet in regions with not more than 18 or 20 inches of rainfall during the growing season is 2 square feet of area in the cross section of the channel for every acre of land that drains into the channel. If very heavy storms occasionally occur, the carrying capacity of the outlet should be larger; otherwise, the water run-off will overflow the channel and cause greater soil losses.

In the northern part of the United States, where the winters are long and cold, one of the problems in connection with water outlets is keeping

FIGURE 17-9. This picture was taken from inside a large city-type bus as it was driven down a grass waterway through the center of a corn field on a rainy day. This ride, part of a conservation tour sponsored by the Soil Conservation Service, dramatically proves how effective such waterways can be in preventing erosion. (Photo by Harry B. Kircher)

FIGURE 17-10. A waterway that is covered with a heavy growth of grass will carry fast-moving surface run-off with no washing. The water is clear—it is free of silt. Yet it is flowing rapidly. (Courtesy, Soil Conservation Service)

the channels from freezing closed. Whenever an outlet can be made on a southern or southwestern exposure, this problem will be greatly reduced. In no case should the outlet be used as a road. Neither should the channel be open for grazing by cattle, because the longer the grass blades, the better the protection afforded the channel.

The closed-tile outlets are a special type of outlet consisting of an open inlet, for the water in the terrace to enter, connected to a closed circuit (usually farm tile). This form of terrace outlet should only be installed when properly designed.

Not only does the use of terraces reduce soil losses and increase crop yields, but it also makes for a more flexible cropping system. The many types of terraces are useful under differing soil conditions. Proper outlets for terraces are important so that no soil erosion occurs as the water moves from the field.

QUESTIONS AND PROBLEMS

1. If the steepness, or grade, of a slope is increased from 3 percent (3-foot drop in 100 feet of horizontal distance) to 8 or 10 percent, how much more water run-off would you expect to find?

2. What causes the greater soil losses if the amount of water run-off is not increased?

3. If the steepness of the slope is increased to 18 percent or more, what is likely to happen to water run-off?

4. Which will cause the larger soil loss: (a) a definite volume of water run-off at the rate of 2 miles per hour? or (b) one-half this volume of run-off at the rate of 4 miles per hour? Explain your answer.

5. If the volume or quantity of water run-off is doubled without increasing the velocity, or speed, of the water: (a) How much more cutting or erosion will take place? (b) How much more soil will the run-off carry?

6. If the velocity of the water run-off is doubled without increasing the volume: (a) How much more cutting or erosion will take place? (b) How much more soil will the run-off carry?

7. Which crops slow down water run-off the most? Which the least?

8. What is strip cropping, and how does it reduce soil washing?

9. What factors help determine the width to make crop strips across a slope?

10. Name the kinds of strip cropping that are used in different situations and indicate some use for each. Which are used in your area?

11. What is the difference between contour tillage and strip cropping?

12. What is the definition of a terrace as used during early times? How does this differ from the definition used at the present time?

13. What are the advantages of using terraces?

14. Describe the difference between bench, ridge-channel and diversion terraces and tell where each is most useful.

15. Explain how each of the terraces described in No. 14 are made. What types of terraces are used near you?

18

Crop Rotations
and Other Practices
in Soil Conservation

The agriculture of some parts of the United States, such as the Wheat Belt of the Midwest and the Cotton Belt of the South, was built upon the production of one crop. The agriculture of most of the country today, however, depends upon the production and use of several crops: therefore, the former one-crop regions are becoming more diversified. When various crops are grown on a farm, they tend to follow a definite sequence. For example, in those areas where corn, small grain and hay are produced, a field that is planted to corn one year will ordinarily be planted to some small grain, such as oats, barley, rye or wheat, the second year. Some hay crop may be planted along with the grain or immediately following its harvest. This may be any legume or non-legume that will survive the winter and make a hay or pasture crop the third year. A common example of a four-year rotation in the Midwest is corn, soybeans, wheat and clover, in a four-year succession. In this rotation the fifth year the clover is plowed and corn planted, thus starting again on the four-year program. A crop rotation may be simply defined as a sequence of crops grown in recurring succession on the same field or area of land.

In recent years, crops rotation practices have changed to less diversification. This trend reflects a change in livestock production and advances in farming technology. Livestock production has become concentrated on a relatively few large farms. As a result, the majority of farms no longer need forage crops. The farming technology of conservation farming, especially no-till, as described in the preceding chapter, has helped keep soil losses to tolerance levels without the need of as much rotation.

A common rotation in the southern Corn Belt today is corn, soybeans and winter wheat, with the beans planted soon after wheat harvest. Many other farmers simply rotate corn and soybeans.

IMPORTANCE OF CROP ROTATION

Notwithstanding advances in technology, crop rotations are vital to agriculture. They aid in the efficient use of plant nutrients found in the soil. This is so because each crop has differing needs for plant food, and what one crop doesn't use before being lost to leaching, another can. As a result, loss of nutrients to leaching is diminished. Crop rotations also aid in the reduction of insect losses. Insects do not have as great an opportunity to increase in number if the host crop is rotated. Often, introduction of another crop may bring in insects which prey upon the insects of previous crops. Furthermore, crop rotations reduce soil and wind erosion when they are used to maintain maximum ground cover.

Crop rotations are generally a useful conservation practice. If ill-conceived, however, they can reduce and eventually destroy our natural resource base; if well-conceived, they can strengthen it.

Definite Rotation Attempted

Most farmers try to follow a definite rotation and even lay out their fields accordingly. Misfortunes such as winter killing of the hay crop, drought damage at certain critical periods during the growing season and attacks of crop-destroying pests and diseases (chinch bugs, Hessian flies, corn borers, smut, rust, etc.) often break into the rotation. When misfortunes strike, the crop sequence is altered to fit the circumstances. Thus, the rotation is different for that period. Conservation-minded farmers, however, soon return to the planned sequence.

Length of Rotations

Crop rotations vary in length from 2 or 3 years to 10 or 12. The usual rotations of five or six years are not uncommon. Longer rotations may consist of two or more years of corn, followed by a year or two of some small grain and two or more years of hay if the land is not subject to erosion, that is, if it is Class I land. Or, rotations may be lengthened by increasing the number of years the fields are in hay or grass if the soil erodes, as in Class IV land.

The need for special crops in some sections of the country may determine the length of rotations. In the eastern part of the United States, there is greater acreage of hay than of other crops. This results from the expansion of the dairy industry close to the consuming East. Farmers there find it cheaper to ship in 20 pounds of grain for every 100 pounds of milk produced and to raise more hay than to attempt to raise both. This rotation, consisting essentially of hay and pasture, may be no longer, however, than many of the rotations used on Midwest farms which ship the grain to the East. Each section of the country has its rotation or system of cropping which meets its special need, either for feed or fibre crops, or for the control of erosion. Here again, the desirable rotation for any area not only must meet the needs of the area for food and feed but also must safeguard the soil.

Rotations Help Control Erosion

It has already been mentioned that soil losses are greatest with intertilled crops such as corn, soybeans, cotton and tobacco, while losses are practically negligible with hay crops. A rotation ordinarily combines into a sequence of years those crops which show small soil losses with those which show greater. The average yearly loss for the complete rotation is thus smaller than losses which occur with the production of corn or small grain alone.

Figures from the five states of Oklahoma, Ohio, Missouri, North Carolina and Wisconsin show the average yearly loss of soil in a rotation of cotton or corn, small grain and meadow or hay crops to vary from a little more than 4 tons per acre for Oklahoma to 28 tons for Wisconsin. Water run-off losses did not show as great a range as did soil losses. The lowest amount of water run-off, slightly over 9 percent of the rainfall, was in North Carolina, which had approximately a 15-ton soil loss per acre, while the highest percent of water run-off loss, over 21 percent, was from Ohio, which showed only around a 13-ton soil loss per acre. The slope of land on which these losses were measured ranged from 7 percent for Oklahoma to 16 percent for Wisconsin (see Table 18-1). The soil loss studies from which these figures were taken tend to bear out the conclusion that the steepness of the slope of the land has more to do with soil losses in a rotation than does the amount of water run-off.

Rotations Add Organic Matter

In addition to reducing soil losses, crop rotations which include legumes and grasses also add organic matter and loosen the soil so that frequently the loss of the soil from the following corn crop is less than that of the second year after the site has been plowed in preparation for small grains. As already noted, under continuous cropping, soil losses from corn are much greater than those from small grain.

It should be remembered, however, that good crop rotations alone will not reduce soil losses to a safe point, except on those fields with slight slopes. Other practices, such as strip cropping and terracing, must be used in connection with crop rotations on hilly and rolling lands.

TABLE 18-1. Average Yearly Water Run-Off Loss and Soil Loss with a Three-Year Rotation

Area	Soil per Acre	Water, Portion of Total Rainfall	Slope of Fields
	(tons)	*(%)*	*(%)*
Statesville, N.C.	15.1	9.3	10
Guthrie, Okla.	4.2	10.2	7
Bethany, Mo.	9.1	16.2	8
LaCross, Wis.	28.0	16.9	16
Zanesville, Ohio	13.3	21.2	12

Rotations and Strip Cropping

Strip cropping makes possible with minimum soil losses the use of crop rotations on fields which are subject to erosion. Also, if it were not for crop rotations, strip cropping would not be as useful as it is in controlling erosion.

Since one of the first requisites for the use of strip cropping is that every other strip be in some hay crop or grass, it is easily understood why experts generally recommend a four-year rotation of one year each for some intertilled crop and grain, followed by two years of hay or hay and pasture. If more hay and pasture are needed, or if hay is needed for longer periods of time, a six-year rotation may be desirable.

BENEFICIAL USE OF FERTILIZERS

Soil losses tend to be cumulative. They remove plant nutrients which are essential for crop production. This reduces the quality of crop growth. This reduction in quality of plant growth, in turn, increases the erosion hazard.

An effective way to reduce soil erosion in combination with crop rotation and other conservation products is to add fertilizers necessary to maintain and increase crop yields. When this is done, it aids in reducing erosion by providing vigorous vegetation.

Fertilizers, which include green manures and animal wastes, should be applied to the soil in accordance with needs. Deficiencies can be determined by taking soil samples and having them tested. Local county agents of the USDA Extension Service should be contacted as to availability and location of soil-testing facilities. When nutrients are applied according to these tests and other conservation measures are employed, the productivity of the soil is increased. This increase in soil productivity not only enhances crop yields but also adds to the volume of organic matter produced, which, in turn, helps increase or maintain the organic matter of the soil. This additional organic matter improves the soil's workability (tilth) and makes the soil more resistant to erosion. Care should be taken not to overfertilize. Not only is this costly and wasteful, but it also could be harmful to the crops. And, if there is an excess, it may pollute the water supplies.

Organic or Inorganic Fertilizer

Fertilizers generally applied to crops are nitrogen, phosphorus and potassium. Law requires that the fertilizer components be indicated on the bag. They are generally stated as pounds available per hundred pounds of material. There are many forms of nitrogen, phosphorus and potassium used in the fertilizer industry. These forms are both organic and inorganic. The form applied is immaterial to the green plant as it absorbs plant food in the elemental form (ions) and thus does not differentiate between organic and inorganic forms. Enthusiasts for using "natural" fertilizers claim, however, that when organic materials are used, the plants receive more trace elements since the nutrients are absorbed more slowly.

Organic Farming and Organic Gardening

There is nothing wrong with organic farming—using only so-called "natural" fertilizers such as manure and decayed vegetation—except for the idea that it would be practical to return to it today. We farmed that way 75 years ago. But, wastes used to fertilize the organic way are generally very low in fertility compared with chemical fertilizers. Also, plowing crops under to restore fertility is a costlier method than applying commercial fertilizers. We simply could not meet our food needs today without a large input of chemicals and fertilizers. The idea that nitrogen added to the soil as a chemical is somehow harmful to plants, whereas nitrogen derived from a legume is somehow "purer" and harmless, has no basis in fact. Dr. Sam Aldrich, agronomist and former member of the Illinois Pollution Control Board, comments: "Nitrogen from plant residues and manure is first converted from organic form to ammonium and then to nitrate. Nearly all nitrogen in fertilizer is in ammonium form and it, too, converts to nitrate." A more justifiable objection is that nitrogen and other nutrients of commercial fertilizers, being water soluble, can add to water pollution if applied unwisely.

Organic gardening can be fun and productive enough for home needs. Furthermore, it is a convenient and useful way to dispose of many wastes. Whether or not organic vegetables are more healthful than those raised the conventional way is debatable. However, there is no question that the debates themselves are beneficial, for they spur more agricultural research.

USE OF HERBICIDES AND INSECTICIDES

In recent years, farmers have been using a variety of herbicides and insecticides to combat weeds and insect pests and to maintain conservation crop rotations. When suitable chemicals are used, weeds and insects are controlled, resulting in greater crop yields and farm production efficiency. Much has been said about the environmental pollution caused by their use. This criticism has some merit because the chemicals developed first had long half lives (long-lasting—slow to disintegrate) and their residual effects plagued the environment. The insecticide DDT, which is toxic to humans and absorbed through the system, is an example.

Wildlife with traces of DDT were found from Florida to Alaska. One conservation organization said DDT really stood for: "Dead Ducks Tomorrow." Fortunately, it is largely outlawed today. Also, indiscriminate use of agricultural chemicals has had a bad effect on the environment. Again, a change for the better has been made. The chemicals now being developed and used have short half lives, with little or no residual environmental effects.

Agricultural chemicals are needed for top agricultural output. They should not be used indiscriminately, however. Advice as to kind and amount of insecticide or herbicide to use can be obtained from the USDA Extension Service, which has offices in nearly all counties.

THE PROBLEM OF GULLIES

It frequently becomes necessary to use a special device or type of construction in order to retard or stop erosion. This is especially true where the water run-off has already done a great deal of washing and where the cuts or gullies are large.

Various practices or devices are used to protect against further cutting away, and frequently the use of a mechanical or special aid, as well as the more commonly used soil conserving practices, is needed to do the best job of keeping the remaining soil in place (see Figure 18-1).

How Gullies Are Made

The most conspicuous damage that can be seen when erosion is severe is in the form of gullies. Gullies are found almost everywhere. In most cases where gullying starts, there will be little or no grass covering the surface, and practically no other plant growth will be found to slow down water run-off.

FIGURE 18-1. The bench terraces on this Iowa farm enable the farmer to produce crops on this land without severe erosion. The earthen dam prevents further gullying and provides a water supply. (Courtesy, Soil Conservation Service)

The depth and shape of gullies, as well as the rate at which they are made, depend upon any one or more of several factors. Some soils, such as wind-deposited (loess) soils and certain types of sandy soils, seem to erode fairly readily, leaving straight-walled cuts which are easily widened to form "U"-shaped gullies. Any soil with a soft subsoil which erodes readily will tend to form gullies of this shape.

If, on the other hand, the subsoil is heavy and absorbs little water, the gullies usually are not as deep as those formed in the lighter subsoils. They ordinarily are "V"-shaped, and their progress in cutting up a field is not as striking as in the case of the formation of the "U"-shaped gullies. If the soil is shallow and underlaid with rock, the depth of washing will be only a few inches through the thin soil to the rock, but the width of the wash may be very great.

A "U"-shaped gully is usually formed by water falling over the edge of a bank. The falling water at the edge of the eroding soil washes away the underlying subsoil. The topsoil then caves in, and the lip of the gully thus gradually moves up the slope. Many times we have watched small "Niagaras" of this type after heavy rains, as they drop to a lower level and undercut the lip of the watercourse as they fall. We probably were not conscious of the damage done to a field as the water cut deeper and deeper channels which backed slowly up the hill. If there were no drop at the edge of the field or if a good growth of grass were maintained, there would be no waterfalls and no gully cutting.

In cases where converging slopes concentrate run-off water, an economical method of preventing gullying is to keep the water-flow path at the slope junction covered with a thick strip of grass which is never plowed. The grass slows the water flow sufficiently to prevent erosion. It is sometimes possible to stabilize a gully by planting the entire ravine to some fast-growing, dense vegetation. Different grasses, vines or shrubs may be used for this purpose, depending upon the soil, the climate and the topography of the area (see Figures 18-2 and 18-3).

Where vine or grass growth is difficult to establish, it may be possible to put in a temporary dam of earth, grass, brush, wire or stones in order to slow down the water run-off until vegetative cover is well started. On the other hand, if the volume of run-off is too large for satisfactory vegetative control, it may be necessary to make a more nearly permanent dam which is large enough to hold the water that accumulates as a result of any heavy rain. The slowed-down water run-off will drop its excess load of soil back of the dam (see Figure 18-1). In order to let most of the water escape from the pond after it has been slowed down and much of the suspended soil has been deposited in the bottom of the pond, a structure known as a drop inlet, which is constructed as an integral part of the dam, will carry the excess water off through a metal or clay tube in the lower part of the dam.

In some situations, diversion ditches are built across the waterway and above the gully. These ditches do not let the water flow into the washed-out gully, but they carry it around and to one side. Diversion ditches should be permanent features of the land and should be so put in that they will not, in turn, be the source of further erosion.

It doesn't take long to fill back of a dam, and if the dam is built high enough, a small acreage of new soil will be created. Unless steps are also taken to stop the erosion from the hillsides, a dam of this sort is but a temporary device for holding back soil and relieving flood conditions. The larger

FIGURE 18-2. Gullies cut on the side hill in a cattle lane. Wherever cattle wear a path smooth, there is every chance for erosion. (See also Figure 18-3.) (Courtesy, Soil Conservation Service)

FIGURE 18-3. The eroded area shown in Figure 18-2 was planted to trees which made enough growth to protect the slope from further washing. The trees are five years old. (Courtesy, Soil Conservation Service)

the dam, of course, the longer it will serve as a pond for holding flood waters and reducing flood and silting damage farther down the ravine.

It is much easier to prevent the formation of gullies than to control them and heal the scars after they have once started. Sometimes this type of erosion may be prevented by the relocation of roadways or cattle lanes so as to follow the contour more nearly. Most gullying is preceded by sheet erosion so that if the land is farmed to prevent this form of erosion, it is possible to keep many of the gullies from forming. When gullies are once started, they require more drastic measures, however, if their devastating progress is to be controlled.

Use of Flumes

Flumes (chutes) are used to carry water run-off down steep hillsides or over the lips of gullies to lower levels. They must be built so as to resist erosion or cutting by the run-off water.

Sod-covered flumes are ordinarily used for dropping the water less than 10 feet (perpendicularly) and for draining small areas of probably not more than 25 acres. In areas where Kentucky bluegrass or Bermuda grass grows well, sod flumes have been used to drain larger watersheds into gullies that have only a few feet drop. Flumes are not built to fill gullies with silt or to stabilize either the gully channels or sides, but only to lower the water to another level. The steepness, or slope, at which a flume may be put in depends not only upon the soil type and the size of the watershed but also upon the height of the waterfall and the type and quality of sod used. The steepest slope for a sod flume is about a 1-foot drop, or vertical distance, to a 4-foot horizontal distance. This means that if the water is to be dropped 4 feet, the flume should be at least 16 feet long. It also should be wide in proportion to its depth because shallow water will not run as rapidly down a slope as will deeper water. In general, the flume should be at least 15 inches wide for every acre of the watershed, and the depth of the water at its maximum run-off should not exceed 12 inches.

Concrete- or stone-constructed flumes are used where the water run-off is too great for sod flumes to hold or where the drop to the lower level is too much. Occasionally, wooden or metal flumes are as satisfactory as concrete. All of these flumes are of a more permanent nature than the grass-sodded flumes, and the costs are much greater. Their slopes may be

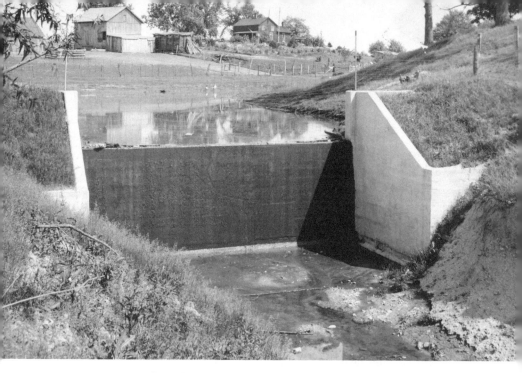

FIGURE 18-4. This 10-foot-deep gully drains a 75-acre area. The concrete dam makes a pond which will ultimately be filled with silt. The flume drops the water 9 feet and slows the rate of flow so that no washing will take place. (Courtesy, Soil Conservation Service)

twice as steep as those of sodded flumes, and they will carry more water run-off if they are properly constructed (see Figure 18-4).

STREAM BANK EROSION

Streams never travel in straight lines. They wind and twist, always seeking out the easiest way to move to lower levels. The greatest force of the water in a stream is exerted against the bank of the outside of each bend, and any deposit of sand or gravel occurs on the inside where the current is quietest. As this process continues, the bends in the stream become more abrupt, and the current cuts more deeply into the bank. The final result is that much of the bottomland along the stream bed becomes so cut up as to be of little use for crop production. Stream bank cutting also may take place on farms where water flows only during times of heavier rainfalls or in the spring when melting snow causes water run-off.

Vegetative Growth Prevents Intermittent Stream Bank Cutting

Ordinarily, it is possible to control the bank cutting that takes place

FIGURE 18-5. This stream started to wash away the bank, and if it had not been stopped, it would have gradually cut across the productive land to the left, forming an ox bow. The bank as shown here has been worked down, and willow cuttings have been planted between the poles held down by posts and wire. (See also Figure 18-6.) (Courtesy, Soil Conservation Service)

FIGURE 18-6. The willow cuttings planted on the eroded stream bank shown in Figure 18-5 have made enough growth to protect the bank from further washing. The cuttings have been in two years. (Courtesy, Soil Conservation Service)

in a stream which flows only intermittently by the use of grasses, shrubs and trees. Before adequate growth can be established, it is frequently necessary to use some temporary obstructions along the eroded bank to check water velocities enough to redeposit the soil lost from the location. After the bank cutting has been checked and enough silt or other sediment has been deposited, it may be necessary to plant the desired vegetation if sufficient cover is not provided by natural growth (see Figures 18-5 and 18-6).

Many Stream Banks Require the Use of Jetties

Jetties are extensions built into a stream from the bank to deflect the water flow. These obstructions, when built correctly in the right places on the curves, direct the stream flow away from the bank and permit some filling with sediment between the jetties. The Ohio State University conducted tests some years ago to determine the best location of the jetties for the control of stream bank cutting. According to this authority, the first jetty should be placed at the point where the flow line of the stream intersects the eroding stream bank "A" on Figure 18-7. A second line should

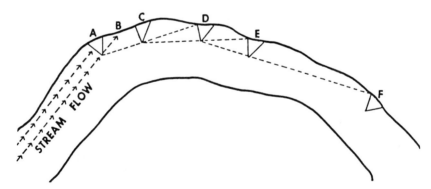

FIGURE 18-7. Jetties for a stream bank to keep it from washing away.

then be drawn parallel to the flow of the stream, but passing through the outer point (toe) of the first jetty. The point where this line intersects the stream bank—"B," should be half the distance between the first jetty and the second jetty, "C." Each succeeding jetty around the bend should be placed at the point where a line projected across the toes of the next two upper jetties intersects the bank—"D," "E," etc. These jetties should point down stream, and the upper edge of each should form about a 45 degree angle with the bank. The top of each jetty should slope downward toward the stream from the bank at about the angle expected for the ultimate bank. It was also found desirable to use low jetties which cost less to build than higher ones but which are as effective in stopping the erosion.

The distance that the jetties should project into the stream depends upon the swiftness of the current and the volume of water in the stream. In no distance should they project more than one-fourth to one-third the width of the stream at flood time. When extended too far into the stream, the jetties themselves may be washed away.

Types of Jetties

Jetties may be made of various materials, depending upon the type of stream which is doing the cutting. On shallow, slow-moving streams, piles of alternate layers of rock and brush have proven satisfactory. The faster a stream moves, the more securely the jetties must be anchored. Loose rocks held in place by woven wire and forming sausage-shaped jetties have proved effective in streams where the rock-brush jetties would not hold. Any one of the fastest-moving streams requires jetties which are firmly tied into the bank and anchored to the bed of the stream so as to be protected from undercutting. These jetties frequently are built as cribs, which are then filled with stone, pieces of cement and the like. Jetties of this type are most expensive to build and are scarcely ever put up by individual farmers to protect their property. Ventures of this size usually are community sponsored and financed for the protection of highways.

RIP-RAP

A rip-rap, or revetment, completely covers the area to be protected and differs from a wall or fence in that it is laid on the slope of the land. It is used where other means of control are practically as expensive without giving the complete protection afforded by a rip-rap. Because it is so expensive, it is used sparingly and is supplemented as much as possible with vegetative cover. Most rip-raps are of a permanent nature, however, and as such may be made of stone laid in cement or mortar. Occasionally, temporary protection is desired until the area can be covered with some tree or shrub growth. In such instances, brush matting or a covering of loose stones is used. When trees or shrubs completely cover the area, the protecting rip-rap is no longer needed.

PROTECTING ADJACENT LAND

Continuously flowing streams usually have a more persistent erosion problem than is found in the ravines which carry water only periodically. One important factor, as both a preventive and a control measure, is the protection of the strip of land immediately adjacent to a stream. As live-stock will eat off the protective vegetation, they should have only limited access to it, and that access should be on level stretches of the stream bank if the best erosion control practices are to be used.

CHANNELIZATION OF STREAMS AND RIVERS

Channelization is the practice of deepening, widening and/or straighten-ing an existing channel in a stream in order to increase its capacity to carry greater volumes of water. This is done to reduce the frequency of flood damage to lowlands adjacent to the stream, to reduce the severity of the meanders (windings) of a river and to improve the navigability of streams.

When meanders are removed, the total length of the river is reduced and the gradient (the amount of fall expressed in feet per mile) is increased. This aids navigation, but it can speed the water downstream faster to add to flooding.

Channelization is a rather controversial practice from a conservation viewpoint. In some places, after the channels had been dug, poor planning had caused the environment to deteriorate. Dredged materials were left in huge piles, with nothing done to prevent them from adding sediment, in great amounts, to the stream. Aquatic life was destroyed, and water qual-ity was reduced. In other areas, the stream banks, which had been stable, became unstable and produced little or no habitat for wildlife.

Today, before any sizeable channelization project is begun by the federal government, the wildlife and environment of the stream are evaluated. And, the project is fully reviewed at public hearings. Environmental considerations are then provided for in the project plans. A channelization project, before approval, should be worthwhile. It should add to our resource base by minimizing flood damage, providing drainage of lands needed for agriculture or providing better transportation potential, and it should not result in costly losses of irretrievable environmental assets.

MANY BENEFICIAL WAYS TO MANAGE OUR SOIL RESOURCES

Crop rotation is a useful practice that increases output and has many conservation benefits. Fertilizers, besides adding to higher crop yields, also can help save the soil if used widely. Herbicides and insecticides have been improved and greatly increase farm efficiency. But, they too must be used with care.

Gullies are a sign of neglect of the land. They are easier to prevent than to control. However, there are many ways to deal with them. Stream bank erosion is a natural process. Various devices can be used to prevent streams from washing away valuable land and property. Channelization of streams and rivers should be done only when it adds to our resource base, considering all environmental costs.

Conservation does pay. Soil losses are reduced, yields are maintained or increased and the soil is conserved to produce food and fibre in the future.

QUESTIONS AND PROBLEMS

1. What is crop rotation? Why is a definite rotation not followed by most farmers?

2. Under what conditions is it safe to depend upon rotations alone to control erosion?

3. What is a common rotation for your part of the state? How is it benefiting the soil?

4. How can adding fertilizers wisely help the soil? What are some of the problems in using commercial fertilizers? What are the advantages? Why would an "organic farming enthusiast" not agree with you?

5. What are some of the pros and cons of using insecticides and herbicides? How can you find out which ones are the best to use?

6. Describe how gullies are formed. When a "U"-shaped gully is formed in one field and a "V"-shaped gully in another, what difference in the soil of the two fields is indicated?

7. No doubt you have seen a gully in the process of being cut or formed. Describe the conditions which apparently are responsible for the gully—for example, a lane along the side of a hill where cattle go to and from a pasture, a cut to reduce the grade of a highway or a plowed field on the side of a hill.

8. What structures or devices are used to control gullies? Under what conditions is it possible to use sod or other vegetative growth to stop or control gullies?

9. What is a drop inlet? What ultimately happens to the pond in back of a dam when a drop inlet is put in?

10. What is a diversion ditch? Should it ordinarily be built as a permanent or a temporary structure? Explain your answer.

11. What is a flume, and what is the reason for using a flume—to fill a gully, to stabilize the channel or to lower water to another level?

12. How can the erosion caused by streams or rivers be controlled?

13. How does rip-rap differ from jetties? Out of what materials may rip-rap be constructed? Which types of construction are commonly used for permanence?

14. Is channelization of streams and rivers a "good" or a "bad" conservation practice? Explain your answer.

19

The City and
Natural Resources

So far, we have considered the nature of wind and water power, fuel and nonfuel minerals, water and forests and soil and vegetation, and we have discussed the conservation of all of these. None of these, as we have learned, is a resource until it is of use to us. Perhaps the most important fact about the "life" of a resource is not so much the stock of that resource provided to us by nature, as the way in which we use it and the rate at which we use it. Nowhere is this problem more focused than in the city. The city is the caldron in which pressures on world resources come to a boil. Events such as war in the oil-rich Middle East, drought in Africa, depletion of forests in South America and failure of the wheat crop in the USSR take their toll in the market places of the world—the cities, where most of us live. Conversely, large cities send their influence far beyond their boundaries. Our way of life in the city has a tremendous impact upon our entire resource base. Some say that the city threatens to destroy it. Others say the city is the generator of resources.

CITY GROWTH

From 1950 to 1985, the number of supercities[1] in the United States increased from 169 to 280, and the total number of residents from 85 million to 180 million. The total population in the United States increased over 4 percent from 1980 to 1985, to 238.7 million, with over three-fourths living in supercities. While the relative size of central cities in many metropolitan areas has declined sharply over the years, central cities were growing more (or losing less) than they did in the 1970's throughout the nation.

The City Seen from Space

So great is the impression of our cities on the landscape that they were clearly visible to the astronauts of *Skylab* when they circled the earth some 270 miles above it in space. Dr. Robert Holz, a member of the scientific team that trained the *Skylab 4* crew in earth observations and who conducted debriefings afterwards, told the American Association of Geographers at its annual meeting in Milwaukee on April 21, 1975: "The development of the city significantly changes the environment and produces a new signature on the landscape."

City Influence Beyond Boundaries

The economic, the social and even the physical impact of cities upon our resources extends far beyond city boundaries. Some urban geographers and sociologists divide our entire country into city regions. What goes on in Troy, Illinois, and Hot Springs, Arkansas, depends very much upon developments in their city regions centered in St. Louis and Little Rock. The outward spread of population from St. Louis has caused Troy to double in population within a decade. The fortune of Hot Springs is tied to decisions about the legality of gambling, which is determined in the state capital, Little Rock. No place is really isolated from the impact of the city.

Even agriculture receives its impulse from cities, according to Jane

---

[1]Supercities are the metropolitan areas (MSA's and CMSA's) defined by the U.S. census. MSA's are central cities that, when combined with suburban neighborhoods, exceed 50,000 population and have close interconnections. CMSA's are those SMA's that are over 1 million in population.

FIGURE 19-1. Most of greater Chicago is depicted in this NASA photo which shows how urban growth has radiated outward from the heart of town at the Loop—a small dark patch near the waters of Lake Michigan. Chicago's huge O'Hare International Airport complex is at center left. Most of the land is occupied by buildings. For many years Chicago sent much of its sewage to downstate Illinois via the Chicago Sanitary and Ship Canal (bottom center) which eventually led to the Illinois River, another example of the widespread impact of a large city. (Courtesy, National Aeronautics and Space Administration)

Jacobs, a sociologist who is a well-known author of books on cities and an editor of *Agricultural Forum.* "Cities came first—rural development later," she writes. She relates that fodder crops were developed in the city gardens of France a century before they were adopted in rural farming. Today, she notes, fattening beef on corn before slaughter began in the city stock-yards of Kansas City and Chicago. Now, the fattening is taking place in rural areas—a transplant from the city. Ms. Jacobs predicts that cities will become ". . . more intricate, comprehensive, diversified, and larger than today's. . . ."[2]

Cities and People

A concern of many of us is that cities threaten not only our natural resources but also our own well-being. We fear that we will become unhealthy and mentally unbalanced if confined to urban living. René Dubois, a famous microbiologist, stated: "Wherever he goes, and whatever he does, man is successful only to the extent that he functions under environmental conditions . . . under which he evolved . . . man does not really 'master' the environment . . . (he creates) sheltered environments within which he controls local conditions."[3] He suggests that there are limits beyond which our lives cannot safely be altered by social and technological innovations. Since by the end of the century, most human beings will be born in urban situations, Dubois points out that "the future will therefore depend upon our ability to create urban environments having the proper biological qualities."[4] He stresses that while people have remarkable adaptive capacity, they still require immense environmental diversity if their full potentials are to be reached.

To those of us reared on the farm or in rural communities, it seems "natural" to assume that living in the country is best for us. But, the city may well be more satisfactory to some people. Herbert Gans tells us that while, for some people, being outdoors provides satisfactions ". . . I have known other people who derive similar benefits from walking through the streets of Manhattan. . . ."[5] He cites the case of tenement residents who when taken to the wave- and wind-swept beaches of Cape Cod, wanted to get back as quickly as possible to their own neighborhood. He comments, "They come from a culture which does not prepare them for being alone and for becoming immersed in nature."

---

[2] Jane Jacobs, *The Economy of Cities*, New York, Random House, Inc., 1970, pp. 17, 250.

[3] William R. Ewald, Jr., ed., *Environment for Man: The Next Fifty Years*, Bloomington, Indiana University Press, 1967, p. 15.

[4] *Ibid.*, p. 21.

[5] Davis W. Fischer and John E. Lewis, eds., *Land and Leisure: Concepts and Materials in Outdoor Recreation*, Chicago, Maroufa Press, 1975, p. 19.

Need for Cities

The reasons for the growth of our metropolitan areas, our supercities, vary. They may be primarily economic. Many of us would prefer to live in the country. But we cannot afford to do so. The city is where both consumers and producers can meet most readily, at less cost to the one and more profit to the other. This is sometimes referred to as the ***advantage of aglomeration***—the advantage of having ready access to a great mass of things all jumbled together. For others, the attractions of the city are what may be called the ***amenities,*** the nonfinancial attractions that make life more fun—major league baseball, national hockey, all kinds of films, stage plays and operas, bowling, ice skating, tennis and golf to choose from and restaurants serving anything from the sukiyaki and curried rice of the East to the *sauerbraten* and *kartoffelkloss* of the West.

From the days of Catal Hüyük, one of the earliest known cities, which existed in the region of present-day Turkey some 8,000 years ago, cities have been with us. The question is not What can we do to disperse city dwellers into villages or How can we get along without them? The question is How can we make cities better? Can we build them so they will enrich our resource base and us?

THE GREEN CITY

First, let us consider what can be done about our present cities. One of the most obvious ways we can make them more healthful is by providing more vegetation and more usable open space. Vegetation is essential to helping purify the air. Open space is needed to permit the sunlight to reach the earth's surface and us, as well as to provide a place for the plants to grow and for us to move around in. Ways of providing more trees and other greenery are to plant them along streets, in residential areas and in parks and recreation areas and to set aside outstanding natural areas.

The addition of trees or gardens to the downtown or commercial districts of cities is being done today in many cities. Not only do the trees and flowers add beauty, but they also are a good indicator of air quality. If the plants do not survive, it may be because of air pollution.

In residential areas, trees and grass are often neglected by the city. Trees have been cut down to make way for utility lines and have been removed in some communities so that buses can conveniently pull up to the curbing. In other towns, trees have been removed because they were diseased—although a good idea, the trees have not been replaced. One reason for this neglect of vegetation is that it saves the city money. It is important for curbside plantings and parkways to be restored or introduced anew.

Providing Cluster Zoning and Parks and Preserving Natural Areas

In new residential areas, green space can be provided by **cluster zoning** (see Figure 19-2). Here, houses are constructed close together on one part of a parcel of land, leaving more space for recreational and park areas on the rest of the parcel. Under the traditional system, house lots are too small to be of much use.

The word today on parks is "bring parks to the people." Neighborhood parks make the city more liveable. They provide a place for sunlight and fresh air. Vest-pocket parks are small islands of trees and flowers that relieve the monotony of asphalt, brick and cement and provide diversity which helps give identity to neighborhoods. A ball diamond or a few tennis courts provide open space and needed recreation areas that can supplement the parks.

Some cities have unique natural areas within their metropolitan boundaries. These should be preserved. For example, giant saguaro cactuses standing just outside Tucson, Arizona, have been set aside as a national monument. These cactuses stand up to 50 feet in height. Beaches, canyons and unique bogs and marshes are other examples of the kinds of natural areas which exist near some of our major cities and should be saved.

THE CBD AND THE CENTRAL CITY

Cities customarily grow outward from a center which becomes the focus of activity known as the central business district (CBD). Surrounding this core area is a densely populated section called the central city. Both of these areas have become blighted in many cities, as both businesses and private citizens have moved to the suburbs. A major urban problem is to restore this rotted core. A program to rebuild the CBD in St. Louis, Missouri,

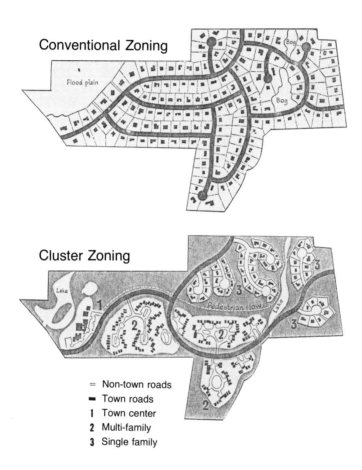

FIGURE 19-2. Echo Hill, a 250-acre development in Amherst, Massachusetts, was first planned as a typical grid-type community (upper). But then, builder-developer William E. Aubin switched to Planned Unit Development (lower) to provide green spaces for community "breathing room." The above diagram appeared in an article by Charles Dole, "Proof of P.U.D. Is in the Living," *The Christian Science Monitor,* April 12, 1968. Adapted by permission from *The Christian Science Monitor,* © 1968, The Christian Science Publishing Society. All rights reserved.

has provided new apartments, office buildings and recreation centers. The ball park, Sportsman's Park, was fashioned anew, renamed Busch Stadium and moved many miles, from the northern part of the city to the downtown. A large apartment project, Mansion House, was built on the riverfront, which the CBD faces. In cooperation, the National Park Service renovated a famous old courthouse, established a museum and built the 630-foot high Gateway Arch with extensive landscaping surrounding it, now one of the top tourist attractions in the United States (see Figure 19-3). A new convention center and five new hotels were built. And, a number of low- and medium-income housing projects were situated just outside the CBD.

Can renovation of the CBD of a city, such as is being done in St. Louis, really revitalize the entire central city? In the case of St. Louis, the program, after some early setbacks, appears to have become successful. The Spanish Pavilion, rebuilt in the city after being moved from the New York World's Fair, was taken over by private interests and converted to a hotel. The Mansion House apartments likewise were converted to a motel. The largest office building ever built in the city was completed in 1977 by the Mercantile Bank. A new riverfront recreational and commercial development, known as "Laclede's Landing," has attracted many visitors and some businesses. Two large apartments were connected in a grass and steel "palace" with specialty shops—known as "St. Louis Centre." A few blocks west of the CBD, a large, abandoned railway station was connected to a recreation and shopping center in 1986 and has become a great success. Throughout the development, efforts have been made to provide open space, greenery and pleasant vistas. The program illustrates an attempt to revitalize the CBD by providing environmental diversity, which Dubois, cited earlier, noted as an essential if people are to reach their full potential.

To upgrade housing in the St. Louis area, the city, several decades ago, undertook the largest, in terms of a single area, land-clearance project in the nation. Some 2 square miles of buildings were razed. Subsequent building has proceeded with a combination of residential and commercial buildings and at least one large manufacturing plant, a printing concern. This project, known as the Mill Creek Valley development, indeed has a variety. Slab housing, modular housing, apartments, duplexes, single-family dwellings—all are represented in the residential section. Commercial structures likewise are varied. And, change is still going on. A major concern is whether or not the various projects, which were added one by one instead of as part of a comprehensive plan, will ever really "jell" as a community.

FIGURE 19-3. The Gateway Arch, rising high above the St. Louis waterfront on the Mississippi River, reminds us of the importance of our magnificent river resources in the history of our nation—especially in the growth of cities. In the late 1700's and early 1800's, water transport dominated the movement of freight and passengers. Then, St. Louis was unmatched for commercial access to the West, reflecting its superb position on the Mississippi River near the confluence of that river with the Illinois and Missouri rivers and not far from its junction with the Ohio River. But, transportation modes changed. While the volume of river freight by barge today far exceeds the amount carried by steamboats years ago, its relative significance has declined, as trains, trucks, and airplanes have taken over. St. Louis, like all large metropolitan centers in the United States, has become a world trade center with access to resources inconceivable a few centuries ago to all but a few visionaries.

In the background is the Old Court House and part of the grounds of the Jefferson National Expansion Memorial National Park. The park development, which includes the Gateway Arch, a museum and the Old Court House, has helped revitalize downtown St. Louis. Almost all of the high-rise buildings shown are relatively new. (Courtesy, St. Louis Convention & Visitors Commission)

In 1987, new management of the complex was being sought to help the area realize its potential for good living.

Other attempts to clear blighted areas in the central city have met with mixed success. Notably successful developments include those by Leon Strauss, who was named St. Louis Construction Industry Man of the Year in 1980, and who has also received the St. Louis award for outstanding community service because of his redevelopment housing programs. His formula for success was attractive housing realized through a package of profitable financing arrangements and imaginative development schemes. The latter based development on the ability to control whole city blocks and thus renovate an entire area rather than isolated units. He also effected innovative plans for rehab housing which considered both aesthetic and functional goals. Unfortunately, by 1988, reflecting the impact of the Tax Reform Act of 1986, the programs of Mr. Strauss' redevelopment corporation and other like developers had been sharply curtailed. Government support in terms of tax abatement and other privileges were withdrawn. Many projects became financially unworkable.

A lesson in disastrous public housing was the St. Louis Pruitt-Igoe project. Hailed when built in 1955–56 as a model of housing to rehabilitate low-income families, the apartments had become quagmires of vice and violence by the 1960's. The project, which housed 10,000 people, has now been torn down. Lack of proper design was one reason for the failure. Oscar Newman, in his book *Defensible Space*, suggests that the major physical flaw in the design of public housing can be fixed. Pruitt-Igoe was a monolithic type of high-rise apartments with no streets through the center. Newman states that projects must be open to view from the outside. This provides onlookers, which adds to safety. Pruitt-Igoe had skip-stop elevators and long hallways and inadequate playgrounds. There was no feeling of territoriality—a sense of pride and responsibility for one's own area of the project, which Newman points out is essential. He also recommends that new public housing projects should be built in middle-income areas and should be kept small (500 units) and low (under 7 stories).

Another problem with Pruitt-Igoe was a lack of social planning and guidance.

Deteriorating public housing remains an urban problem in St. Louis and other cities. The nation has some 10,000 public housing projects, many of them in problem areas. A ray of hope for improvement is a new government program empowering renters to manage their projects themselves.

Less than 20 projects, however, have taken this step. Results have been mixed. In St. Louis, the experiment has been quite successful at the Cochran public housing project, as shown by its full occupancy and sharp drop in crime. Successful management involves tenant instruction, rules and rule enforcement. The goal is to change people's attitudes and to form a good neighborhood—the basic answer to pleasant urban dwelling.[6]

AIR QUALITY AND THE CITY

All of us have been concerned about the quality of air in the city, but how many of us have realized that the impact of the city on air masses extends far beyond its boundary? Here again, let's consider St. Louis as an example, for it happens to have been the center of a unique national project—a five-year project, 1971–1976, called METROMEX (Metropolitan Meteorological Experiment). The project involved 35 scientists from a number of different private and public research agencies.

The project found that two counties to the east, and thus downwind from St. Louis, get 10 to 30 percent more rainfall in the summer than comparable regions outside the city's influence. The net effect is to increase crop yields by 2 to 5 percent. Individual rainstorms can dump as much as 300 percent more water than those formed elsewhere. While the added rainfall is found to be beneficial to crops, the thunderstorms that often accompany it—especially those with hail—are harmful.

An adverse effect of the city on air quality has been increases in ozone levels sometimes far from the central city. In 1980, Edwardsville, Illinois, led the state in EPA ozone readings—exceeding both state and federal standards. Yet, Edwardsville lies about 20 miles east of the major industrial areas of St. Louis and has virtually no industry of its own. In recent years, high ozone-level records have been associated with communities in Lake County, Illinois, well north of the Chicago hub. The readings, of course, depend upon various factors of the specific location and the number of air monitoring stations. Even though ozone diffuses rapidly, all parts of a community do not necessarily have uniform air quality.

---

[6] Art Levine and Dan Collins, "When Tenants Take Over," and Michael Bose, "Beating Blight in St. Louis," *U.S. News & World Report*, August 4, 1986, pp. 53, 54.

While some of these effects are because of added heat from the city, as well as air pollution, we must wonder about the potential impact of our other large metropolitan areas on the surrounding countryside. The battle against air pollution in cities, where auto exhausts and factories are concentrated, is a matter of life and death (see "Air Pollution and Resources," Chapter 23).

PLANNING CITY GROWTH

Planned Unit Development

Rehabilitating the old sections of cities is one opportunity to better use our natural resources. It is sensible and economical to continue using those land areas now occupied by cities for urban purposes. Both in redeveloping large sections of our old cities and in providing for new growth, a new, unified type of development known as Planned Unit Development (PUD) is being practiced.[7] This is one way of avoiding the urban sprawl of the past, in which building often proceeded without regard for environmental conditions or for total community needs.

In this type of development, a large area of land, say, several square miles or more, is developed as a unit over a span of years. The development may include commercial and industrial as well as residential sections (see Figure 19-4). The character of the physical conditions of the land—drainage, existing vegetation, soils, etc.—is taken into account in the planning. Thus, a more harmonious adjustment to the resource base is possible than under the traditional piecemeal method in which residential subdivisions, shopping centers and industrial establishments were sometimes located so that they compounded problems of adjustment to the landscape rather than solving them (see Figure 19-5).

What Will Happen to Farm Land?

Several million acres of farm land on the edge of cities are taken out of agriculture and put into buildings and streets and other urban uses each

---

[7]For a technical definition, see Robert W. Burchnell, *Planned Unit Development: New Communities, American Style*, New Brunswick, New Jersey, Center for Urban Policy Research, Rutgers University, 1972.

year (see Chapter 14). Will PUD's continue to take over the farms? One way of preventing this is being tried out in Suffolk County, Long Island. The citizens of the county have decided to buy the right of farmers to sell their acreage to developers. *Time* magazine points out how it works: "If a farm is worth say $6,000 per acre to a developer but only $1,500 per acre to a farmer, the county will pay the difference—$4,500—for the 'development rights.' In return, farmers who join the program must agree to keep the land in farms forever."[8]

FIGURE 19-4. The swimmer in the foreground is standing beside a community swimming pool overlooking a lake in the Cottonwood Village section of the Cottonwood Planned Unit Development. Modular housing is in the background. This is one of the lower-cost communities of the development. (Courtesy, Merrill Ottwein, The Cottonwood Companies, Edwardsville, Illinois)

Another method to save farm land, proposed for the Green Spring Valley of Maryland, is having the PUD try to include in its boundaries those farms which are to be kept in crops as well as the area that is thought environmentally suited for housing. Whether used for crops or housing, the land could then be purchased at the same price per acre by the developer. And, the developer would be legally bound not to build on the farm acreage.

---

[8]"Planning City Growth," *Time*, April 21, 1975, p. 48.

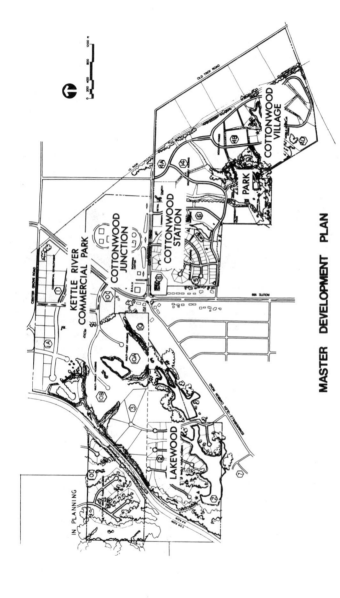

MASTER DEVELOPMENT PLAN

FIGURE 19-5. This master development plan of the 813-acre Cottonwood Planned Unit Development, located near Edwardsville, Illinois, illustrates how unit planning can provide variety and natural areas. Cottonwood Village features modular homes and several different styles of conventionally built single-family homes and townhouses. Cottonwood Station features homes in a medium-price range, clustered to provide more usable open space. Cottonwood Junction is a shopping center with an enclosed sports complex. Kettle River is subdivided for commercial ventures. Lakewood and its annex, Ginger Creek (not identified in drawing), have luxury single-family homes and townhouses. Many acres of heavily wooded parkland with nature trails and numerous lakes provide the residential areas with a natural setting. (Courtesy, Merrill Ottwein, The Cottonwood Companies, Edwardsville, Illinois)

SOIL, SEWAGE AND THE CITY

Suitability of Soils

Too often urban development has ignored the requirements of soil. Probably the most important investment most of us make in our lifetime is the house in which we live. The soil on which we build may be very undesirable for this use and thus may create many problems. Soil characteristics that should be considered are the seasonal water table, flooding potential, slope, shrink-swell potential, potential frost action and bedrock depth. These factors have an influence on the ability of the soil to support a house without its having cracked walls, foundations and driveways. They also indicate the potential for wet basements as well as flooded houses. Obviously, we should investigate soil conditions prior to building; otherwise, our "dream home" can become a nightmare.

Adaptability for Sewage

Another matter that must be taken into account besides the suitability of soils for supporting buildings is their adaptability for sewage. Otherwise, our homes as a place to live may become very disappointing.

Centralized sewage systems are the best. But, many areas are beyond public sewers and must dispose of household sewage on site through septic tanks into a buried filter field, if development is permitted. The success or failure of these systems depends on the soil. Soil characteristics important for this use are (1) permeability (the ease with which air and water move down through the soil), (2) height of the water table, (3) flooding potential, (4) slope of the land and (5) depth to bedrock.

Soil may not be permeable enough or too permeable to accommodate septic systems satisfactorily. If a soil is not permeable, water and the effluent will not be absorbed by the soil. When this occurs, the disposal area becomes fully saturated, and the area becomes unsightly and unhealthy. If the soil is too permeable, another hazard may exist. The effluent will flow rapidly downward and possibly contaminate the ground water.

The level of the water table has a direct bearing on the efficiency of waste disposal. Soils vary considerably in seasonal wetness and seasonal water tables. If a soil has a very high water table, additional water in the form of sewage effluent cannot be added to it without overflow. Generally, soils having seasonal water tables below 6 feet have few or no problems, while soils having seasonal water tables less than 4 feet have serious problems. Soils have inherent properties that can be mapped so as to indicate seasonal water tables, enabling us to avoid problems.

Flooding is an obvious hazard for any form of sewage disposal. When soils become flooded, sewage-disposal fields associated with septic tanks become inoperative, creating a serious health hazard as well as making household plumbing useless.

The slope of the land is also critical to efficient sewage disposal in septic tank systems because it affects the layout of the disposal area. The steeper the slope, the greater the chance of the sewage effluent migrating to the surface by lateral movement. This is offensive to the eyes and nose and can be fatal.

If bedrock is at the surface, it would be difficult to install a septic tank disposal field as well as to have the bedrock absorb the discharge. If the bedrock is fractured, the discharge might move downward as well as laterally to contaminate ground water supplies. It is important to have at least 4 feet of soil to filter the effluent.

Septic systems generally are not a satisfactory way of disposing of sewage. In many areas, especially urban, they should be prohibited.

NEW TOWNS

When PUD's are developed to such an extent that they actually are small cities, they are referred to as "new towns." Such complete communities have been built in the United Kingdom for over three decades. And, others have been developed on the continent of Europe. Over a decade ago, we in this country began building what we called "new towns," but only recently have some of the projects really qualified for this designation.

A new town may be defined as a new community planned to be largely self-contained, providing homes, services and jobs for its citizens, in a physically, socially and economically balanced environment. New towns differ from PUD's in that they are much more ambitious in extent—often proposing to accommodate 100,000 or more people eventually—generally requiring planning for a much longer period of time and massive government financing.

Both new towns and PUD's are adaptable to meet the requirement for the rehabilitation of central cities. They could be located smack in the center of the city, for example, after land clearance. Thames-Meade, a British new town, is located in a former factory area on the Thames and within the London Metropolitan Area, for example (see Figure 19-6).

FIGURE 19-6. Thames-Meade is a new town located within the London metropolitan area. Note the high-rises in the background and the two- and three-story dwellings on the right. An office building is in the center background. To the left is a lagoon for run-off water, which also is used for recreation. Some 40,000 people live here. (Photo by Harry B. Kircher)

New towns are worth considering. In 1972, a three-year private study commissioned by the late Laurence Rockefeller concluded that the federal government should adopt a national policy calling for the creation of new towns. The study suggested free-standing new towns as well as those to be located within cities or on the edge of cities, or located to expand growth of small towns. There is no question that the chance to plan for diversity, including the amenities and reducing the adverse environmental effects, is appealing. However, experience with new town development in Great Britain has been mixed. Those towns built nearest metropolitan centers have been the most successful. But, in a free society, while government can encourage people to occupy new towns and establish business there, it cannot make them do so. Ways need to be found to keep alive opportunities for private initiative and preferences in planned communities in order to ensure their success.

THE PLACE OF SMALL CITIES AND TOWNS

While the discussion here has been of supercities because they are the major problem areas today, there is no intention to deny the importance of smaller cities and towns in accommodating resource development. In a study of such communities in the Eighth Federal Reserve District, a region comprised of all of Arkansas and parts of six other states, author Kircher showed how these cities met manufacturing, trade, recreation and other needs of the region. He concluded that they were a vital part of the region's economy. As these cities grow or reconstruct, application of unit development principles will help them relate to the natural resource base better.

If the tide of population movement from country to city could be reversed, some of the pressures would be taken off the city. In fact, some of the social maladjustments of the city have occurred because country job seekers got "lost" in the metropolis. As has been noted however, just the reverse has been taking place.

Megacounties

In fact, many small towns have been engulfed in the last three decades by development of heavily populated regions, called "megacounties" by *Time* magazine. Fairfax County, Virginia; Johnson County, Kansas; and Orange County, California; are examples cited by *Time*.[9] All adjoin large cities. All enjoy great wealth but suffer environmental problems as natural open spaces vanish.

Author Kircher visited Orange County in the spring of 1987. He found elaborate shopping centers and health care facilities and beautiful restaurants and homes. Recreational possibilities included horseback riding trails, tennis courts, swimming pools, golf courses and, of course, the ocean beaches. Residents have just about every amenity and can meet almost every need without having to drive into the central city of San Diego. Offices

---

[9]"The Boom Towns," *Time*, June 15, 1987, p. 14 ff.

and manufacturing plants of multimillion dollar corporations along with bustling trade outlets and fat retirement checks support high incomes with little unemployment. But, the crowding of people into a geologically unstable and climatically semi-arid environment has created problems. Houses built on unstable rock and soil slide downhill in torrential rains; others built adjacent to wooded canyons burn up in wind-driven fires during the dry California summers; and many quiver uneasily from frequent earth tremors. Overall is the impending threat of a water shortage—for the county is heavily dependent upon imported water.

The National Council on Development for the 1980's, agreed in the first phase of its work that physical development should include the following two points: (1) communities should be more compact, both in developing and existing populated areas, and (2) a balance should be developed between employment and residential uses in existing urban centers as well as in new satellite communities. The Council recommended that by various land-use controls, ". . . 'urban villages' [be encouraged] within towns and cities where diverse housing and related services lay in close proximity to a commercial and industrial core."[10]

CITIES ARE NATURAL—WE HAVE MADE THEM UNNATURAL

In this chapter, we have been able to touch upon only a few of the ways to deal with cities so that they will be more of an element of strength in use and development of our natural resource base.

Cities are here to stay. Barring a nuclear war which might wipe us all out, cities are bound to grow, and their influence on our resources is bound to increase.

We can improve our present cities. We must. Otherwise, chaos threatens to overwhelm us. City and regional planning are absolutely essential to the wise use of our urban resources and the protection of our rural resources. Well-designed and well-implemented plans will protect not only the city dwellers but the farmers, ranchers, lumber-producers and other rural dwellers as well.

---

[10]"Policy Trends, Harmonizing Design with Policy," *AGORA*, Newsletter of the Landscape Architecture Foundation, Vol. 1, No. 1, Autumn 1980, p. 3.

Planning does not necessarily mean **government** planning. It is a trick, but one that must be performed if we are to develop resources to the best advantage, to preserve wise local discretion in planning, while at the same time assuring that reasonable regional and national land-use needs are not being shortcut. And, we need to preserve the ingenuity and initiative of private businesspersons, while still protecting our irreplaceable resources. PUD's are generally private, not government, ventures. And, even government projects are generally planned with the help of private consulting firms and are built by private builders.

City planning should proceed on the basis of sound ecological assessment of the soil, water, air and other resources. Modern schemes of interrelated design and long-range development, such as those of PUD's and new towns, are promising ways of helping check the chaotic, wasteful metropolitan growth of the past.[11]

Despite the importance of elements of design and the necessity of building in harmony with nature, it must be noted that some of the most pressing problems of our cities are social. Our resources, it will be recalled, depend just as much upon our societal as upon our technological abilities. In the city, our societal abilities especially appear to be most wanting: ". . . many cities large and small are now prowled by cold-eyed youths who mug and kill without emotion or remorse."[12]

The need for rebuilding cities is especially critical to minority groups and to individuals who are economically deprived. John E. Jacob, president of the National Urban League, in an interview in *The Christian Science Monitor* stated that reviving U.S. cities is the league's primary objective. "We were founded on the basis of helping the rural blacks adjust to urban life," he said. "Our clients are no longer . . . country blacks coming to northern cities to escape the segregated South. Today we have to seek the restoration of the inner city without having minority residents give it up to . . . gentrification."[13]

---

[11] For more information on conceptual, scientific and design approaches to problems posed by nature and urban development, see *Landscape and Urban Planning;* An International Journal of Landscape Design, Conservation and Reclamation; Planning and Urban Ecology; Amsterdam; Elsevier Science Publishers; 1988.

[12] "The Menace of Any Shadow," *Time,* December 22, 1980, p. 32.

[13] Luix Overbea, "Urban League Leader Focuses on Revival of U.S. Cities," *The Christian Science Monitor,* Midwestern ed., July 17, 1987, p. 6.

Cities over 8,000 years old have been discovered. Who knows how many were washed away in the muds of the Yangtze Kiang, blown away by desert winds or drowned in the rising seas? Like all other living things, humans have their communities. The largest of them are cities. If we can preserve their health and vigor, we will thrive. If we let them disintegrate into chaos, our entire resource base will be threatened.

QUESTIONS AND PROBLEMS

1. How do cities influence our resources in the country? Give two examples.
2. Where would you rather live—in the country or in a city? Why?
3. Why do people want to live in cities?
4. How can we make our cities "greener"?
5. How does cluster zoning make better use of our land resource?
6. How is St. Louis rejuvenating its central business district (CBD)?
7. What are some problems of trying to rebuild the central city?
8. What was the Pruitt-Igoe project? What did its failure teach us about better planning for cities?
9. How can a Planned Unit Development (PUD) result in better use of our land resource than we had without it?
10. What is a method of planning or of buying land that can help prevent agricultural land from being taken over by nonfarm development?
11. Why is it important to know about the soil in cities?
12. Can new towns solve the problem of rehabilitating cities? Explain your answer.
13. Are small towns and cities still needed for resource development? Explain your answer.
14. Do you agree or disagree with the conclusion that "cities are natural"? Explain your answer.

20

Why Wildlife
Is Important and
How to Save It

When the term *wildlife* is mentioned, some of us immediately think of deer, bears or water birds which can be hunted during the "open seasons"; to others, it brings to mind songbirds, rare plants of the woods, the virgin forests or lovely flowers that can be enjoyed only as long as they are left in their native habitat; while, to still others, it means the fish of our streams, lakes and seas. The term *wildlife*, indeed, includes all nondomesticated plants and animals: mammals, birds, reptiles, amphibians and fishes—all *vertebrates*— and *invertebrates*, such as shellfish, crabs, starfish, insects, spiders, worms, corals, sponges and numerous one-celled animals. Wildlife is so rich and varied a resource that the surface can only be skimmed here. Our concentration will center on the wild animals and the way in which non-specialists can help conserve them.

"Life today, despite the process of elimination /which has occurred throughout geologic time/ is not poorer but richer and more varied than in any previous epoch," Marion Newbigin, a zoologist, botanist and geographer, has written in *Plant and Animal Geography*.[1] How much

---

[1]Marion Newbigin, *Plant and Animal Geography*, London, Methuen, 1950, p. 24.

longer our rich and varied wildlife will remain so appears to be in ques-tion, however, unless we do a better job of taking care of it. Within the last century, 9 mammals, 31 birds and 6 fishes have been exterminated in the United States. Since colonial days, 62 animals have become extinct. It is sad that these animals are gone, for the record shows that we can do wonders in restoring wildlife. Deer may be more plentiful in North America now than when Europeans first settled here. Antelope, elk and turkeys are examples of wild game that have been brought back from dan-gerously low levels to number in the hundreds of thousands.

The United States is a world leader in programs to rescue endangered species by controlled breeding, *U.S. News & World Report* observed in its April 17, 1978, issue. Since 1966, when Congress passed the Endangered Species Preservation Act, the federal Office of Endangered Species has set up recovery teams to bring back over 50 species of wildlife from near extinction (see Figure 20-1).

However, today over 270 mammals, over 200 birds and many other animal and plant species are threatened with extinction. In fact, close to 1,000 species are listed by the U.S. Fish and Wildlife Service as being endan-gered. (See Table 20-1 showing the breakdown for 1985.)

TABLE 20-1. Endangered and Threatened Wildlife and Plant Species — Number, 1985[1]

	Mammals	Birds	Reptiles	Amphibians	Fishes	Snails	Clams	Crustaceans	Insects	Plants
Endangered species, total	273	216	74	13	45	4	24	3	8	73
U.S. only	20	59	8	5	30	3	22	3	8	67
U.S. and foreign	19	13	6	–	4	–	0	–	–	5
Foreign only	234	144	60	8	11	1	2	–	–	1
Threatened species, total	26	4	25	3	17	5	–	1	4	14
U.S. only	4	3	8	3	14	5	–	1	4	10
U.S. and foreign	–	1	4	–	3	–	–	–	–	2
Foreign only[2]	22	–	13	–	–	–	–	–	–	2

[1] *Endangered species* — Those in danger of becoming extinct throughout all or a significant part of their natural range. *Threatened species* — Those that will probably become endangered in the foreseeable future.

[2] Species outside U.S. and outlying areas as determined by the U.S. Fish and Wildlife Service.

FIGURE 20-1. The beaver, the wild turkey and the Canada goose are examples of the kinds of wildlife that have increased in numbers in response to management practices in recent years. (Courtesy, U.S. Fish and Wildlife Service)

JUSTIFICATION FOR WILDLIFE

Why save wildlife? To some people this seems an absurd question. However, for those who do not see its absurdity, the question must be asked, and answered, so thay they will understand why wildlife is important.

Wildlife can be justified for reasons we have chosen to call the four "E's." These are Economic, Esthetic, Ethical and Ecological.

Economic value of wildlife.—Wildlife has a tremendous dollar-and-cents value. There is income from the sales of fish and furs and savings from eating wild game. But, this is only a small part of their worth. Billions of dollars are spent each year for hunting, fishing and other forms of recreation related to wildlife. More billions are saved by the control of environment for wildlife.

Hunting expenditures in the United States increased from about $2.1 billion in 1970 to $8.9 billion in 1980. Big game hunting accounted for about 60 percent of these expenditures; small game, 31 percent; and waterfowl, 9 percent.

Sport fishers almost quadrupled their fishing expenditure during the 10-year period—from $7 billion to $27 billion. Of this amount, fresh water fishers spent about four times as much as salt water fishers.[2]

In 1985, almost 59 million Americans went fishing, according to preliminary figures by the U.S. Fish and Wildlife Service and U.S. Bureau of the Census. Angling expenditures were $28.2 billion.[3]

The value of furs and hides harvested from wild creatures in the United States totaled $0.38 billion in the early 1980's.[4]

Especially important to all of us is the value of wild animals, birds and reptiles in helping control the spread of insects and other pests. The economic worth of such benefits is difficult to measure. Certainly, direct benefits are several billions of dollars. Indirect benefits are as valuable as life itself. The bottom line is that without the help of these creatures in

---

[2]U.S. Fish and Wildlife Service and U.S. Bureau of the Census, *1980 National Survey of Fishing, Hunting, and Wildlife Associated Recreation*, Washington, D.C., 1982.

[3]Report on 1985 survey (see footnote 2, above) by Duncan Barnes, "Editorial," *Field and Stream*, June 1987, p. 5. This survey is conducted every five years.

[4]Organization for Economic Co-operation and Development (OECD), *The State of the Environment 1985*, Paris, France, OECD, 1985, p. 137. Members of the OECD environmental group were 17 European countries, Australia, New Zealand, Canada, Japan, Turkey and the United States.

maintaining nature's balance, food crops would be devastated, life would be untenable and our entire economic system would collapse.

Esthetic value of wildlife.—No one can measure the value of beauty, but we all can recognize it. We spend billions of dollars each year on cosmetics to make ourselves "more beautiful." We pay fortunes to architects to design beautiful buildings. For many years, U.S.–made automobiles were sold on the basis of their beautiful lines. President Lyndon Johnson proclaimed "beauty" a national goal in the 1960's. What is more beautiful than wildlife? We value birds for their beautiful plumage, song and flight. We value antelope and deer for the beauty of their graceful movements. Much of the joy of fishing is in the beauty of the leaping trout. How beautiful are flickering fireflies on a quiet summer night—even the deep "Hrumm, hrumm" of Mr. Bullfrog is beautiful. How drab life would be without the beauty of wildlife!

Ethical reasons to save wildlife.—We have a "moral" responsibility to pass along to our children and grandchildren our wildlife heritage. Furthermore, we should not be wasteful. The Indians' use of buffalo for food, shelter and clothing was a wise use of a resource. But, our reducing the numbers of buffalo in wholesale slaughter from over 50 million to less than 1,000 in a few years was unethical.

Ecological value of wildlife.—Last considered of the four "E's," but the most important to our material well-being is the ecological worth of wildlife. As explained in Chapter 23, in which some of the principles of ecology are discussed, all lifeforms on earth are interdependent in what is referred to as the "web of life." When we wipe out various species of wildlife, we are destroying some of the richness of our own life. Carried far enough, it means total destruction for us too.

In *food chain* relationships, animals eat plants and people eat animals. If the balance of nature becomes upset, people will be also. When ranges were overgrazed by cattle, the soil was exposed and eroded away, and sagebrush took over from the grasses or sandy, rocky wastes developed. Then, the land could support neither cattle nor wild animals, and certainly not people. Insects and reptiles can be as important to our well-being as large animals. We stamp them out without thought.

The interrelationships of plants, animals and land to people is illustrated by problems of the Florida Everglades. This large wet land is dependent upon reliable amounts of steady, slow-moving water to maintain its fragile ecosystem. Soon after it became a state in 1845, Florida began to convert the Everglades to agricultural use by ditching. This action exposed the rich organic peats, resulting in drying, fires, land subsidence and erosion. Shallow acquifers in southern Florida lost their water supplies, which allowed salt water to creep into them. The establishment of the Everglades National Park in 1947 halted some of the destruction. But, by 1973 some 40 percent of southern Florida's wetlands were gone. With them went many of the native plants and animals.[5]

In the 1980's, concern for the ecosystem of the remaining Everglades has been translated into action. Authorized in 1976 and completed in 1987, the Kissimmee River was restored to its original meandering channel from which it had been diverted. This river, located north of the Everglades, is a major source of water for Lake Okeechobee, whose waters in turn are vital to the Everglades. Through ditching, the river had been shortened to half its length with disastrous results for the lake and consequently the Everglades. The restored river and the conservation projects, including the closing of a number of canals, are intended to help the Everglades.

Congress tried to protect our coastal areas against harmful development by passage of the Coastal Zone Management Act of 1972 (CZMA). It provided funding for planning coastal zone management. During the 1970's and early 1980's, a number of states took advantage of this act to adopt new laws and regulations or to improve the implementation of existing laws. But, Charles E. Little writes bitterly in the summer 1987 issue of *Wilderness* that: "Our efforts to promote coastal-zone planning [are] virtually defunct after fifteen years of trying; schemes to support state-level planning. . . failed so often that finally even the conservationists got bored with them . . ."[6]

Another reason for preserving wildlife, one not included in the four "E's," is their inspirational value. Whose spirit has not been uplifted by the cheerful chirping of chickadees on a dreary winter's day or by the sight of the wavering "V" of Canada geese high in the air as they wing southward? We characterize our friends by referring to them as "courageous as a lion," "sly as a fox" or "wise as an owl."

---

[5]William C. Reffalt, "A Nationwide Survey, Wetlands in Extremists," *Wilderness*, Washington, D.C., The Wilderness Society, Winter 1985, pp. 34–35.

[6]Charles E. Little, "Letting Leopold Down," *Wilderness*, Summer 1987, p. 47.

NOT ALL WILDLIFE BENEFICIAL

A few years ago, author Kircher and some friends were camping near Fishing Bridge in Yellowstone National Park. The cook was assigned the job of sleeping in the back of the stake truck, which had the food supplies. Late one night, a black bear decided to investigate some interesting scent it had caught, so it clambered up the tailgate of the truck. The cook, suddenly awakened, was almost startled out of his wits to find himself suddenly face to face with a black bear. Fortunately, he just happened to have a baseball bat handy. He proceeded to give the bear a "friendly" tap on the nose, with the fervent prayer that he had convinced it to dine elsewhere. At that point, the cook was convinced that at some times and some places wildlife are not especially beneficial. It took many years for certain animals to be domesticated successfully. A wild animal cornered, desperately hungry or sick (for example, rabid) can be dangerous. A word to the wise is sufficient!

Some wildlife which have gotten out of balance with nature appear to be mostly destructive. Large flocks of blackbirds—red-winged blackbirds, common grackles, cowbirds, rusty blackbirds and starlings— make a lot of noise, have an odor and can carry disease. They are a problem to farmers. One theory for their destructiveness is that they have been forced out of their habitats to become a nuisance in cultivated areas. Another is that the flocks have grown out of size because the birds' natural predators—hawks and crows—have been so greatly reduced in numbers. No conclusive theory or solution to the problem has been found. The situation emphasizes the point that in our world, so heavily settled by people, more wildlife management than ever before is needed.

PROVIDING HABITAT FOR WILDLIFE

The *American Dictionary of the English Language* defines *habitat* as "the area or type of environment in which an organism or biological population lives or occurs." What kind of habitat is it that enables wild animals to survive? It is an environment which includes shelter, food, water and range—a place to move around in. The greater the diversity of habitat, the greater will be the diversity of the wildlife there.

Vegetative cover provides shelter for wild animals, so the first step in building up an area for animal habitat is to restore cover, if needed. This step also reduces erosion and helps hold the rain on the soil until it can be absorbed.

Generally, vegetation cover benefits both wildlife and soil. Even weed growth will afford temporary shade and some food for birds and small animals. In an area with sufficient rainfall, where vegetative cover has been lost, nature itself will start the process of restoration, although it may be relatively unsuccessful if problems such as acid mine drainage, wastes or steep erosion slopes are present. Under favorable conditions, grass and shrubs will start fairly soon from seeds carried to the area by wind or birds. Seedlings from trees such as cottonwoods and maples may also drift into the area and start growing at about the same time as the shrubs.

In an area with little rainfall, the problem of establishing vegetation cover is more difficult. Furrows plowed on the contour help hold the rainfall on hillsides, and the use of baffle strips in freshly cut ravines slows down water run-off. Check dams accomplish the same result, or even sodding some strips across the watercourse may help in reducing the speed of water run-off and in restoring some plant growth.

Another consideration in wildlife preservation is to provide suitable places for animals to build homes and to live securely from their enemies. This again means shrubs and trees for some animals, good grass for others and, for still others, a soil in which they can make holes or runways.

Habitat must also provide food. We should realize, however, that some types of plants are much more beneficial to wildlife than others. Some plants are valuable for domestic livestock and erosion control but are of little value to wildlife for either food or cover. Planting beneficial species makes more sense than planting just anything to hold the soil in place. Landowners should ask the USDA Extension Service advisors in their areas for recommendations of specific plants (see Figures 20-2, 20-3 and 20-4).

Farmers can increase wildlife habitat by leaving a few rows of unplowed crops next to fence rows or wooded areas. Food plots which, after being plowed, provide stubble which will stand up above the snow are most valuable for wildlife. Good intentions do not feed wildlife if the food is buried.

An adequate range for certain wild animals is beyond the capacity of all but a few extremely wealthy persons to provide. Lord Estes, for whom the town of Estes Park, Colorado, was named, once controlled an area of many square miles in the very heart of the Colorado Rockies. While a number of large farms and ranches are still held in the United States today, most of us must leave the provision of range for wildlife such as antelope, buffalo, deer and elk to the federal government. Because these animals move freely from public to private lands, unaware that they may be "trespassing," we must make sure that any small landholdings we may have or may use enhance habitat for wildlife.

If farm land owners and operators do their part, they can help relieve some of the stress on wildlife caused by the expansion of human activities by allowing some diversification and providing some set-aside areas for wild-life. Upland wildlife such as ring-necked pheasants, bobwhite quail, Hungarian partridges, cottontail rabbits, white-tailed deer, waterfowl and many types of songbirds thrive in diversified farm land (see Figure 2-2). But, they must have undisturbed nesting and winter cover.[7]

Wild pheasants need more than space to roam. Major problems that face them are clean farming and no-till farming practices. Clean farming practices call for the elimination of hedge rows and idle land. No-till farming, as was noted in Chapter 16, requires use of toxic herbicides and insecticides which eliminate nearly everything alive except the seeds of the crop sown. Without weeds and insects, there can be no pheasant nests and no pheasant chicks.[8]

Small animals such as foxes, opossums and raccoons may travel only a few acres or a few miles in search of food, while others such as beavers and muskrats may occupy a particular pond. In these cases, small landowners may be able to meet all their needs within their own landholding.

Third, there must be a supply of water available. Animals in the desert or on the semi-arid plains have special systems which permit them to adapt to a very low water supply, or they obtain it from somewhat unusual sources, such as cactuses. Or, nature has equipped them to travel long distances in search of water. In the former case, the water-gathering plants upon which they depend must be protected or provided. In the latter case, an adequate range, perhaps hundreds of square miles, needs to be provided. In the humid eastern part of the country or in the mountains and on the seacoasts of the West, the water supply needs to be kept uncontaminated by poisonous wastes and chemicals. Small landowners may be

---

[7]Letter to Harry B. Kircher from Ron George, Wildlife Research Biologist, Iowa Conservation Commission, February 27, 1980.

[8]Jim Bashline, "Pheasants in Frigid Weather," *Field and Stream*, November 1987, p. 108.

FIGURE 20-2. The cottontail rabbit, the coyote and the raccoon are illustrations of wildlife that have adapted to the ways of civilization. They survive in excellent farming conditions. (Courtesy, U.S. Fish and Wildlife Service)

FIGURE 20-3. This land was completely overbrowsed by deer. No food is left within reach of even the largest animal. (Courtesy, Wisconsin Conservation Department)

able to increase the availability of water by damming creeks or even drilling wells to create lakes.

More information on the specific requirements for providing habitat is given in the next chapter.

Wildlife Need More Than Waste Acres

The large number and great variety of our wildlife require many kinds of food and shelter. Because of these varied needs, desirable numbers of the different species cannot be maintained by limiting them to the use of severely eroded land alone. It is for this reason that wildlife conservation must include many localities and environments for the maintenance of a satisfactory wildlife population. There are many small pieces of land in all agricultural areas that are not useful for crop production but which are more or less ideally adapted as homes for wildlife. These small acreages serve most wildlife purposes best if they are fenced so as to keep domestic animals from rooting up, grazing or trampling the vegetation. Where this is done, the owners in many areas will be rewarded within a few years by the return of animal wildlife as well as woods or prairie flowers.

FIGURE 20-4. During some winters the number of deer lost by starvation has been enormous. These trees show they have been so heavily browsed during the summer that little growth is left for winter deer browse. (Courtesy, Wisconsin Conservation Department)

THE STRUGGLE FOR SURVIVAL

The importance of predators (enemies) to the survival of any one kind of wildlife should not be overlooked (see Figure 20-5). Nature provides that each form of life becomes food for some other form. The simplest, smallest forms of aquatic (water) plants are consumed by exceedingly small, or microscopic, animals. These, in turn, are devoured by somewhat larger

FIGURE 20-5. Every form of life lives off some other form. Without predators, other enemies and disease, any one species could well populate the earth. It is only because of this dependence of one form of life on another that a balance in nature is kept. Without predators such as mountain lions and lynxes, our deer population would require hunting seasons on does to help keep the deer population in check; and without foxes, hawks and owls, rabbits would be a worse plague than the locusts of Biblical times. (Courtesy, U.S. Fish and Wildlife Service)

FIGURE 20-6. If you look closely, you will see a day-old baby elk which hid itself in this manner twice within an hour. Hiding places were selected by this baby elk where protective mottling of sunshine and shadow was most effective. Its mother was not near. Open range is required for natural perpetuation of elk. (Courtesy, National Park Service)

animals, which are later eaten by still others. When the wildlife population maintains a fairly definite proportion year after year, it is said to be in natural, or biological, balance.

This struggle for survival serves two purposes. First, the stronger, more alert of each group survive, making a hardier race, since the weaker or less cautious individuals are the ones that become food for others.

The second purpose served by this struggle for existence is to prevent the dominance of any one species. The increase in insect life during one summer would swarm the earth were it not for the enemies of insects—parasites, weather and disease. Disease is an enemy that is always a threat to overabundance of animal life. Rabbits could take over the country except for predators such as foxes, coyotes, hawks and owls. Nature's balance among the various kinds of life is maintained mostly because of the continuous pressure of wildlife upon its food supply—other living things.

The Kaibab Deer Incident

One of the great lessons in game management was learned on the Kaibab Plateau, "high country" bordering the Colorado River in northwestern Arizona. Here a mesa, relatively cut off from the rest of the countryside, was the home of some 3,000 Rocky Mountain mule deer. In 1906, to preserve this herd from the fate which was rapidly befalling other wild game in the United States, President Theodore Roosevelt set aside 1 million acres of this area as a national game preserve. About 6,000 predators of the deer—coyotes, mountain lions, bobcats and wolves—were destroyed. The management program appeared to be a great success. Within about 10 years, the deer herd doubled. Two years later, it doubled again. By 1923, the herd had reached 100,000 head, according to some estimates. But, there was no glory in the numbers. By then, it was obvious that something had gone wrong. Deer carcasses were lying around by the thousands. Thousands of animals were gaunt from malnutrition and disease. The trouble was easy to find. There was little to eat. The trees and bushes had been chewed up. In what the National Wildlife Federation has called "The Terrible Lesson of the Kaibab," two sterling principles of wildlife management were learned: (1) that predators along with plant eaters must be protected on game refuges and (2) that when people upset the "balance of nature," they must actively manage the habitat. Failure to carry out either of these principles means that game refuges become death traps (see Figure 20-6).

WILDLIFE MANAGEMENT

Among the approaches that have been made to the problem of conserving our wildlife, two of the commonly recognized methods date back to colonial times. They are hunting restrictions and wildlife refuges (see Figure 20-7). Today, we recognize that these alone cannot do the job. All landowners must provide habitat where possible.

Hunting

Management of wildlife today commonly involves hunting. Trapping, too, may be included. Hunting is widely approved. But, it should be done with the reverence of the German *Maester Jaeger* (master hunter) who in accordance with his code of honor . . . "protects wildlife and hunts as a proper huntsman, seeing the Creator honored in the creatures."[9] This reverence for wildlife parallels that of the Native American who also regards wildlife as sacred. Professor Fred Voget, an internationally respected scholar of native North American ethnology and cultural change, writes of the Crow Indians:

> The view of the world expressed in Crow contemporary philosophy contains the idea that individuals are linked to the world through a personalized cause and effect. . . . The world is alive with power, *maxpe*, and whatever moves, grows, and lives does so because of this special *maxpe*. . . .
>
> To overcome omnipresent threats to life and limb, men need to cooperate with and seek out the protection of the power holders and power dispensers in the world. Men need the *maxpe* of the eagle, which never misses, or of the bear, which is courageous, overpowering, and smart in fighting and eluding enemies. Then there is the buffalo, the fearless and fearsome charger, ever ready to turn and bowl his enemy over, and tough to subdue even when mortally wounded. In the ant one finds the busy and tireless industry that never ends despite the work load, while the quick mobility and near invisibility of the dragon-fly is a power to have ready at any time.
>
> Man's animal, bird, insect, tree, and rock associates are not to be ignored but respected for their powers and solicited for assistance in living out one's natural life.[10]

Hunting Restrictions

The idea that all game belong to the sovereign or the state originated in Europe, where only the rulers or owners of vast estates were privileged to hunt. Before the Magna Carta, which in 1215 granted definite privileges and liberties to the English day-workers, the killing of a stag cost the hands, the eyes or even the life of the offender. Or, the offender could be

---

[9]Freely translated from the German:Das ist des Jägers Ehrenschild
Dass er beschützt und hegt kein Wild,
Weidmännisch jagt, wie sich's gehört,
Den Schöpfer im Geschöpfe ehrt.

[10]Fred W. Voget, *The Shoshoni-Crow Sun Dance*, Norman, Oklahoma, University of Oklahoma Press, 1984, pp. 294–295.

FIGURE 20-7. Canada geese over Crab Orchard Refuge in Illinois. Refuges help in perpetuating wildlife but should not be looked upon as a solution to abundance. (Courtesy, U.S. Fish and Wildlife Service)

imprisoned for "a year and a day." Even after this date, severe penalties continued to be enforced against laborers for the possession of any kind of wildlife, though they no longer lost life or limb because of this.

The drastic restrictions to hunting were not brought to this country, though the idea that all wildlife belongs to the state was accepted. The earliest game regulations were for the purpose of legalizing the hunting by colonists that was taking place after they once learned how to live "off the land."

Early Colonists Not Hunters

It is interesting that the early colonists were faced with a lack of food amounting to starvation conditions, even though they were surrounded by an abundance of wildlife. Some say that they were too "civilized" to make use of the plentiful wildlife of the woods, the seashore and the streams. The chances are that neither English nor Dutch colonists knew anything about hunting or fishing, because these privileges belonged only to the rulers in their parent countries. Few, if any, had ever caught a fish or killed a wild animal. They knew nothing about "living off the land." It was only with the help of the Indians and through the severe school of experience that they finally learned to adapt themselves to the use of food supplied by the abundant wildlife around them.

Hunting Permits Required

Hunting privileges were granted as early as 1629 by the Dutch West Indies Company, and in the Massachusetts Bay Colonial Ordinance of 1647, provisions were included for the right of hunting. In 1677, Connecticut passed laws regulating seasons for hunting and prohibiting the export of game, hides or skins. As early as 1700, all the colonies, except Georgia, had established closed seasons on deer. In Virginia, for example, the killing of deer out of season provoked a fine of 500 pounds of tobacco. Deer

FIGURE 20-8. These white cedar woods are good winter deer browse. As long as green growth is found in quantity within easy reach of deer, there will not be starving deer in the area. Is it more humane to let deer starve, protect predators which in turn will keep down the numbers or permit hunters to reduce the deer population? (Courtesy, Wisconsin Conservation Department)

were not to be hunted by firelight, and running deer with dogs was prohibited in New York as early as 1788. The early colonists also regulated the hunting of game such as bobwhites, wild turkeys, woodcocks, ruffed grouse, heath hens (now extinct) and muskrats.

Closed Seasons

There are so many different kinds of wildlife protected today that we can scarcely realize the vast numbers of all kinds of birds and animals that were once killed just for the fun of killing. Yet, it was only about a hundred years ago that closed seasons, or complete protection of certain birds and animals, became common. In 1818, Massachusetts declared a closed season on snipes; in 1821, New Hampshire protected beavers, minks and otters. Maine protected moose in 1830, while the first prohibition of spring duck shooting was enacted by the Rhode Island assembly in 1846. In 1850, both Connecticut and New Jersey provided general protection to all small songbirds and to the "small owl" for the first time. The first hawk to receive protection was the osprey, or fish hawk, in New York in 1886. These regulations are evidence that, although early in our colonial history we were conscious of the importance of conserving the wildlife of the country, most of the laws protecting it were enacted only quite recently.

Obviously, game laws are not effective unless they are observed. If hunters disregard these regulations, they threaten the very survival of various species of wildlife and of the sport of hunting itself. A good hunter will do even more than the law requires by following the old saying: "Limit your kill; don't kill your limit!"

Hunters and Fishers Pay for Wildlife Protection Today

Paradoxical as it may seem, it is the hunters and fishers today who support game protection programs. They are the ones who buy hunting and fishing licenses and pay for special permits and stamps which largely fund state wildlife programs. And, thanks to the Pittman-Robertson Federal Aid in Wildlife Restoration Act passed in 1937, 11 cents of every dollar they spend on arms and ammunition is siphoned off by federal tax and given to the states for use in wildlife restoration. Over one-half billion dollars has been distributed to the states from this source for habitat development and enhancement programs as well as hunter safety education programs. And, at least another one-quarter billion dollars for wildlife has been realized from duck stamp sales to hunters and a 10 percent excise tax on fishing rods, creels, reels, artificial lures, baits and flies under the Dingell-Johnson Act of 1950. In 1985, Congress amended this act to add a 10 percent tax on flasher-type fish finders and trolling motors and a portion of the motor fuel tax. The new amended act was expected to raise a billion dollars within the decade following its passage.

In 1985, fishers spent over $28 billion for sport fishing and hunters over $10 billion for hunting. It is estimated that over 100 million persons participated in wildlife associated activities.

Hunters' organizations have also provided valuable direct help and management aids for wildlife. For example, the Migratory Waterfowl Hunters Association has set thousands of nesting boxes for wood ducks, helping bring them back from critically low numbers.

Ducks Unlimited (DU) is another "doer" conservation organization. Since 1937, the group has constructed over 2,900 waste control projects in North America. These waterfowl habitat areas cover nearly 4 million acres and cost $225 million. If a person were to hike around every marsh conserved by Ducks Unlimited Canada, the distance traveled would be well over 15,000 miles—a distance two-thirds around the world at the equator.

South of the border, Ducks Unlimited de Mexico has now developed some 45 wetland projects encompassing 240,000 acres of waterfowl wintering and nesting habitat. Many other conservation projects have been and are under development by this 580,000 member organization.[11]

How about trappers? Furs are a valuable resource and wild animals should be controlled in accordance with the limited environment. Trappers, operating of course within regulations and with regard for the environment and approved practices, perform a valuable service. George Reiger in his conservation article in the June 1986 issue of *Field and Stream* argues that "the only long-term way to [protect wild America] . . . is to provide economic values for the wild country and creatures in it. One of the least harmful ways to provide those values, while at the same time protecting the land, is to perpetuate trappers on the land. . . ."[12]

Reiger's view that wildlife must be treated in most cases as an economic resource is the same as the view of many conservationists (over 40 per-

---

[11] Peter H. Coors, "1985: The President's Report," *Ducks Unlimited*, May–June 1986, pp. 24, 25.

[12] George Reiger, "Conservation: The Nature of Film," *Field and Stream*, June 1986, p. 16.

cent) from 65 countries who were questioned in an exclusive international survey by the National Wildlife Federation. The Federation observed that the theme that wild resources must pay their own way is "perhaps the most controversial and contested theme in the survey."[13]

Game Refuges Provide Valuable Help

Another approach to the problem of conserving our wildlife is through game refuges. This is one of the systems used by some of our Indian tribes in their efforts to have plenty of game. Theodore Roosevelt told of the Creek Indians putting aside large tracts of land where persimmons, haws, chestnuts, muscadines and fox grapes were plentiful and where bears could feed and fatten unmolested. They called these tracts "Beloved Bear Grounds." Then at certain times the tribe would move in and kill large numbers of bears, which were their main source of animal food and oil.

Most of the wildlife refuges established during colonial days were private preserves, such as the deer parks of Virginia, North Carolina and Maryland. These refuges accomplished little except within restricted areas, and by 1800, most of them had ceased to exist.

The first state game refuge was established in California in 1870, and the second was established in Indiana 33 years later in 1903. This was also the date of the establishment of the first federal wildlife refuge for colony-nesting birds, that is, birds that live and nest in groups. Among the birds protected during the next five years were the gulls, terns and pelicans. The first federal refuges for migratory waterfowl were set up in 1908 in Oregon—the Lower Klamath and Malheur Lake refuges.

The story of some of these large refuges is one of both hope and disillusionment. Large areas were drained for agricultural use at great expense and later were again partially restored as refuges when they were found not to be profitable agricultural ventures. Other refuges were left in their original state and provided nesting places, feeding grounds and shelter for migratory birds.

According to the U.S. Fish and Wildlife Service, in 1986, there were 428 refuges in the Wildlife Refuge System, occupying over 88 million acres of land. These refuges have been established to accommodate mammals, waterfowl and both migratory and nonmigratory birds.

---

[13]Jonathan Fisher and Norman Myers, "What We Must Do to Save Wildlife," *International Wildlife*, Vienna, Virginia, National Wildlife Federation, May–June 1986, pp. 12–15.

These Measures Only Partially Effective

The use of closed seasons and bag limits helps control the numbers of the various species of game which are killed yearly, and because both season and bag limits can be changed, the yearly kill of game by hunters can be adjusted to reflect the change in population of the various species. This is only a partial answer to the wildlife conservation problem, however. Private landowners must cooperate in habitat provision, as noted in the next chapter.

The same limitation applies to game refuges or sanctuaries. They are especially useful in offering some protection to wild game by furnishing them with safe havens during their breeding seasons. Rick Messenger, site superintendent of a government wildlife refuge on the Mississippi River near St. Louis, notes three major habitat requirements for waterfowl: nesting, migration and wintering. Each has different needs which the manager helps provide by protecting certain areas, planting desirable vegetation for feed and raising and lowering water levels as required. With good management many more waterfowl can be supported on a unit of land than under all but ideal wilderness conditions.

The hope was that these refuges would provide surplus numbers of the various kinds of wildlife which would move out from the refuges to populate other areas. While this does take place to a limited extent, we cannot expect that less than 1 percent of the total land area of the country can supply game for the other 99 percent.

One of the reasons why this kind of program cannot by itself take care of wildlife needs is the impossibility of raising sufficient numbers of wildlife in these restricted areas. Many forms of wildlife will not thrive in restricted areas, while others do not tolerate crowding. They demand ranging, feeding and nesting space out of proportion to their size and capacity for eating. For example, the production from 2 or 3 acres of cropland will furnish a year's supply of feed for a cow, or another animal of like size, but the number of pheasants to be found on this same acreage of land will ordinarily not exceed one bird. Yet, this bird can make use of only a fraction of the feed and protection afforded by this amount of land.

Another question about the value of refuges is that certain species may be so reduced in numbers that their existence is in real jeopardy. Such species may have lost the vitality or "biological potential" necessary to perpetuate themselves under any circumstances. For example, some biologists believe that once passenger pigeons were reduced in numbers to a certain point, they were headed for extinction because they seemed to have lost their desire to nest.

All Landowners Must Provide Habitats

Probably the main disadvantage in the use of refuges as a solution to wildlife problems is failure to give proper consideration to the most beneficial use of other land which would best be used for wildlife habitat. Wildlife is part and parcel of nature's balance. Its conservation cannot be limited to federal or even state or local government ownership of all the land that should be used for wildlife. If the problem is to be handled effectively, it must be the responsibility of every landowner, whether that owner be a public agency or a private individual. Some farm land should be used.

Although we already have 88 million acres of land in the Wildlife Refuge System and millions more in state refuges, there are still many millions of acres in privately owned farms and ranches that could best serve as wildlife habitats. These acreages could not be combined into larger pieces even if the government were willing to buy them. Besides that, our government[14] now owns approximately two-fifths of all the land of the country (see Table 20-1). It is a question of whether the welfare of our people is best served by further concentration of land ownership in these various units of government, except in the case of wetlands.

TABLE 20-2. Our Land and Its Ownership, 1982

Ownership	Acres (in millions)	Percent
Private	1,329	58.7
Indian land	51	2.2
Public land	885	39.1
Federal	730	32.2
State and local	155	6.8
Total	2,265	100.0

Source: U.S. Bureau of the Census, *Statistical Abstract of the United States*, 1986, 106th edition, 1985.

---

[14]"Our government" in this sense includes all federal, state, county and municipal units.

DEVELOPMENT OF WILDLIFE RESEARCH
AND EDUCATION PROGRAM

The federal government has developed an exceptional system for education about wildlife in the past five decades. The nation's first fish and game management teaching program was set up at Iowa State University (then, a college) at Ames in 1931. Such programs have since become established at many other state universities. Cooperative wildlife research units have been set up at various locations in the country. Fish and wildlife specialists have been added to the staff of the USDA Extension Service in many states. Both the Extension Service and the Soil Conservation Service have specialists in plant life. Many states have upgraded the status of their wildlife field personnel from that of game wardens, largely enforcing hunting laws, to conservation officers who spend much of their time researching and teaching conservation.

NONGAME PROGRAMS

A serious weakness in some game management programs is their neglect of nongame wildlife species. Some progress has been made in the last few years, but there is much to be done. The value of nongame animals for their consumption of insects and other pests has been noted (see Figure 20-9). They are an important link in the food chain and indispensible to functioning of the ecosystem. Many nongame species, such as songbirds, add brilliant color and fascinating sound to our lives. Those who overlook proper care of nongame species in their concern for game animals should remember that the latter, like people, depend upon nongame animals for a viable environment.

WE'RE NOT OUT OF THE WOODS

Wildlife is important to us for both its economic and its non-economic value. There is little question about that. But, as far as "saving" wildlife is concerned, it is perhaps appropriate to use the well-known expression "We're not out of the woods, yet." You will recall that we have pointed out several times that dense woods are **not** the best habitat for animals.

FIGURE 20-9. Contrary to some popular opinion, owls and hawks, like the red-tailed hawk shown here, are among our most beneficial birds. Their food consists mainly of small mammals, especially rodents. If an occasional hawk or owl becomes a nuisance to farmers by preying on chickens, the conservation agent should be consulted. He/she may destroy it or catch it and move it to a distant location. Hunting of these birds of prey is both foolish and illegal. They do more good than harm. (Photo by Carol S. Sutherland)

We still haven't found all the answers to "saving" wildlife, nor are we doing nearly as much as we should be. The next chapter suggests one way in which we may improve the record by providing better habitats.

QUESTIONS AND PROBLEMS

1. What different forms of life are included as wildlife?

2. Give some comparison that may show the economic value of our bird life.

3. Does wildlife serve a better purpose because of its economic value to us or because of the non-economic values we derive from the various forms? Explain your answer.

4. List the requirements for the continued support of wildlife.

5. Describe the struggle for survival among wildlife. What is meant by natural, or biological, balance? What are predators? Explain their purpose or use in maintaining the biological balance.

6. The statement is frequently made that certain pieces of waste, badly eroded or cut-up land, are useful only for wildlife. Explain why this statement is or is not true.

7. In attempting to "manage wildlife," colonists imposed what two restrictions that limited the killing of game?

8. List the probable reasons why the early colonists of this country were faced with starvation, even though the woods and streams around them supported an abundance of wildlife.

9. Why are closed seasons, reduced bag limits and game refuges only partially effective in maintaining the wildlife of this country? What kind of land in this country would serve its best use if devoted to wildlife?

10. If we are to have the variety and amount of wildlife which the land of this country will support, who must assume the responsibility of bringing this about?

11. Name some game birds and wild animals that are surviving in your agricultural neighborhood.

12. What game birds and animals have disappeared in the last century? What wild flowers? (Check the library for information.)

13. What is "The Terrible Lesson of the Kaibob" deer incident? What principles of wildlife management did we learn from it?

14. How do hunters help pay for conservation? How can nonhunters help?

15. What responsibility does every landowner have if we are to have an effective conservation program?

21

Providing Wildlife Habitat

As stressed in the last chapter, providing habitat—a space in which wildlife can find adequate shelter and food—is an especially critical conservation problem today. So great is the pressure for development of land for houses, factories and commercial buildings that little thought is apt to be given to providing a home for wildlife. Productive land use and wildlife habitat have often been thought to be incompatible—that both cannot exist in the same place. This is not necessarily so. We are not proposing to put a herd of buffalo on the plaza at Rockefeller Center, New York, or grizzly bears in the Chicago Loop. But, songbirds are at home in Central Park, and gulls thrive along the Chicago River. Conversely, wide open spaces that are inhospitable to humans may be equally undesirable for wildlife. Unreclaimed strip mines with acid waters and barren soil are an example. This chapter is devoted to a consideration of habitat possibilities.

WILDLIFE HABITATS ON FARMS AND RANCHES

The management of wildlife areas on farms and ranches need not reduce total crop production. It should not require the diversion of land now used for crops, except for small acreages that are best suited for use by different forms of wildlife. It does require a knowledge of the best use of certain pieces of land and a program that provides for their most suitable utilization.

In many cases the only steps required are protection from fire and from grazing or use by domestic animals, while in others additional steps should include some tree or shrub planting. A third conservation measure pertains to the control and use of water, that is, ponds and streams on the farms.

Millions of acres of potential wildlife land are located on privately owned farms. Much of this land could be improved by relatively inexpensive treatment or handling. The major categories listed by the Soil Conservation Service in which land-use practices valuable to wildlife could be improved are the better management of marshes, ponds, stream banks, field borders, mined-over areas and various odd acreages that are often otherwise unused.

Most states offer some type of program for wildlife habitat on private lands. Such programs focus on the landowner or operator as decision-maker or implementor. Most of them are voluntary and small in scale, particularly as applied to farms. "They include various types of plantings, borders, shelter-belts, seeding of marginal lands, food or cover plots, and possibly water related practices," Charles Deknatel notes (see Figure 21-1).[1]

Wildlife can be increased on well-developed farm and ranch land eventhough the land contains no waste corners, wet spots or stony knolls. Windbreaks of trees, which help reduce wind erosion, furnish shelter for small game and songbirds; strip cropping in many instances provides nesting spots for birds; fence rows, if not cleaned of all grass and shrub growth, are havens for both game birds and songbirds. Even on ranches and in range country, if range land is so managed that a good growth of native grasses is maintained, prairie chickens, sage hens and even the elusive antelope may again appear.

One of the problems of wildlife in ranch country is the competition for forage. Elk, deer and antelope compete with cattle for grass and other forage. A buffalo requires about as much roughage as a steer, so that for

---

[1] Charles Deknatel, "Wildlife Habitat Development on Private Lands: A Planning Approach to Rural Land, Use," *Journal of Soil & Water Conservation*, November–December 1979, pp. 260–261.

every animal of this type, the feed for one steer is gone. The ratio of other animals to steers is two elk, four deer, four bighorns and four antelope. Unless the rancher is getting a handsome income from dude ranching, wildlife without control may be an unbearable expense.

FIGURE 21-1. Idle corners, when left to grow to brush and weeds, and especially when planted to corn, sorghum or other grains, make ideal food patches and cover spots for quail, pheasants, Hungarian partridges, rabbits, etc. It costs little to encourage wildlife on good farm land. (Courtesy, Wisconsin Conservation Department)

PONDS AND LAKES FOR WILDLIFE

During the past few years, tens of thousands of ponds and small lakes have been built in this country. They are built ordinarily to provide water for farm livestock, to slow down or stop water run-off from farms or to encourage scenic water sports—not to promote the production of fish and

FIGURE 21-2. This farm pond in West Virginia is made with a dirt dam. It is the source of many meals of pan fish caught during times of recreation and play. (Courtesy, U.S. Fish and Wildlife Service)

other wildlife. Yet, with but little change, these water bodies could be made to produce some fish and to become the homes of ducks, muskrats, shore birds, etc. (see Figure 21-2).

Managing Ponds and Lakes

When planning a pond or a lake, one should seek the advice of the local agent, soil conservation agent or state game representative since there are so many factors to be considered. Requirements for the plains area of the Midwest will be used as an example here.[2]

---

[2]The following information is summarized, in part, from Alvin C. Lopinot, *Fish Conservation Teacher's Manual*, Illinois Resource Management Series, Springfield, Division of Conservation Education, 1965.

A pond in the Midwest should have a water area of at least ½ acre, a depth of 8 to 10 feet in 25 percent of the area; a spillway; a watershed of sufficient size to maintain the water level unless water can be pumped in from a nearby stream; a well-constructed dam; no excessive erosion and pollution in the area; and no excessive brush, trees or aquatic vegetation.

Stocking with Desirable Fish

The pond should be stocked with fish that can maintain themselves in balance with the food supply and other fish. In the Midwest, one of the successful combinations has been largemouth bass and bluegill. The bluegill use the microscopic plankton and insects as food. The bass eat the bluegill. If bluegill are stocked before bass, they may become so overcrowded that the bass cannot control them. They will prevent the bass from multiplying by eating bass spawn and fingerlings.

Certain species of fish are undesirable for stocking ponds. There may be exceptions, but in general, bullhead, carp, green sunfish and crappie will spoil the pond or lake for better game fish. The bullhead and carp keep the water muddy as they feed on the bottom. The other two varieties multiply so rapidly that they generally soon overpopulate the pond. And, they eat bass eggs, young bass and the food that bass need.

Avoiding Weeds and Siltation in Lakes and Ponds

Midwest lakes generally do not need to be fertilized. Unfertilized lakes should support from 200 to 400 pounds of fish per acre of water each year. This is more fish than will generally be caught in ordinary family sport fishing. The water does require weed control, however. Most pond vegetation is of little value for fish production because it uses nutrients in the water that would otherwise produce phytoplankton as food for the fish. Besides, the resultant "scum" (algae) not only looks bad but also often smells like rotten eggs and may actually be poisonous to fish, birds and even livestock. Pond weeds may also favor mosquito breeding. Chemical control of algae and weeds is possible. USDA Extension Service specialists should be consulted for advice.

The best conservation practice, however, would be to use a natural rather than a chemical agent. Sterile triploid grass carp, which feed heavily on algae and plant weeds, stocked in low to moderate numbers, have been a very effective lake clarifier. Such stocking, however, may be illegal in your state. The state conservation agency can give advice on such stocking.

One of the best non-chemical methods to improve water quality in a small lake is to install an aerator. Some excellent manufactured models are available. Or with ingenuity, considerable work and the purchase of a pump, hose, spraying unit and other necessary parts, a person can build one himself/herself.

A pond must be protected from siltation, or it will not last long. Besides, muddy water is not favorable to game fish. Worst of all, the fish cannot see the bait on the hooks! The erosion controlling practices we have discussed in connection with soils should be practiced, and livestock should be kept away from the shore and off the dam.

Harvesting the Fish

Finally, harvesting the fish should be adequate to maintain balanced pond conditions. When we catch small panfish in a well-established lake, we should not throw them back in. Keeping them will leave more food for the remaining fish and will help prevent overstocking. Of course, if the lake is understocked, it would be wise to throw back the medium-size fish, which will provide better breeding stock. Also, in ponds stocked with bluegill, sunfish and bass, we should fish out the first two species, as compared to the number of bass, in the ratio of 4 to 1. In any case, we should not take more than the daily limit allowable by law.

Providing for Fish, Waterfowl and Fur Bearers

If, rather than fish, the main purpose of the pond is to provide for fur-bearing animals and water and shore birds, fencing the pond is desirable. This will allow undisturbed nesting, resting and feeding grounds for wildlife. In this case, there should be some shrub and tree growth at or near the shore. It is possible, of course, to have both fish and other wildlife in the same area. The number of each will naturally be smaller than if the whole emphasis is on the production of one or the other, because conditions for the production of both kinds of wildlife are a compromise of the requirements for either form of life if produced alone.

FIGURE 21-3. A group of students on an observation field trip look over a wildlife conservation area on a Corn Belt farm. The area was established on part of an acreage too wet to farm in most seasons. The pond helped drain the land so part of it could be put back into production. It now provides good fishing. Multiflora rose and a mixed planting of maples, pines, and other trees, shrubs and grasses provide feed and cover for wildlife. State of Illinois conservation agent Don Hastings led the group. (Photo by Harry B. Kircher)

WETLANDS FOR WILDLIFE

Our first thought about marsh lands and inland swamps is that here are sources of virgin soil which will produce well when once the water is removed. We become convinced that their value for producing cultivated crops far outweighs their value as producers of muskrats, waterfowl and shore birds. Drainage projects follow. Water is removed, and the water table is lowered. Farms are set up, and crops are produced. But, in many instances, the costs of operating these units are high, and productions are disappointingly low. (See Figure 21-3.)

Next, we condemn all marsh and swamp drainage projects as failures. There are moves toward restoration of the marsh areas and many drainage projects are given up. Farmers move out of the areas, and wildlife again takes over. Examples of this change in attitude are found in the restoration of Lake Mattamuskeet in North Carolina, Thief Lake in Minnesota, Horicon Marsh in Wisconsin, Seney Marsh in Michigan, Lower River Flood Plain in North Dakota and Lake Malheur in Oregon. After several years of disappointing experience, these areas were found to be more valuable as wildlife habitats than for intensive agricultural use.

It happens that neither of these two extreme viewpoints is entirely correct and neither is entirely incorrect. Some marshes have been drained and are being used profitably as farm land. Some marsh lands in Louisiana, which for some unexplained reason were poor places for wildlife, were drained and found to be poor cropland. Later when they were restored as wildlife habitat, they proved to be excellent homes for fish and other wildlife. Others have been dismal failures when drained and cannot now be restored to their original use as habitats for wildlife.

Probably the outstanding example of this experience was the Lower Klamath National Wildlife Refuge in southern Oregon and northern California. Fifty years ago, this area contained over 80,000 acres of marsh land, and it was one of the greatest nurseries for waterfowl and shore birds in the western states. Literally hundreds of varieties of birds were found nesting there, and millions of birds were estimated to have made it their summer home.

Then, this wetland was destroyed to accommodate the popular belief that once freed of surface water, this area would add to the agricultural wealth of the West. A by-pass was built above the lake so that no more water flowed in, and within four years, the lake had dried up. Peat fires started and in many instances burned to a depth of 6 feet. The result was that instead of having myriads of wildlife or thousands of dollars' worth of agricultural production, "a vast alkaline ashy desert" was formed "from which clouds of choking dust arose, often obscuring the sun." A waste area was the result.

Unfortunately, the Lower Klamath refuge is not an exception to the loss of wetlands. More than 120 million acres of an estimated 215 million acres of wetlands that existed in America during colonial times—about 56 percent—have been destroyed. And, losses continue at the rate of more than 450,000 acres annually.

In late 1985, the preceding alarming facts were reported by the U.S. Fish and Wildlife Service in a massive study, begun in 1979, called the *National Wetlands Trends Analysis*. This report focused on the period between 1950 and 1970, using comparisons of aerial photographs to measure changes that had taken place. The following trends were reported.

Inland wetlands and lakes.—There was a net loss of vegetated wetlands (inland marshes, forested wetlands and shrub swamps) of 11 million acres, nearly all the result of agricultural production. Non-vegetated wetlands (ponds and inland mudflats) increased to 2.3 million acres, largely the result of the building of farm ponds. A net gain in deep water habitats (inland lakes and reservoirs) of 1.4 million acres occurred, largely as a result of construction projects.

Coastal wetlands.—There was a net loss in vegetated wetlands (coastal marshes) of 372,000 acres, mostly due to conversion into the open water of bays and sounds, and an overall gain in sub-tidal deep water habitats (bays and sounds) of 200,000 acres.

Most threatened wetlands.—Inland marshes, forested wetlands and coastal wetlands are the most threatened, according to the report. Some causes of destruction are natural, but most are human-made.

As for the future, the *National Wetlands. . .* report is guardedly optimistic. The U.S Fish and Wildlife Service is working, through a variety of programs, to conserve existing wetlands. But it believes that our wetlands will inevitably shrink under cropland and urban pressures.[3]

We all can help save these valuable lands by purchasing "duck stamps." Revenue from the stamps is used in the acquisition of leasing of prime wetland habitats. The Migratory Bird Hunting and Conservation stamp program has helped in the purchasing and maintaining of our national system of more than 400 refuges, which cover over 80 million acres.[4]

Much of Our Wetland Should Never Be Drained

Each marsh, whether large or small, must be studied carefully, and

---

[3]For an excellent analysis of the inventory, see Fred Tetreault, "Liquid Assets," *Outdoor Highlights*, Springfield, Illinois Department of Conservation, March 16, 1987, pp. 3–7.

[4]Peter Steinhart, "For Wildlife, the Struggle Continues," *National Wildlife*, April–May 1986, p. 8.

its most profitable long-time use determined only after all possibilities have been explored. It is for this reason that no general statement can safely be made as to the best use for all wetland. Certainly, much of it should never be drained.

Wetlands are hard to measure and define. Official estimates of the original wetland acreage in the lower 48 states have ranged from 137 to 215 million. That would be about 5 to 10 percent of wilderness America. By 1988, we had probably lost well over half of the original amount of our wetlands. David Wallace said of such estimates in *Wilderness* magazine:

> It's probably fair to say that the coterminous United States had lost well over a third of its wetlands by 1950, and that, at a yearly loss rate of between 380,000 and 450,000 acres since then, it has now lost over half. The Fish and Wildlife Service's *1984 National Wetlands Inventory* estimates that fifty-four percent had gone by the mid-1970's, so depending on one's preferred estimate of the original, we now have between 90 and 140 million acres left.[5]

Wetlands support 19 species of small game, 7 species of big game, 11 species of fur animals and hundreds of nongame mammals, birds, amphibians and reptiles. Wetlands provide many of the basic food elements of the nation's commercial fisheries as well, a study by the National Association of Conservation Districts reports.[6]

The loss of wetlands through drainage, dredging and filling is often called "reclamation." To environmentalists, it has really been "desecration"— desecration of nature.

STREAM BANKS CAN AFFORD WILDLIFE SHELTER

Most of our stream banks continue to wash away, and the beds of streams move from one location to another. Stream bank erosion has other bad effects in addition to its destruction of excellent cropland. It frequently undercuts trees, bridges and houses. It destroys highways and railroads.

---

[5]David Rains Wallace, "Wetlands in America, Labyrinth and Temple," *Wilderness*, Washington, D.C., The Wilderness Society, Winter 1985, pp. 13, 16.

[6]National Association of Conservation Districts, *A Summary: Non-federal Natural Resources of the United States*, Washington, D.C., circa 1979, p. 11.

It covers good land with sand and gravel, and it loosens silt, which is carried downstream to be deposited in back of dams, thus destroying the capacities of the dams for impounding water.

Probably the easiest and cheapest way to control most stream bank erosion is through the use of grass, shrub or tree growth along the banks. Almost any bank which is to be kept from eroding must be sloped. There are few exceptions to this rule. The slope should not be greater than a 1-foot rise for each 1½ feet of horizontal distance. After the bank has been sloped, it should be planted without delay. Shrubs and grass offer better protection of the slope than does tree growth.

Occasionally, it is necessary to direct the force of the stream away from a bank by laying stone rip-rap from the bank several feet out into the bed of the stream. Work of this kind is quite technical and should be attempted only under the direction of a conservation specialist. It is only when stream banks furnish shelter and security, along with some food supply, that wildlife is encouraged to stay there. All of these steps, helpful to the perpetuation of wildlife, are also desirable soil conservation measures. (See also "Stream Bank Erosion," Chapter 18.)

WILDLIFE HABITATS IN THE CITY

If we are to provide for wildlife in large metropolitan areas, we need to maintain food, shelter and water. It is generally possible, as in some rural areas, to establish a natural area and then just help it regenerate itself. Potentials for wildlife habitats vary from suburban back yards to large city parks or the type of village commons set aside in many modern residential developments.

A homeowner's own back yard can be a wildlife habitat. It may be as simple as filling a bird feeder and providing a bird bath. Planting bushes and trees for nesting and food requires more space and time. The homeowner can also provide bird houses if careful thought is given to the type needed and the best location. In this planning, publications such as the National Wildlife Federation's book *Gardening with Wildlife* should be obtained.

Planning for larger urban open-space areas should be done with the help of landscape gardeners and wildlife experts. Management practices similar to those for farms and ranches and lakes and ponds are often

applicable. All of us can take a part as citizens by seeing to it that our public lands are managed to the best of their wildlife potential. Private abuses
of habitat can be stopped by good zoning and properly enforced anti-
pollution laws.

WILDLIFE'S FUTURE DEPENDS ON EVERYONE

No other resource is so dependent on the action of each of us as
individuals as is our wildlife resource. Whether landowners or not, we are
directly influencing wildlife by our support or lack of support of environmental programs. How each of us acts toward wild plants and animals wherever and whenever we encounter them will determine how rich and varied
wildlife will remain. Private owners, of course, have a special responsibility.
They must provide habitat if we are not to suffer continued losses of wildlife. But, let us remember, as citizens we are all stewards of about two-
fifths of the land in the public domain.

An excellent example of citizens' support for wildlife is the program
of the Iowa Conservation Commission. The Commission has initiated a private lands incentive program to encourage the establishment of an agricultural crop that is both economically desirable to private landowners and
beneficial to nesting wildlife. The Commission is planning to spend a total
of $1 million derived from the sale of wildlife habitat stamps to cost-share
the establishment and proper management of switchgrass pastures.

Effective conservation of wildlife, like conservation of other natural
resources, requires three steps: (1) research, (2) education and (3) action
with nature. Knowledge and enthusiasm are not enough. We must act!

QUESTIONS AND PROBLEMS

1. How much should agricultural production be decreased in order to develop
   good shelter and food patches for wildlife on well-improved farm land? How
   can potential wildlife land now in farms be fairly readily improved so as to
   support some form of wildlife? List the kinds of treatment that are desirable.

2. On what other parts of the farm besides marsh lands, stream banks, odd acreages, etc., can wildlife be given shelter and still not reduce the production
   of the farm?

3. Ponds and lakes have served what purposes in the past? What kinds of wildlife can be supported in and around these water bodies?

4. Why is it desirable not to have silt-filled, muddy water drain into ponds and lakes?

5. How would you go about managing a pond or lake for better fishing?

6. What kind of information do you think you need to obtain in order to manage a water body properly?

7. How can you have both fish and waterfowl or fur-bearing animals in the same pond area?

8. Under what conditions is it desirable to confine the access of cattle or other livestock to a limited part of the shore?

9. Whom should you consult for information on management of lakes and ponds for wildlife?

10. Why should much of our wetland never be drained?

11. What is the simplest way to control erosion on most stream banks and to make them useful as wildlife coverage?

12. In order to secure the best land use, which specialists should share in the planning of wildlife habitats?

13. What game birds or game animals are found in your area? What nongame species?

14. How can their numbers be increased?

15. How can wildlife habitats be created in the city?

16. What, in the final analysis, is going to really determine how well wildlife management is provided for?

22

Natural Resources
from the Seas

We are very fortunate in the United States in having excellent access
to the seas of the world. Our shores are lapped by the waves of three
out of five of the world's oceans—the Atlantic, the Pacific and the Arctic.
We also border on the Gulf of Mexico. Our long coast line is another advantage, for the most abundant sea life is to be found in coastal waters. Also,
here we can most easily reach the bottoms, if desired, to tap mineral
wealth, as in the case of offshore oil deposits. In previous chapters we
have discussed how the oceans may be thought of as the basic reservoir
for the hydrologic cycle and thus the basic source of all our water supply;
how ocean currents, waves and tides might be harnessed for energy; and
how there is a possibility of desalting ocean water and drinking it. This
leaves unanswered the question of how to extract minerals from the sea
water and how to increase our food supply coming from the oceans.

SEA WATER – A REMARKABLE RESOURCE

All of us who live near or visit the sea marvel at the differing colors
of the water, enjoy the fun of splashing or swimming in it and appreciate
its ability to support us in boats on its surface and to maintain sea life

within its depths. But, how many of us have thought of it as a remarkable combination of minerals, organic substances and gases, whence all life on earth is said to have issued?

Many Minerals in Sea Water

Among the elements present in sea water are sodium, chlorine, magnesium, sulfur, calcium, bromine and some 40 more. The list is so long that the sea would appear to be an almost unlimited source for minerals. The trouble is the cost. Most of these minerals can be obtained more easily on land by mining beds laid down millions of years ago in ancient seas now vanished. A notable exception is salt, a combination of sodium and chloride, which is easily gotten by evaporation. Magnesium also is obtained from sea water. Both of these are also produced from mines. Commercial mining of magnesium taken from the sea floor has been under consideration for a number of years. Sands containing potassium-bearing minerals have been used as fertilizers.

PLANT AND ANIMAL LIFE OF THE SEA

The plant and animal life in the waters of the sea occur in an amazing variety and number of shapes which are distributed very unequally from place to place. This is not surprising when we recall the the seas cover 71 percent of the earth's surface. They are said to provide some 300 times more living space than all land surfaces and fresh waters combined. Of all this life, we see only a small part. And, we use only the larger forms of this rich sea life directly for food.

Life in the seas falls into three fairly distinct major categories, according to ability to move about. These are (1) the benthos (from the Greek *bathys*, "depth of the sea"), the sitters and creepers, which, in general, move slowly along the bottom of the oceans; (2) the nekton from the Greek *nēktos*, "swimming"), the swimmers, which are able to move through the waters at will; and (3) the plankton (from the Greek *planktos*, "drifting"), the drifters, which drift with the currents or other outside forces. The neuston (from the Greek *neustos*, meaning "an inanimate object which moves through the water like a boat"), the skimmers are a fourth major group of water life, mostly found in lakes and ponds, for they rest on the film at the water's surface, which must be relatively smooth.[1]

Higher plant life is completely absent in the open ocean. A flowering plant of the pond-weed family, called "eelgrass," however, lives on most ocean shores where wave action is not severe. But, this is an exception. The oceanic equivalent of our abundant land vegetation is found in microscopic plants located in the upper zone, reached by the sunlight.

Two of the aquatic life groups are very familiar to all of us, for we eat them for dinner. In the first group are oysters, clams and crabs. The swimmers, the second group, include fish, shrimp and whales. The third group, the drifters, is by far the largest in volume and numbers. But, many of them are almost too small to be seen by the naked eye. One of the most important varieties of animal plankton is only 3/16 inch in length. One, however, with the impressive name of *Giant astracod*, is 3/8 inch or more long. Plant plankton may resemble those that form green "blankets" on our fresh water lakes and ponds. Plant plankton are at the base of the food pyramid for other forms of aquatic life. They are the principal photosynthetic agents of the seas.

FISH – A DESIRABLE FOOD

Earliest history records the importance of fish as a human food, and in times of shortage of other foods, fish have saved people from starvation. Following World War I, the children of some European countries showed the effects of a poorly balanced diet in their retarded physical growth. The children of Finland, on the other hand, appeared robust and healthy, even with a restricted diet.

A study of the reason for this satisfactory child development in contrast to that of other countries with no worse diet showed that the whole fish diet was the answer. The people who ate the whole of the smaller fish apparently were supplied with those trace elements in food which are necessary for early normal human development.

---

[1] For an ecological coverage of the ocean and its life, see William A. Anikouchine and Richard W. Sternberg, *The World Ocean, An Introduction to Oceanography*, 2nd ed., Englewood Cliffs, New Jersey, Prentice-Hall, Inc., 1981. Author Kircher included information gathered from his former professor at the University of North Carolina, Robert E. Coker, in this section.

THE EARLY COLONISTS USED FISH

The New England colonies turned early to fishing as a source of food and also in order to have something to sell to foreign countries for the items they in turn wished to buy from those countries.

There are many reasons why the New England colonists became fishers. The rapidly increasing demand for fish both in America and in Europe opened a market for anyone with fish to sell, and the New England colonists were much nearer the banks along the American side of the Atlantic where the fish were found than were European fishers. Thus, it was much easier for them to reach these new fishing grounds and to start fishing operations between the severe storms which swept the banks than for European fishers who required weeks of oceangoing travel to reach the banks.

As mentioned earlier, the colonists took up shipbuilding because of an abundance of timber and a familiarity with maritime activities. It was natural, therefore, for them to combine fishing with their other work, such as farming, lumbering and shipbuilding.

Best Fish Required by Foreign Markets

As a result of the large catches of fish, the colonists developed some unusual trade relationships. By the middle of the eighteenth century, the New England fishers found it profitable to salt a catch so it would keep. It was then sorted into three classes for the three markets available. The largest, fattest fish comprised the first class, and they were sold locally, probably because they were most difficult to cure thoroughly. Fish at this time were salted and sold whole. No attempt was made to dress the fish before salting.

The second class of fish were the best quality, were a nice size for curing and carried the proper amount of salting. These fish were sold on the European markets where demand for this quality of fish was good.

The third class, which amounted to nearly one-half the whole catch, included those fish which were small, bony, too salty, broken or otherwise damaged in handling or those which were off-flavor because they did not have enough salt. The market for these fish was the West Indies, where the manual labor for raising sugar cane was done by Negro slaves brought in from Africa. These slaves seldom lived longer than six or seven years in this work, so the owners did not pay much for the food supplied to them.

Fish Traded for Molasses, and Rum for Slaves

A second unusual feature of this fish trade was that the West Indies planters needed a market for their by-product known as molasses. A deal was made whereby the third class of fish was traded for the useless molasses. The New Englanders found that a gallon of rum could be made from a gallon of molasses, and the rum would sell for 10 times the cost of the molasses. So, the New England trader sold stale or overslated fish for molasses and then traded the rum, which was made from the molasses, for gold or slaves in Africa. The slaves were then sold to plantation owners in this country who needed cheap labor for cotton production. Thus, the early fishing industry, through these ramifications, was a source of both wealth and human degradation, the latter being a major cause of the Civil War.

From 1975 to 1984, the catch of principal species of fish in the United States increased from 3,779 million pounds to 5,408 million pounds. Use

FIGURE 22-1. These fish, caught in the Atlantic, are being taken from the pocket of a pound net and loaded onto a boat. Fishing in our coastal waters can be further increased. (Courtesy, U.S. Fish and Wildlife Service)

was divided almost equally between human food and industrial products. The Gulf states led by far in the size of catch, with the Pacific states catching about 60 percent as much. If the entire East Coast is counted as a unit (New England, Mid-Atlantic, Chesapeake Bay and South Atlantic), its catch exceeded that of the Pacific Coast. The value of the U.S. catch was about $2 billion in 1984. Imports of fishery products have been about half our total consumption for many years.

The finfish catch exceeds shellfish in weight but not in value. In principal species, the humble but delicious shrimp ranked first in value 1984. Salmon was valued about 20 percent less (see Figures 22-1 and 22-3 and Table 22-1).

FISH SUPPLY SMALL SHARE OF OUR NATION'S FOOD

Fish are a valuable addition to our diet, as has been noted. But, they provide a relatively small share of our total food supply. The total yearly catch of fish in this country amounts to some 7 billion pounds, or about 30 pounds for every person in the United States. With imports, it is possible that we get somewhere near the world average of 10 percent of our food consumption from fish. Most of this supply comes from the oceans on both sides of this country, rather than from inland lakes and rivers.

MANY FISH SPECIES DISAPPEARING

We think of the vast oceans which cover almost three-fourths of the surface of the earth as containing inexhaustible quantities of sea food. This is far from true. Many of our fish species are getting scarce.

The halibut of the Atlantic were once a most important sea food. Now only negligible quantities are caught, and they have all but disappeared from our tables.

The shad, also of the Atlantic Coast, are spoken of as among the most prized fish for the table. Until recently, they were among the three most abundant species of fish on the whole Atlantic Coast. A year's catch of nearly 50 million pounds was not uncommon. Not only were shad used fresh for immediate consumption but also many were salted and kept for winter use. Now, the great shad runs are history. Many factors have contributed to their disappearance. Overfishing, the construction of dams which blocked them from their spawning grounds in the tributaries of all the Atlantic Coast streams and water pollution by industrial waste, together, have practically exterminated this valuable species.

The haddock, which were quite numerous in 1930, have declined so much that the current catch is less than half of what it was then.

Other fish, such as salmon, spend the greater part of their lives in the ocean depths. It is only at spawning time that they leave these ocean haunts and return to fresh water streams where they deposit their eggs. When the young hatch, they swim to the ocean. During these migrations, the fish have been taken in such great numbers that there is fear of destroying the industry.

The salmon industry was known as the lifeblood of Alaska until the establishment of our vast military network there and the development of petroleum resources. The salmon industry alone is worth many times as much to this state as the production of gold. The permanence of the industry depends upon a continuation of the migration of these yearly supplies of salmon to the streams of the country.

Only a few thousand whales remain of the millions in the seas when Herman Melville wrote his famous novel, *Moby Dick*. The decline is the result of waste and greed. It is indicative of the human ability to destroy animals, no matter how large and powerful they are. Whales are the largest mammals in the world and range the oceans from the north to the south polar regions. Studies have indicated that if international limits on whaling could be agreed upon, whalers would be able to harvest tens of millions of dollars worth of whales annually without endangering the species. But, the agreements arrived at so far have not been effective.

FISHERIES IN TROUBLE

Our nation is having serious difficulties in its conservation of fisheries. Michael Weber of the National Audubon Society reported in the fisheries chapter of the society's prestigious annual assessment of wildlife and the federal government's conservation record, released in June 1986. Donald L.

Rheem gave this version of highlights of the chapter in *The Christian Science Monitor,* June 18, 1986:

> Overfishing of some species like cod, striped bass, haddock, and lobster not only affect recent catches, but also potentially disrupt the balance of species within the ecosystem. This may result in reduced long-term yields for many species.
>
> Georges Bank, one of the world's richest fishing grounds, suffers from declining haddock populations and a herring population deemed commercially extinct. Atlantic salmon are now so depleted that recorded catches are rare in the U.S. In the Gulf of Mexico, the stock of King mackerel appears near collapse and billfishes and swordfish are near or past their maximum yield, according to the report.[2]

RELATIVE IMPORTANCE OF FRESH WATER FISH

Most of the fish from our fresh water lakes and streams are caught in recreational or sports activities. The value of these activities to those of us who spend time at them cannot be measured in terms of the food value of the catch. Sport fishing is a relaxation for tired, tense people from coast to coast.

The amount of fresh water fish is much less than that of ocean species. It has been estimated that fresh water fishing contributes less than 2 percent of the seafood in our national diet (see Figure 22-2). This does not count the raising of fish in ponds.

FISH FARMING IN THE SEA OR ON "LAND"

The raising of fish in fresh water ponds or the providing of beds for shellfish in bays or estuaries (those parts of the river where the tides mix with the river current) for the market has been increasing in importance in the United States. Farm-raised catfish have become a $200 million industry. Farmers in the Mississippi Delta, which has 85 percent of the

---

[2]Donald L. Rheem, "The Audubon Society Assesses Troubled State of U.S. Wildlife," *The Christian Science Monitor,* June 18, 1986, p. 4.

TABLE 22-1. Fisheries — Catch and Value of Principal Species, 1975 and 1984[1]

Species	Catch 1975	Catch 1984	Value 1975	Value 1984
Fish				
Cod, Atlantic.............................	56	97	13	36
Flounder	162	220	44	124
Haddock	16	26	5	18
Halibut	21	48	16	25
Herring, sea	131	179	6	26
Jack mackerel	37	23	2	2
Menhaden.................................	1,803	2,891	49	117
Ocean perch, Atlantic....................	32	12	3	4
Pollock.................................	21	64	2	9
Salmon, Pacific	202	691	107	392
Tuna....................................	393	212	107	118
Whiting.................................	42	46	4	7
Shellfish				
Clams (meats)	113	133	43	116
Crabs	306	313	81	187
Lobsters, American	30	44	51	114
Oysters (meats)	53	48	45	81
Scallops (meats)........................	14	59	23	128
Shrimp	347	302	226	488

[1] Catch in millions of pounds live weight, value in millions of dollars. Data exclude landings by U.S. flag vessels at Puerto Rico and other ports outside the 50 states and production of artificially cultivated fish and shellfish. 1980–84 preliminary.

Source: U.S. National Oceanic and Atmospheric Administration, *Fishery Statistics of the United States,* annual, and *Fisheries of the United States,* annual, Washington, D.C.

world's output, produced about 250 million pounds of catfish in 1986. Arkansas, Alabama and Louisiana are other major producing states. Could this be "the best thing that's happened to the South since cotton"?[3]

Fish farming in ponds 3 to 5 feet deep, and ranging in size from less than 1 acre to more than 15 acres, has been practiced in China and India for centuries. The waters of these ponds must be fertilized in order to produce the plankton so necessary for the life cycle of water life. In Japan, where quite favorable conditions prevail, the yearly production

---

[3] See Julia Reed, "A Fish Tale Worth Telling," *U.S. News & World Report,* November 10, 1986, p. 66.

of fish farms is estimated to be about 6 percent of all seafood sold there.[4]

It should not be assumed, however, that fish farming is as simple as putting fish in the water and just letting them multiply. Owners of large fish farms must use many chemicals and equipment to keep the fish productive and healthy and, of course, fed.

FIGURE 22-2. These carp are being taken from Lake Mattamuskeet, North Carolina, by a commercial fisher. Carp represent one of the many types of fish caught in inland waters. (Courtesy, U.S. Fish and Wildlife Service)

Fish are also produced in salt water under controlled conditions such as in large pens or by propagation on protected sea beds. Such fish production is commonly called **aquaculture.** It accounts for about 10 percent of the world's annual commercial fish harvest.[5]

---

[4]T. V. R. Pillay, "The Role of Aquaculture in Fishery Development and Management," *Journal of Fisheries Research Board of Canada*, Vol. 30, 1973, pp. 2202—2217.

[5]Gary D. Stauffer, "Fishing Industry," *The World Book Encyclopedia*, Vol. 7, Chicago: World Book, Inc., 1988, p. 183.

Some of our favorite seafood is produced by aquaculture—more than half of the catfish, crawfish and oysters we buy and a somewhat smaller share of the salmon. And, there could be many more! A 5- to 10-fold increase in aquaculture by the year 2000 is feasible, according to conclusions of the FAO World Conference on Aquaculture, held in 1976.[6]

FISH CATCH MAY INCREASE

New devices have been developed for locating schools of fish by the noise they make. The adoption of other special equipment and up-to-date techniques in fishing has resulted in some of the largest catches of fish known. In fact, the world's fish catch has tripled since World War II, according to the UN Food and Agriculture Organization.

On December 22, 1980, President Carter signed the American Fisheries Promotion Act. Martha Blazall, director of the Office of Utilization and Development at the National Marine Fisheries Service, maintains that "the act will expand foreign trade and seafood products and provide more effective monitoring of foreign fish operations."[7] U.S. fleets could support a catch about three times as large as at present, the National Marine Fisheries Service reports.[8]

CYCLE OF LIFE IN THE SEA

The problem of trying to increase the food resource from the sea is not so much that of catching fish as it is of knowing just where to break into the cycle of life in the sea. There is a balance which over the years is maintained between the production of plankton, which grow in greater or lesser abundance in the sea, and of other higher forms of life, which in turn are fed upon by still higher forms. Through a series of what scientists call "predations," these lower forms of plant life are transformed into successively higher forms of life.

The plankton composed of plants is the only part of the sea cycle which

---

[6]Council on Environmental Quality and the U.S. Department of State, *The Global 2000 Report to the President: Entering the Twenty-First Century*, Vol. II, Washington, D.C., 1980, p. 112.

[7]D. K. Plot, "U.S. Fish Industry Lands a Whopper—New Law to Haul Up Productivity," *The Christian Science Monitor*, December 29, 1980, p. 7.

[8]*Ibid.*

FIGURE 22-3. From Bristol Bay, Alaska, come more than half the world's harvest of sockeye (red) salmon. The estimated catch of fish and shellfish from the bay has been worth over $10 billion. Bristol Bay encompasses 40,000 square miles of the Bering Sea. The herring catch is the latest bonanza. Some skippers have grossed up to $145,000 in three hours. (Photo © Dan Guravich; information adapted from article by John Hemingway, "Blending Old Ways and New in Bristol Bay," *Exxon USA*, Vol. XXV, No. 1, Exxon Company, USA, 1986)

creates organic matter from inorganic materials in the open seas. This is done in the presence of sunlight in a manner similar to that used by any green-leaved land plant. Animals do not possess this ability, so they must feed either upon plants or upon other animals that have first fed on plants.

There is a good deal of confusion over the term *plankton*. The drifting life of the sea is called **plankton.** There are both plant and animal drifters. **Algae,** a group of plants that make their own food from inorganic substances and generally contain chlorophyll, comprise the bulk of the **plant plankton.** Not all algae are plankton. Some are fastened to the sea bottom or coasts, and of course, some are common to us on inland water bodies or moist surfaces. Some algae are quite large. Kelp, a brown seaweed, for example, may be 100 feet in length. **Animal plankton,** which are generally minute in size, feed upon the plant plankton. Some plankton have such a mixture of plant and animal qualities that both botanists and zoologists claim them.

Each time some form of life consumes some other form, there is a wastage or loss of organic matter. The amount of the lowest form of animal life which is produced from eating plankton is much less than the amount of plankton consumed, and every time another form of animal life consumes some simpler form, there is another loss. The volume, or poundage, of fish produced may not be more than 0.001 of the volume of the original plankton which was consumed by the lowest form of animal life in this final step in the cycle of life in the sea.

If we wish to increase the total quantity of food produced from an acre of water, we should catch the smaller fish. Where this is systematically done, the total poundage of fish produced per acre of water can be greatly increased. And, if some economical way could be found to make human food out of plankton, the total production of food from water could be increased. But, if we want the larger fish, we must be content with less food than if we use the smaller-sized fish. In any case, conditions must be such that a large amount of plankton is produced if a large fish crop is to be obtained. The same principle holds for small ponds and lakes (see Figure 22-4).

FIGURE 22-4. This 78-acre lake on the campus of Southern Illinois University at Edwardsville serves a multiple purpose. It provides for fishing. The school's heating and cooling plant uses its water. Up the lake from this spot there is a swimming beach. In addition, the lake serves as a scenic outlook for student housing. (Photo by Harry B. Kircher)

Importance of Plankton Production

The preceding paragraphs stressed the importance of having plankton in water where fish are to be produced. If an acre of the ocean bottom produces a yearly supply of 50 pounds of fish, the overlying waters must produce from 25,000 to 50,000 pounds of plankton during the same time. And, since plankton are not produced farther below the surface than sunlight actually penetrates, it is readily understood why ponds need not be deeper than 5 or 6 feet to produce immense amounts of this microscopic plant life.

A second requirement for plant growth is heat. Also, so that the largest quantities of fish can be produced, the proper kinds and amounts of plant food or nutrients must be present in the water.

If it were possible to convert plankton directly to our food supply, and we could harvest tremendous quantities, where would the higher forms of fish life get their supply of food? Thus, if we break the food chain relationship, we might lose our present fish resource. We might imperil the entire ecology of the seas, resulting in eventual loss of the plankton. We might end up with less food than ever before.

OUR NATION'S UNDERWATER BOUNDARY EXTENDED

Our nation's underwater boundary was greatly extended in 1964. At a United Nation's law-of-the-sea conference in 1958, it had been agreed that the limit of sovereignty over the sea bottom should be at whatever line is drawn by a 600-foot depth of water. Sovereignty implies not only the ownership but also the right to develop. By this agreement, which became legal in 1964, the offshore land area of our nation was extended by one-third its former total extent!

Our territorial control has been extended even further. In 1976, the Fisheries and Conservation Act set up a mechanism to control all fishery resources within 200 miles of our shores. Research to supply needed information for this purpose and advice on policies are supplied by the National Oceanic and Atmospheric Agency (NOAA), established in 1969.

MORE REGARD FOR NATURE'S CYCLES NEEDED

Modern technology has made possible more thorough study of the oceans' depths and marine life. New research efforts are being made in this direction. We have extended our territorial waters and are attempting to stop the pirating of them by other nations. Also, more fish farming may add to our food supplies only if it is not polluted. Thus, the sea may eventually yield more than its present share of our food supply. However, this is going to require more regard for nature's cycles of life than we have shown in the past. Otherwise, it will yield less.

QUESTIONS AND PROBLEMS

1. Why don't the minerals in sea water presently constitute our major mineral resources for industry?

2. What are the three major groups of plant and animal life in the seas? Give an example of a form of life in each.

3. Which form of plant or animal life in the sea is most basic? Why?

4. Why is fish a desirable food?

5. What are the reasons why the colonists took up fishing along the Atlantic shore?

6. How did the colonists dispose of the three classes of salted fish?

7. Is our present resource of fish increasing or decreasing? Give some cases which support your answer.

8. Do we get a major portion of our food supply from fish of the sea? How important are fresh-water fish compared with those from the oceans?

9. What is meant by fish farming?

10. Explain how the cycle of life in the sea operates. If we could convert plankton to a commercial food crop, how might it threaten life in the sea?

11. How have our national underwater boundaries been extended?

12. If we should let our soil erode away so that our agricultural production fell off by a third or more, would we be able to make up the deficiency by increasing our output of food from the sea? Explain your answer.

23

The Ecological Approach to Natural Resources

Although various resources have already been discussed, we have learned that they are all closely interrelated. The study of how living organisms and the nonliving environment function together as a whole is called *ecology.* Scientists call this interrelated whole an *ecosystem.* We can only develop natural resources for our maximum benefit by considering our place as part of this ecosystem.

THE SCIENCE OF ECOLOGY

Ecological relationships are a fundamental basis of life on earth. One principle of ecology is that living organisms—animals, including human beings, and plants—and their nonliving environment—rocks; minerals; gases, including air; and water—are inseparably related. The dependence of animals upon one another was expressed well many years ago by the famous writer Jonathan Swift:

> Big fleas have little fleas
> Upon their backs to bite 'em
> And little fleas have lesser fleas
> And so, *ad infinitum.*

415

With apologies to Mr. Swift, we might add in order to include the full concept of ecology:

> Big fleas like to live on dogs
> And dogs are man's best friend;
> But, without grass and sun and sky
> They'd all die in the end.

The face of the moon gives us a good idea of what an unbalanced natural system looks like. With no atmosphere, there is searing heat or numbing cold—nothing in between. No processes have allowed photosynthesis. Without this process and other factors, there are no lifeforms. The moon's environment is entirely unsuitable for life.

We don't need to go to the moon, however, to find examples of unbalanced systems. While human ecology is still very imperfectly understood, it seems a reasonable assumption that the crowding of people into vast, box-like apartments, without recreation space or elbow room from neighbors, does not provide a balanced environment. These prison-like structures destroy a sense of belonging and home, which even exists in some of the poorest, most run-down small dwelling units which they have replaced. This imbalance apparently has helped account for a rise in crime and delinquency.

Another principle of ecology is that all life is dependent upon the continuous inflow of the concentrated energy of light and radiation. We need the sun! To the extent that we limit energy receipts from the sun by air pollution, or in other ways, we are limiting life.

A third principle of ecology is that most of the world obtains its food through the process of plant photosynthesis and microorganism photosynthesis. Thus, the survival of this minute plant and animal life in our environment is one of the keys to our survival.

Ecologists note a fourth principle, that all living matter has limiting conditions. Some of these limiting substances may be very small and essential, such as the traces of minerals needed in our diet. Others may be large and essential, such as rainfall and light. Development of an ecosystem is limited by the essential factor available in the **least** quantity. To put it simply, a chain is as strong as its weakest link.

The final principle of ecology that we will note here might be called the **community principle.** A community—that is, a group of animals or plants living together in the same environment—has a community character that is dependent upon the total relationships of the community. That is to say, the community is more than the sum of its individual members. When one member of a community is destroyed, it affects the character of the entire community. Under balanced conditions, each species finds it place and a diversity of species assures that no single one will dominate. The various life cycles support one another. A pond which has a balanced plant and animal life, as explained in an earlier chapter, is a good example of a small community. Our whole world may be thought of as a large community.

That nature tends to strike a balance between living things does not mean that change is not going on constantly. As we have studied various resources, we have learned that all nature is changing. The land is eroding; ponds are drying up; and plants and animals reach a peak of growth and then die. A succession of various types of communities follow one another. We cannot wholly prevent change. But, we may be able to slow it down or to speed it up to work in our favor.

Unfortunately, we have been ignorant of or have chosen to ignore the principles of ecology. As a result, we are facing the many resource problems which we have already noted and others which we will now consider.

AIR POLLUTION AND RESOURCES

A key problem of our environment is that we are destroying the availability of our remaining resources by polluting them. Once we thought of atmosphere as an unlimited, self-renewing resource. Now, we realize that it is a relatively thin film of gases subject to contamination.

Excessive air pollution could result in the flooding of most of our seacoast cities. If carbon dioxide reaches the atmosphere faster than it can be absorbed by the ocean or converted back into carbonates and oxygen by animals and plants, some scientists believe that we may experience a gradual warming trend which would melt the polar ice caps and raise the ocean levels 100 feet or more. New York and Los Angeles would be among the cities drowned out.

Another view of air pollution is that solid particle emissons may be helping form a cloud cover on earth which would cool the atmosphere and bring continental glaciation and cold climate far south of its present limits. Much of the northern United States would become uninhabitable. We would again be in the Ice Age.

Whatever the long-term effect of air pollution, the immediate effect has apparently, among other things, shortened human life. Several classic cases prove this point. At Donora, Pennsylvania, on October 26, 1948, a heavy, soot-laden fog began to blanket the town. Before it was washed away by rain four days later, over 5,000 of the town's 14,000 residents had become ill. Twenty died! On December 5, 1952, a great black smog began to envelop London, England. During the five days before it lifted, 4,000 more deaths took place than would have normally occurred in that period of time. In the 1950's and the 1960's, both New York and Chicago experienced apparent "killer" smogs.

While these are now historic accounts, their lessons should not be forgotten, for severe air quality problems still plague us. Of 41 SMSA's studied from 1975 to 1977 by the Council on Environmental Quality, 5—New York, Chicago, Denver, Los Angeles and San Bernardino—Riverside—Ontario—had "unhealthful" ratings (over 100 on the Pollution Standard Index of the EPA) for 30 percent of the year. There were 11 cities that had over 100 days in this category, and 20 cities with over 50 days.

In 1970, Congress passed the Clean Air Act, which was designed to control industrial sources through federal administration. But, there was not sufficient participation by state and local authorities to control area sources of pollution effectively. Nor were actual control and maintenance aspects satisfactorily addressed.

In 1977, the act was amended to become known as the 1977 Clean Air Amendments, which put emphasis on state responsibilities for clean air. Specific goals were set for attainment, and more attention was given to controlling non-industrial sources. As the Environmental Quality Index of the National Wildlife Federation shows (see next chapter), the nation's battle for purer air may have lost ground in 1987. But, earlier Federation reports and those of the Environmental Protection Agency and the Council on Environmental Quality, indicate that the trend in prior years was favorable.[1]

Recently, acid rainfall has been causing special concern. The Council on Environmental Quality in its *Tenth Annual Report* declared:

> Acid rain is a major environmental problem on both sides of
> the Atlantic Ocean. Although the problem is currently confined

---

[1]Council on Environmental Quality, *Environmental Quality, The Tenth Annual Report of the Council on Environmental Quality*, Washington, D.C., 1979, pp. 17–50.

to the Northern Hemisphere, it appears likely that the problem will also occur in the Southern Hemisphere. It is considered a primary environmental threat in the Scandinavian countries and a source of marked concern in Japan and Canada. As required by the National Energy Plan in 1977, the President commissioned a study on potential environmental impacts of increased coal use. The study report, known as the Rall Report, identified acid rain in the United States as one of the six environmental problems requiring closer scrutiny. . . . Although acid rain may have some unquantified benefits, the adverse effects of acid rain are of great concern. In the eastern half of the United States, the average pH of rainfall is now between 4.0 and 4.5. Some rainfall has a pH as low as 3.0. This is about equivalent to the acidity of lemon juice. In the eastern half of the United States, the acidity of rainfall appears to have increased about 50-fold during the past 25 years.[2]

Industry is often accused of being the main culprit in causing air pollution, but we are all guilty. While the fumes of manufacturing plants are certainly a major air polluter, so are those of burning dumps, back yard and municipal incinerators, jet planes and especially automobiles. Whatever the causes, it is clear that clean air can no longer be taken for granted. Nor should dirty air be tolerated. Cigarette smoking has become a national health hazard. Now, concerns are being expressed about the effect of heavy concentrations of tobacco smoke upon nonsmokers. Federal, state and local laws have been adopted which require that public places provide nonsmoking areas.

What can be done about air pollution? Three principal steps that might be taken, suggested by a committee of the American Association for the Advancement of Science, are (1) filter the effluents, (2) modify processing to eliminate pollution and (3) cooperate better with nature. Industry could use more solar energy (Figure 23-1) and so can we. For example, awnings over south and west facing windows can be raised to permit more direct sun heat to warm the house in winter and lowered to keep rooms cooler so less air-conditioning is used in summer. Since less power will then be used by the power company, such practices will cut down on their emission fumes. We can mulch leaves instead of burning them, returning to nature the organic matter and eliminating smoke. We can keep the engines of our automobiles tuned up, thus burning fuel more efficiently and emitting less exhaust gas.

---

[2] *Ibid.*, pp. 70–71.

FIGURE 23-1. Inexhaustible solar energy already is relieving our dependence upon exhaustible resources of coal, oil and gas. One way to put the sun's energy to use is by a photovoltaic system. This 200-watt peak capacity unit supplies power to a weather station in the Illinois climate network at a remote location west of Peoria, Illinois. (See also Figure 8-3.) (Courtesy, Illinois Department of Energy and Natural Resources, Springfield, Illinois)

The acid-rain air pollution cleanup could be very profitable to business and labor involved. Legislation to reduce sulfur dioxide emissions from coal-fired utilities would result in a net gain of some 195,000 U.S. jobs and $13 billion in annual sales for U.S. companies, according to a study by Management Information Services. The gains, however, would not be evenly distributed among states. High-sulfur coal-producing states would be paying out, in all likelihood, more than they would benefit dollarwise.[3]

PESTICIDES — FOR BETTER OR WORSE?

There are two major categories of pesticides: insecticides, chemicals to control insects, and herbicides, chemicals to control undesirable plants.

---

[3]"A Sweet Side to Acid Rain," *Time*, February 16, 1987, p. 49.

Chemical insecticides and herbicides have greatly reduced disease and increased crop and livestock production through their reduction of insect pests and undesirable plants. In some 40 years of managing a midwestern cash grain farm with a few livestock, author Kircher directed a constant battle against insects such as corn borers and cut worms on the one hand, and weeds such as fox tail and cockleburs on the other. Such pests can reduce yields of crops severely or even wipe them out. Diseases which can be carried by insects or noxious plants can, of course, kill livestock.

In recent years, U.S. manufacturers have produced over $4 billion a year of synthetic organic pesticides to help farmers here and abroad control the thousands of detrimental plants and insects that plague them.[4]

Insecticides have become a major worry because of their ability to persist in the environment. Traces of these poisons have been found all over the world. Although the insecticide DDT was banned in 1972, it has been found in 584 of 590 samples of fish taken from 45 U.S. rivers and lakes, according to a study conducted by the Bureau of Sport Fisheries and Wildlife. Insecticides such as the banned DDT and its chemical relatives are nerve poisons. Their particular threat to human life is that they do not break down readily into less lethal forms. Thus, they ***persist.*** They last from insect to fish, to animal, to human, and so on, however the food chain might operate. Opponents argue that they will become concentrated in harmful amounts in humans, causing pesticide-related illnesses and death. "Our ability to detect infinitesimal traces of pesticides in food, air, and water surpasses our understanding of how they may affect our bodies,"[5] Allen Boraiko writes after interviews with chemists at the Harvard Biological Laboratories and with other experts in government and business.

Therefore, pesticides must be used with caution, and the United States and other developed nations must stop exporting toxic pesticides, often those banned in their own countries, to developing nations. Information on pesticide use is available from the various USDA extension offices which are located in every state in the United States.

Progress must be made in improving alternative methods of pest

---

[4] See U.S. Department of Agriculture, Agricultural and Stabilization Service, *The Pesticide Review* (an annual publication) for specific figures. Data also available from the Bureau of the Census, *Statistical Abstract of the United States* (annual).

[5] Allen Boraiko, "The Pesticide Dilemma," *National Geographic Magazine,* February 1980, p. 183.

control. One such method is biological warfare in which harmless insects may be used, for example, to eliminate harmful ones.

SOLID WASTE DISPOSAL

For thousands of years, we have regarded the land surface of the earth and its underground extent as practically limitless. It was inconceivable to think that there would not always be a site suitable for a city location, that highways would ever cover enough ground to affect agriculture or that we would not have plenty of waste land or underground areas in which to dispose of our garbage and trash. But, that day has already arrived! A million or more acres a year of farm land are being buried beneath our superhighways each year. While we talk of building new cities in the middle of open plains—a most costly process, our solid wastes clutter the countryside.

The amount of solid waste generated in the United States has been increasing at an annual rate of between 1 and 2 percent over the past quarter century. If this trend continues, our nation is heading for unmanageable waste accumulation. In some cities, this has already happened. Chicago has only four years before its 33 dumps will be full. Los Angeles dumps should reach capacity by 1995. Some New England towns run trucks 24 hours a day to Pennsylvania and Ohio. Towns on Long Island ship as far west as Michigan.[6]

In 1988, U.S. municipal waste, which includes industrial and commercial wastes, had attained an annual rate of over 1,400 pounds per person.[7]

Matter cannot be destroyed. It merely becomes transformed, as we noted in Chapter 1. Simple burning of trash is not the answer to the waste disposal problem, for this would simply be turning solid waste pollution into air pollution. But, controlled burning with proper equipment has been providing useful energy, as was noted in an earlier chapter. We need to find additional methods of turning waste products into useful resources, thus taking care of their disposal in a beneficial manner. Recycling is such

---

[6]Stephen Budiansky with Robert F. Black, "Tons and Tons of Trash and No Place to Put It," U.S. News & World Report, December 14, 1987, p. 58.

[7]Estimates of rates of growth and current rate by author Kircher on the basis of data from the Council on Environmental Quality, and the Bureau of the Census.

a method; however, on the average, less than 10 percent of our consumer solid waste is being recycled.

Hazardous Wastes

A serious conservation problem is solid and liquid materials that are hazardous to all forms of life. About 60 million tons or more are generated yearly in the United States. Because many of these materials endure for years, in hundreds of places they have leaked into surrounding rural and urban areas and adversely affected the health of plants, farm animals, wildlife and people. Prior to passage of the Resource Conservation and Recovery Act of 1976, disposal of these wastes was inadequately done by the industries that generated them. There was inadequate or nonexistent identification, responsibility, knowledge of dump locations or standards for operators of dump sites. In some cases, hazardous material has been dumped into streams or sprayed along roadways.

Federal regulations now require generators of hazardous wastes to obtain permits for temporary storage, to use appropriate containers and labels for them and to document each load leaving the plant with a shipping manifest to ensure it arrives at a licensed waste storage facility. Transport companies must also document and handle each shipment according to EPA regulations, and storage facility operators must obtain permits and meet federal and/or state storage, handling and disposal regulations. Standards are established for wastes on the basis of four measurable characteristics: ignitability, corrosivity, reactivity and toxicity.

One of the earliest cases of toxic waste damage, which became widely publicized, is the Love Canal area of Niagara Falls, New York. The canal was dug by William Love in the mid-1800's in an attempt to connect the Niagara River above Niagara Falls with Lake Ontario. The project was abandoned and that portion of the canal already dug filled with water. In the 1940's, Hooker Chemical Co. and other industries started using the canal as a dump for drums of toxic wastes. The site was sold for $1 to the local school board in 1953, and the deed disclaimed responsibility for any future problems which might come from the wastes. Testimony by a former Hooker Chemical Co. official before the House of Representatives Commerce Investigations Subcommittee in 1979 revealed that the company did not warn nearby residents of the toxic chemicals because it feared legal action.

Problems of strong chemical odors and chemical burns suffered by children who played in the area appeared in the late 1950's and early 1960's. In 1978, the state health commissioner, after complaints from local residents, investigated and then ordered the site fenced off, the leaking chemicals removed and the worst parts of the canal capped with clay. Residents of the area were found to have an unusually high rate of birth deformities, miscarriages and liver ailments. Eventually, more than 80 toxic compounds, 11 of them suspected carcinogens, were identified in the materials that had leaked from the corroded drums. More than 200 families were evacuated from the area at partial to full public expense.

Another striking example of the deadly impact of improperly disposed of hazardous waste is Times Beach, Missouri. Late in 1982, the people of this small town on the bank of the Meramec River, a few miles southwest of St. Louis, discovered that their area was severely contaminated with an extremely toxic chemical—dioxin. In the early 1970's, a trucker who had been hired to oil 10 miles of unpaved streets had mixed some waste sludge from a chemical factory with the oil and then spread it. High incidents of cancers, miscarriages, seizures and kidney difficulties resulted. After many months of negotiation, the state purchased many town lots at around $90,000 each, and most of the inhabitants left. The town is now abandoned.

About 60,000 potentially harmful chemicals are manufactured and used today in the United States. Old and some not-so-old dumps are leaking these into the environment with serious threat to public health at possibly 10,000 locations. Cleanup, started under the five-year "Superfund" of $1.6 billion, which expired in 1985, may eventually cost $300 to $400 billion, shared by the federal government; state, county and municipal governments; and industry. A strengthened Superfund bill was finally passed by Congress in 1987. Future disposal of hazardous materials should be paid for by the companies that produce them, either directly, or through tax assessments to government agencies.

In *Fortune*, Jeremy Main writes that future industry expenditures may, indeed, exceed those of government.[8] Private companies that make cleaning up hazardous wastes a business may reap high profits. But, as he points out, the risks are great.

---

[8]Jeremy Main, "Who Will Clean Up by Cleaning Up?," *Fortune*, March 17, 1986, pp. 96–102.

RECREATION AND OPEN SPACE

The availability of our space resources cannot be properly evaluated simply by calculating density figures, that is, the number of persons or machines, or some other units, per given area. The question that always should be asked is What kind of area? Is the area productive land, snow-covered waste or rocky, sandy desert?

Certain kinds of land use are much more demanding of space than others. And, our space requirements per person are constantly changing. We can stack people layer on layer in apartments. Little land is used per person. But, if too many apartments are placed side by side, where will the children play? With more urban growth, we have more concentrations of people in small areas and thus more need to provide recreation space near these concentrations. The move into the city may provide some available nearby space if farm land is abandoned on the outskirts of town, or at least becomes available for recreation because it is hilly and not very productive agriculturally. This has happened in many communities. But, some areas may have limited use for recreation. They may be flat, uninteresting lowlands, suitable for ball parks, but not attractive to the eye. Scenic spots and clear streams are apt to be destroyed by suburban sprawl and industrial blight unless definite conservation plans are made and carried out to preserve them. We need to consider quality as well as quantity.

The crowding of humanity has spread far beyond our cities. Wallace Stegner, a novelist and historian who has written widely about conservation, described the plight of our national parks in this way in 1965:

> . . . Old Faithful Yellowstone National Park at eruption time is a mob scene in a parking lot; Yosemite Valley on a summer weekend is like Times Square without electric signs. In California's splendid system of state parks and beaches a summer traveler can rarely get a camp site, and if he does he may well find himself squatting in a rural slum . . . [9]

Unfortunately, overcrowding still remains a problem in 1988.

---

[9] Wallace Stegner, "Whatever Happened to the Great Outdoors?," *Saturday Review of Literature*, May 1965, p. 37.

FIGURE 23-2. Vacationers Tom Watson and Nancy Branch look over the crystal clear waters of a lake in the high Sierras of California. Even such apparently remote areas must be protected from excessive use and from abuse, or their natural systems will be destroyed. Predictions call for 250 million annual visits to national parks by the year 2000. (Photo by Susan Kircher)

Fortunately, the concern about overcrowding has been reflected in public policy. More camp grounds have been provided in national forests. Visitors have been bused into some parks to reduce the load of cars. Despite accelerating travel costs, people continue to visit the parks in near-record numbers. Nevertheless, the National Park Service Director, Russ Dickeson, urged in 1980 that national park system growth be slowed and that only areas with true national significance be added. He pointed out that expansion of the system has been so rapid (52 natural and recreational areas in 20 years) that maintenance is lagging behind (see Figure 23-2).[10]

A report on the status of outdoor recreation was prepared in 1986 by the President's Commission on Americans Outdoors, chaired by Lamar Alexander, governor of Tennessee. Despite general improvements in the environment since the 1960's, one staff paper in the report describes "a tenuous balance between degradation, restoration, and conservation of resources. For some resources it is a continual struggle just to maintain the status quo." A major concern of the Commission is how to raise money for needed care and improvements of recreational areas and facilities.[11]

PHILOSOPHY OF ECOLOGY

As we review the contradictory record that our resource strategy has wrought, we are forced to realize that we, while molders of nature, are also part of nature. We have sought out many inventions which have freed us from drudgery and have helped compress time and space. We would not turn the clock back to the day when we had to have water by bucket from the nearest stream, to fire up the cook stove with wood and to saddle up the family horse and race for the doctor everytime there was an emergency. On the other hand, we wish we could bring back the tall trees, clear streams and clear sky. We are part of nature. We are inseparably related to other living organisms, dependent upon a continuous flow of energy from the sun and food energy through photosynthesis.

We must operate within limits our systems can tolerate. Of course, a few of us can exist for a limited time in space capsules like the astronauts. And, at least one scientist has visualized that we may build great cities in like manner. Cities would be enclosed in great balls which might float on the ocean or even in space. To many of us, not only is such an idea fantastic, but it is also repugnant. Even if it were possible, would life be worth living without the wonders of life in its natural state—without flowers and trees and birds and wild animals, the sky above and the earth beneath our

---

[10]"Wildlife Digest," *National Wildlife*, Vienna, Virginia, National Wildlife Federation, October—November 1980, p. 28-A.

[11]Donald L. Rheem, "Preserving America's Outdoors," *The Christian Science Monitor*, July 1, 1986, pp. 5, 6.

feet? Ecology teaches us that even an artificial system cannot go on forever outside nature's cycles. It must at some point depend upon nature's reserves. And, in wholly unnatural surroundings, how long could we remain sane?[12]

CONSERVATION VERSUS ECOLOGY

What is the difference between a conservational and ecological viewpoint? The basic difference is in the action implied by the words. *Conservation* implies doing something—"conserving." The "doing" may be a "setting aside," or an increase in the efficiency of use. For wilderness areas, for example, we noted that the action of withholding these from commercial and industrial use is a conservation action. The history of conservation and the development of modern concepts are covered in the next chapter. The point we want to make here is that while conservation involves education and research, finally something must be done—or there is no conservation.

By contrast, *ecology* simply means the study of the environment. The word itself does not imply that there will be a follow-through to action, even though ecologists are often leaders in conservation.

Professional conservationists should understand, at least within the limits of their specialty, the principles of ecology. They should always be conscious that one change sets another in action—that the web of life is, indeed, fragile for some communities. It is only as strong as the weakest strand that supports it.

Ecologists, on the other hand, do not need to understand how to bring about effective conservation. They do not need to know how to correct erosion problems, build ponds, economize in the use of minerals, and so on. Nor do they need to practice conservation to be ecologists. They may choose to analyze the "balance of nature" of an endangered natural community, such as a particular pond or woods, without worrying about how it might be saved, or whether it should. The world of human action can remain entirely outside their field of study. Hopefully, however, their studies will be used by conservationists both in establishing goals and policies and in setting a plan for action.

---

[12] A wide selection of books on environmental psychology and design is available from Cambridge University Press, 32 East 57th Street, New York, New York 10022.

To narrow-minded ecologists, people are intruders. They are apart from nature. They upset nature's balance. To these zealots, *conservation* is a bad word. Certain conservation practices may encourage tilling the soil, diverting water, harvesting wild animals and cutting forests. But, to the zealots, God made trees and little green apples, but not tractors, houses and barns. They see people as just bad actors.

Conservationists know that conservation means the best use of our natural resources for quality of life, taking into account the natural system. This may involve setting some resources aside. But, it is a positive concept that finds proper use a good idea. Without modern agriculture, supported by good conservation, even our country would be short of food today.

Conservation does not mean going back to the illusory "good old days." As noted, we would not want to. Firing the furnace, shoveling manure, milking cows or digging ditches by hand never was great sport. New methods and instruments must be adapted to achieve more, not less, productivity while still not abusing our resources. Under good conservation, corn yields have jumped from 50 to over 200 bushels an acre on some farms on the rich prairie sod of central Illinois after a century of cropping. Some range land and stripped land have been reclaimed. Smoke abatement has been achieved in some of our cities. Some forest land in both the East and the West has been restored.

Conservationists must stamp out the idea that nature without people is a benevolent system in which all works together in harmony and love. A slogan for a brand of cigarettes many years ago, even though we use it in a different context, fits well: "Nature in the raw is seldom mild!" People may be irresponsible rogues at times, but they are not irredeemable. They can be redeemed by practicing conservation. ***Conservation*** is a good word.

ENVIRONMENTAL PROBLEMS WORLDWIDE

The problem of maladjustment to the environment is not ours alone in the United States. It faces industrialized nations everywhere and has spread to the developing nations. Pollution and waste disposal problems face the Soviet Union and Japan, East and West Germany and the United Kingdom. Thus, the problem is not a matter of the particular kind of government and economy we have. The problem is more basic. We must change our goals. We must tailor our resource planning to the interconnectedness of all things. We must view the world as a unit. Pollution of air and water, spoilage of the landscape and needless waste of mineral resources may hit certain parts of the earth especially hard. But, like the ripples from a stone dropped in a pond, they eventually reach to every shore.

QUESTIONS AND PROBLEMS

1. How might an ecological approach to a natural resource, such as coal, differ from a strictly economic approach?

2. What is the ecological relationship between grass, beef cattle and humans?

3. How does the environment on the moon differ from that on earth? What does this suggest about our care of our environment?

4. Make a list of 10 ways in which we benefit directly or indirectly from the light and radiation of the sun. Give a satisfactory substitute for as many of these as you can.

5. Look up the word *photosynthesis* in a good reference book. Why is this process essential to our lives?

6. How does the life in a well-balanced farm pond illustrate the community principle of ecology?

7. Why does the population explosion have a greater impact on our resource base than just the increase in the numbers of people suggests?

8. What particular actions would you suggest to reduce air pollution in your neighborhood?

9. In what ways would you suggest solid waste might be put to use?

10. How would you suggest that recreation facilities be improved in your county?

11. What is the difference between a conservational and an ecological viewpoint? Are they in conflict?

12. Why do we need to be concerned about ecological problems outside our own country?

24

Conservation—
Everybody's Opportunity

The decade of the 1970's was one of remarkable progress in increasing environmental awareness and action. In 1970, the Environmental Protection Act, one of the most far-reaching pieces of environmental legislation ever passed by any nation, was enacted. Also, in 1970, an unprecedented nationwide expression of environmental concern by citizens—Earth Day—occurred. Throughout the United States, meetings and demonstrations were held about environmental problems. We, as a nation, were more concerned about conservation of natural resources than ever before in our history. But, our ardor for nature appeared to wane during the 1980's. By 1988, because of abuse, misuse, inadequate action and just plain neglect of the environment, we were falling far short of the conservation goals we had set earlier. Progress in solving old environmental problems, such as soil erosion, water pollution and vanishing wildlife, still lagged. And we were searching for ways to solve more newly recognized problems such as destruction of forests by acid rain, of our planet's ozone shield by manufactured chemicals and of life by the escape of radioactive materials from nuclear power plants. The international community was seeking ways to absolve the threat of nuclear war and to lessen the prevalence of conventional war.

For an overall view of the status of the environment as the year 1988 began, the *20th Environmental Quality Index* (EQI) of the National Wildlife Federation is highlighted. A brief history of conservation development and philosophy follows.

20th ENVIRONMENTAL QUALITY INDEX

Early in 1988, in its *20th Environmental Quality Index*, its review of national environmental developments for the past 20 years, the National Wildlife Federation concluded that "things are getting better and worse at the same time."

The introduction to the index shows that environmental concerns and developments over the past two decades have been mixed. The Federation states:

> The nation has reduced by 25 percent the amount of visible particulates—such as smoke and soot—that once clouded its industrial cities. But the Environmental Protection Agency has now discovered that the most unhealthy particulates are tiny specks of ash and dust, one-tenth the diameter of a human hair. Unlike their larger relatives, these particles easily evade the body's natural defenses. As a result, they deposit toxic, cancer-causing substances directly in human lungs. Equipment to reduce this just-realized threat may cost industries responsible nearly two billion dollars during the next seven years.
>
> Catalytic converters and no-lead gas have dramatically reduced the amounts of lead, nitrogen dioxide and sulphur dioxide in the air. But another pollutant for which automobiles are partly responsible, ozone, is proving much more intractable. An estimated 80 million Americans face daily lung irritation from this persistent poison.
>
> Our success in reducing so-called point source pollution—the sewage that fouls a specific section of river, the smokestack that darkens the skies downwind, the noxious car exhaust that taints a city neighborhood—has unmasked a far more formidable category of problem [*sic*]. This is pollution that does not come from a single source and which may travel large distances. The DDT used in South America may end up in Lake Erie, for example.[1]

---

[1]National Wildlife Federation, *20th Environmental Quality Index*, Vienna, Virginia, 1988, in the February–March 1988 issue of *National Wildlife*, p. 39.

The Federation notes that "two decades of EQ Indexes also offer a glimpse into the changing face of the environmental movement."

> In the beginning, Americans were slow and reluctant to wake from their long daydream of endless growth, limitless consumption and irresponsible waste. The call to awareness was the strenuous work of a few visionaries who struggled to persuade their dubious countrymen, as the prophets of the Old Testament once did, to repent and reform.
>
> Then came an orgy of revelations and alarms about the fragility of the environment and the incompatibility of limitless appetites with limited resources. The indifference of the 1960s gave way to shock, determination and then action. All of this was celebrated in a grim but exuberant national town meeting called Earth Day in 1970. More importantly, the rush of feeling was translated into a flood of federal legislation aimed at cleansing our water and air and protecting wildlife.
>
> But as the EQ Indexes of the subsequent years show, we were as naive in our confidence as we had been in our ignorance. . . .
>
> Not only were the [environmental] problems more difficult than expected, but as the 1970s gave way to the 1980s, public interest lagged. There were no more Earth Days, no charismatic national leaders calling us to environmental awareness. The environmental movement, it was said, was moribund.
>
> Yet something else was happening. The protesters and writers and speakers of the early days had been replaced by the lawyers and scientists of the Environmental Protection Agency, the Council on Environmental Quality and a number of highly organized national organizations supported by steadily growing memberships.
>
> As a result, environmental concerns have been made part of the fabric of our institutions. . . . [2]

Jay D. Hair, president of the Federation, commented in regard to the 20-year review, "The greatest accomplishment of the environmental movement since Earth Day has been putting our strong desire for environmental protection at the heart of the quality of life in our society."[3]

The following are some of the conclusions reached in the Index about the state of the environment in 1987.[4]

---

[2] *Ibid.,* p. 39.

[3] *Ibid.*

[4] *Ibid.,* pp. 40–46.

WILDLIFE

Some species have recovered, but many suffer from toxins and land loss.

Duck numbers still down—While the populations of many species of breeding ducks in North America increased in 1987 over the preceding year, they are still well below their historic levels.

Vanishing species—In a study of nearly two dozen national parks, researchers found that more than 40 populations of mammals have vanished since the parks were first established.

AIR

While some pollutants have declined, most cities still have dirty air.

Unfit to breathe—Some 76 million people in the United States live in areas where they breathe dangerous ozone levels. Millions more breathe unhealthful amounts of pollutants.

Fouling the parks—In many of the national parks that are regularly monitored by the Department of the Interior, air pollution now obscures scenic views more than 90 percent of the time.

WATER

Can a stronger U.S. law stop the flow of run-off pollution?

Leaking into ground water?—Less than 10 percent of 5,000 potentially dangerous types of wastes are regulated. As a result, many may be handled improperly.

Tough problem to stop — Last year, Congress finally authorized funds to fight one of the nation's most nagging water problems—run-off pollution from farms, city streets and mines.

ENERGY

Controversy erupted over plans to drill for oil in the Arctic.

Coal mining increasing—Partly due to higher oil prices, a record amount of coal—897 million tons—was mined in 1987. Coal now generates about 55 percent of the nation's electricity.

More efficient appliances — An important law passed in 1987 requires manufacturers to build refrigerators and many other major appliances that use far less energy than the current models.

FORESTS

The pressure is on to cut more timber on public woodlands.

Shrinking forests—As many as 18.8 million acres of forests could be lost by 1995 in the South, where almost half the nation's timber is produced, predicts a federal study.

Bad business—In recent years, the United States has consistently lost money selling timber in 76 of 123 national forests. One reason: the high cost of building logging roads.

SOIL

Progress is being made in the battle against soil erosion.

Protecting the soil — Farmers in eight states have enrolled more than a million acres of highly erodible cropland in the federal government's Conservation Reserve.

QUALITY OF LIFE

Americans remain committed to cleaning up pollution.

Survey — The Federation's magazine, *National Wildlife*, surveyed its readers with the question: Is the quality of your environment better, about the same, worse than five years ago? Those responding rated their environment as follows: better, 13 percent; about the same, 50 percent; worse, 37 percent.

BEAUTY AS A GOAL

During the past several decades, the value of establishing the preservation and attainment of beauty as a national conservation goal has been further implemented by the restoration of historic buildings and by city beautification projects. President Lyndon Johnson, with the ardent support of his wife, lead a crusade to preserve and enhance the country's beauty in 1965. In the *Conservation Yearbook* of the U.S. Department of the Interior for that year, he is quoted as follows:

> A few years ago we were greatly concerned about the Ugly American. Today we must act to prevent an Ugly America. For once the battle is lost, once our national splendor is destroyed, it can never

be recaptured. And once man can no longer walk with beauty or wonder at nature, his spirit will wither and his sustenance be wasted.[5]

NEPA AND EIS

President Richard Nixon recognized the environmental crisis of our nation in his State of the Union Address, January 22, 1970, saying:

> The great question of the '70's is: shall we surrender to our surroundings or shall we make peace with nature and begin to make reparation for the damage we have done to our air, to our land and to our water?

Shortly before the speech, he had signed the National Environmental Protection Act (NEPA) into law on New Year's Day. The purpose of the act was "to declare a national policy which will encourage productive and enjoyable harmony between man and his environment. . . ." The heart of the law is the requirement that all government agencies prepare Environmental Impact Statements (EIS) on any proposed actions which might significantly affect the quality of the environment.

As the decade of the 1970's began, starts had been made in cleaning up the air. Congress set up a National Center for Air Pollution Control and granted money to carry out improvements. Exhaust control devices had been installed on new automobiles. In New York, Chicago and other cities, laws on air pollution were being enacted and enforcement was begun. Young people were demonstrating in high schools and colleges for an environmental cleanup. As noted earlier, the Clean Air Act was passed in 1972 and amended in 1977 to make it more effective.

We began to try to control noise pollution. Construction of a jet airport that would have threatened wildlife of the Florida Everglades was stopped. We began to consider how we might control the sonic booms of high-speed aircraft or at least limit their flight patterns so that they do not shatter the glass and structure of houses, not to mention the nerves of the inhabitants.

---

[5] U.S. Department of the Interior, *Quest for Quality, Conservation Yearbook*, Washington, D.C., 1965, p. 94.

PROVISIONS FOR OPEN SPACE

During the 1980's, steps have been taken to preserve and care for more open space for recreation, enjoyment of beauty and possible scientific values. Additional areas of redwood forests have been made national parks. A number of streams have been designated wild rivers, to be preserved in their natural state. Magnificent stretches of beach on Cape Cod on the Atlantic and at Point Reyes on the Pacific and other areas have been set aside as national parks. The system of national trails has been extended. However, no open-space event could match the outstanding one with which the 1980's began—the conservation protection given millions of acres of land in Alaska, as noted in Chapter 12.

THE BUSINESS CLEANUP

Business has also made progress in avoiding waste and pollution. Some steel companies and electric power companies have installed devices to eliminate most of the air pollutants caused by their heating operations. More water is being recycled. Some mine operators have built settling basins to precipitate wastes in the sludge from mines rather than dumping them into streams. Oil companies are capturing and using much of the excess gas that escapes from oil wells, which they formerly burned off, and mining companies are doing more reclamation (see Figure 24-1).

Businesses should view abating pollution and in other ways improving the relation of industry to the environment as an economic opportunity, for the equipment to process wastes will need to be manufactured. In any case, the ultimate cost of such improvements will be paid by the consumer.

As noted in Chapter 19, in the past two decades, businesses have helped rehabilitate old housing in many cities, have built innovative recreational and shopping centers and generally have made cities more pleasant places in which to live and work.

THE AGRICULTURAL TURNABOUT

In the past five decades, agriculture has made the dramatic turnabout from robbing the soil to farming on the basis of land capabilities. Forestry

FIGURE 24-1. (Top) The wheat field being harvested in the foreground is on a reclaimed surface coal mine in Randolph County, Illinois. During one crop season, the yield averaged 37 bushels per acre, with some plots yielding 60 bushels, as verified by the University of Missouri. Nine inches of topsoil and 39 inches of reconditioned soil known as "agricultural root medium" have been replaced. The structure barely visible on the horizon is the shaft of an underground mine, which is a slope-type mine reaching coal too deep to strip. (Courtesy, Peabody Coal Company) (Bottom) This watery playground was once a coal mine. The surface-mined area, near Huntsville, Missouri, was revegetated and turned into a private development within three years. This picture was taken 16 years after reclamation. (Courtesy, National Coal Association)

turned the corner from "cut out and get out" policies to management on a sustained yield basis. State and federal agencies adopted rules and recommended practices from pesticide use that lessened the danger to our biotic system.

Conservation and the 1985 Farm Bill

In late 1985, Congress passed a farm bill which has been called "the most fundamental change in soil conservation policy of the past 50 years."

This legislation is intended to lead to the retirement of some 40 million acres of our most erodible cropland. Nationwide, some 104 million acres, or about one-fourth of all cropland, will be eligible for the program. Farmers who wish to participate in the Conservation Reserve, as it is named, will submit bids on the annual rental payments they would accept. If their bids are accepted, they will sign 10-year contracts with the U.S. Department of Agriculture agreeing to replace cultivated crops with perennial grass, wildlife plants or trees. In addition to rental payments, participating farmers will receive 50 percent cost-sharing to help establish cover crops.

Each year the program is expected to save 750 million tons of soil from erosion, to reduce stream sedimentation by more than 200 million tons and to cut the amount of pesticides applied annually by about 60 million pounds. Also, it is hoped that at least 5 million acres of reserve land will be reforested.

The 1985 farm bill also contains a "sodbuster" provision, which requires farmers to follow an approved conservation plan to qualify for participation. Likewise, a "swampbuster" stipulation makes farmers ineligible for farm program benefits if they produce commodities on wetland that has been substantially altered or drained for that purpose.

Another aspect of the bill is the authority given to the Farmers Home Administration to write off delinquent debt partially in exchange for easements. The easements, lasting 50 years or more, would convert highly erodible cropland to less intensive uses.

Major threats to the successful execution of the program appear to be: (1) funding may be cut back because of budget cuts made under the Gramn-Rudman Act; (2) the local SCS, ASCS and soil conservation district offices may be overloaded with the task of implementing the policy; and (3) some of the final changes in the bill may have blurred its intent; thus, the law may be further weakened in design through the regulatory process. A long-term monitoring and evaluation program is needed to protect the validity of the program. The responsibility for this rests with the nation's private conservation and farm organizations.[6]

Individual farmers need to have a cooperative attitude also. In order for them to be eligible for farm subsidies, they must have a soil conservation plan in place by January 1990, and the plan must be in practice by January 1995.

LAND-USE PLANNING

By the 1980's, states had begun to recognize the need for statewide land-use planning. We, as a nation, had found out that helter-skelter private development based solely on the profit motive and governmental planning based largely upon political expediency threaten our prime agricultural soils, our forests and wilderness areas, our free-flowing streams, our Great Lakes and coastal waters and other natural resources. They cost us money and even our lives. Houses had been washed over cliffs by torrential rains in California, engulfed by swirling flood waters in Illinois, Mississippi and Pennsylvania and smashed by waves under the fury of hurricanes in Texas, Louisiana and Florida. California experienced some moderately severe earthquake tremors, and the Mississippi Valley area was warned to be prepared for a quake someday. Government agencies and private research organizations studied the problem and devised emergency plans for the future.

It was becoming increasingly clear that many of our losses were unnecessary. They could have been prevented or, at least, modified, had good land-use plans been made and implemented.

Slow Progress in Land-Use Planning

Congress is well aware of the need for land-use planning, but progress

---

[6]This material is based on three articles in the *Journal of Soil and Water Conservation*, January–February 1986, as follows: Robert J. Gray, Director of Policy Development for the American Farmland Trust, "Proving Out: On Implementing the Conservation Title of the 1985 Farm Bill," pp. 31–32; John R. Block, former Secretary of Agriculture, "Conserving Soil Conservation," pp. 30–31; and Duane Sand, Farming Project Director for the Iowa National Heritage Foundation, "Good News and Bad for Soil Conservation," p. 32.

has been slow. In 1980, after many years of debate, it still had not succeeded in enacting a land-use bill into law. A bill proposed would have provided $100 million a year to help states set up a nationally coordinated state planning program. The bill was endorsed by the National Association of Counties, the National Governors' Conference and all major environmental groups. However, opponents presented the bill as undermining state and personal property rights. And, the administration determined there was no money in the budget to implement the plan.

Meanwhile, at the state level, land-use legislation has continued to face opposition as the complications of such programs have become evident. On the other hand, almost all the states have considered, initiated a study of or enacted some kind of state land-use law.

Many citizens, unfortunately, still view land-use legislation as more of a threat to private property than as a protection of resources. Of course, zoning does affect land prices, and some ordinances can be very inequitable in the eyes of landowners. Ways must be found, such as those pointed out in Chapter 19, to reward those who forego selling their land at higher prices for residential, industrial and commercial use, in order for it to remain for needed environmental use. Who can blame a landowner for feeling it is unfair if his/her neighbor's 100 acres of, say, Class III or Class IV land can be sold for industrial purposes for $500,000, while the landowner is told his/her Class I land can be sold for agricultural purposes only, which would bring a price of $200,000 or less?

ECOREGIONS — AN ECOLOGICAL SYSTEM

The ecoregions classification adopted by the U.S. Forest Service (see Figure 24-2) illustrates how an ecological system can be developed for land-use planning.[7]

The U.S. Forest Service explains:

> There are a number of different kinds of regions depending upon objective or purpose. Just as a region based on agriculture

---

[7] A more detailed map and a booklet explaining the system are available from the U.S. Forest Service, Rocky Mountain Forest and Range Experiment Station, 240 West Prospect Street, Fort Collins, Colorado 80526. The authors are indebted to Dr. Robert G. Bailey, who is credited with the design of the map in Figure 24-2 and who cooperated in supplying other information.

is an agricultural region, one based on ecosystems is an ecosystem region or *ecoregion*.

To date, most work based on the ecosystem concept of resource management is at a detailed level. There are at least two reasons why a regional view of the ecosystem is needed: (1) to permit detailed data to be aggregated into more generalized units for decisionmaking at higher levels; (2) to provide an integrating frame of reference needed to fully interpret the more detailed information.

This map was developed to meet these needs. Maps based on classification of climatic types, vegetation associations, and soil groups have been widely used, but no comparable broad-scale synthesis of these maps has been commonly accepted. This map is an attempt to fill that gap.

Because land is a complex of surface attributes, in other words, an ecosystem, the classification should reflect spatial patterns as well as properties. How a piece of land will behave cannot be predicted fully in terms of local controls or single factors acting in isolation, but is in part determined by relationships with adjoining areas. There is thus intrinsic advantage of assessing land in terms of interacting units at various scales of grouping. The process of grouping objects on the basis of spatial relationships rather than solely on similarity of taxonomic properties is called *regionalization*.[8]

OTHER PROBLEMS STILL TO BE SOLVED

Many conservation problems remain to be solved. Water pollution from offshore oil seepage or leakage from oil tanker vessels still occurs. Conservationists and lumber producers disagree as to the best policies to protect our forests. Many of our farmers still have not signed up for conservation programs. Most of the many small privately owned woodlands in the nation are sitll not being well managed for productivity of timber. Municipalities continue to be faced with crime, housing and traffic problems. Sewage improvement programs, however, have moved toward completion.

President Gerald Ford's administration was dedicated to getting the nation through the energy crisis with a minimum of monetary inflation. Environmental actions, the President felt, had to be shelved for the time

---

[8] U.S. Forest Service, *Ecoregions of the United States* (map), Washington, D.C., 1976. See also Robert G. Bailey, compiler, *Description of Ecoregions of the United States*, U.S. Forest Service, Washington, D.C., 1978.

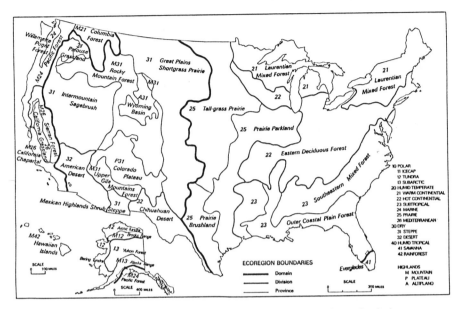

FIGURE 24-2. Ecoregions of the United States. (Courtesy, U.S. Forest Service)

being, if necessary, to accomplish these other objectives. In a message prefacing the *Fifth Annual Report of the Council on Environmental Quality*, in December 1974, he wrote:

> . . .'. today, millions of our citizens share a new vision of the future in which natural systems can be protected. . . . We must also recognize that, even with a strong conservation program, we will still have to mine more coal, drill for more oil and gas, and build more power plants and refineries. . . . [9]

Beautifying the landscape received more publicity than action in the first half of the decade. A bill for highway beautification was stripped of its effective provisions by the time it passed Congress. Cities were having trouble passing bond issues to provide money for buying land for parks and other recreation facilities before the land was built up. Thousands of miles of abandoned strip mines remained unreclaimed.

---

[9] Council on Environmental Quality, *Fifth Annual Report of the Council on Environmental Quality*, Washington, D.C., 1974, Preface.

President Jimmy Carter began his term of office with a strong conservation stand. And, in the following years, he supported wilderness preservation and preservation of public lands in Alaska. But, as the nation entered an economic recessionary period in 1980, he proposed sharp cuts in many conservation programs, including those supporting solar energy, habitat protection and mass transit acquisition.

Conservation Cutbacks and Signs of Hope

Emphasizing productivity while attempting to control inflation and increase defense spending, President Reagan cut back conservation programs. By the year 1987, during his second term in office, the environmental record improved as an aroused public and a more environmentally oriented Congress made themselves heard. But, there remained many grievous shortcomings in policy and action.

On the encouraging side, during the 1970's and 1980's, state and local governments made considerable gains in environmental planning. Hawaii became the first state to adopt statewide planning. California established an outstanding long-range energy plan. Missouri and Illinois supported strong conservation programs for wildlife and recreation.

Land-use controls, furthermore, were at last coming to communities in the last bastion of unbridled private land development—the Southwest. Pinal County, Arizona, of which Florence is the county seat, is a good example. "The county," *The Arizona Daily Star* editorialized in June 1987, ". . . took a giant common-sense step into the future . . . with a six-month moratorium on the county's practice of letting developers do much of their land planning for them."[10]

During the moratorium, the county hired a professional planner. In 1988, he was busy developing needed policies, procedures and plans for land-use and water conservation.[11]

Large and environmentally questionable water projects continued in 1986. Heading them was the Tennessee-Tombigbee Waterway, the biggest, most expensive, and one of the most controversial federal navigation projects in the nation's history. Its cost of $1.8 billion was $600 million more

---

[10] *The Arizona Daily Star*, June 3, 1987, p. 1c.

[11] Interview with Dean Brennan, Planner, Pinal County, Florence, Arizona, April 4, 1988.

than the McClellan-Kerr Waterway in Arkansas and Oklahoma cost to complete. The waterway connects the TVA system (the Tennessee River) with the Tombigbee River. The cut through hills to do this was accomplished by the U.S. Army Corps of engineers, which moved 307 million cubic yards of dirt—96 million more than were moved for the Panama Canal. Mobile, Alabama, at the southern terminus of the waterway has spent $232 million modernizing its port facilities in anticipation of increased waterway traffic.[12]

Another new navigation project of the same magnitude in cost as "Ten-Tom" is the new Lock and Dam 26 being built by the Corps on the Mississippi River just upstream from St. Louis, Missouri. The old lock and dam had become outdated, resulting in long delays for tows. Building of the new facility was fought in court by the railroads, who argued it was economically unnecessary, and by conservation organizations, who feared adverse environmental impacts. Their suit was lost, and construction was well along in 1987.

NASA PLANS FOR NEW
ENVIRONMENTAL UNDERSTANDING

In mid-1986, NASA officials proposed an extensive program of earth surveillance by orbiting satellites that would greatly enhance our understanding of the environment. The space vehicles would track weather, map the land, trace Earth's gravitational and magnetic fields, probe the atmosphere and monitor ocean currents.

NASA's Earth System Sciences Committee (ESSC) had been working on this proposal for the past three years. The National Oceanic and Atmospheric Administration (NOAA) and the National Science Foundation (NFS) have joined in its presentation. Besides U.S. satellites, those from Japan, the Soviet Union and possibly India and China would be involved. Operation of the system by the mid-1990's is anticipated.

ESSC chairman Francis P. Bretherton of the National Center for Atmospheric Research noted that expected planetary changes:

---

[12]Carolyn Bennett Patterson, "The Tennessee-Tombigbee Waterway—Bounty or Boondoggle?," *National Geographic Magazine*, Vol. 169, No. 3, 1986.

. . . will take climate and our natural environment outside the range
of historical experience. Our children and grandchildren throughout the world will have to develop new definitions of what is normal,
to adjust their expectation of floods and drought, to alter their
supplies of food and water to cope with new realities. . . . We must
start now to lay the foundation of knowledge and understanding
for our successors to act upon.[13]

HISTORY OF THE PHILOSOPHY
OF CONSERVATION

As we consider the many resource problems we have studied, it
sometimes seems as though the battle to save our environment has just
begun. But, as long ago as 1748, a book on conservation farming practices
by Jared Elliot, a minister, was published in the United States. Elliot's book,
and several others which soon followed it, however, had little impact at
that time.

Saving for Future Use

The earliest concept of conservation evident in the policies of our nation
was that of "saving for future use." In the 1800's, the word *conservation*
was applied mostly to our forests. National concern over forest conservation was aroused by the report in 1871 of a committee appointed by the
Commissioner of Agriculture, that in less than two centuries nearly one-
half of our original forest land had been cleared. Up to that time, it was
the common belief that our natural resources were practically inexhaustible. Our forests, in particular, were assumed to be large enough to meet
all future needs for lumber and wood. Trees were as common as weeds
and were destroyed with little more regard. It came as a shock to learn
that we might not always have timber for every use!

The first step as a follow-up of this report was the creation of a Division
of Forestry within the Department of Agriculture. This division immediately
began to publicize the disappearance of our forests and to call attention

---

[13]Robert C. Cowen, "NASA Urges Intense Earth Surveillance," *The Christian Science
Monitor*, June 30, 1986, pp. 3, 4.

FIGURE 24-3. Conservation includes preservation and wise use of natural resources. This is a view overlooking the Estes Park, Colorado, area, with peaks of the Rocky Mountain National Park in the background. The Rocky Mountains provide not only excellent habitat for wildlife and recreational sites for humans but also forests, range land, water and minerals. (Photo by Harry B. Kircher)

to the need for definite government action to preserve this most useful resource.

In 1889, Congress passed a bill giving the President of the United States power to set aside land for forest preserves. This power was used sparingly, but it did much to stress the importance of the fast disappearing forests to our national welfare. After Theodore Roosevelt became President, he set aside more land for national forests than had all preceding presidents.

As time passed, we became aware of the need for saving other natural resources. We began to fear that coal and iron ore reserves would not last forever. New oil fields were discovered, but the production from the older fields dwindled. Finally, we became conscious of the loss of our soil and of its possible effect upon future production of food. Thus, gradually, over the period of two generations, we enlarged the meaning of the word *conservation* from its limited use in connection with the preservation of our forests to include preservation of all those natural resources which are useful to us in our complex way of living (see Figures 24-3 and 24-4).

FIGURE 24-4. This picture symbolizes the time, mostly past, when the sky was filled with fumes from escaping gas or the wasteful burning gas from wells to enable them to produce oil more readily. The belching smoke is caused by the burning waste from drilling operations— oil, mixed with mud, water and the chemicals used in drilling a new well. The flare is caused by the burning of natural gas which is produced with the oil and thus is not marketable. It is burned as a safety precaution but should be returned to the reservoir to maintain pressure and to make it possible for a higher proportion of the petroleum in the reservoir to be recovered.

Prevention of Waste

A second meaning we have come to associate with the word *conservation* is "prevention of waste." We Americans have been prodigal with our natural resources, as the previous chapters of this text have shown. We now understand that in addition to saving our forests for use in the future, we need to eliminate present waste in harvesting and using wood, which has been estimated as amounting to two-thirds of all timber cut. We have come to realize that besides concern about the extent of our natural gas reserves, we should worry about the amount we are losing in the wells (see Figure 24-5). A few years ago the daily waste of natural gas from one oil field alone was enough to supply the needs of 10 cities the size of our national capital.

Wise Use

A third concept of conservation is that it deals not only with savings and prevention of waste but with *wise use* as well. In fact, good conservation, in some cases, requires that a use rather than a savings be made. Thus, many mines when once opened must be kept operating, or they will fill up with water, or the timbers supporting the structures above will give way, and the remaining reserves will be lost or at best recovered only at greatly increased costs. When timber of our commercial forests reaches what foresters call maturity, it should be cut, or it will deteriorate and become worthless for commercial purposes.

TODAY'S CONSERVATION PHILOSOPHY

Conservation today not only incorporates the three principles of savings, waste prevention and wise use but also stresses the interaction of the whole environment, including people. It also emphasizes the need to be concerned with the quality of life. Quality of life should be set above quantity of things as a goal in developing resources. A wealthy person who is seriously ill is the object of pity, not envy. Our national wealth of resources will do us little good if badly polluted, nor can world prosperity be realized.

Ways that developing and industrialized countries could work together to achieve long-term economic growth without harming the environment were considered in a three-year study by a commission set up by the United Nations. Its massive report, issued in the spring of 1987, includes recommendations that governments integrate environmental concerns into decision making and reform international economic relations to strengthen cooperation on environmental issues.[14]

Today's conservation stresses the human benefits to be derived from environmental resource management. Realized to its fullest extent by government and business, by all of us, conservation principles can help us achieve freedom from want, good health, peace and individual dignity. Through conservation, the world could achieve a true quality of life for all.

---

[14] Timothy Aeppel, "Economic Goals vs World Environment," *The Christian Science Monitor*, April 27, 1987, p. 6.

FIGURE 24-5. Wise use. Some land can be used for the production of cultivated crops and still not be lost through erosion, while other land can best be kept in place through the production of grass or woods. The stripped areas are growing crops such as corn, oats and hay, while the land that shows no strips is in grass. Still other land is wooded, and the accumulating leaf mold and small undergrowth in those woods, if they are not pastured, serve as sponges to prevent surface run-off and erosion. (Courtesy, Soil Conservation Service)

Conservation Defined

The "new" conservation, as defined earlier in the Preface and in Chapter 2, is "the management and use, which may include preservation, of natural resources for quality life—life in harmony with aesthetic, ecological, economic and ethical principles."

This definition includes four major parts. First, conservation of natural resources means **action,** action to conserve natural resources through management or use. Research, while absolutely essential to conservation, is in itself not a conservation action. Education, likewise, while a key to realizing conservation, is not, unless applied, conservation.

Second, conservation includes both **preservation** and **use** of natural resources. Whether it is better to consume a resource or to preserve it is often a difficult conservation question.

Third, conservation is for maintaining and advancing the **quality of life** everywhere. Conservation is an international discipline. Some actions are obvious—we remove a Copperhead snake from the woodpile in the interests of our own lives. Some are complex—how do we discipline and reform humans who are destroying—or about to—our ecosystem, which would destroy life in all the world?

The fourth part of the definition provides the **principles** that need to be observed for quality of life. Quality of life is in harmony with biological cycles; exists in an economic environment which assures the best allocation of resources for human welfare; is not crushed by waste, lack of foresight and unfairness; and is pleasing.

In practice, ecological and ethical considerations should not be compromised and should come first. But, what is ethically acceptable and ecologically significant is sometimes difficult for us to agree upon. When economic and aesthetic considerations clash, it may be almost impossible to find a compromise. But, we have to try. Sometimes there is a clear best alternative (see Figure 24-5). Sometimes we only have a choice of the "least bad" of several alternatives. Sometimes taking no action is best.

TWO VIEWS OF OUR NATURAL RESOURCE BASE

Those who are concerned with our natural resource base fall into two major groups: optimists and pessimists. The optimists emphasize the limitless nature of energy and the potentials of human intelligence. They believe that human ingenuity can meet resource needs and that people are too intelligent to continue plundering the earth to their own ultimate destruction. The pessimists emphasize the exhaustible nature of our natural resources and the "creature" nature of humans. They fear that the rising rate of population growth and of abuse to the environment cannot be halted.

It is helpful to consider both the optimistic and the pessimistic outlooks. A Pollyanna attitude leads to disregard of unpleasant facts, postponement of action and overconfidence. An alarmist view of our energy potential leads to fear, paralysis of action and an attitude of defeat. What is needed is a concerned yet confident view that inspires firm action and perseverance. The accomplishments of genius are said to be 1 percent inspiration and 99 percent perspiration. But, the job can be enjoyable and rewarding.

"Reports on the future of energy by the Andrew W. Mellon Foundation, the Ford Foundation, the Resources for the Future Project, and Harvard Business School agree on just one point: The 'key energy resource' is conservation," Mel Maddocks writes in *The Christian Science Monitor*. "Alternatives are what make the world 'thinkable.' Alternatives, multiple choices, second and third ways break the fatalism produced by Fearful Prognostications. One begins to subscribe to patience, to look for improvements rather than The Answer—to think small, if you will."[15]

What needs to be done is to realize the land ethic of Aldo Leopold, co-founder of The Wilderness Society and father of modern game management in the United States. He wrote:

> All ethics so far evolved rest upon a single premise: that the individual is a member of a community of interdependent parts. His instincts prompt him to compete for his place in the community, but his ethics prompt him also to co-operate. . . . The land ethic simply enlarges the boundaries of the community to include soils, waters, plants and animals, or collectively: the land.
>
> We can be ethical only in relations to something we can see, feel, understand, love and otherwise have faith in. A land ethic, then, reflects the existence of an ecological conscience, and this in turn reflects a convention of individual responsibility for the health of the land.[16]

PROFITS FOR MORE RESOURCES—THE LAND ETHIC FOR BETTER RESOURCES

Since profitability should not be the only reason for resource development and allocations, some environmentalists have hinted that if we are to conserve our environment, we should do away with the private profit system. Such a policy would be doing away with a major incentive to resource development. While it is true that our country's productivity would not have been possible without an outstanding natural resource base, a major incentive that sparked that development was private profit. The abuses that went along with that development are shocking. But, as many examples in this text have shown, government has done much to throttle the kind of uninhibited rapaciousness evident in our early history. And, private industry has done much to clean up its own act. An indication

---

[15] Mel Maddocks, *The Christian Science Monitor*, November 14, 1979, p. 13.

[16] Aldo Leopold, *Sand County Almanac*, as reported in *Toward an American Land Ethic*, Washington, D.C., The Wilderness Society, 1980, p. 3.

of better business of ethics is the increasing employment of women in responsible jobs at pay equal to that of men in like positions (see Figure 24-6).

It seems strange to hear some people say that the answer to the environmental problem is to have *more* government. We need *better* government, not more. And, we need honest business to go along with it. What is needed is an acceptance of the land ethic by all of us. Profit means more resources. The land ethic means better resources.

FIGURE 24-6. Andy Bajerski is pictured during a moment of rest from her job of driving a 100-ton truck for the Leahy Mine of the Amax Coal Company at Campbell Hill, Illinois. In recent years, more and more women have won increasingly responsible jobs in natural resource development. (Photo from Amax Coal Company; courtesy, National Coal Association)

WHAT CAN WE DO?

But, a person asks, "What can I do? I am so small and the world so large!" First of all, we should practice conservation at home and on our jobs, be it school or work; and we can practice conservation at play. Second, we should be advocates of conservation in the groups to which we belong— church or club, fraternity or sorority, labor union or chamber of commerce, League of Women Voters or National Association for the Advancement of Colored People, and to our personal friends and acquaintances. Third, we should join and support conservation organizations such as the National Wildlife Federation, the National Audubon Society or our state society, the Sierra Club and The Wilderness Society. It is through these and like organizations that we can gain the clout to achieve conservation goals. Already such organizations have helped save San Francisco Bay from pollution by dumping, wild rivers from being tamed, wilderness areas from being scarred by mines, treasured wildlife from being wiped out and all of us from being exterminated by DDT.

FIGURE 24-7. Looking at a Pacific sunset from Waikiki Beach on the island of Oahu, Hawaii, leads us to reflect upon our responsibility to help advance the conservation goal of freedom from fear, want, sickness and war for all peoples of the world. (Photo by Harry B. Kircher)

Finally, we may be able to help conserve our resources by preparing ourselves and finding jobs directly in conservation work. Whether forest ranger, lawyer specializing in environmental law or regional planner, we would then have the satisfaction of knowing that our job was helping all of us to survive.

THE BATTLE FOR NATURAL RESOURCES

Young people will inherit the resource base. They must be willing to fight for it. Battles are generally destructive of life and property. The battle to conserve natural resources is an exception. It is a battle to preserve life.

It is a battle to benefit all of us. It is a battle which upholds rather than ridicules ideals. Unfortunately, it is youth who will pay the steepest price should the battle not be won—should we humans continue to disregard the demands of the ecosystem, should we continue to slight ecological, ethical and aesthetic needs in deference to economic demands.

The grand lesson of the foregoing pages is that our natural resource base is amazingly bountiful. Were it not, the human race would not have survived. What a beating it has taken from us! Yet, over the years remarkable resources have been developed that had never before been dreamed of. And, the process continues. Sure, there are and will continue to be "bads," such as droughts and floods, hurricanes and tornadoes, insect pests and bacterial scourges to challenge our existence. But, over the centuries, we have learned more and more how to cope with such natural disasters. They are not the real problem to realizing a high-quality life. The critical problem—the real enemy to achieving abundant life, liberty and happiness—is us.

The world, as we observed in the very beginning of this book, is embraced by the *noussphere*—a word coined to represent the realm of intelligence, inspiration, ingenuity and knowledge. Our resources depend upon how well we relate to this powerful stream of energy. Moreover, it is how well we mix this power with a precious ingredient known as "love"—love which encompasses tolerance, respect, care, forgiveness, compassion and humility. This is the way to conservation of the world and of ourselves.

QUESTIONS AND PROBLEMS

1. Did the EQI show that our environment was improving or deteriorating? What are some of the problems?

2. How did NEPA and EIS attempt to protect the environment?

3. What are several conservation actions taken by government, business and agriculture during recent years to help protect the environment?

4. What are the advantages of statewide planning? Why should anyone object to it?

5. What was the early meaning of *conservation*, and to what resources did it mostly apply?

6. In what circumstances is it good conservation to continue to use a resource?

7. Which methods of conserving a resource would you suggest for: (a) a forest, (b) an oil or a gas well, (c) a river and (d) the soil?

8. Name four natural resources found in your area and tell how you think each could be better conserved.

9. How does our present concept of conservation differ from that of a century ago?

10. What can you do to help conserve our resources?

25

The Human Body
and Natural Resources[1]

Humankind is classified as a human resource (see Chapter 1). But, that unique collection of organic and inorganic matter and gases which we call the body is also a natural resource. Its elements are free gifts of nature. And, however great our wealth of "other" natural resources may be—of what value is this to us humans if we ourselves are weak and sickly? So, we conclude our study of natural resources with a chapter noting the interlinkage of this resource and other natural resources.

Humans are, of course, more than physical bodies. Without the marvelous spark of energy we call life, the body is just a collection of earth materials—it is no longer a human being. And, without the inspiration which ignites our mental processes and the power to think, which enables us to store and increase knowledge, humans would be just another animal species living largely by instinct. Life may go on after death, but while we are here on earth, it is through the human body and the agents it manufactures that we are able to express ourselves, creating or destroying resources. The health of our bodies is dependent upon the extent to which we intelligently manage and live with our other resources.

[1]The authors are especially indebted to Diana Friesz, an environmental control specialist in private industry, and Richard Nicol, M.D., for help in researching this chapter.

THE HUMAN BODY

As we noted in Chapter 2, the earth has four major systems or spheres—the atmosphere, hydrosphere, lithosphere and biosphere—which have their smaller systems. The human body is a system within the biosphere with 11 major systems of its own: the skeletal, muscular, nervous, vascular, digestive, respiratory, endocrine, lymphatic, urinary, integumentary and reproductive systems. Each system integrates with the others in an attempt to maintain a constant internal state, despite variations in the external environment—a process known as *homeostasis.*

Effects of the external environment upon homeostasis, and subsequently upon human health, can, of course, be beneficial or destructive. Good health occurs when the processes of adaptation to changing environmental factors proceed within the limits of the homeostatic mechanisms' ability to adjust (see "The Science of Ecology," Chapter 23). Many such adjustments, for example, constriction of blood vessels to prevent heat loss, rapid breathing to compensate for rarified air and scarring to aid the healing process, are readily made. Disease occurs when the steady state between organisms and the physiochemical environment (air, water, food), biological environment (bacteria, viruses, plants and animals, including other humans) or social environment (work, leisure, cultural habits and patterns) is upset. Homeostatic mechanisms may be taxed beyond their limits by the rapid and severe changes possible in the external environment, such as pollution, insecticides and harmful radiation.

Although death from infectious diseases has shown a precipitous decline since 1900, death and sickness from environmentally related respiratory diseases and cancer have shown an equally precipitous rise.[2]

AIR AND HEALTH

Air is essential to life on earth. Most cells of the body derive the bulk of their energy from chemical reactions involving oxygen obtained from the environment by breathing. Carbon dioxide, despite its low concentration in air (less than $\frac{1}{600}$ that of oxygen), plays a vital role in the

---

[2]John H. Dingle, "The Life of Man," *Scientific American,* September 1973, Vol. 229, pp. 82–83.

cellular process. It is a waste product of cellular respiration, and it also serves to regulate the rate of breathing. The presence of carbon dioxide in the form of carbonic acid functions to control the acidity-alkalinity balance of the blood. All of the major components of air, and some of the minor ones, are of biological importance in maintaining human homeostatic conditions.

Unfortunately, as we are only too aware, air pollution has become common (see Chapters 19 and 23). The principal components of air pollution are carbon monoxide, sulfur oxides, nitrogen oxides, hydrocarbons, photochemical oxidants such as ozone and particulate matter.

A common disease attributed to air pollution is emphysema. This disease attacks the membranous walls of the alveoli. Alveoli are clusters of tiny cup-shaped hollow sacs, lined with blood capillaries servicing as the sites of gas exchange in the lungs. Oxygen diffuses inward and carbon dioxide outward across the delicate membranes. Pollutants cause the thin alveolar walls to lose their elasticity and tear apart. Nonfunctioning air spaces are left. The area in which gas can exchange is restricted. Oxygen deficiency results.

Bronchial asthma and chronic constrictive ventilatory disease, a condition related to emphysema, are also aggravated by air pollution. Some researchers even believe that there is a link between air pollution and the common cold. Air pollution is also a contributor to lung cancer. Carbon monoxide is another pollutant which is a killer if in sufficient concentration because it deprives the blood of oxygen. The oxygen-carrying capacity of the blood is the result of the affinity of the hemoglobin, an oxygen-bearing protein, in the red blood cells for oxygen. Carbon monoxide combines with hemoglobin even more readily than oxygen, and once combined, the new "carboxyhemoglobin" molecule is no longer able to carry oxygen. Thus, a person may die from asphyxiation even in the presence of oxygen if the carbon monoxide concentration is high enough. People trapped in heavy rush-hour automobile traffic are exposed to much higher than normal concentrations of carbon monoxide. Drivers may suffer loss in reaction time, alertness and visual acuity.[3]

---

[3] To amplify this discussion of air and water and health, see the following which served as sources: Charles Robert Carroll and Dean Miller, *Health, The Science of Human Adaptation*, 3rd ed., Dubuque, Iowa, William C. Brown Company, Publishers, 1982; Norman S. Hoffman, *A New World of Health*, New York, McGraw-Hill Book Company, 1976; and Kenneth E. Maxwell, *Environment of Life*, 3rd ed., Monterey, California, Brooks/Cole Publishing Co., 1980.

Sulfur oxides and nitrogen oxides may also result in air pollution. While sulfur oxides are derived from the combustion of coal which contains sulfur, nitrogen oxides are the product of the high-temperature combustion of coal, oil and gasoline. Both of these types of oxides damage human health by causing irritation of the eyes and respiratory passages, which may be permanently damaged by long exposure.

Hydrocarbons are another air pollutant we have cited. Although there is no evidence linking hydrocarbons directly to human disease, hydrocarbons are a major constituent of smog. And, smog can bear many irritants, besides contributing to mental depression and accidents related to poor visibility.

Photochemical oxidants, the most well known of which are ozone and peroxyacetyl nitrates (PAN), are known to be irritants to the eyes, nose and throat. They may cause headaches, coughs, shortness of breath and thickening of the bronchiolar walls.

Any matter in the air, which is not a gas, but which is either a solid or a liquid, is referred to as particulate matter. Many substances can adhere to particulates so that often it is not the particulates themselves but what they carry with them into the lungs that is harmful. Particulate matter can damage especially the microscopic hairlike parts lining and projecting from the respiratory passages, called cilia. Their whiplike motion cleanses the respiratory tract of pathogenic microorganisms and dirt. If damaged, they lose their capacity to function properly, and the underlying cells of the respiratory system structures are vulnerable to disease.

Among other extremely hazardous pollutants carried in the air which may impede homeostasis are asbestos, beryllium and mercury. Asbestos has been widely used for many industrial purposes, including brake linings in cars. The inhalation of asbestos fibers has been linked to malignant diseases of the lungs, such as bronchogenic cancer and mesothelioma.

The metal beryllium is used in rocket fuels, missile guidance systems, nuclear reactors and atomic weapons. Inhaled beryllium leads to progressive lung disease and death.

Mercury, commonly used in the manufacturing of paint, pulp and paper, batteries and mildew-proofing, may also pollute the air. Air-borne mercury can affect the central nervous system and cause weight loss, insomnia, tremors and psychological disturbances.

As was widely publicized upon the installation of catalytic converters in U.S. automobiles, high concentrations of lead in the air are associated with emissions from motors burning leaded gasoline. Excessive lead inges-tion can seriously impair the nervous system. Lead poisoning in ghetto chil-dren who eat paint and plaster which contains lead is evidence of this problem.

WATER AND HEALTH

In the chapter on water (Chapter 10), we noted that despite the abun-dance of water, we often face shortages, especially of water of a desirable quality. No substance is more essential to the human body. The human body contains up to 90 percent water, depending upon age, with the body gener-ally dehydrating as it ages. If we lose more than 20 percent of the water of our bodies, we will die. Even a healthy person can live only a few days without water.

But, it is more than just the quantity of water that is vital to our bodies. It is its quality! Ordinarily, water has many dissolved salts, sugars and other substances. These substances in the water are what make it so valuable in the human body. Water transports enzymes into the digestive tract and provides the lubrication for circulation, digestion and excretion. Food must be dissolved before it can enter the bloodstream of animals. Even carbon dioxide and oxygen must be dissolved in the liquid portion of the blood before it can be used by the body.

Water should be free of harmful bacteria and excesses of various substances for healthy use. It is impossible for the human body to maintain homeostasis while utilizing polluted water. Illnesses such as typhoid, cholera, dysentery, gastroenteritis and infectious hepatitis can result from the action of microorganisms present in the water. The bacterial contamination of water supplies is a common disease hazard in the United States today (see Chapter 10).

Some cardiovascular conditions are related to the consumption of contaminated waters. Increased sodium intake from polluted waters puts a strain on the heart and circulatory system. Nitrates, which may enter the human system through contamination by sewage and wastes from domestic animals and by run-off from agriculture, are especially harmful to newborn babies. The digestive tract of infants contains bacteria which convert otherwise harmless nitrates into toxic substances. The result is a blood disease, *methemeoglobinemia*, that can lead to death due to suffocation.

ENERGY FROM THE SUN AND
THE HUMAN BODY

In Chapter 2, we noted that without plant life, our bodies could not obtain the sun's energy. Energy is transmitted to humans from the sun indirectly through plants by the process of photosynthesis. The carbohydrates (carbon, hydrogen and oxygen) thus synthesized are essential to our metabolic processes. Some are quick energy sources for the body. Others are stored and broken down for later use.

The simple sugars (monosaccharides) may reach our system through candies or baked goods, or fruits and vegetables. Two sugar units per molecule (disaccharides) may be derived from sugar cane or sugar beets (sucrose), corn, potatoes, wheat and rice (maltose) and milk (lactose).

Another important product of photosynthesis is cellulose, which forms the basic structure for wood and cotton, so useful to shelter and clothes for our bodies.

Another family of natural resources essential to life are proteins and amino acids, consisting primarily of carbon, oxygen, hydrogen and nitrogen. Amino acids are fundamental units of proteins. Some, but not all, amino acids can be synthesized by our bodies. Others, however, must be derived from the food supply. In volume, meat and eggs are principal protein foods in the United States, but grain and dairy products are also major contributors.

We are also turning more directly to vegetable products for our supply of fats. Fats are vital to humans. But, an excess of the wrong type may be linked to cardiovascular disease. Traditionally, we obtained fats from butter and other animal products which are saturated (filled with hydrogen atoms on both sides of carbon atoms). Saturated fats may accumulate readily in our bodies, thus increasing cholesterol, a soapy-like substance which is a part of tissue. In recent decades many consumers have switched to vegetable oils which are unsaturated (have some free carbon atoms not linked with hydrogen atoms) and, therefore, accumulate less fatty tissue in the human body than animal products. Such oils include coconut, cottonseed, peanut, soya bean and sunflower seed.

Finally, the health of our bodies is dependent upon a proper balance of enzymes, vitamins and hormones. These resources comprise less than 1 percent of the weight of the body. But, they are extremely critical to our health.

Enzymes are proteins produced by living organisms which function as biochemical catalysts. Essential to certain body processes, enzymes enable the body processes to perform with less energy. Hormones are substances formed by one organ and conveyed to another, which is then stimulated to function by their chemical activity. Vitamins are complex carbon, hydrogen, oxygen compounds which are essential in small amounts for the control of metabolic processes.

In sum, our bodies are critically dependent upon the natural resource base for food, shelter and clothing and the complex chemical compounds which determine health.

PESTICIDES, METALS AND HEALTH

Manufactures from natural resources may be either a boon or a bane to humans. Insecticides have benefited human health by controlling insects and increasing food production (see Chapter 18). Malaria, which is transmitted by the *Anopheles* mosquito, and typhus, carried by the human body louse, have been virtually eliminated from the United States with the help of insecticides.

Insecticides have been a hazard to human health by interfering with the functioning of the central nervous system; damaging the respiratory and digestive tracts, skin and eyes; and adversely affecting mucous membranes, the rate of metabolism and the condition of visceral organs.

Among chemical compounds that have been in global food chains are high concentrations of a group of industrial herbicides, known as the polychlorinated biophenyl, or PCB's. PCB's are insoluble in water, soluble in fats and oils and very resistant to either chemical or biological degradation. In short, they tend to persist. In 1979, officials were stil discovering new victims of a 1973 incident in which PCB was accidentally mixed with animal feed. Thousands of domestic animals and possibly millions of humans were affected.[4]

Our knowledge of the effect of pesticides (both insecticides and pesticides) on humans is seriously deficient. But, we know the toll is great.

---

[4]Lawrence H. Hall, "A Plague of Poisons," *National Wildlife*, August–September, 1979, pp. 29–32.

Dr. Malcolm Hargraves, senior consultant at the Mayo Clinic, believes that more fatalities are caused by pesticides than by automobile accidents.[5]

Only small quantities of some substances can cause serious damage to the body. Asbestos fibers, for example, are suspected of causing cancer. And even low levels of cadmium, a widely used heavy metal, can be a threat to health.

The toxicity of some chemical wastes was dramatically revealed when chemicals from an old canal channel, called Love Canal, erupted to the surface of the ground in a residential area in New York State, as noted in Chapter 23. Unfortunately, the proliferation of such wastes throughout industrial regions of the United States is alarming.

DRUGS AND TOBACCO AND CONSERVATION

The abuse of drugs, in many forms, in the United States has become so serious in recent years that it is a major threat to the goal of conservation—a quality life for all humankind. To cite one example, the number of cocaine-related emergency room admissions in the United States in 1985 was almost 10,000, according to the National Institute on Drug Abuse. The death toll from this drug has risen sharply—it was over 600 persons in 1985. As newspaper headlines have proclaimed, cocaine, heroin and some synthetic drugs can injure the heart and lungs or cause brain damage and paralysis. This can lead to death.

More insidious than hard drugs is the effect of alcohol. Moderate drinking is condoned by some doctors, and for some persons and for some medical conditions, it is beneficial. The jovial drunk has been a source of humor from William Shakespeare to Noel Coward. So, many of us fail to take the drinking problem seriously. However, too much alcohol dulls the nerves and stultifies the brain. As many as half of all fatal automobile accidents are alcohol related. Productivity losses because workers drink are heavy. Over time, the liver and/or other vital organs can be adversely affected by excessive alcohol consumption.

Cigarette smoking is another example of an outside substance, in this case nicotine, that may for a long period of time appear to yield only

---

[5] Oliver S. Owen, *Natural Resource Conservation, An Ecological Approach*, 4th ed., New York: Macmillan Publishing Company, 1985, p. 427.

pleasure. But, the damage to the heart and lungs is taking its toll. By the time alarming symptoms become evident, the addicted smoker has great difficulty in stopping.

If we were conservationists, we would (1) take care of our bodies and not abuse them and (2) support private and public organizations which promote health and fight drug abuse, a problem which is international and needs to be met by worldwide as well as nationwide, state and local action.

NOISE AND HUMANS

At a certain point, even noises can become hazardous to human health and hearing. For urban dwellers, sounds from automobiles, jets, construction activities, power mowers, motorcycles, office machines, televisions and stereos may combine to create a harmful level of noise. The Environmental Protection Agency has summarized some of the physical effects of exposure to high levels of sound in the following symptoms:[6]

1. Blood vessels in the brain dilate.
2. Blood pressure rises.
3. Blood vessels in other parts of the body constrict.
4. Pupils of the eyes dilate.
5. Blood cholesterol levels rise.
6. Various endocrine glands pour additional hormones into the bloodstream.

It is difficult to link noise directly with a specific disease or mental disorder, but there appears to be little doubt that it is a contributing factor to such disorders.

RADIATION AND THE BODY

Today, the advent of nuclear power as an energy source has brought a new threat of radiation exposure to humans (see Chapter 7). As has been noted, improper radioactive waste disposal and the vulnerability of nuclear

---

[6]U.S. Environmental Protection Agency, *Report to the President and Congress on Noise,* Washington, D.C., 1971.

power plants to sabotage by terrorist groups are some of the potential threats to human health from radiation. Of course, there is always the potential holocaust of nuclear war!

Assessing the risk of exposure to radioactivity involves extremely complex relationships. A number of theories and measurements have been explored. But, the various assumptions and conclusions are still controversial. That is to say, while there is no question as to the carcinogenic property of radiation, there are questions as to the ways to assess its potential threat.

Radiation may be transported by many means. Radon, the product of the decay in uranium tailings, may end up in the lungs. Water may also be an important pathway for radionuclides which move into ground or surface waters. Humans may be exposed to them directly by eating fish, or they may be exposed indirectly by drinking affected water or by bathing in it. A third transport medium for radionuclides is plants which humans may eat either directly or indirectly by their eating the meat of animals that have consumed such plants.

As to health effects, most theories attribute damage to breakage or mutalism of the DNA within the cell nucleus. If sufficient energy is deposited in an organ, excessive cell death may occur. Even low levels of radiation may lead to leukemia, cancer or shortened life span.[7]

HUMAN REPRODUCTION AND CONSERVATION

Human life is very precious. It is not uncommon in some societies to measure wealth in terms of how many children a person has. Furthermore, some nations count their strength in terms of numbers of people. Certainly, the birth of a baby—the wonder and excitement of new life—should be a reason for great joy. Too often, however, the joy is mixed with apprehension. How will we be able to feed and care for this child? Will the child enjoy good health? Will he/she have a happy life? Fear of the worst can lead to the worst—infanticide.

Does conservation mean population control? "Yes" is the easy answer.

---

[7] Douglas J. Crawford and Richard W. Leggett, "Assessing the Risk of Exposure to Radioactivity," *American Scientist*, September–October 1980, pp. 524–536.

"How" is the difficult one. Population control is carried out by two general means: (1) social controls and (2) individual family planning.

Social Controls of Population

The government has two major options in population control policy: (1) an intervening, activist policy in which the government dictates what shall be done and (2) a guiding, assisting incentive and penalty policy in which the individual has choices. Clearly, in the United States, the second option is the one consistent with our dedication to individual freedoms.

An activist policy for population control may advocate actions such as government euthenics and enforced abortion programs. Such abhorrent programs have actually existed. We must be on guard that they never happen here.

A guiding, assisting policy of incentives and penalties might advocate actions such as:

1. Lowering taxes for single people.
2. Taxing large numbers of children in a family, or at least not giving tax deductions for them.
3. Providing recognition of two-child families.
4. Encouraging marriages at a later age.
5. Supporting birth control education and other family planning information.

Individual Family Planning

In the United States, founded on the principles of individual liberty, the final decision on birth control should be left up to the individual. It is the government's duty, however, in accordance with its responsibility to provide for the health, education and welfare of its citizens, to encourage and facilitate family planning consistent with conservation goals. Such planning is not necessarily negative. The nation might desire an increase rather than a decrease in the birth rate. The goal should be to maintain a rate of population growth sustainable under anticipated resource development and resource base capacity.

Ecology teaches us that life moves in a cycle and is subject to complex interrelationships. Humans have been granted intelligence to adjust to these relationships. If religion does not, commonsense should warn us that wanton misuse of our ability to procreate only results in eventual human misery. Rightly used, this wonderful gift enriches our resource base.

THE BODY, OTHER RESOURCES AND THE FUTURE

Will humankind sink or swim? Will we be able to overcome the resistances to more abundant resources, including a healthier body, or will we be overcome by them? The world's futurists, those scholars and others who make it their business to predict the future, appear moderately optimistic. After reviewing many of the reports of scholarly, government and business organizations, including the 50,000-member World Future Society, *U.S. News & World Report* concluded: "Despite the downbeat nature of many current forecasts, many scholars come to a loose consensus that humanity's historic ability to cope with perils will emerge and the world will somehow survive.[8]

As for the human body specifically, it should be recalled that life spans have been extended dramatically within recent years, from an average of 40 years to an average of 74 years-plus within the experience of most older people alive at present.

Prognosticators, reviewed by *U.S. News & World Report* in the preceding article, believe that many of the most dramatic breakthroughs in technology in the future will be in medicine. Already on the drawing boards or in the testing stage are a diet supplement that can improve memory, a totally safe and nonfattening artificial sweetener and a drug that retards the aging process.

Some researchers believe, according to the report, that severed limbs may, within a few decades, be regenerated by using electrical impulses to spur the growth of new tissue. And, more and more defective body parts will be replaced by artificial implants.

The fervor to increase life expectancy is especially intense in life-affirming California. Longevity organizations abound. One approach to rejuvenation research is to modify the DNA biomechanism that causes aging. Other approaches include age-reducing therapies and modified diets.

---

[8]"What Next 20 Years Hold for You," *U.S. News & World Report*, December 1, 1980, pp. 51–53.

Would increased life spans mean a new population explosion? Physiology Professor Roy Walford, who wrote *Maximum Life Span, The 120-Year Diet*, points out that if every couple, starting 8,000 years ago, had produced only two children, the world population would be less than ½ billion today, rather than its present 5 billion. Our solution to overpopulation should be birth control, not life control, he contends.

Would a longer life span just prolong the miseries of old age? Not if biologists are successful. Their aim is to increase the span of the healthier middle years. Nor need we worry about living forever. Assuming the present rate of accidental fatalities continues, even if we abolish death by aging, our average life span would be 200 years—our maximum, 600, according to Walford.[9]

David Lilienthal, former chairman of the TVA, first chairman of the Atomic Energy Commission and a successful businessman, who died in January, 1981, at the age of 81, was passionate about the future of the United States, as the *St. Louis Post-Dispatch* reports:

> "If we make up our mind, if we get the lead out, we'll find this is the greatest underdeveloped country in the world, and that it doesn't have to be timid and fearful of growth," he told the *Post*.
>
> "Human energy, 'drive, brainpower, creativity, imagination,' puts other energy to work for human use," he said. "Utilize this energy and you solve the problems of producing power for factories and homes, as well as the other essentials of life, including the development of a rich culture and sound government."[10]

We sympathize with Mr. Lilienthal's sentiments. But, there is a catch. It is true that if we develop our highest human energy potential, we will realize the highest potential for our other resources. But, the catch is that unless we develop our other resources wisely, we cannot reach our highest human energy potential.

QUESTIONS AND PROBLEMS

1. Identify some major natural resources which aid the respiratory system. Explain how each of these resources actually affects the system.

---

[9] Jerry Lazar, "Do You Dare to Live Forever?," *California Magazine*, July 1987, p. 49 ff.

[10] "To Lilienthal, Human Energy was Nation's Greatest Asset," *St. Louis Post-Dispatch*, January 18, 1981, Sec. 8-F, p. 1.

2. Define *homeostasis* in your own words, after consulting several sources to help you better understand the process. Why must homeostasis be maintained by the body?

3. Name the six principal components of air pollution. Which appears to be the least serious to the human body in direct effects? Can any component be the most serious? Explain.

4. Cigarette smoking is said to be a contributing factor to emphysema. Describe how it may affect the alveoli of the lungs.

5. What is particulate matter? Describe how it may affect the lungs.

6. Name a substance which affects the nervous system. Bring a report to class relating at least one instance of mercury poisoning in humans. (Check the *Reader's Guide to Periodical Literature* for titles of articles.)

7. Why is water so important to the body?

8. How does polluted water threaten our health?

9. Insecticides can be beneficial or harmful. Give two examples, one illustrating, on the one hand, how an insecticide has benefited humans and, on the other, how it has harmed them.

10. Give an example of a chemical which persists in the human system.

11. Is it possible that noise alone can be harmful? Explain your answer.

12. Why is excessive radiation a threat to the body?

13. What facts lead us to be encouraged about the future prospects for human life, despite the problems of pollution?

14. What must we do if we are to develop our highest human energy potential?

26

Careers in the Environmental Sciences and Conservation

ENVIRONMENTAL/CONSERVATION CAREERS

The purpose of this chapter is to provide you with a general overview of careers in the environment and conservation fields, referred to hereafter as environmental/conservation careers. These careers include the whole range of enterprises, from the physical sciences to environmental services, which are devoted to actions that help protect the ecosystem and help develop resources in accordance with conservation principles. As this text has emphasized, the earth is one great interlinked system. Persons whose jobs are very remote from the physical handling of earth materials may have careers directly related to the environment. Thus, the financiers or politicians who release or withhold funds or help defeat or pass certain legislation may be the ones who really decide whether forests are cut or saved, streams dammed or left wild and land kept in farms or developed for factories.

THE MARKET FOR
ENVIRONMENTAL/CONSERVATION JOBS

The outlook for environmental/conservation jobs is good. *Fortune* magazine called the 1990's "the decade of the of the environment." Industry, it expects, will create many jobs related to environmental protection in order to comply with stricter environmental legislation and liability provisions. Even now, the environmental service industry is estimated to be over $100 billion annually and growing by 10 percent per year. Some areas of greatest demand in recent years have been environmental engineering, solid waste management and public health and safety. Hazardous waste sites identified for the Department of Energy will take 30 years to clean up, according to official estimates. And, enforcement of the Clean Air Act will provide many new jobs.

The outlook for employment is not as bright for nonprofit environmental groups. Contributions had levelled off at the time of this writing. And, even though such groups were offered relatively low salaries, they were swamped with applications for the jobs.

Underlying the strength of the environmental market is the support of the general public shown by public opinion polls and voting records.

PICKING AN
ENVIRONMENTAL/CONSERVATION CAREER

The balance of this chapter is designed to help you in the choice of a career from the broad environmental/conservation field. First, you might want to prepare yourself by taking an aptitude test which your school should be able to furnish you. Then, before looking at careers specifically, you might want to consider whether you favor inside or outside work or private or public employment.

Indoor or outdoor. — Do you want to spend most of your working hours indoors or outdoors? Some of you may have clear preferences. The preference of our friend Floyd comes to mind. He loved to farm and farmed to live. Planning for his retirement, he built a fine brick house in town, but he never really used it. At 80 years of age, he still spent most of his time in his house on the farm and, when he felt like it, worked in the fields. By contrast, our friend Earl liked living in a suburb near the school where he taught. Earl was not interested in being in the country. In fact, he did not even like yard work. When he retired, he stayed right where he was except for travel. Neither person would have been happy in the other's career. That is the inside-outside of it. Of course, in a career you may pick, such as that of a forester, you may enjoy starting out as a ranger who rides a horse into the woods, but when your bones begin to creak, be satisfied to become a supervisor who straddles a chair in the office.

Government or private business. — Another basic choice is whether you want to work in government or private business. Perhaps you like both and it is just a matter of which presents the best job opening at the time. Author Kircher's career is an example. He started in private business, a farm cooperative, as an office manager and associate editor. After war had disrupted his career there, he accepted employment as a senior bank clerk with an agency of the federal government, the Federal Reserve Bank, eventually transferring to research and an editing job. Then, after completing a graduate degree, he became a teacher of conservation, planning and geography at a state university, managing a farm on the side and writing professionally. The thread that held his career together was writing. In your case, it might be an accounting or engineering capability that would carry you through several careers.

People oriented, machine or nature oriented? — Do you really prefer to work with people or do you prefer tinkering with machines or building things? Or, do you choose to be with plants or animals? In the first instance, you would enjoy careers in politics, sales or teaching. In the second case, you would enjoy most being an engineer or a manufacturer. In the third, you might choose to be a research biologist or farmer. You may move from one emphasis to another. Associate author Gore started out after graduation with a state geological survey and completed her career teaching earth sciences and conservation.

Should the job market determine your choice of a career? — The job market may well determine the job you take. And, if you take a job just to be employed and like it, you may make a career of it. Many have. But even though circumstances may force you to take the first job that comes along, that job need not necessarily determine your life career. If you want a job that is more environmentally/conservation oriented, keep looking. And keep training. Go to night school. Participate in conservation organizations, and read the literature. Improve your knowledge of environmental problems. Develop your skills in the job you have, and make a good record so that you will have good references when you have the opportunity to move into an environmental job. Then, do it.

Selected Careers

Introduction

Environmental/conservation careers are divided into three major sectors in the discussion which follows. In each of these groups, various careers are evaluated: (Group I) careers that deal directly with the environment, (Group II) careers in industries that change nature into manufactured products and (Group III) careers in the environmental service industries.

Because of the interrelationships, some careers may involve work in more than one sector. Thus, a soil scientist (Group I) may also be a teacher (Group II). Or, a top executive in a large, integrated corporation may be in coordinating mining (Group I), manufacturing (Group II) and sales (Group III).

Since the scope of environmental/conservation careers is so great and a complete description of a job might involve endless detail, the authors have taken some liberty in the combination of jobs they have used and in generalizing and being selective in the presentation of job characteristics. And, not all jobs are covered; however, after studying these descriptions and using them for background and as examples of methodology, you can, with the help of a good library and a few interviews, adequately appraise any job not included here. In fact, even for those careers included in this chapter, you may conduct further research in the careers that interest you most.

Earning estimates are very general. If you want dollar figures, you should consult publications such as those of the Bureau of Labor Statistics and Civil Service Commission or business magazines. Neither jobs in the trades such as carpentering and plumbing nor various jobs done by un-skilled workers are covered, although they certainly have a major impact on the environment.

DESCRIPTION OF ENVIRONMENTAL/CONSERVATION CAREERS

Careers Dealing Directly with the Environment

Conservationist

Requirements. — To qualify for a government position with a conservationist rating, one needs a bachelor's degree with emphasis in subjects such as botany, biology, field crops, forestry and agricultural economics.

Characteristics. — After graduation, as a conservationist, you usually are required to spend at least one year in a training program. Much of your work is likely to be outdoors identifying land-use problems and proposing solutions. You must consider benefits both to the landowner and to society. To solve some problems assigned you, you will need the cooperation of other specialists such as agronomists, foresters and wildlife biologists.

Advantages and disadvantages. — A conservationist is in the open air much of the time working directly with environmental problems. These may be local in nature but their solution will benefit the community. You work directly with landowners and can see the results of your efforts. Your initiatives are recognized by co-workers and management.

Disadvantages are that it can be a tough job requiring ingenuity, persistence and a positive attitude. You are often working one-on-one. You are expected to attend meetings and training sessions and to keep up-to-date with practices and research, doing much of this on your own time.

Earnings. — Salaries are generally compatible to those of others in similar fields of work. They are commensurate with experience, but experience comes slowly and so may raises. The job generally requires transfer from one geographic area to another.

Farmer/Rancher

Requirements. — To become an owner/operator of a farm or ranch, you need to be able to make a large investment in land, equipment and, unless the operation is limited to crops, livestock. Today, many such operations are big business. Adequate capital may be difficult to acquire unless it is inherited. If you are a tenant operator on a highly productive farm, however, you may be able to save enough money to eventually buy land of your own. If you do this with heavy borrowing, it could be disastrous.

To be successful at farming or ranching requires experience and training. This generally begins with childhood on the farm or ranch. Further agricultural education continues at high school in rural areas. You may want to get more education. You can obtain more education at land grant universities with offerings of instruction in such disciplines as agronomy, animal husbandry and field crops. Valuable instruction can be obtained also from junior colleges and from workshops and seminars offered by government agencies and some corporations.

Characteristics. — This career requires both labor and management skills. As a farmer/rancher, you often work alone and must be able to make decisions. You will operate and make minor repairs on machinery, decide which crop varieties to plant and what kind of tillage and fertilizer to use. If you raise livestock, you need to understand feeding, disease prevention and shelter needs of the animals. To be successful as a farmer/rancher, you need to understand financing and marketing. Modern farmers increasingly are using computers to help decide the effectiveness of pesticides, fertilizers, and irrigation applications and to keep records. Above all, you must have initiative to get the job done and to know where to get information and help when needed.

Advantages and disadvantages. — As an owner/operator of a farm or ranch, you are your own boss. Your rewards are generally related to your initiative, persistence, skills and hard work, but you cannot control nature. You need to farm the land within the limits of its soil capability and to pray for favorable weather, controllable animal and plant diseases and minor insect infestation. You need to follow conservation practices that work with nature, not against it.

Other disadvantages are that you have no control over the market unless you retail your crops and livestock. Loans may be too costly or not available to you.

Earnings. — Profits from farming and ranching are extremely variable from year to year. They are subject to weather conditions, land and animal diseases and insects, finance costs and prices of fuel and other production inputs over which the owner/operator has little, if any, control. On the positive side, many farmers and ranchers earn a good income and own property which has been in their families for generations. And many feel that this occupation is richly rewarding as a way of life.

Forester

Requirements. — To become a professional forester, you will need a bachelor's degree in forestry. Major courses likely would include forest insects and diseases, plant pathology, forest soils and woodland management. Others might be courses such as water management, computer science and surveying. Junior colleges sometimes offer courses leading to an associate degree in forestry.

Characteristics. — Most of the work would be outdoors in all kinds of weather and you might often be alone. Tasks include marking trees for marketing or stand improvement, identifying insect damage and plant diseases and recommending control practices. You would help plan for and participate in the prevention and control of forest fires. You would recommend varieties of trees for ornamental or commercial plantings. And, the preparation and/or delivery of speeches and/or writing of articles about forest needs and practices may be assigned to you.

Advantages and disadvantages. — Foresters work outside, generally in rural areas. You may work alone much of the time so you can have real pride in your initiative and accomplishments.

Of course, the kind of isolation you may experience is boring to some. And, if you have a fear of poisonous plants and snakes and do not like wild animals, this is no career for you. Furthermore, as a beginner assigned to outdoor work, you should enjoy roughing it.

Earnings. — Beginning salaries have been comparatively low compared to those in other scientific fields with comparable training. And, many applicants have applied for more jobs than were available. Those who love the outdoors find the job rewarding and with initiative and hard work can get promotions with salary increases.

Mining

Geologists, mining engineers and others who make a career in mining, including the petroleum industry, are discussed under headings "Other Careers in the Natural Sciences," "Engineering" and "Manufacturing and Other Environmental Businesses."

Advantages and disadvantages. — Few industries can be more exciting at one point or more disappointing at another than the petroleum and mining industries, especially in exploration and discovery operations. If you have ever stood on a drilling rig in Texas, felt the vibrations of its operation with the expectation that oil or gas might be found at any minute or, conversely, experienced the sudden silence when the drills stop because it is a dry hole, you know what is meant by excitement and disappointment.

In this field, you have the opportunity, when you are conservation oriented, to help obtain maximum economic production with minimal environmental costs.

Earnings. — Mining is one of our basic industries; therefore, while the market may be either boom or bust, some employment always continues. You have to decide whether you like the industry well enough to share in the risks. Good jobs and big profits still can be realized.

Soil Scientist / Researcher

Requirements. — You will need at least 15 semester hours of soil courses and/or related subjects, such as organic chemistry, physical chemistry and clay mineralogy, leading to a bachelor's degree. Generally, to qualify for research in both private and government enterprises, you will need advanced courses leading to a Ph.D.

Characteristics. — The work may either be in the confines of a laboratory, with limited contact with field employees, or be divided between time indoors and outdoors. Usually you will be involved in problem solving, using or creating techniques for investigation. The findings of research soil scientists are used directly and indirectly by those in other related fields. Ability to communicate well with others is, therefore, essential.

Advantages and disadvantages. — In this job you generally have a fixed work schedule which is not affected by the weather. You work with others. You have the excitement of doing original research. On the negative side, the work may seem too confining. Problems you are asked to solve are not always clearly defined, and insufficient time may be allocated to fully carry out the desired research. Sometimes budgets are insufficient to supply adequate laboratory equipment or facilities.

Earnings. — Salaries are generally in the middle-income range. Some researchers, however, may receive sufficient exposure and success to achieve a high income. As a consultant, you may also earn extra income.

Soil Scientist / Soil Classifier

Requirements. — See "Soil Scientist/Researcher."

Characteristics. — Even as a college graduate, you usually are required to spend at least one year in a training program before you are qualified for this job rating. The work generally is done on the land, examining and identifying the properties of soil types and their locations in accordance with standards set by the Soil Conservation Service. Also, you may be asked to determine the soil percolation properties for on-site sewage systems and to identify the basic engineering properties of soil. These observations generally are recorded in notebooks and their locations plotted on aerial photographs for use by others.

Advantages and disadvantages. — The job requires the ability to work outside in adverse weather conditions and where pollen can irritate you. It requires strength to extract the soil auger in places where power equipment cannot be used. In urban areas, residents often resent your presence on their land and it takes diplomacy to allay their suspicions. On the positive side, miles of walking in the fresh air is good for your health. And, you are your own boss once you get out of the office.

Earnings. — The salary is somewhat low in the beginning, but with training and experience it increases. Within five years, you can expect it to be comparable with those of others in research.

Wildlife Management and Research

Requirements. — While an appropriate college or university degree is required for professional status by most agencies today, you may be hired as a trainee in game management programs (especially in the summer) before completing your education. These jobs provide excellent experience, give insight into the nature of the work and may lead to eventual permanent employment. Today, requirements have been upgraded. Instead of a "warden" largely responsible for law enforcement, you might be called a conservation agent or wildlife biologist and spend much of your time in educational activities and research. Some training in biological science is essential.

Characteristics. — You might compare this career to that of a forester. Both would likely start in the outdoors, with desk jobs available as you move up the ladder. In this occupation, you likely would be involved in estimating wildlife populations (especially game animals), studying habitats and making recommendations for conservation requirements in order to establish hunting seasons and bag or head limits. And, you might be called upon to help enforce hunting and fishing laws.

As a wildlife biologist, you would do laboratory research. Or, you may "sting" ponds, make fish counts in streams and make recommendations for management. You probably would be asked to cooperate in educational programs such as a series of lectures at schools and speeches to hunting and fishing clubs and other organizations. While some private jobs are available, the chances are that your career would be with the state or federal government.

Advantages and disadvantages. — Obviously, this is a career with great appeal to those who love wildlife and take pleasure in directly contributing to its conservation. A disadvantage of government employment can be frustrating because of the red tape involved and because of the possibility that you might have to work under incompetent or ill-informed political appointees. And, you may not be able to find a job in the geographic area or the type of activity you prefer. But, this is often the case with other jobs as well.

Earnings. — Pay was formerly relatively low for wildlife management jobs, which largely were political. Now that qualifying tests and/or college degrees are required, the pay scale has increased to respectability. Those hired under civil service provisions may expect to receive tenure and a schedule for advancement and increases in pay.

Wildlife professionals are generally dedicated to this work and do not measure its value in dollars and cents.

Other Careers in the Natural Sciences

Natural sciences is a broad category which includes as a group some of the other major natural science specialties and some of their common characteristics. Those specializing in this field who are included here are: biochemists, biologists, geologists, hydrologists, materials scientists, physicists and public health physicians.

Requirements. — Practicing natural scientists have studied a minimum of four years in college, and a large percentage have one to three years of university graduate study. Do not let this extensive educational requirement scare you because of costs. Teaching of the natural sciences requires much assistance in preparation for class demonstrations, laboratory exercises and research; therefore, universities provide many graduate assistantships in this field. If you can obtain one, it probably will provide your tuition and some monthly pay. Also, assistantships provide excellent training and often lead directly into a job upon graduation.

Job characteristics. — Natural scientists are attracted to this field because they are curious about how nature works and want to develop or master various techniques of finding out. Careful observation and analytical skills are necessary. If you plan to enter this field, you should be fascinated with observing patterns and relationships in the biosphere and with developing and testing hypotheses about them.

Some branches of geology, hydrology, soil science (see separate discussions of these specializations) and biology require work outdoors involving mapping, sampling and testing. Most sciences require laboratory work. More and more scientific work in the environment requires teamwork with scientists from different disciplines and with non-scientists. An example is the preparation of environmental impact statements. If you are a chemist or an ecologist, you probably will develop and test new and perhaps better materials. You will try to find chemicals which are safe for people, domestic animals, plants and wildlife. And, as an environmental/ conservation careerist, you will be looking for materials that have a minimal environmental impact in their manufacture and use and can be recycled or made of recycled materials. As a chemist or materials scientist you would be developing non-toxic products and ways to safely destroy toxic wastes. Along with physicists, you might try to develop new and practical ways to use inexhaustible energy sources, using energy-efficient machines and energy-conserving chemicals and materials.

As a biologist, ecologist, geologist, biochemist or hydrologist, you might be required to locate and measure our water supplies and to keep them clean.

As a geologist or hydrologist, you would locate, measure and produce mineral and water resources. And, in accordance with law and management decisions, you would monitor sites to see that this is done with minimal environmental damage and safe disposal of wastes.

As a medical scientist, you would protect public health by identifying and isolating germs. You would also study diseases which may attack domestic and wild plants and animals. And, you would develop new genetic materials to protect and improve crops and livestock. Biologists also engage in this kind of research.

Advantages and disadvantages. — Major advantages to you of a career in the natural sciences is the excitement of discovery and/or development of materials which help all of us and the environment and the satisfaction of devoting your life to proving hypotheses and imparting knowledge rather than acquiring wealth or power.

A major disadvantage of a natural science career is that if teaching, you may have little time after your teaching duties for research. Also, research can be frustrating. Experiments fail, observations become tedious or do not correlate, and your work may never be recognized or appreciated.

Earnings. — Potential earnings are very good for a natural scientist, but it may take many years to advance to a high wage. As noted above, graduate assistantships provide help to get you started, but you may have to eat popcorn for lunch! Some scientists increase their incomes by receiving consulting fees, or as a result of successful research which has commercial application, they may even become wealthy.

CAREERS IN ENGINEERING AND OTHER NATURE-TRANSFORMING INDUSTRIES

Engineering

Introduction. — There are many different kinds of engineering careers, but they have many common characteristics, so we are going to discuss engineering as a career in general.

Each specialty, of course, has some unique requirements. These descriptions should help you decide if you like the field and which careers you want to investigate further.

Requirements. — Professional engineering requires a four-year higher education degree and the passing of a state examination for a license. Master's degrees are the most common final university level of formal education. Your success in getting a job and advancing will also heavily depend on experience.

If you do not like or appear unable to master mathematics, choose another career. Computer skills are also necessary in today's market. Engineers say that they are assigned or accept objectives and are expected to use proven ways or devise new means to achieve them. But, this is true of most endeavors. It is called "problem solving."

Characteristics. — Almost all lines of engineering offer a great opportunity for an environmental/conservation career. Engineers plan, design and build roads, dams, mines, oil production and transportation facilities, and commercial and residential buildings, including all the mechanical elements. As an environmental/conservation engineer, you would design these works so that they minimize environmental impacts and maximize resource values.

Some engineers build and operate electrical generation facilities and are responsible for waste heat and product disposal, which should be done in a sound manner, and chemical engineers provide for the production, storage and handling of materials. They need to safeguard the public from those that are toxic or harmful. Mechanical and industrial engineers can make especially significant contributions to conservation by designing energy-efficient and cost-efficient engines and appliances.

As an engineer, you might spend much of your time in an office or a drafting room; however, certain projects require outdoor work. Likely, there will be a mix as you get different assignments or move on to more responsibility.

Advantages and disadvantages. — Once you have served your apprenticeship, you will have the satisfaction of being creative and of seeing your ideas become reality. At the top level, you can be relatively independent. And, you are in a very respected profession.

But, all is not gold. You may spend many years doing routine, lackluster assignments before you achieve enough stature to be inventive. But, you may be able to set up your own company and become very successful. This is called "realizing the American dream." It does happen. Your enterprise would require access to capital funds. If these are not available, you might start a consulting engineering firm, which would need relatively little capital. Consultants are often needed for environmental conservation projects.

Regardless of how successful, you will find that an engineering enterprise can be very frustrating because of difficulties in obtaining raw materials, getting delivery on time, labor strife, keen competition and government regulations.

Earnings. — Depending upon the business climate, engineers generally have relatively high earnings. Employment with large firms is considered reliable with paid benefits and retirement programs. But, massive layoffs are also possible. Top salaries for large firms are staggering.

Earnings in successful small firms are also relatively good, but employment, unless you are the owner, may be unreliable. Such firms may live from contract to contract.

Engineering jobs offered by local, state and federal agencies are apt to be under civil service, offering more job security than small private businesses, but less pay.

Manufacturing and Other Environmental Businesses

Requirements. — A good high school education is adequate for a career in a small business, including manufacturing, but large businesses often start their screen of job applicants at the college level. One very prosperous small businessman of author Kircher's acquaintance left school in the fourth grade. This does not mean, of course, that he stopped learning then. To be a successful businessperson, you need to develop your skills of being a good judge of people and knowing how to deal with them. And you need to develop a sense of values. One way to develop this is by working at odd jobs during your youth. New and innovative ideas and willingness to take a risk are ingredients of success that you especially need in environmental/conservation type businesses. You also need management and accounting skills. Many schools from small business colleges to universities offer business training.

Characteristics. — In business, you may find yourself in a "dog-eat-dog" highly competitive situation or one so boring that you fall asleep at your desk. In the first case, you may develop stomach ulcers; in the second, a bad case of being overweight. In between are jobs which offer opportunity, yet are steady.

Business owners and managers have many opportunities to make handsome profits by manufacturing and/or marketing "earth safe" products. These range from renewable energy devices to non-toxic and recycled materials of all kinds. As noted under engineering, you may set up a consulting service. Your specialty might be environmental management.

Advantages and disadvantages. — A great advantage of running a small business is being your own boss. And, you will reap the profits! Careers in large businesses, including manufacturing firms, may provide more job security and less job trauma, but not necessarily. On the other hand, many small businesses fail their first year. Inadequate financing and marketing can doom a venture to failure regardless of the quality and environmental worth of the product.

Earnings. — Successful businesses in the environmental/ conservation field can be very profitable. Good discussions and analyses of businesses, large and small, are carried in such business magazines as *Forbes*, the *Wall Street Journal* and in numerous trade journals. Women who were formerly badly discriminated against are earning pay equal to that of men, holding more and more top management positions, and now many women own their own businesses.

Waste Water and Drinking Water Treatment Plant Operator

Requirements. — Entry requirements are attendance at a technical training center for water treatment operators or a college/university degree in sanitary or civil engineering and certification. In past years, many water treatment plant operators were political appointees with high school educations so training centers were set up to help these people update their knowledge and pass certification exams, now required by most states. To be certified, a combination of education and experience is required plus passing the examination.

Characteristics. — As a water treatment plant operator, you are responsible for the treatment of either sewage waste water or purification of fresh water to meet public health standards. Or, you may be treating water to reach specifications of a manufacturer. The machinery and equipment must be monitored and maintained and regular lab tests run on the effluent. You should keep up with the technical literature and attend refresher training courses.

Advantages and disadvantages. — Today, water plant employees generally enjoy the security of civil service contracts. Both kinds of plants, if properly financed and managed, are modern, clean, orderly places in which to work. Once certified, you will enjoy professional standing and association with others in this specialty. Old plants, however, may present many operational problems which cannot be corrected until engineering improvements are made. As a manager of such a plant, you have to bear the brunt of public dissatisfaction with the operation.

Earnings. — At the entry level, salaries are relatively low. But, most jobs are under a salary schedule providing regular raises until a salary is reached comparable to those in other technical jobs.

Careers in Environmental Service Industries

Banking

It may seem strange to some that banking is listed as an environmental career, but not if you consider that one of the major problems of conservation projects is financing. The world badly needs experts in banking and finance who will devote time and ingenuity to devise ways to provide funds to meet environmental needs.

Characteristics. — Commercial banking may be entered at any educational level from high school to university. With a high school education you will begin your banking career as a teller or clerk. While employed you will have many opportunities for education through on-the-job training by attending banking classes sponsored by the American Association of Banking or by attending night school at a university. With more education you can advance more rapidly.

Government financial agencies also provide many opportunities in financial jobs with almost guaranteed pay raises, vacation time, sick pay and retirement provisions. You may best qualify for government jobs after first working in a private institution, but the situation may also be vice versa.

Banking can be a very exciting or a very dull career, depending upon the position you hold and your own outlook. At the entry level, you will probably perform relatively routine tasks under close supervision. As you demonstrate your capacity for responsibility, you may become a loan officer. With leverage in the granting of commercial loans, you have the chance to exert much influence on conservation in your community. As an accountant or financial manager in businesses or government agencies, you would have similar opportunities by controlling budgets and expenditures affecting environmental projects.

Advantages and disadvantages. — Most banking is inside work done in very clean and often attractive surroundings. If you like contact with the general public, you will have plenty of that in commercial banks.

Even at the entry level, you are performing a valuable and respected serv-ice. At advanced levels, you may have the opportunity to shape the growth of your community, or even your state or our nation, for a quality environment. On the down side, you may become saddled with tedious work with little chance for advancement. Then, it is time to move to an-other bank or another career.

Earnings. — At entry levels, salaries were traditionally low at banks at the clerical level, but often relatively high for officers. The presumption was that at lower levels, you were adequately rewarded because the work was steady and secure. Failures of banks, savings and loans and other financial institutions in recent years have probably destroyed this image. Fortunately, salary levels, across the line, have improved along with other job benefits. Also, unlike the past, there are many opportuni-ties for women in banking and other financial careers today. Many have become bank officers in what was once almost exclusively a man's domain.

Government

Introduction. — At the beginning of the chapter, it was pointed out that one of the basic choices you have to make in choosing a career is whether you want to work in private business or for the government. Following is a discussion of some of the careers you might be able to fol-low in government and some of the characteristics of a government job.

Requirements. — Requirements for environmental/conservation jobs in the government cover almost the entire spectrum of requirements for the careers noted in this chapter, from ties to a particular politician or po-litical party to a highly technical education.

Characteristics. — Government jobs might be characterized as being of almost infinite variety. In some form, they would express all the activi-ties we have discussed in this chapter. Working conditions and employ-ment benefits for big government and big private business are apt to be very similar. But, while you can be sure that the federal government is not going to stop operating, even the largest private businesses have failed. Government agencies, of course, are terminated from time to time, and political jobs last as long as your party is in power. In general, competitive pressure is greater in private enterprise than in government. And, you have opportunities for bonuses, high salaries or other earnings and rapid advancement in private business that are not realized in professional government jobs.

If you want to stay in private enterprise, yet want to work with government, you might become a lobbyist. Lobbyists, widely used by conservation organizations, have the job of persuading politicians at both the state and the federal levels to pass environmentally sensitive laws, set up and control agencies for administration, enforcement, etc. Such a job demands knowledge of environmental facts and conservation needs and the ability to communicate effectively.

Advantages and disadvantages. — A major advantage of working for the government in most professional jobs is steady employment secured by civil service provisions and the opportunity to serve your country directly. But, you will miss the excitement of being tossed about by the ups and downs of the market place, characteristic of private businesses. And, you can never completely be your own boss in government.

Earnings. — In private business, you have the chance of a reward in dollars relative to your individual achievement. In government, as a scientist, your research is the property of the government, and you will probably not have as much opportunity to advance in salary and to be promoted. Business careers, however, are generally more risky. Presumably, the more risk you take, the greater your prospective earnings and your prospective losses.

Journalism

Requirements. — A good liberal arts education is a sound background for writers. To write well in the environmental/conservation field, you should also take some science courses and maybe even get a second degree in science. A college degree may be necessary to get a job on a publication, but will not necessarily make you a good journalist. You can be taught how to present ideas and describe events. You need to have "drive," initiative, an inquisitive mind, self-motivation and persistence. Typing skills are an absolute essential. Computer skills (especially word processing) are also needed for many jobs.

Characteristics. — Environmentally knowledgeable writers are needed to provide reliable information about environmental problems to the general public. As a journalist, you will likely work for the mass media — newspapers, magazines, television or radio. Or, you may write public relations and advertising copy for businesses or do technical writing for the government.

Advantages and disadvantages. — You should expect to put in long hours, staying up all night, if necessary, to meet publishing deadlines. Or, you may be "tied" to a desk doing rewrites or editing and spending much of your time doing research in the library. This can be tedious work. But, conducting interviews or investigating events outdoors can be very exciting and enjoyable. You can enjoy great satisfaction from seeing your writing published and being able to influence sound environmental laws and practices.

Earnings. — The range of salaries and potential earnings is great. Freelancing is risky business. Metropolitan newspapers, national magazines, advertising agencies and some company journals pay very well. Good environmental writing is in demand.

Law

Requirements. — To practice law, you need a law degree and must pass the bar examination. Those entering the environmental/conservation field should have some background in the physical sciences, although a student in a graduate program in environmental law at the University of Texas, who had been a geologist, told author Kircher that he did not think his physical science background was really essential. Perhaps he will feel differently after he has been in practice.

Characteristics. — Upon entering law, you may have to put in long hours of case study for a number of years with little individual recognition until partners senior to you leave the firm or retire. But, after some experience, you may be able to start a small law firm of your own. Environmental law is a relatively new field and there will be increasing demands for it.

Legal experts are needed to deal with resource use, waste disposal and pollution problems; to assist with interpretation of government regulations; to help formulate water and mining laws; and to settle disputes on public land claims.

As a lawyer in environmental law, you will often develop the contacts and communication skills which will make it easy for you to step into politics as a champion of the environment.

Advantages and disadvantages. — Beginning law practice may be discouraging because of long hours and lack of recognition. But, the legal profession is respected and, if promotions are not forthcoming in a reasonable time, you should have plenty of opportunity to change employers or set up your own office. As noted in the preceding paragraph, you also have the option of running for public office. The public generally accepts your legal training as a good qualification.

Earnings. — For lawyers at the top of their class, even starting salaries can be very good, and successful lawyers in private practice have high incomes. Others may be paid relatively low until vacancies permit them to move up in their partnership. Lawyers are often in a position to be the first to know of good investment opportunities which will enhance their incomes.

Planning

Introduction. — Over 7,000 delegates attended a national meeting of planners in Dallas a few years ago. Included were architects, builders, engineers, professional city and regional planners and real estate developers. Planning is truly a diversified field involving both government and private businesses. Environmental planning is a relatively new field.

Requirements. — A higher education degree and generally a high professional standing are needed for this career. For example, city and regional planners for full membership in the American Association of Planners are required to have an acceptable education background, experience in the field and certification by passing an examination.

Characteristics. — Since it is such a diverse field, the character of planning varies widely from discipline to discipline and from place to place. Much of your work could be in an office or drafting room going over plans or drawing them up, making or supervising the making of maps and researching codes and ordinances or government documents.

Field work might also occupy considerable time, although after initial inspection of land, you might turn the job of detailed mapping over to survey crews. And you may arrange for experts in various earth science specialties, such as geology, hydrology and soils, to make studies for you.

The planning process involves setting goals and objectives and identifying the problem, determining land use capability of the site and capital improvements on it, consideration of the site's accessibility and services available to it, drawing up of the plan, critiquing the plan (a government project probably involves holding hearings), getting final approval, implementing the plan and setting up a schedule for review of the plan in the future.

Advantages and disadvantages. — The thrill of being an environmental planner is seeing plans you have developed to protect and/or enhance the environment become adopted and implemented. The frustration is that you may have neither the power to grant final approval of the plans nor the satisfaction to see them adopted and carried out. The final decisions are generally up to either the politicians or the officers of the private corporation that hired you.

Earnings. — Some planners enjoy lucrative private contracts, and others have well-paying government positions. Entrants to the field, however, may have to endure years of low pay while they are considered as being in training.

Public Health

Requirements. — A college degree is needed with concentrations in the area in which you are specializing.

Characteristics. — The public health field needs engineers, physicians, chemists, biochemists, technicians and others dedicated to public health. Your job in this field would be to enforce safe standards for air, water and food quality, to regulate sewage and industrial waste treatment and to research the reactions of humans and wildlife to various chemicals such as those in pesticides. You would try to determine the tolerance of organisms to various chemicals and to help arrange for monitoring them. Your work will vary in accordance with your particular specialty.

Advantages and disadvantages. — The satisfaction of performing essential and lifesaving services is a source of great satisfaction. The problem of not being able to achieve desired goals because of limitations of research, politics, lack of funding and failures in implementation is very frustrating. Some research is quite tedious, but other research is exciting.

Earnings. — Professionals in the public health field are generally well paid and have good job security.

Teaching

Introduction. — An environmental program may be said to have three elements: research, teaching and action (work on the land). Especially in our democracy, environmental science and conservation education of the general public are essential so that we have an overwhelming demand for a quality environment and for the kind of actions needed to achieve it.

Requirements. — To teach in the primary grades or high school, you must have a teacher's certificate. Today, four years of college also is generally required. An advanced degree is needed to enter the field of college or university teaching.

Characteristics. — Conservation is generally taught as a part of other subjects at the elementary and high school levels and is apt to be stressed in the environmental sciences. Teachers need to be leaders in asking for and introducing conservation and environmental science into the curriculum at the high school level where it is oftentimes very weakly presented even in such states as Illinois where teaching of conservation is mandated by law.

At the college and university level, you may be able to teach courses in general conservation or in your environmental specialty or even to get an entire program of environmental study adopted.

Environmental teaching should be reinforced by laboratory exercises and field trips. Conservation teachers should support conservation organizations and participate if local chapters are available. They should help students organize clubs that are environmentally oriented. Where the situation is favorable, they should have the students develop an outdoor laboratory (hopefully with the help of the school board and parents).

Advantages and disadvantages. — Advantages of teaching include the pleasure and excitement of working with receptive students and association with colleagues who have common interests. Also, teachers today have generally good working conditions, a salary schedule and known conditions for advancement and fairly generous vacation periods. During the teaching year, on the negative side, a teacher may have to work day and night in order to grade papers, prepare examinations, complete various reports and attend meetings. Discipline problems, teaching overloads, poor classrooms and facilities and excessive extracurricular assignments occur in some schools.

Earnings. — It is well known that one does not go into teaching to make money, although administrators and some university professors who may get extra income from outside consultation and/or research have relatively high incomes. In some rural areas and regions of the country, teaching at the elementary and high school levels is poorly paid.

The unique reward of being a teacher is your satisfaction in sharing knowledge with your students and seeing them grow in ability and understanding. As a teacher of environmental subjects, you are especially pleased when your students enter environmental work and promote conservation.

Agricultural Education Teacher or Extension Advisor

Requirements. — You will need a bachelor's degree to get into this field. Course work would include agronomy, field crops, chemistry, entomology and botany. The job requires an internship or other on-the-job training.

Characteristics. — As an agricultural education teacher, you would primarily teach in the classroom, but might offer or participate in short courses and help in community programs. Extension advisors offer short courses and spend time advising farmers on the farm. If you were holding this job, you would also write and supervise the distribution of bulletins, manuals, press releases and reports. And, you would prepare and deliver reports and speeches. Your job is to provide environmental/

conservation information to students, farmers, ranchers and others involved or interested in agriculture. In this field, it is all important to know how to deal with the mass media. And, you must spend much time keeping informed and answering questions, often over the telephone, from the general public.

Advantages and disadvantages. — This is a good job for you if besides having agricultural knowledge, you like to deal with people. Working hours are relatively fixed, but will include meetings and courses in the evenings and on weekends. Lack of acceptance of new ideas by those whom you are trying to reach can be frustrating. (Refer to the career heading "Teaching" for other characteristics which apply.) These two occupations are not well recognized outside the agricultural community, but what difference does that make to you if you spend most of your life in a farming community?

Earnings. — The salaries vary, depending on the size of the program and area served. They are generally competitive with those of others in the field.

CONCLUSION

Environmental/conservation careers are available to accommodate almost any interest from A to Z, architecture to zoology. To have such a career, you do not have to take the vow of poverty. Many jobs in the environmental field pay quite well. Also, environmental jobs are on the increase. The best payoff is the satisfaction you receive from knowing that you are gainfully employed in helping other people and the environment.

Hopefully, the preceding pages have helped you identify the career field in which you are most interested. You may even have narrowed your choice to one particular specialty.

It is hoped, however, that nothing that has been said here will limit your career goals. Even after you have completed your education and stand with diploma and teaching certificate or other credentials in hand, approach your job with an open mind. A career may open for you even more promising than the one you selected. My friend John, after completing military service as a marine fighter pilot, decided to become a dentist. He enrolled in a suitable program, but several months into the school year his instructor found that the models of teeth John had prepared were extremely crude. At first, the instructor thought John was just careless. Then he checked John's hands and found the fingers broad and stubby. "How will you get those into someone's mouth?" he asked. John gave up dentistry and took up geography. He graduated with a Ph.D. and specialty in cartography. Soon he became a cartographer for NASA and helped chart plans for the first moon landing—more thrilling than drilling!

Then again, you may find yourself so satisfied with your job that you devote your entire working days to one career. Associate author Wallace was raised on a farm, got his education in agriculture, specializing in soils, and has spent his entire working days, even after retirement, measuring, mapping and analyzing soils or teaching or writing about them.

No matter what kind of job you may have to take to meet pressing needs, keep the goal of an environmental/conservation career in mind. Opportunity in fields of resource use and conservation will knock many times. Your future in an environmental/conservation career is limited only by the boundary of your ideas and imagination, your desire to serve and your persistence and enthusiasm.

Goethe wrote, "In the realm of ideas, everything depends on enthusiasm; in the real world, all rests on perseverance."

QUESTIONS AND PROBLEMS

1. Are only graduates from agricultural colleges qualified to work in the environmental/conservation field?

2. Name at least five occupations in the environmental/conservation field that are not directly related to agriculture.

3. What occupations, related to the environment, can be found in high schools?

4. Discuss the problem of becoming a farmer/rancher.

5. Is the outlook for an environmental/conservation career favorable or unfavorable?

6. Into what three sectors have the authors divided environmental/conservation careers?

7. What is the major advantage of a career in the natural sciences?

8. Name an advantage and a disadvantage of a career as a small manufacturer of an environmentally sound product.

9. Name three careers in the environmental/conservation service industries.

10. Which environmental/conservation career appeals to you most? Why?

Glossary

accelerated erosion: the erosion process progressing at a rate exceeding natural rate, thus causing a deterioration of the resource. The degree of destruction is determined by degree and kind of acceleration.

acid rain: rain with a low ph (potential of hydrogen—a measure of acidity or alkalinity. The numeral value of 7 is neutral—decreases with acidity, increases with alkalinity).

air: a colorless, odorless, tasteless mixture of gases with approximately 78 percent nitrogen, 21 percent oxygen and some argon, carbon dioxide, neon, helium and other gases.

air pollution: contamination of the air by undesirable gases and particulate matter. The most common pollutants are carbon monoxide, sulfur oxides, nitrogen oxides, hydrocarbons and photochemical oxidants, such as ozone.

algae: any of various primitive, primarily aquatic plants that lack true stems, roots and leaves but usually contain chlorophyll. Seaweeds are a common example. Algae often cover the surface of stagnant ponds in summer.

alluvial deposits: material transported and deposited by water. As an example, alluvial valleys are generally formed by materials settling out of flood waters.

amino acids: acids consisting primarily of carbon, oxygen, hydrogen and nitrogen. They are fundamental units of proteins.

animate and inanimate energy: living and nonliving energy—examples, a horse and a lump of coal.

annual crops: common field crops (corn, soybeans, cotton, peanuts, etc.) that are grown, tilled and harvested in one year from seed.

anthracite: hard coal. Contains a very high percentage of fixed carbon and a very low percentage of volatile matter. It burns with little smoke and has a high heating value.

atmosphere: the gaseous mass surrounding the earth.

biennial crops: crops, such as clover, that take two years to reach maturity from seed.

biomass: weight of biological tissue (principally vegetation). It can be used directly for energy by burning or converted to alcohol or petroleum-type fluids.

biosphere: those regions of the earth that support self-sustaining and self-regulating ecological systems. The sphere in which all living things exist.

bituminous coal: called soft coal to distinguish it from the hard anthracite coal. A high heat value coal containing a high percentage of fixed carbon and moderate to high percentage of volatile matter.

breeder reactors: reactors which produce more fuel than they consume. There are two kinds: liquid metal-cooled fast breeder reactors (LMFBR) and gas-cooled fast breeder reactors (GCFBR).

BTU: amount of heat, the British Thermal Unit. The amount of heat required to raise the temperature of 1 pound of water 1°F at or near 4°F, the point of water's highest density. The burning of one kitchen match provides about 1 BTU.

carbonaceous: rock containing carbon or carbon compounds.

catalyst: a substance, usually present in relatively small amounts, that modifies, precipitates or increases the rate of a chemical reaction without being involved, changed or consumed in the process.

chain reaction: a process which, once started, produces enough energy and/or materials to keep it going, frequently at an accelerating pace.

chlorophyll: green plant pigments essential for photosynthesis.

clay: a mineral particle with a diameter smaller than 0.002 mm.

clearcutting: the cutting and removal of all the trees from a large area in a forest for commercial purposes, rather than just selected trees.

cluster zoning: zoning regulations which permit housing to be built exceptionally close together, provided that the open space thus sacrificed is used for open space elsewhere in the subdivision area.

commercial forest: an environment of soil, water and climate capable of producing commercial grade saw logs within 50 years.

conservation: the use of a resource in such a way that the resource does not diminish in value, productivity or integrity.

conservation of natural resources: the management and use, which may include preservation, of natural resources for quality life—life in harmony with aesthetic, ecological, economic and ethical principles.

conservation tillage: tillage practices which involve the least disturbance of the soil and provide plant residues on the surface. The residues provide resistance to erosion as well as rain drop dispersion of soil particles.

deuterium: an isotope of hydrogen found in sea water. Can be used to make fuel for nuclear fusion reactors.

DNA: deoxyribonucleic acid—the biomechanism that causes aging in the body.

ecoregion: a region based on ecosystems.

ecosystem: a community of living organisms and their nonliving environment interacting as a collective entity.

elasticity of demand: expansion or contraction of demand for a product in response to price changes. If goods do not sell when their price is dropped sharply, demand is inelastic and vice versa.

eluviation: the process of removal of clay matter and/or chemicals from portions of the soil.

environmental impact statement (EIS): a statement of the effect development would have on the environment. Required for major projects contracted by the government.

enzymes: proteins produced by living organisms which function as biochemical catalysts.

erosion: the process of wearing down the land surface. This is done by water running and/or wind blowing over the land surface. It is a natural process.

evaporation: loss of water vapors from a water surface into the atmosphere because of heat.

evapotranspiration: evaporation (loss of water vapors to the air from a water surface because of heat) along with transpiration (loss of water to the air through the pores of the skin or stomata of plant tissue)—a process which accounts for much of the water circulating in the hydrologic cycle.

externalities: used in economics to identify side effects of economic activity which are not taken account of by the market place—example: smoke from a factory.

fertilizer: organic and/or inorganic compounds applied to soil to replenish, maintain or enhance the nutrient supply. Nutrient content of fertilizer is expressed in terms of soluble nitrogen, available potassium and phosphorus. It is marketed as pounds per hundred, e.g., 10-10-10. The first number is nitrogen, the second is phosphorus and the third is potassium.

fixed carbon: in coal, the percentage of weight remaining after complete distillation at 950°C, less the ash content.

fission: splitting. Term is applied to atomic fission, a splitting of atomic nuclei by high energy neutrons, which releases large amounts of energy.

fossil fuels: those derived from the accumulation of plant and/or animal material (fossils) in past geologic ages.

fusion: term used in atomic energy field to describe the forcing together of the nuclei of lighter weight elements to produce heavier elements. This process releases large amounts of energy and is believed to be that which produces the energy of the sun and other stars.

game: with reference to wildlife means wild animals, birds or fish hunted for food or sport.

geothermal: pertaining to heat within the earth.

habitat: the space in which one lives, as applied to wildlife, means an area providing adequate shelter, food, water and range.

homeostasis: a state of physiological equilibrium in the body or any organism.

humus: decayed plant materials.

hydrogenation: as applied to coal, the process of liquefying coal and obtaining crude oil from it which can be converted to gasoline or lubricating oil.

hydrologic cycle: the cycle as water moves from the oceans overland where it is precipitated as rain or snow, recharging the earth's surface and ground water supplies and then returning to the oceans through evapotranspiration and runoff.

hydrometallurgy: recovery of valuable metals from dilute water solutions.

hydrosphere: the earth's major stratum of water, including ground, surface and atmospheric water.

illuviation: the process of accumulation of clay matter and/or chemicals in portions of the soil.

inorganic fertilizer: compounds consisting of chemical elements that when applied to the soil provide plant nutrients for the growing of living plants.

ion: an electrically charged atom. Ions occur in solutions, melts and in places where high energy can impact the atoms.

isotope: a chemical element which exists in more than one atomic weight and has an isotope for each differing weight. Weight differences between isotopes of the same element are caused by different numbers of neutrons in the nucleus. All isotopes of the same element contain the same numbers of protons (positively charged particles) and electrons (negatively charged particles), so that they are identical in their chemical behavior, though they have slight physical differences.

jetties: extensions, which may be made with cement, lumber or even old automobiles, built into a stream from the bank to deflect the water flow.

land ethic: adoption of moral principles toward nature, especially practicing conservation of nature (the land).

leach: to remove some chemicals, such as calcium, from the soil by the passing of liquids (water, weak acids, etc.) through the soil.

legumes: crops, such as clover, alfalfa, soybeans, that can extract nitrogen from the air and fix or stabilize it in nodules on the roots.

levee: a raised, longitudinal, manufactured structure commonly made of dirt, built to prevent water from overflowing, especially rivers. Term also used for small ridges as in an irrigated field and for landing places on rivers.

lignite: low-grade coal with a woody texture, containing much moisture and having low-heating value. Often called brown coal.

limestone: rock made up of calcite (calcium carbonate), commonly formed of broken shells.

lithosphere: the strata of rocks in the earth. The solid part of the earth.

loess: materials settling out of wind storms. Finer materials (clay size) may be transported long distances. Dust from Texas, during the Dust Bowl era, was transported as far as the northeastern part of the country.

long-wall mining: mining coal along the wall of a rectangular room dug underground. Mine waste is dumped behind the drilling machinery as mining proceeds, filling the space behind the operator. Eventually the roof will warp downward, permitting moderate subsidence on the land surface over the mine.

megacounties: counties so densely populated that they are called *mega* (Greek, from *megas*, great).

metabolic processes: the physical and chemical processes involved in maintenance of life.

muck: organic matter decomposed to the point where the plants forming the muck cannot be identified.

mulch: a layer either organic or inorganic on the surface which has a different porosity than layer below, which reduces water losses through evaporation.

National Environmental Protection Act: (NEPA): an act of the federal government which requires that an environmental impact statement be prepared for any major project affecting the environment.

natural erosion: erosion progressing at a rate in nature that does not reduce the integrity of the resource.

non-commercial forest: an environment of soil water and climate incapable of producing commercial grade saw logs within 50 years.

nongame programs: programs to support songbirds and other wildlife which are not or should not be hunted.

noosphere: the human mental sphere.

no-till: also called zero-till. Seed is drilled into the soil. Neither plowing nor discing is used.

noussphere: the field of energy expressed by intelligence, inspiration, ingenuity and knowledge.

OCS: Outer Continental Shelf.

organic fertilizer: plant matter that when decomposed provides plant nutrients for the growing of living plants.

overburden: in mining or quarrying, the soil and rock having no commercial value, which lies above the valuable deposit and must be removed to obtain the valuable material.

ozone: a gaseous derivative of oxygen (O_3), formed by electric discharge or exposure to ultraviolet radiation.

peat: carbonized vegetation formed by decay of vegetation below the water surface of bogs. It contains much moisture, has a low-heating value and is an early stage in the formation of coal.

perennial crops: crops, such as alfalfa and the grasses, that will provide ground cover from seed for several years when properly managed.

pesticides: chemicals that are used to kill unwanted and/or injurious plants (herbicides) and animals (insecticides)—especially noxious weeds, insects and rodents.

photosynthesis: the process through which the sun's energy is transferred through chlorophyll in the presence of water to become free oxygen and food sugar.

photovoltaic cell: a cell which is capable of producing voltage when exposed to energy, especially sunlight.

plankton: the drifting life of the sea—may be either a plant or an animal. Drifting algae are an example of plankton.

Planned Unit Development (PUD): development of a relatively large area of land as a unit with a master plan rather than helter-skelter development.

plant nutrients: nutrients necessary to produce green plants. The essential nutrients are generally considered to be: nitrogen, potassium and phosphorus. However, other nutrients, not in sufficient supply, may adversely affect plant growth (such as boron for alfalfa).

potable: drinkable.

potential energy: the energy that a physical system is capable of expressing but is not released.

radioactivity: spontaneous or induced disintegration of atomic nuclei, releasing radiant energy and high velocity particles.

range lands: large areas of open grasslands used primarily for grazing livestock.

recharge: addition of water to an underground reservoir. It may be by natural processes of rain and river water infiltration or in an "artificial" way through pits or wells constructed by people.

regolith: the earth's crust, derived from the Greek; *rega*, meaning "covering" or "blanket" and *lith* meaning "stone."

reserve: valuable mineral material which has not been produced and is still in the ground. Reserves are subdivided into *proved*, which have been measured from drilling data; *probable*, which are indicated to be present by a favorable combination of geologic factors adjacent to known deposits; and *possible* or *potential*, which are thought to be present from some evidence and favorable geologic factors.

residual deposits: these deposits are formed from materials in the place where they now reside.

resource: something of use to humans. Something that can be turned to for help or support.

resource base: all of nature providing potential to become a resource.

resources—functional concept of: a term, coined by Eric Zimmermann, that resources are a function of (determined by) our wants (creature and societal) and abilities (technological and societal) acting upon the resource base.

resources—exhaustible: resources available only in limited quantities. There are two kinds: irreplaceable and replaceable (renewable). Examples are minerals and wildlife.

resources—inexhaustible: resources which do not diminish with use; solar energy is a prime example.

sand: a mineral particle which has a diameter greater than 0.05 mm.

sandstone: rock made up of sand grains cemented together. Sand grains range in size from 2 to 1/16 mm.

secondary recovery: oil recovered from an underground reservoir after or during primary recovery. Water, gas, heat and solvent injection into the oil reservoir rock are some methods of secondary recovery or enhanced oil recovery. Recovery of once-used material for reuse, such as newspaper or scrap metal salvage.

slope-percentage: the vertical drop in feet in a horizontal distance of 100 feet. Example: if in a horizontal distance of 100 feet the vertical drop is 7 feet lower, the percentage is 7 percent.

shale: rock made up of very small (less than 1/256 mm) clay particles cemented together.

silt: a mineral particle with a diameter between 0.05 and 0.002 mm.

societal arts: the skillful applications of principles and methods that enable us to live together as a society— examples: practice of good education and government, ethical business and benevolent religion.

soil: that portion of the earth's mantle that is able to support some form of plant growth.

soil depletion: the removal of plant nutrients and organic matter from the soil.

soil productivity: the ability of a soil to produce an acceptable yield of selected crops using acceptable agricultural methods.

soil texture: composition of sand, silt and clay in various proportions. Soils with a high percentage of clay are said to be "heavy" or "clayey." Conversely, soils with a high percentage of sand are said to be "light" or "sandy."

soils—transported: these are soils formed from materials that have been moved from places of origin by glaciers, wind, water or gravity.

superconductors: ceramic compounds (metal and oxygen) through which electric current can flow with little resistance.

supertrees: trees grown from seedlings from the fastest growing, tallest, straightest and healthiest trees in the forest.

surface mining: sometimes called open pit or strip mining. Open mining, especially of coal, removes topsoil and other earth materials to reach the mineral resource.

synfuel: gas, gasoline, oil, etc., derived from coal or other organic material by chemical processing in factory installations.

technological abilities: abilities to apply science to the solution of problems, especially to meet industrial or commercial objectives.

thorium: a metallic element that is a resource for nuclear energy, especially if breeder reactors are used.

transpiration: removal of water from plants through the surfaces of the leaves, a natural process of plant physiology. Also, removal from animals through the pores of the skin.

vadose water: water held in the topmost layer of the earth—the source of most soil moisture for plants.

weathering: chemical reaction of rock minerals with atmospheric chemicals and water to form new minerals chemically stable in contact with the atmosphere.

wetlands: lands that have water at or on the surface of such duration that they are unable to produce the common crops on an economical basis. They are thought to be impractical to drain unless a drainage project, involving several land owners, is initiated.

wilderness: an unsettled, industrial, unspoiled, uncultivated natural region; such lands set aside by our federal government in the National Wilderness System.

wild river: river remaining in its natural condition—a river officially designated as such in our National Wild Rivers System.

Recommended General Sources for Environmental Information

No text can cover in detail the encyclopedic array of information available today on the environment. From the hundreds of sources consulted by the authors, the following publications, selected because they present in a forthright manner a wide coverage of environmental concerns, are recommended for the establishment of a small reference section in the library for use by students. This listing is not meant to discourage those who have the means of supplementing these publications with others appropriate to their fields of interest and geographic location. A more complete list of references and aids is given in Lytle and Kircher, *Investigations in Conservation of Natural Resources* (Danville, Illinois: The Interstate Printers & Publishers, Inc., 1979), the student laboratory manual designed to accompany this text.

American Association for the Advancement of Science (AAAS), *Science,* 1515 Massachusetts Avenue, NW, Washington, D.C. 20005. This weekly journal reports the latest scientific experiments. It contains excellent book reviews and informative editorials and letters to the editor.

Conservation Foundation, *Letter, A Monthly Report on Environmental Issues,* 1717 Massachusetts Avenue, NW, Washington, D.C. 20036. Published bi-monthly, this letter analyzes specific environmental topics in detail. Other valuable publications also are available.

Council on Environmental Quality, *Annual Report,* 722 Jackson Place, NW, Washington D.C. 20006. This annual report is one of the most comprehensive reports available on environmental actions during the past year.

National Wildlife Federation, *National Wildlife,* 8925 Leesburg Pike, Vienna, Virginia 22184 (also publishes *International Wildlife* and special reports).These monthly magazines carry beautifully illustrated articles on timely environmental concerns. They include other topics besides wildlife. Monthly magazines published by the Audubon Society, Nature Conservancy, Sierra Club and The Wilderness Society should also be added to the library if the budget permits.

Resources for the Future, *Annual Report and Resources* (a brief journal published three times a year), books, and discussion papers. Resources for the Future, 1616 P Street, N.W., Washington, D.C. 20036. This non-profit private organization studies the most pressing resource problems. Its journal and reports discuss the highlights of the organization's findings and review the books subsequently published.

In addition, students should have readily available the following:

The National Atlas of the United States of America, U.S. Geological Survey, Department of the Interior, Washington, D.C., 1970 (for sale by the Superintendent of Documents, Washington, D.C. 20402). In this magnificent atlas, students can find many of the basic geographic relationships essential to understanding environmental interrelationships. (Of course, a current school atlas should be available too.)

Statistical Abstract of the United States, 1986, 106th ed., U.S. Bureau of the Census, Department of Commerce, Washington, D.C., 1985 (for sale by the Superintendent of Documents, Washington, D.C. 20402, or from any Department of Commerce district office). The *Statistical Abstract of the United States* is an approximately 1,000-page national inventory. Social and socio-economic data, such as status of older people, women and minority groups; characteristics of unemployed; number of households comprise about one-third of the statistics. Business and industry and associated statistics comprise about one-fourth of the data. Agricultural, transportation, communications and other data and a section of recent trends and methodology and reliability complete the volume. (Of course, new editions also should be used when they become available.)

Index